EMPATHIC TEACHING

By the same author

Joseph Conrad: Writing as Rescue
The Talking Cure: Literary Representations of Psychoanalysis
Narcissism and the Novel
Diaries to an English Professor
Surviving Literary Suicide
Risky Writing: Self-Disclosure and Self-Transformation in the Classroom

Empathic Teaching

Education for Life

JEFFREY BERMAN

University of Massachusetts Press
AMHERST AND BOSTON

LC 2004019703
ISBN 1-55849-467-7 (cloth); 1-55849-468-5 (paper)
Designed by Jack Harrison
Set in Electra with Avant Garde display type
Printed and bound by The Maple-Vail Book Manufacturing Group

Library of Congress Cataloging-in-Publication Data

Berman, Jeffrey, 1945–
  Empathic teaching : education for life / Jeffrey Berman.
      p. cm.
  Includes bibliographical references and index.
  ISBN 1-55849-468-5 (pbk. : alk. paper) — ISBN 1-55849-467-7 (library cloth : alk. paper)
  1. English language—Rhetoric—Study and teaching—Psychological aspects. 2. Report
writing—Study and teaching (Higher)—Psychological aspects. 3. Teacher-student
relationships in literature. 4. English teachers—Psychology. 5. Teacher-student
relationships. 6. Empathy in literature. 7. Empathy. I. Title.
  PE1404.B4643 2004
  808'.042'071—dc22

                                                                    2004019703

British Library Cataloguing in Publication data are available.

To the memory of beloved Barbara;

to the two oncologists who prolonged
her life and eased her suffering,
Fred Shapiro, M.D., and
Glenn Dranoff, M.D.;

to the therapist who helped us
accept the inevitablitity of
death, Edward Dick, C.S.W.;

and to our family, hope for the future,
Jillian and Alex, Arielle, Dave,
and Nate the Great.

Almost always, when a person realizes he has been deeply heard, his eyes moisten. I think in some real sense he is weeping for joy. It is as though he were saying, "Thank God, somebody heard me. Someone knows what it's like to be me." In such moments I have had the fantasy of a prisoner in a dungeon, tapping out day after day a Morse code message, "Does anybody hear me? Is anybody there?" And finally one day he hears some faint tappings which spell out "Yes." By that one simple response he is released from his loneliness; he has become a human being again. There are many, many people living in private dungeons today, people who give no evidence of it whatsoever on the outside, where you have to listen very sharply to hear the faint messages from the dungeon.

Carl Rogers

CONTENTS

ACKNOWLEDGMENTS

A sentence from the Talmud describes the people to whom I am most indebted for this book: "Much have I learned from my teachers, even more from my colleagues, but most from students, most of all." I could not have written *Empathic Teaching* without my students, who not only gave me permission to use their writings but also educated me about their extraordinary lives. Like the venerable Mr. Chips, I believe that "Schoolmastering's so different, so important," and in the last thirty years I have been privileged to teach thousands of undergraduate and graduate students, men and women, young and old, many of whom have become friends. Teachers never know when a former student will appear whose life has been changed by a course; such students inevitably change their *teachers'* lives. Ben Gordon is one of these people, and I would say that I am grateful beyond words were it not for my belief that no matter how imperfect, language *can* express one's deepest appreciation. I also want to thank those students who were in my English 300 (Expository Writing) and English 226 (Literature and the Healing Arts) courses, including Cheryl Bencivenga, Shauneen Creighton, Gabrielle DiFabbio, Marie Donlon, Sarah Harrington, Gary Holtz, Gwen Hood, Stephanie Jordan, Teresa Lauless, Barbara Lee, Fernando Luciano, Brian McAuley, Lewis Michelson, Sheryl Miller, Tony Ortiz, Tamara O'Shea, Molly Ripton, Jason Rosenfeld, Daphne Ruoff, Jarrod Schneyer, Eleanor Schulz, Sheila Soskin, Andrew Tartaglia, and David Weiner. Gladly would they learn and gladly teach.

I wrote much of this book during my wife's terminal illness. Barbara was always my first and best editor, and though she was not able to read this manuscript, her influence on my life and work is profound and ever-lasting. She taught me to be an empathic listener, as she was, and to listen carefully to those who do not often speak. I am grateful to my children for their emotional support during this dark time. My older daughter, Arielle Berman Albert, and son-in-law, David Albert, both clinical psychologists, taught me a great deal about attachment theory and trauma theory, respectively. I acknowledge with great pleasure Arielle's doctoral dissertation, "Parental and Peer Support as Predictors of Depression and Self-Esteem among Late Adolescents: An Attachment Theory Perspective," and Dave's doctoral dissertation, "Prevalence and Patterns of Post-Traumatic Stress Disorder among Persons with Severe Mental Illness." My younger daughter, Jillian Berman, and son-in-law, Alex Willscher, both lawyers and federal prosecutors, gave freely of their wise counsel and helped me stay out of trouble.

As usual, my friend and mentor Jerome Eckstein, professor emeritus, University at Albany, read every word and offered countless substantive and stylistic suggestions. My colleague Randall Craig did not need to read the manuscript to help me: during the many years of our friendship, I have tried to internalize his capacity for rigorous criticism and respect for measured language. I am grateful to my department chair, Professor Gareth Griffiths, for his many acts of kindness. As with *Risky Writing*, Anne Jung has been an exemplary empathic reader and listener: she was the first to read the entire manuscript and helped me to overcome my doubts about the completion of this project. I hope that one day I will have the pleasure to thank in person Mary Ellen Elkins for her insightful responses to the manuscript and for her comments on PSYART, the electronic listserv moderated by Norman Holland. Judith Harris, author of *Signifying Pain: Constructing and Healing the Self through Writing*, and professor Peter Rudnytsky, professor of English at the University of Florida and editor of *American Imago*, strengthened the manuscript by offering detailed suggestions for revision. Were it not for their endorsement, this book might not have been published. Others I wish to thank include Dr. Benjamin Kilborne, Dr. Sybil Nadel, Professor Daniel Rancour-Laferriere, and Professor Dawn Skorczewski. Mark Bracher, professor of English at Kent State University and founding editor of *JPCS: Journal for the Psychoanalysis of Culture and Society*, and Marshall Alcorn, professor of English at George Washington University, have taken a special interest in my work and have demonstrated in their own teaching and writing the value of both the talking cure and the writing cure. Thanks also to Ellen Keegan and Lucille Ouimet, who have audited several of my courses and who agreed generously to help me read page proofs.

I regard the University of Massachusetts Press, which now has published four of my books, as part of my extended family. Once again Clark Dougan, senior editor, has gifted me with his professional expertise and friendship. Anne Gibbons has been a superb copy editor for my last two books; I hope I have taught my students as much about grammar and style as she has gently taught me. And Carol Betsch has been an attentive and efficient managing editor.

Part of the discussion of Norman Holland's *Death in a Delphi Seminar* appeared in the fall 1996 issue of *Psychoanalytic Books*. The discussion of May Sarton's novel *A Small Room* was the basis of a keynote talk entitled "The Teaching Cure" given at the Psychoanalysis and Narrative Medicine

Conference at the University of Florida at Gainesville on February 21, 2004. A section of chapter 4, "Crying in the Classroom," appeared in the April 3, 2003, issue of the *Chronicle of Higher Education* and was reprinted in *Student's Book of College English*, 10th edition, by David Skwire and Harvey S. Wiener (Longman Publishers, 2004). Another section of chapter 4, "'The Void (of a Father) in My Life': Sabreena's Story," appeared in the spring 2004 issue of *Transformations: The Journal of Inclusive Scholarship and Pedagogy*, published by the New Jersey Project, William Paterson University. Sections from "Empathy and Its Vicissitudes," "Risky Teaching," and "Crying in the Classroom" first appeared as talks given at the Association for the Psychoanalysis of Culture and Society Conferences at George Washington University in 2004, at George Washington University in 2002, and at Rutgers University in 2001, respectively.

EMPATHIC TEACHING

Introduction
MAKING A DIFFERENCE IN STUDENTS' LIVES

A teacher affects eternity; he can never tell where his influence stops.
  Henry Adams

"We all love to instruct, though we can teach only what is not worth knowing."
One need not agree entirely with Lizzy Bennet's gloomy assessment of education in *Pride and Prejudice* (236) to conclude that in the nearly two hundred
years since Jane Austen wrote the novel, we are no closer to agreeing on what
is "worth knowing." Nor can we agree on the best pedagogical methods. Many
teachers would endorse Harvard educator Richard Light's observation in
Making the Most of College that they enter the profession to make a difference
in their students' lives (105), but how is this achieved? I received a letter from
a former student in October 2002 that addresses this question:

Dear Professor Berman,
  *Perhaps you remember me from the creative writing class you taught circa
spring 1983. It was a good group, and I came away with confidence I never
received prior. I spent many years concerned that my desire to write was vanity
and self-delusion. The class was an important bulwark against that despair.*
  *I took several more of your classes—Freud and the Literary Tradition,
Narcissism and the Novel, Thomas Hardy. I was a distracted, uneven student, but I found the classes stimulating, received some good grades and
graduated SUNY with better grades than I'd received since elementary school.*
  *The next time I saw you was at your talk at Borders, on Wolf Road, following
the release of your book* Surviving Literary Suicide *in 1999. It was a tremendous
stroke of luck that I saw the promotional flyer. I read your book in something
akin to a hypnotic trance, and was fascinated by your talk. I knew the tragic
story of your friend's suicide, but hearing it again prompted me to reread dozens
of letters from my former girlfriend, a suicide at 23, and a person I had known
my entire life. I'd been lugging them around for 14 years, unread since her death.
I was shocked upon rereading them to see how clear it was that she was suffering
from manic depression. I sat on my bedroom floor and wept.*
  *In your talk, and the questions afterward, I caught repeated references to
Kay Jamison and William Styron, and bought their books. Reading them, I
began to wonder if I might have manic depression.*

1

The 1990s were a terrible decade for me, filled with loss, divorce, alcoholism, financial devastation, health trouble, depression, despair and near suicide. At 23, a doctor told me I probably had manic depression, but a family member was skeptical and I did not pursue it. By 36, my life had deteriorated to an intolerable degree, and suicide seemed a serious possibility. I finally sought an evaluation from a psychiatrist, and was diagnosed with manic depression, probably rapid cycling type II.

I started medication. To my amazement, under the treatment I lost all desire to drink alcohol almost immediately. Keep in mind, I was a serious alcoholic for 22 years. That was over three years ago.

My doctor tried a series of medications to better control my illness and titrate dosages. A subsequent drug had another surprising effect: after years of consuming Herculean amounts of caffeine, I quickly lost desire for it, and gave it up completely. The alcohol and caffeine experiences say interesting things about brain chemical imbalance and self-medication, but that is another topic.

Sober and stabilized, I saw the absolute chaos of my life: the debts, the broken relationships, the legal problems, the lost time and dreams, the exploitations by others. I was in shock. I was overtaken with bouts of severe depression. My wife had left me, and her lawyer was sending me letters asserting that my illness was concocted. I am a child of a difficult divorce, and projected much of my own pain onto my toddler son; as soon as he left from a visit I dropped to the floor in tears. No one seemed available to help me. I found myself on my bedroom floor, I'm not sure how long, curled in a ball, moving only with great difficulty. The mental anguish I felt far exceeded any physical pain I ever experienced. The only time I found relief was playing with my son, until he left for his mother's house, and I disintegrated again. I became suicidal, and as I sank, I struggled with the problem of my responsibilities as a father. I couldn't find a way to commit suicide and be available to my son, and the dilemma paralyzed me. In my depression, I thought I could find some sort of intellectual solution to what is obviously an impossible choice. I told my doctor my situation, and he said it was time for the hospital. He arranged for me to be admitted the same day, and feeling lonely, scared and desperate, I drove through a severe February blizzard to get there.

The psychiatric hospital saved me; within two days they had me stabilized, and the killer cloud began to lift. I also found great support at Alcoholics Anonymous, where people who had seen much greater hells told their stories of suffering and recovery. A kind friend ran my business while I took a year off to heal and stabilize. Though some members of my social circle stepped away, certain people dazzled me with their commitment to do whatever they could to help. My step-brother, who lives out west, generally speaks to me occasionally and visits once a year. While I was sick, he called every day, often several times, with thoughtful counsel and support. You never know who will emerge to help you.

After several months spent trying to understand life from a normal perspective, I began to write. I became reacquainted with my voice, my stories, my style, and my personal convictions about what makes good writing. In the psychiatric hospital I couldn't clasp a pencil, but gradually everything I started to say as a young man came back to me, now with new urgency.

The enclosed book is the first finished piece. Others are underway. Please accept this copy as a validation of your faith in my writing skills, and as a gift in gratitude for the ways, major and minor, intended or unintended, that you personally helped me recover from my untreated condition. Life is good: I have a wonderful family, including my true love Randi (she did the beautiful book design), and a beautiful seven-year-old son, Richard.

As you read the book, you may be amused to see that you are in it (see the Saul Bellow poem).

I remember the Saul Bellow visit to Albany quite well, and was intrigued to see in the latest SUNY glossy that his visit marked the formal opening of William Kennedy's New York State Writers Institute. This fact was lost on me at the time.

Regardless of your appearance as a character, one could say that you appear throughout the book, in that it probably would not exist if not for you.

> *With gratitude and best regards,*
> *Ben Gordon*

I carried the letter in my briefcase a few days before opening it, and when I did, I couldn't remember my former student. Since 1983 I have taught more than three thousand men and women, and although I learn the names of all my students during the semester, many of those names fly out of my head as soon as the semester ends. Ben mentions seeing me at Borders, but I didn't recall speaking to him afterward. Was I having a "senior moment," unable to remember the obvious, or had he not reintroduced himself to me after the talk? It was not until I read the poem about Saul Bellow that I recalled my former student and the curious incident that led him to meet a famous writer who played such a decisive role in his life:

> *Saul Bellow Saved My Life*
> *he came to the university to give remarks*
> *as part of a prestigious literary series*
> *my professor invited several students*

to attend a special reception
more intimate than the big speech.

The night before the reception
I had nothing to wear
the bottom half of my suit was missing
my dress shoes crushed by a guitar amp
and smelling of stale beer
my daily clothes were balled in the hamper
it was midnight
we had no washer

I went to bed and dreamed
I was late to meet Saul Bellow
As I entered the auditorium the door creaked
making him lose his place
everyone was staring at me
under the red light of the exit sign.
I woke up smelling charcoal
there was a greasy haze
hanging halfway between floor and ceiling
from the kitchen, a warm orange glow

the toaster oven
set on smoulder
was busy torturing some morsel to death
the paper towels blackening and flaking away
a plastic cup melting
In the room adjacent
my housemate
passed out drunk

I put everything out in the snow
the toaster oven hissing as it sank
through the brittle crust
then I cracked a window
and went to sleep

In the morning
I assembled some ridiculous outfit
and went to meet Saul Bellow
my professor greeted me with a solemn smile
To distract him from my clothes
I told him about my dream
and awakening to the imminent conflagration

he heard me out, then said
you must tell this story to Saul Bellow

I stared down at my manure stained boots
while my professor extracted the great man
from a crowd of admirers.
With my teacher as escort
he climbed the carpeted stairs of the auditorium.
his tailored suit said
this is not a man
who owns a toaster oven

I tried to rush through it
but Bellow was in no hurry to release our
handshake
as I told him how I awoke to squelch the blaze
his eyes fell to my t-shirt
left at the house by someone's old girlfriend
and donned in bleary morning haste, it read
FRANKIE SAY RELAX

I'm glad I came, he said. (Gordon 34–35)

My first thought after reading Ben's poem was that it was nervy of me to introduce a student to Bellow, reputed to be an intimidating presence both on and off the stage. Ben's presence must have emboldened me, for I do not usually have the temerity to approach luminaries. I doubt that Bellow long remembered the incident; surely I had not. Yet both the anticipation of meeting Bellow and the actual meeting with him proved to be a transformative experience for Ben. The dream about Bellow, the night before the talk, prompted Ben to rouse himself from sodden slumber to extinguish a fire that might have taken his life. And Ben's encounter with a Nobel laureate, who listened to his story and affectionately shook his hand, was the inspiration for a lively poem written nearly two decades later—a poem that has helped to confirm his own identity as a writer.

Warm Teachers

Ben's writings piqued my interest, for I received them precisely as I was struggling with the question of how teachers make a difference in their students' lives. I was curious about how he remembered my classes. What made them different from his other college classes? How had I given him confidence? How did my talk about suicide initiate a series of events that radically changed his life? Assuming that my memory was not faulty, I was curious why he hadn't introduced himself to me at the Borders reading. Finally, I wondered whether Ben's dream about Bellow literally saved his life —and, if so, how he explained this mysterious premonition. And so I telephoned Ben and asked him if he was willing to elaborate on these questions. He agreed without hesitation and within a few days sent me a ten-page email:

Your classes were unprecedented in my time as a student. To understand the effect of your classes on me, it may be helpful to see what came before.

When I was a sophomore in high school, there was a buzz in homeroom that the smartest kids in school had received invitations to a special assembly. A friend showed me his invitation. All the brightest kids in the advanced classes had them too. I was not invited.

I decided to attend regardless, and no one questioned my presence. The assembly turned out to be a briefing about a new gifted students program, to begin the following year. The school's most dynamic teacher spoke at length about building lasers and working with scientists. It sounded exciting, and I signed up in June and was there in September, without anyone questioning me.

I did well in the program, advancing my study module rapidly, and was held as an example to classmates. In fact, only my module, a group of three, achieved significant accomplishments—such as a study of alternate energy sources, and a program-wide weekend field trip to Cape Cod to visit an experimental energy study facility, where we viewed eco-friendly concepts under development. The trip was attended by all the study groups in the program, and a cavalcade of parents, chaperones, and school bus drivers.

One day, I was chatting with the program teacher, and he disclosed that he knew I had wriggled into the program. I asked him why I wasn't invited, like the others. He said, "You had the highest IQ but the lowest grades." At the time I was failing trigonometry and doing poorly in some other classes. He told me that my math teacher was questioning my participation. Soon after, I was caught talking to a girl in one place when I was supposed to be in another, and the program teacher, in an uncharacteristic burst of anger, ejected me from the program. My experience of an inspiring teacher leading me to academic success was destroyed. I spent senior year in exile, until late May, when the gifted program teacher passed me in the hall and said how much they missed me in the program. He walked away before I could respond.

I became wary of teachers. At my first college, a small liberal arts school in Ohio, I found the teachers eccentric, odd, and isolated. Most seemed frustrated that they had landed at a school surrounded by cornfields to the horizon, far from any city. I not only did not bond with any teachers, but found them aloof and in direct contradiction to the warm fuzzy descriptions of student-teacher collaboration described in the catalog. Some were so bad I simply stopped attending their classes.

I left that school for SUNY-Albany in the middle of my sophomore year. SUNY-Albany, at the time, did not advertise intimate contact with teachers. I signed up for English and journalism classes, with a vision of myself becoming a professional journalist. To my surprise, I encountered dynamic teachers like Fred LeBrun and Bob Miner, who were not only engaging teachers, but friendly and sociable as well.

Journalism students were not numerous, and I became friendly with several. On one occasion, Bob Miner invited the class to his home for dinner. I went, and although everyone seemed a lot more relaxed than me, I felt like part of a group. It was a dramatic contrast to the experience of my first college.

My success in these classes, including an introductory creative writing class, gave me confidence to approach you at your office about the advanced creative writing course you taught, for which instructor permission was a prerequisite. I found you warm, interested in my accomplishments, and identity, and though you soon had to rush off to teach, you invited me to join the course before departing. I looked forward to the class all through break on the strength of your warm and welcoming personality. I contrasted it with some of the more bizarre faculty I encountered and was delighted I had taken the initiative to find you and obtain permission to join the class.

People run from warm to cold. I prefer the former. My response as a student varies based on the persona, however: I want to please the warm person, and I dread, fear, or hate the other. Fear doesn't motivate my schoolwork as much as create contempt, but working on an assignment for a teacher who acknowledges your efforts, knows your name, and recognizes some distinguishing aspect of you as a person is exciting.

In one class you invited us to propose essay questions for the final exam, offering points toward an A on the exam if your question was selected. You chose one of the two I submitted. It was exhilarating taking the test, feeling successful and recognized. The question I submitted was one of the first pieces of writing that I wrote and rewrote many times, teaching me the value of self-editing. I still remember that question on The Catcher in the Rye:

> On two occasions (in the mummy room at the Museum of Natural History and again on the stairs at Phoebe's school), Holden encounters the word "fuck" carved as graffiti, and he is outraged, concerned that "some little kid like Phoebe" might see it and wonder what it means. What aspect of his relationship with his sister, and children generally, drives Holden's strong reaction, especially given his propensity for using off-color language himself?

The "fuck" question came to me almost immediately after you announced the competition. How many students use the word "fuck" on a final exam question submission? Of course, there had to be a certain genteel aspect about it: one couldn't simply deploy a "fuck" quote and expect an easy A. Holden's relationship with Phoebe, Jane, and children generally is one of the great debates among the novel's readers and scholars. The question of Holden's swearing seems mild now but was hot at the time. Why does he get so upset? I thought it would be a good question, and I honed it. Because it was short, I didn't have time for a colossal mood swing, so the experience and practice were rewarding; the piece came out well, and I thought you'd enjoy it even if you decided not to use it. (By the way, I thought it was brave of you to use it.) When you did indeed use it, it was a fine moment for me. I thought I sensed classmates who weren't as well prepared sweating over my contribution to the exam.

In your Creative Writing class the first piece I wrote included a sex scene, though not a graphic one. Yet there was something evocative about it, and at the next meeting of the class, several of my female classmates were in a tizzy. One told me she had circulated the story on the whole wing of her dorm and all her friends thought it was wild and great. I thought I was about to be asked on a date, then you arrived and spoiled it. Still, the discussion of my story was lively, and I felt like my first effort was warmly received.

I remember the Creative Writing class as a small, interesting, alert-looking group, bright-eyed; the teacher's permission prerequisite seemed to enhance everyone's feeling of "glad to be there" and there was a detectable good feeling, rather than the more typical sense of resignation encountered at many classes. This class was a privilege, not a chore.

We read our own work in alternate weeks, to allow ample discussion time. It was always especially exciting to present one's own work, though there were others who were interesting to follow. It was sometimes a knock when someone had rushed an assignment, or was not at all a developed writer, requiring tutoring in basic aspects of composition. It was also frustrating when a depressed period impaired my own work, and I squandered the chance to present something I thought was decent.

It's important to remember what 302 was not. There was no eccentric, goofball professor, past his prime or burned out, spending more time explaining the cryptic symbols of his unique term paper grading system than teaching. There was no snobbery. There was no smug self-satisfaction. There was no locking the door to prevent classroom access to students arriving late, regardless of reason. I was once locked out when the teacher misread his wrist watch, and stood there for ninety minutes, listening through the door.

I was presented a copy of Sister Carrie as a token of apology. Perhaps one day I will cool off and read Sister Carrie.

I don't think anything I wrote for the class after that was as good as the first one. I began wrestling with questions of identity, voice, theme, and mission as a writer. I hadn't found mine and became self-conscious. Nonetheless, you took me aside after class as the semester was ending, and told me that the other students in the class were "in awe" of me. I had received kind compliments from several classmates, and made a few friends, but this was stunning news.

Following college, writing became an increasing struggle. Depression, and its cousin, Why Bother?, plagued me. I began to doubt your news of my classmates' awe and felt intimidated by it. I produced several hundred pages of material, including a few book drafts, but they were often more therapeutic than readable, and rewriting and editing were especially difficult. I sent a manuscript out, and had an agent offer to shop a book based on the first five chapters, but I lacked the energy to follow through. I was married at the time, and my wife resented my writing time, preferring that I join her watching television. I tended to write for an hour every night while drinking and knock off as the alcohol sapped my determination.

I was isolated. I missed the camaraderie and encouragement of your class. I often thought that if I could only write something worth presenting to you, it would draw me into a circle of people who shared my aspirations.

Your classes taught me the difference between a friendly community and a narrow world of ego one-upmanship. It is more important to me to share news of success with people who truly helped me than it is to outwit an editorial collective or schmooze some editor so that my poem can appear, 18 months from now, surrounded by a bunch of crap, to be read by twenty people.

I don't like isolating my poems that way — it's like sending one child to boarding school and keeping the rest home. My books are intended as total works, from title to narrative order to design. A friendly community, if you will.

I found such community at AA. I found qualities that are rare, and often intimidating to uninitiated people, including, at the time, me. The lack of judgment of others. The brutal, rugged honesty. The support for members in crisis. The disparate people united in the quest for sobriety. The way people listen when you talk. The way they avoid offering advice, focusing instead on listening and letting the person find their own right answer, or perhaps sharing aspects of their experience where others might find lessons.

I went through a gradual but substantial personality change. I was ashamed of the many times I drove drunk, and amazed by the tales people told of jail, broken families, stealing, lost jobs, living in cars, hiding bottles.

I heard many variations of how it started out to be so much fun, then evolved into despair, misery and ruin. One man's children would not speak to him, ten years of sobriety later. Many attendees had numerous DWI's and were prohibited from driving. They rode to meetings with relatives or with other attendees.

The AA mantra, which intimidates some people but really is just a ritual to set the tone, speaks about forgiving and asking forgiveness of those we have harmed. We learn not to judge others, and also not to judge ourselves. We learn to forgive others, and gradually ourselves. Many times I have entered an AA meeting with dread and emerged lightened and peaceful. At AA, I made real, new adult friends for the first time since college, as opposed to the bars where everyone is your friend when you're buying. At my first meeting, two men approached me afterward, aware from my comments that I was a first-timer. They introduced themselves and gave me scraps of paper with their home numbers. One took my number—and called me, just to talk, shortly after I returned home. Those two men are my best friends from AA to this day. Without their outreach, I don't know if I would have returned for a second meeting.

A question that does come up is, What if the doctor who diagnosed me at 23 had managed to get me into treatment? He gave me a referral and the phone number of a psychiatrist. It is easy to make a fetish out of this question, pointing fingers, especially when one considers what unfolded later. But the responsibility is mine. I heard the doctor, and I could have taken his advice or not. I was an adult. I could have read up on the condition, followed through. I remember being relieved that at a minimum, I had one physician's diagnosis. Why did it take me all those years, until that night when you spoke at Borders and my subsequent purchase of the books by Jamison and Styron, to nail it?

Affirming Teachers

Ben implies in both his letter and email that what he valued most from my courses was not any particular knowledge or skill that he acquired but a recognition of his worth as a person and the inspiration to develop his creative powers. The Albany professors he singles out for praise were all welcoming and friendly, making him feel an important member of their classes. I believe that nearly all students would agree with his preference for "warm" professors to "cold" ones: "I want to please the warm person, and I dread, fear or hate the other." Nearly all would agree with his next sentence as well: "Fear doesn't motivate my schoolwork as much as create contempt, but working on an assignment for a teacher who acknowledges your efforts, knows your name, and recognizes some distinguishing aspect of you as a person is exciting."

Good teachers, in Ben's view, validate their students and help them to feel a sense of community with their classmates; they are also concerned about their students' well-being. Ben values those teachers who are interested in *all* their students, not simply the *best* students. "I experienced classes where it was clear that the teacher was addressing half the students, and the rest were filling seats. This is disconcerting. I speak from the vantage point of a frequent seat warmer, the person who was not brought along, who did not 'get it' and so fell behind." Ben's preference for teachers who can appeal to a broad range of students supports Kenneth Eble's observation in *The Craft of Teaching*: "Professors gravitate to the bright, well-prepared students. They are easier to teach, and they appear to profit most from instruction, which may simply mean they are most like the professors. But in the increasingly pluralistic colleges and universities of the next decades, the master teacher is likely to be the one who can provide contexts for many kinds of students" (199).

In addition, Ben believed that students felt "safe" in my classes. This feeling of safety persisted even when he was not doing well in one of my courses:

I had a difficult time in the Thomas Hardy seminar, though I did well in the other three classes. I had trouble getting excited about Hardy, as well as keeping up with the reading. (This was the final class I took at SUNY, and my psychological and situational problems were worsening by then.) Yet, I felt safe. In most classes, failure to complete homework is grounds for humiliation or bad marks. In a Jeff Berman class, falling behind is viewed as a chance to explore the reasons, starting with something mild, like, "Have you formed impressions on the portion you've read so far?" Or, "Do you find Thomas Hardy slow going?" In my case, you asked (privately) if the reading load was too difficult. Under the circumstances, it was.

Survival Narratives

Ben's letter and email constitute a survival narrative in which he describes the causes of his illness and the actions that led to his ongoing recovery. He attributes his recovery to several factors: his treatment in a psychiatric hospital and finding the medication to control his mood disorder; his involvement with Alcoholics Anonymous; his reliance upon loving relatives and friends; and his reading of *Surviving Literary Suicide*; *Darkness Visible,* an account of William Styron's clinical depression that brought him to the brink of suicide; and *An Unquiet Mind,* in which psychologist Kay Redfield Jamison chronicles her struggle with manic depression. He neither glorifies his illness nor avoids responsibility for his actions. Nor does he romanticize writing. He states that in the psychiatric hospital he "couldn't clasp a pencil," much less write, and it was only when he spent "several months trying to understand life from a normal perspective" that he was able to express himself in poetry and prose. One of the most moving passages in the letter occurs when he describes the realization that he could not commit suicide without betraying his commitment to his son. He ends the letter by affirming the rich possibilities of life and his indebtedness to those who helped make his recovery possible.

Ben's poem reveals his ability to capture the wildly comical and conflicting emotions he experienced immediately prior to and during his meeting with Saul Bellow. He was embarrassed by his disheveled clothes and fearful that he would arrive late to the auditorium, thus disrupting the reading. The kitchen fire, caused by a toaster oven that was busy "torturing some morsel to death," dismayed him. He was self-conscious in the presence of his professor, who unexpectedly escorts him to the featured speaker whose "tailored suit said / this is not a man / who owns a toaster oven." Finally, he was astonished that Bellow "was in no hurry to release our / handshake / as I told him how I awoke to squelch the blaze." However strange Ben's dream was, reality is more bizarre: who could have dreamed that a great writer would be interested in hearing his story? That Bellow *was* interested continues to astound Ben, and he ends the poem with Bellow's simple but heartfelt words, "I'm glad I came." Ben does not doubt the sincerity of these words. "One can read plenty into tone of voice, but the sensation he gave me with his clasp and speaking tone made me feel he realized that it was conceivable he indirectly saved me from disaster. In my more grandiose moments, I like to think his words were also a vote of confidence. He had the inflection just right. I can still hear it, and feel the veins on his hands. I felt like I was talking to my grandfather."

Though the word appears in neither his emails nor his poem, Ben's writings are suffused with shame, the most virulent emotion, that which is unspeakable. Leon Wurmser, a leading psychoanalytic theorist, has suggested that the word "shame" covers three concepts: the *"fear* of disgrace," the *"affect of contempt* directed against the self," and an "overall *character trait* preventing any such disgraceful exposure" (67–68; emphasis in original). Shame can be so intense that one wishes to disappear: hence the title of Benjamin Kilborne's book *Disappearing Persons: Shame and Appearance*. Kilborne defines Oedipal shame as "feelings of profound defeat (failed competition), annihilatory self-criticism (failed self-worth), helplessness (failed cries for help), rage, and basic threats to self-image and psychic viability" (3)—feelings that may be inferred from Ben's description of his life in the 1990s. And yet if many of the experiences about which Ben writes in "Saul Bellow Saved My Life" arise from shame or its less intense counterpart, humiliation, he is able to transmute this dark emotion into a carefully wrought poem, thus triumphing over defeat. Kilborne quotes a revealing exchange between two major poets that is relevant here: "When Auden was asked by Stephen Spender whether he (Spender) was any good as a poet, Auden replied frigidly, 'Of course. Because you are so infinitely capable of being humiliated. Art is born of humiliation'" (58).

Making a Difference

Ben reveals at least five important ways in which teachers make a difference in their students' lives. First, he implies that teachers instill confidence in their students, affirming, in his own case, the desire to write. A teacher is, in an unexpected way, a "con artist," not by cheating, exploiting, or deceiving others—as we see in the portrait of the sham psychologist Dr. Tamkin in Saul Bellow's *Seize the Day*—but by raising their confidence so that they fulfill their potential. This confidence arises from the teacher's trust in his or her students, allowing them to pursue their own interests and express themselves freely. Ben observes in the first paragraph of his letter that my class helped to convince him that his desire to write was not based on vanity or self-delusion. "The class," he notes, "was an important bulwark against that despair." Writing, as both Styron and Jamison affirm, may arise from despair, in the process transmuting suffering into art. The "stories of suffering and recovery" Ben heard while in AA helped him to regain control of his life, and his own stories and poems may have the same impact on readers.

Second, Ben implies that teachers help students to personalize knowledge. Michael Polanyi demonstrates in his 1958 book *Personal Knowledge* that "into every act of knowing there enters a passionate contribution of the person knowing what is being known, and . . . this coefficient is no mere imperfection but a vital component of his knowledge" (viii). Personal knowledge is experiential knowledge that is relevant to life, and it often implies traumatic knowledge, awareness of an event or experience that produces overwhelming grief, guilt, suffering, or loss. My disclosure of a beloved mentor's suicide in 1968 moved Ben deeply and helped him to understand his own suicidal feelings and those of his deceased girlfriend. To pursue traumatic knowledge, he turned to other authors who have written on suicide. Hearing my talk and reading *Surviving Literary Suicide* motivated Ben to seek professional help for a number of problems that, in retrospect, seemed related to manic depression. From his readings he acquired insights that illuminated the past, clarified the present, and suggested a new direction for the future. Acting on his new knowledge, Ben pursued professional help, stopped drinking, built a support system, and began to build a new life.

Third, teachers who make a difference in their students' lives are friendly and accessible. They minimize the status differences between their students and themselves, and they remain interested in their students' academic and personal success. They present course material in ways that are understandable and relevant to their students, and they challenge students without intimidating them. They stimulate students' curiosity by raising questions for further study, and they encourage learning outside the classroom.

Fourth, teachers who make a difference are willing to acknowledge what they have learned from their own life experiences, including, when appropriate, events that are rarely spoken about in the classroom. My willingness to talk about my mentor's suicide, and its profound impact on my personal and professional life, was one of the turning points in Ben's own life. By opening up myself, I allowed him to explore aspects of his own life that needed to be addressed.

Finally, teachers who make a difference in their students' lives remain part of their lives, even when students no longer see them. Students internalize these teachers, who then become attachment figures, incorporating them into their lives. Ben notes that the "vote of confidence" he received from me in the early 1980s helped to sustain him throughout the 1990s, when his life was falling apart. "I carried it with me, even in the psychiatric hospital. I recall telling other patients that when I recovered enough, I intended to write." This helps to explain Ben's statement that although I appear in only one of his poems, "one could say that you appear throughout the book."

Confronting Traumatic Knowledge

Traumatic knowledge may be frightening: there are periods in one's life when one is receptive to such knowledge and other periods when one is not. Ben implies this when he acknowledges that years earlier he was unable to act on a physician's recommendation to see a psychiatrist. Dark knowledge has a transformative power for good or for ill: it may liberate or imprison. The central ambiguity in Robert Penn Warren's novel *All the King's Men*—"the end of man is knowledge" (9)—can be read in antithetical ways: knowledge is the goal of life, but certain types of knowledge may be fatal. (As the speaker in T. S. Eliot's poem "Gerontion" asks, "After such knowledge, what forgiveness?") Students may not always be emotionally ready to understand a book that speaks to their own situation. At times a novel, poem, or memoir may be too disturbing for a depressed reader to understand, while at other times a reader's depression may paradoxically protect him or her from becoming even more depressed by a book's dark themes. Ben hints at the latter possibility in his comments on *Darkness Visible*:

I recently re-read Styron. I felt very low the first time, and I didn't remember much from my reading a few years ago. My re-reading was during a time of medication change, because depressive symptoms were reemerging and my doctor and I were making medication adjustments. I wanted to review what Styron had to say.

Because I was not in a crushing depression like the first time I read the book, I was frightened. I did not like reading a report of such a comprehensive collapse, as if it might be contagious and I might again succumb. But I also remembered that during my first reading, when the depression had rendered me virtually catatonic, Styron's state didn't seem particularly different than my own, and at that time it was comforting, especially since he recovers.

An Education for Life

Teachers seldom know when they have influenced their students' lives. Students themselves may not know this until years later. A teacher's influence may last for decades, even for a lifetime, as Henry Adams suggests (300). Nor is this influence limited to a particular academic subject. Teachers who make a difference prepare students for an "education for life," helping them to cope with the ordinary and extraordinary challenges that may occur unexpectedly. A. S. Neill, the influential teacher who founded Summerhill School in England in 1921, also asserted that education should be a "preparation for life" (24), but he did not believe that "teaching in itself matters very much" (5). Many academic novels satirize the educational philosophy of institutions that prepare their students for life by dispensing with class work. In his 1954 novel *Pictures from an Institution*,

Randall Jarrell mocks the educational philosophy of Benton, a small liberal arts college for wealthy female students. "Benton teachers pointed out that they were preparing their students for Life, which is not spent in classrooms listening to a teacher lecture" (84). Unlike the utopian Neill and the cynical Jarrell, I believe that students can pursue an education for life in the classroom. An education for life implies what Deborah Britzman calls "difficult knowledge," knowledge that arouses intense resistance in students, who must work through fears, prejudices, and doubts. An education for life involves, to use Daniel Goleman's term, acquiring "emotional intelligence," which he characterizes in his best-selling book as self-awareness, impulse control, persistence, zeal, self-motivation, and social deftness. Ben's education for life implies knowledge not only of the disabling mood disorder from which he had been suffering, and from which his friend had apparently been suffering when she ended her life, but also knowledge of the ways in which he could survive the wreckage of the 1990s. If psychiatry helped him to become sober and stabilized, reading and writing helped him to create his voice, identity, and calling.

I am always appreciative when students *tell* me that I have made a difference in their lives, and I'm even more appreciative when they *show* me this difference. There are many ways to demonstrate this difference, and Ben did so through the precision of his language and his ability to create what George Steiner calls a "counter-world": *"Language is the main instrument of man's refusal to accept the world as it is.* Without that refusal, without the unceasing generation by the mind of 'counter-worlds'—a generation which cannot be divorced from the grammar of counter-factual and optative forms—we should turn forever on the treadmill of the present. . . . Ours is the ability, the need, to gainsay or 'un-say' the world, to image and speak it otherwise" (228; emphasis in original).

Students Who Make a Difference

Teachers who inspire students are in turn inspired by them. Just as I validated Ben's writing skills decades ago, so does his gratitude inspire my teaching. Inspiration is often reciprocal: each of us has provided the other with a lasting gift. The reciprocity extends to writing, for just as I appear in Ben's volume of poems, so does he now appear in my book, a student who has made a difference in my life. Ben has gifted me in many ways: by affirming my teaching, by reminding me of the ways in which my courses have been transformative, by presenting his volume of poems to me, and by allowing me to use his writings. He has also made possible the pleasure of collaboration. Ben and I emailed each other over a period of several months, asking each other questions, comparing perspectives, recommending books and articles to read, discussing the process of publication, recalling other students who were in his classes, and collaborating on this introduction. Ben read and commented extensively on the many versions of this opening chapter, expanded upon his ideas, and suggested substantive and stylistic changes. We began this collaboration as teacher and former student but soon became coworkers and friends.

Ben and I each bore witness to a traumatic experience. Each of us bore witness to suffering, and each felt a compulsion to bear testimony. Each of us took a risk in writing about these events and reading them. For the teller, there is the risk of retraumatization; for the reader or listener, the risk of empathic distress. In narrating and hearing these stories filled with pain and shame, we each played the role of the Ancient Mariner and the Wedding Guest in Coleridge's great poem of sin and redemption, *The Rime of the Ancient Mariner*. Just as the Ancient Mariner's story of crime and punishment stuns the Wedding Guest, leaving him sadder and wiser, so did the story of my mentor's suicide shock Ben. If this seems an exaggeration, recall his opening letter to me in which he describes reading *Surviving Literary Suicide* "in something akin to a hypnotic trance" and then rereading his deceased friend's letters, which he had been carrying with him for fourteen years: "I sat on my bedroom floor and wept." Each of us entrusted risky self-disclosures to the other; each of us experienced not only therapeutic relief but also greater understanding of and connection with the other. Each of us taught and learned from the other in a process of lifelong, interminable education.

Idealizing a Teacher

To what extent does Ben idealize my teaching? Consider, for example, his following statement: "In the best teaching, there is a level of intimacy required: the teacher must learn the students' names (and the students each other's), there must be an effort to prevent anyone from falling behind or being left out, promising students should be nurtured, and suggestions for study and career ideas should be presented to students who repeatedly demonstrate that they are off trajectory and don't realize it. Distinguishing better teachers from best teachers: I believe the best will brook no 'ego affirmative actions,' in which a teacher wishing to seem like a great humanitarian convinces everyone they will excel if they choose to pursue the subject being taught."

I endorse nearly all of Ben's statements about teaching, but I am acutely aware of how often I fall short of being an "ideal" teacher. Sometimes I honor his injunctions in the breach. For instance, although I learn the names of all my students, I soon forget many of them. Moreover, I doubt that all of my students learn each other's names except in small classes. Ben might regard these as minor academic imperfections, as do I, but others are more consequential. It's understandable for a teacher to forget a student from the distant past, but less understandable when that student has taken *four* courses with that teacher, as Ben did with me. He is perhaps too kind to express disappointment over my lack of recall, but it must have been disappointing nevertheless.

And yet, to judge from his later response to this paragraph, Ben was not disappointed that I initially could not remember him. "Let me state clearly: I did not expect you to remember me, particularly without some references to period and memorable events. What mattered to me most was that I tried, in my own way, to validate your faith in my writing by sending you a book I wrote. I am not 'too kind to express disappointment' over your lack of recall, since I never expected it. Had you maintained a clear memory of me, I would have been flabbergasted." Nor was he long disappointed with me after I rejected his request to direct an independent study course with him in his senior year. "My initial preparation was poor, but I approached you first, followed by another professor, and was rejected by both of you pretty quickly. I suspect you get more of these requests than you can handle, and that they take too much time to handle. I was a bit hurt when you turned me down, but I would have turned me down too, and I can be so damn sensitive. Knowing what I know now, it's hard to imagine you finding the time. I sense if you granted me one request, you would be swamped with others."

Apart from forgetting many of my past students, some of my present students find me far from ideal. I see myself as a "warm" teacher, as does Ben, but I know from the anonymous evaluations I receive at the end of the semester that some students are suspicious of my empathy, believing that the self-disclosures I encourage are inappropriate for the classroom. I try to make a difference in all of my students' lives but succeed with only a few. My empathy for certain students has its limits. I enforce a strict attendance policy in all my courses, and when students exceed the maximum number of cuts, I fail them unless they have compelling reasons for their absences. Sometimes I telephone them to find out why they have stopped coming to class, and sometimes I don't: I'm not consistent about this. I doubt that many of those students who receive a failing grade regard me as an excellent teacher. I try to nurture my students, but I seldom give suggestions for "career ideas" to those who are "off trajectory." Similarly, while I don't believe in flattery, I have bestowed high praise on students who have later told me that they found it impossible to live up to my great expectations—a problem at which Ben himself darkly hints.

Unlike psychoanalysts, teachers are not required to help others understand the personal and interpersonal implications of idealization, but they are frequently the recipients of their students' tendency to perceive them unrealistically, and consequently teachers must decide how to respond appropriately. The unequal nature of the teacher-student relationship encourages idealization; teachers may seem to their students the repository of knowledge, wisdom, and experience. Similarly, teachers may idealize their students, seeing them as the embodiment of ideal beauty, innocence, and youth. The intensity of the student-teacher relationship may lead to romantic or erotic fantasies. Acting on these fantasies is as disastrous to the student-teacher relationship as it is to the patient-analyst relationship. The challenge for the teacher, no less than for the analyst, is neither to encourage nor discourage idealization but rather to accept it as part of the process of education.

One way to accept idealization as an inevitable part of education is to acknowledge its existence. Students see only one side of their teachers' lives. They see my "teacherly" self: the person who loves to be in the classroom, who is passionately devoted to reading and writing, and who feels most empowered when he empowers others. Students may also see my "writerly" self when I construct an argument (and, by implication, a "writing" voice) while trying to maintain the reader's interest. But students rarely see my anxious, insecure self. They don't know that I can't read a road map, speak another language, play a musical instrument, load software into a computer, program a VCR, or type with more than two fingers. They have never seen me spend two hours replacing a headlight in my car, only to discover that I replaced the wrong light. In class I may acknowledge these flaws in a wry, ironic voice, but students don't see them as they actually occur.

Rescue Fantasies

Teachers who make a difference in their students' lives need to know not only how to motivate students to do their best work but also how to motivate themselves as well. They also need to recognize the fantasies behind their motivation, especially their rescue fantasies. Otherwise, they may

make *too much* of a difference in their students' lives. The magnetic Dick
Diver in F. Scott Fitzgerald's novel *Tender Is the Night* is an example of a
psychiatrist who makes too much of a difference in his patients' lives. Dick's
rescue fantasy consists of his messianic belief that he can cure through
love. "Save among a few of the tough-minded and perennially suspicious,
he had the power of arousing a fascinated and uncritical love. The reaction came when he realized the waste and extravagance involved. He sometimes looked back with awe at the carnivals of affection he had given, as a
general might gaze upon a massacre he had ordered to satisfy an impersonal blood lust" (27). Therapeutic or pedagogical strategies based on rescue fantasies are likely to fail because of the loss of necessary detachment
and objectivity. Curing or teaching through love creates boundary violations and involves the therapist's or teacher's unanalyzed projections onto
the patient or student, respectively. One of Freud's clearest discussions of
this phenomenon appears in *An Autobiographical Study*:

> In every analytic treatment there arises, without the patient's agency, an
> intense emotional relationship between the patient and the analyst which is
> not to be accounted for by the actual situation. It can be of a positive or of a
> negative character and can vary between the extremes of a passionate, com-
> pletely sensual love and the unbridled expression of an embittered defiance
> and hatred. This *transference*—to give it its short name—soon replaces in the
> patient's mind the desire to be cured, and, so long as it is affectionate and
> moderate, becomes the agent of the physician's influence and neither more
> nor less than the mainspring of the joint work of analysis. Later on, when it
> has become passionate or has been converted into hostility, it becomes the
> principal tool of the resistance. It may then happen that it will paralyse the
> patient's powers of associating and endanger the success of the treatment. Yet
> it would be senseless to try to evade it; for an analysis without transference is
> an impossibility. (42)

Countertransference is identical to transference except that it refers to
the *analyst's* projections onto the patient (or the teacher's projection onto
the student). Freud was understandably reluctant to write about countertransference, fearing that it would undermine the public's image of the
analyst. Nor was Freud always aware of his own countertransference. Anyone who reads *Fragment of an Analysis of a Case of Hysteria*—better known
as the story of Dora—will see the extent to which he projected onto his
patient his own unconscious sexual and aggressive feelings. Since Freud
first wrote about transference and countertransference nearly a century
ago, analysts have published scores of books and articles on the subject.
Glen Gabbard begins his book *Countertransference Issues in Psychiatric*

Treatment by citing a survey of private practitioners and academic psychiatrists that concluded that one of the most highly regarded skills in psychiatry is the ability to "recognize countertransference problems and personal idiosyncracies as they influence interactions with patients and be able to deal with them constructively" (xiii). Analysts must themselves be analyzed before they practice so that they become aware of their own projective tendencies, yet despite this long and expensive process, countertransference issues continue to bedevil analysts and their patients. As Gabbard and Eva Lester note in *Boundary Violations in Psychoanalysis*, "many individuals who choose careers as psychoanalysts or psychotherapists feel they were insufficiently loved as children, and they may unconsciously hope that providing love for their patients will result in their being idealized and loved in return. In this manner, analysts may regulate their self-esteem through their work with patients." Gabbard and Lester quote another analyst's observation that the "desire to cure and the desire to be cured are 'two sides of a very thin coin'" (87).

Boundary violations—acting in ways that transgress the appropriate distance between self and other—are probably as common in teaching as in psychotherapy. A "pedagogy of love," advocated by Jane Gallop, is as dangerous to students as a "therapy of love" is to patients; the teacher, no less than the therapist, must guard against messianic fantasies. Freud's warning in *The Ego and the Id* that the analyst must avoid the temptation to "play the part of prophet, saviour and redeemer to the patient" (50n) also applies to the teacher. Teachers must be aware of their own rescue fantasies, which may have the effect of limiting students' freedom to choose their own direction in life.

To reject a pedagogy of love is not, however, to rule out the power of love in the classroom. Love is surely one of the most ambiguous words and phenomena, and there are many kinds of love: parental and filial love, fraternal and sororal love, marital love, friendly love, patriotic love, spiritual love, intellectual love, romantic love, and sexual love. Love may be selfless or selfish, healthy or pathological, insightful or blind, constant or volatile, self-preservative or self-destructive. Love may be a bulwark against hate or quickly dissolve into hate. In *Songs of Innocence and of Experience* William Blake depicts the contrary states of love: a little clod of clay proclaims that "Love seeketh not Itself to please, / Nor for itself hath any care, / But for another gives its ease, / And builds a Heaven in Hell's despair," to which a pebble in a brook replies: "Love seeketh only Self to please, / To bind another to Its delight, / Joys in another's loss of ease, / And builds a Hell in Heaven's despite" (211). Just as psychoanalysts have acknowledged recently the therapeutic role of "analytic love" (see the essays by Vida and Shaw), so should teachers acknowledge the role of "educational love": the value of teachers' warm feelings for their students, including affection, trust, respect, goodwill, and tenderness. As Max van Manen observes in *Researching Lived Experience*, "[w]e can only understand something or someone for whom we care. In this sense of how we come to know a human being, the words of Goethe are especially valid: 'One learns to know only what one loves, and the deeper and fuller the knowledge is to be, the more powerful and vivid must be the love, indeed the passion'" (6).

The desire to be in the classroom is a desire to be with our students, to engage with them, to teach and learn from them. To nurture our students is to believe in them, to give them our best, to remain connected with them, in effect, to love them. This kind of love makes possible a relational model of education, where teachers and students interact intellectually and emotionally. A relational model enables a pedagogy of self-disclosure, where teachers and students share aspects of their lives with each other. I am not suggesting that teachers and students should embrace each other the way they embrace each other's ideas, but I am suggesting that, as Ben points out, most students prefer warm teachers who remain part of their students' lives. Without implying anything transgressive, I believe that teachers can not only love to teach but also love their students, provided that they observe professional boundaries and remain committed to their students' well-being.

In the last two decades, literary theorists have explored the pedagogical implications of transference and countertransference. In *Self-Analysis in Literary Study*, edited by Daniel Rancour-Laferriere, several psychoanalytic critics discuss how their teaching and scholarship have been shaped by unconscious forces. Teachers are not required, as analysts are, to engage in a long psychoanalysis—even Freud came to realize, in his late essay "Analysis Terminable and Interminable," that no analysis is ever complete—but self-examination is central to any humanistic discipline. In perhaps the most often quoted pronouncement in literature, Socrates declared that the "unexamined life is not worth living." Or as Kierkegaard observes in *The Sickness unto Death*, "The only life wasted is the life of one who so lived it, deceived by life's pleasures or its sorrows, that he never became decisively, eternally, conscious of himself as spirit, as self" (57). Self-analysis is especially important for those who wish to make a difference in their students' lives—a difference that will be genuinely helpful and enduring.

Approaching Teachers

Given his feelings for my teaching, why didn't Ben speak to me after the Borders talk? He offers several reasons, including a cautionary statement about the limits of empathy:

I was depressed, even though I was excited to see you and hear your talk. Depression robs me of assertiveness and self-esteem; I think I secretly hope someone will swoop in and save me from misery. I'd been depressed for months, and it only worsened in the months to come.

It was terrific to see you, hear you. Afterwards, many people wanted to thank you, speak with you, or have you sign a book. There was a line, and some people took more than their fair share of time. Lines, crowds, and waiting make me edgy. I browsed and watched with one eye, hoping it would thin out. The problem is that the last person in line thinks the line is done and that they can have your attention indefinitely. You and the young lady who was last seemed to be enjoying a rich conversation, and I didn't want to stand there like the grim reaper, pressing you both to wrap it up. I could handle it more gracefully now, but the low energy and low self-regard accompanying my depression made it impossible.

I also didn't know if I was prepared to articulate everything I wanted to say. When I look at notes I scribbled inside my copy of Surviving Literary Suicide, *I see that the clarity of my thinking and analysis were inconsistent. It was probably better that I did not approach you at that time.*

When I read Surviving Literary Suicide, *I wrote all over the book. There are some interesting questions in my notes, for example, a response to the Hemingway quote on page 134, in which he says, "If I can't exist on my own terms, then existence itself becomes impossible." I responded, "Where was the reporter in him when he said this?" It's as if I was arguing to myself that bearing witness and curiosity about what will happen next are sufficient reasons to continue with life.*

There is another note inside the book which seems to have been written at your Borders talk, during the question and answer session that followed. "JB is a person who conveys a feeling that he cares deeply about you, and everyone else—he says he's never been depressed/suicidal. Listening to him I am struck by how jealous I feel when he turns his empathy exuding rays on someone else. It's like I can't trust people like this to be loyal to me." This is followed by a note to myself comparing the loyalty of two women platonic friends with the lack of loyalty of my wife, who was then divorcing me. I might add, abandoning me in my hour of need. Today, I understand why she left, but the cruel timing and the legal jihad she launched showed a remarkable lack of perception and compassion.

I considered writing you with comments about your book, but years ago, when some of my own writing drew reader mail, it boggled me. I found the letters either shallow, flattering ("I loved your magazine"), or seeking to gain something. Only a few people told me what the book meant to them emotionally, how it made them feel—the only comments that interested me. I became stuck on the notion that it would be impossible to articulate my thoughts without appearing incompletely informed, and that I would have to take steps to strengthen myself psychologically and familiarize myself with certain material (for example, Sexton) as a prerequisite. I was also concerned, given your friend's suicide, that I not reenter your life at a time of great instability in mine.

I thought it possible we would meet again, anyway. I hoped I would find my way back to writing and that I would share it with you, and that maybe we would talk. And I felt if I failed, no one would know but me, and it seemed it would not matter.

There is a cautionary tale here which applies to the question about how you were different from other teachers. An empathic, friendly teacher seems more likely to be approached by students (and ex-students!) wanting to talk. There are limits to the time the teacher can budget. What are the implications for the student who approaches hesitantly, lingers while others chat merrily away, and finally gives up, feeling that outside the classroom, the empathy of the teacher is neutralized by difficulty in obtaining personal access? What if the student is seriously depressed, and interprets the failure to obtain access as de facto rejection and alienation? (Scheduled teacher-student meetings outside class time seem to address this issue, and have the benefit of familiarizing the student with one-on-one discussions with the teacher).

We all carry a mental list of people we can rely on in an emergency. For a depressed student who is perhaps far from home, the list may be short. One of my manic-depressive friends, prior to a trial suicide attempt, approached a favorite professor for counsel; the professor restated his role as a professor and only a professor; thus there was "nothing he could do." (My friend's account.) My friend barely survived his second suicide attempt, awakening alone after a two day coma, startled to find himself intact, though his head was throbbing and for a day he was without eyesight.

Jamison speaks to this in her book Night Falls Fast, *particularly about the dangers facing young people at colleges far from home and family contact. They are in foreign surroundings at the age range when mental illnesses such as manic-depression often manifest or blossom. Increased drinking may bring out latent conditions. Jamison writes about families shocked and devastated when their children leave home, healthy and expectant, and fall victim to sudden declines in mental health that culminate in suicide attempts or death.*

CDC statistics about suicide rates as relative causes of death in the college student age cohort demonstrate that we have a major public health issue to confront. But as your work is exploring, we also have strategic and moral issues as we consider teachers as highly visible figures in loco parentis, and the implications of their empathic natures and training on the population sitting in front of them.

Ben later told me that he did not want to convey the wrong impression about the sentence he wrote inside *Surviving Literary Suicide* during the Borders talk: "Listening to him I am struck by how jealous I feel when he turns his empathy exuding rays on someone else." It was not a lack of trust that he felt toward me but rather a feeling of neediness in the grip of severe depression. "It's like dangling a bucket of water out of reach of a thirsty man. It's not your job to fix my depression, but warmth, love, and kindness go a long way. This puts pressure on people with these qualities when they are confronted with a depressed person soliciting their assistance. How much can they help? How many people can they help? At what point does it drag the empathic person down? Obviously, a sensible policy is support, reference to pertinent materials, and phone numbers of psychiatric referral centers and hospitals. Any school should be able to provide at least this much, relieving professors of overwhelming obligations."

Ben's decision not to speak with me after my talk suggests his protectiveness of me, his unwillingness to burden me with the depression he was experiencing at the time. His wish not to be like the "grim reaper" is representative of most students, who don't want to impose themselves on their professors. Some of the problems Ben raises have no easy answers, as when he states that students may feel rejected when they cannot approach a professor outside the classroom. Unaware that he was in the audience, I was unable to "swoop in" and rescue him from misery. Nor would I have done so even if we spent a few minutes talking at the bookstore. Yet a teacher doesn't need to be on a student's "mental list" of people to rely upon in an emergency to know how to respond effectively to a crisis. As Ben himself notes, there are many ways a teacher can help a student who is at risk, including listening attentively, suggesting appropriate readings and self-help groups, and making a referral to the counseling center.

Empathic Listening

Empathic teaching implies empathic listening, and Ben told me in a later communication that he had come across a paragraph in Andrew Solomon's

Noonday Demon: An Atlas of Depression that he wanted to share with me: "In an important study done in 1979, researchers demonstrated that any form of therapy could be effective if certain criteria were met: that both the therapist and the patient were acting in good faith; that the client believed that the therapist understood the technique; and that the client liked and respected the therapist; and that the therapist had an ability to form understanding relationships. The experimenters chose English professors with this quality of human understanding and found that, on average, the English professors were able to help their patients as much as the professional therapists" (111). Although I had not heard about the 1979 study to which Solomon refers, I was not surprised, since students have been telling me for years that they have experienced therapeutic relief from many of their writing assignments. In addition, without playing the role of a therapist, I have often received comments from students stating that they found my classes therapeutic — comments that are consistent with the findings of Hans Strupp and Suzanne Hadley, the authors of the study quoted in *The Noonday Demon*. Strupp and Hadley conclude that the results of their investigation were "consistent and straightforward. Patients undergoing psychotherapy with college professors showed, on average, quantitatively as much improvement as patients treated by experienced professional psychotherapists" (Solomon 451–52). An important qualification made by Strupp and Hadley, but not emphasized sufficiently by Solomon, was that the college professors (who came from a variety of disciplines, including English, history, mathematics, and philosophy) were selected "on the basis of their reputation for warmth, trustworthiness, and interest in students" (Strupp and Hadley 1126).

Teachers can thus have an important therapeutic role without being therapists. Nor was I surprised by the many dangers facing college students. These dangers demonstrate, in Ben's words, that educators have a "major public health issue to confront." Few college teachers regard their role as in loco parentis, but given the fact that college students are visiting counseling centers in record numbers, there is now a greater need than ever for educators to make a difference in their students' lives.

Neither Ben nor I could know in advance the significance of my invitation to meet Bellow, but in retrospect, he viewed the invitation as a "lifeline":

The night I had the Saul Bellow dream, I remember the tossing and turning that accompanies nightmares, the dazed awakening, and the odd odor. My sense of smell is poor, so when I smell something burning, it's wise to investigate.

I recently read that firefighters are trained to regard carbon monoxide as

one of the greatest dangers when fighting a fire, often forming first and kill-
ing sleeping people. Toxic materials in smoke may or may not cause some-
one to awake before they sicken. The same article discussed how deaths from
carbon monoxide poisoning are surprisingly common, and recommends CO
detectors in every home. In retrospect, it's scary to contemplate slumbering
away adjacent to a slowly smoldering kitchen counter that is burning but
not blazing.

My illness might conceivably have played a role in awakening me to the
fire. Manic depression, to me, comes with non-manic high energy levels that
seem to exceed what is common. My mother once remarked that as a child I
always seemed twice as alive as everyone else—but also that there was some-
thing wrong, which to her frustration she could not decipher. Even moder-
ately depressed, I am a loving father, a hard worker and a prolific writer; a
friend, also mentally ill, jokingly calls me "the machine" when I am at work.

If the senses of manic depressives are somehow more acute, at least some
of the time (and this would include such "senses" as imperviousness to pain
or hypersensitivity to touch), it is possible that we are more likely to wake up
during a nocturnal blaze, before it is a full conflagration.

Many people report finding themselves awakening a moment or two be-
fore their alarm, day after day, even if they set the clock to different times
depending on their schedule. My anxiety about the Bellow visit was sub-
stantial; I didn't want to disappoint you after you graciously invited me to be
included, but the clothing issue was humiliating, I always had trouble being
on time to school (a 45 minute drive) and was concerned about being late,
and I didn't know what a person like myself with low self-esteem should do or
say. I also hate fawning, and was worried that there would be people crawl-
ing all over Bellow, as there were people seeking your attention following
your talk at Borders.

If you remove the Bellow aspect from my concerns that night, it is possible
something else would have happened to save the house from possible disas-
ter. But I have times, like any person, when I am oblivious and ignorant of
even the most basic goings-on around me. Other times I feel pushed away, if
only by low feelings, and sometimes I actively repel sensory input from my
proximity. A depressed state might have kept me asleep and oblivious, with
consequences.

It is very important that manic depressives keep to a strict sleep schedule,
for example midnight to eight a.m. The wardrobe issue kept me up late,
throwing off my sleep, and the dream state may have come at an odd time,
coinciding by chance with my housemate's pyrotechnics. Waking to sup-
press the fire further damaged my sleep that night. One of my memories of

the Bellow event is how drained and unsteady I felt, even though it was of
great importance and excitement to me.

   I think the most important lesson is that caring about somebody and be-
ing involved with them, regardless of the nature of the relationship, creates a
net around them that can save them from disaster and misfortune. The invi-
tation to meet Bellow is an example. It pulled me up from my sorry station
and condition. It was a lifeline.

   Before a patient is released from a psychiatric hospital, the staff help you
review who will be in your support network, how you will communicate with
them, and what kind of schedule you will keep so that they will remain
involved in your life. Without it, some people die.

   The only straight answer to your question is "maybe." Much of the action
took place in the subconscious, so an empirical conclusion may be impos-
sible. Let me distill my answer to this: I am very glad you invited me to meet
Saul Bellow.

The Pedagogy of Self-Disclosure

And I am very glad that Ben wrote to me, for his letters and poetry confirm
that students value teachers who take a personal interest in their lives. There
are many ways for educators to make a difference in their students' lives, and
in what follows, I describe the teaching that has made the greatest impact on
my students: the pedagogy of self-disclosure. In my last three books, I describe the risks and benefits of self-disclosure. *Diaries to an English Professor*
(1994) explores the ways in which undergraduate students use psychoanalytic diaries to probe conflicted issues in their lives. *Surviving Literary Suicide* (1999) investigates how graduate students respond to suicidal literature—novels and poems that portray and sometimes glorify self-inflicted
death. And *Risky Writing* (2001) describes how teachers can encourage college students to write safely on a wide range of subjects often deemed too
personal or dangerous for the classroom: grieving the loss of a beloved relative or friend, falling into depression, confronting sexual abuse, depicting a
drug or alcohol problem, encountering racial or religious prejudice. Nearly
everyone has difficulty talking or writing about these issues because they
arouse shame and tend to be enshrouded in secrecy and silence. Few teachers encourage their students to write about these risky issues, but *not* to write
about them may be riskier to students' health.

   Teachers who are interested in the pedagogy of self-disclosure should themselves be willing to self-disclose, lest the process remain one-sided. Most
students find me self-disclosing. When appropriate, I talk to my students

about my experiences as a student, teacher, son, husband, father, and now grandfather. The word "appropriate" is important, for there is an art to self-disclosure. Disclosing too much about one's life may reveal egotism or exhibitionism, while disclosing too little may reveal guardedness or aloofness. W. W. Meissner's observation that a psychoanalyst's disclosure to a patient should be both disciplined and spontaneous applies equally well to a teacher's self-disclosure to a student. In my books and classes, I disclose the guilt and grief arising from my friend's suicide, the shame I experienced when I almost did not receive tenure in the 1970s, and my ambivalence about being Jewish. These self-disclosures reveal my vulnerability and help my students to see me not simply as their teacher but as a human being. I also disclose positive experiences: my deep love for my wife and children, my passion for teaching and writing, my lifelong interest in literature. I don't discuss all of these experiences and feelings in every class; like most people, I try to be selective about when, where, and how I self-disclose. I rarely know in advance when I am going to self-disclose in a class. I have never regretted a self-disclosure to a student, and it is rare for students to say that they have regretted a self-disclosure to their classmates. My self-disclosures encourage my students' self-disclosures, resulting in a sharing of knowledge that becomes part of an education for life.

Students have permission in all of my classes to use the pronoun "I" when writing their papers. This hardly seems earth-shattering, yet few of my own undergraduate and graduate professors encouraged me to write in the first person, and it was not until the end of my third book that I seized this opportunity. Many teachers still believe that allowing students to use the first person pronoun produces narcissistic or solipsistic writing. This may occur, but it is worth the risk. Students, especially in the social sciences, are often surprised when I give them permission to use "I" in a paper, but there is a compelling educational reason to do so. The interpreter is always part of the interpretation, and forbidding the use of the first person generally leads not to greater "objectivity," which does not exist, but to the failure to locate one's point of view, which is always subjective. "The academic bias against subjectivity," notes Parker Palmer, "not only forces our students to write poorly ('It is believed . . . ,' instead of 'I believe . . .') but also deforms their thinking about themselves and their world. In a single stroke, we delude our students into thinking that bad prose can turn opinions into facts, and we alienate them from their own inner lives" (18).

In his book *A Way of Being,* the distinguished psychologist Carl Rogers cites a psychoanalyst friend who observed, in Rogers's words, that "no person has more than one seminal idea in his or her lifetime; all writings by that person are simply further explications of that one theme." To which Rogers responds succinctly, "I agree. I think this describes my products" (79). Without comparing myself to Rogers, I agree that this describes my own products. I would like to believe that I am returning voluntarily to this idea, exercising my agency, but it might be, as Nadine Gordimer observes, that "We do not choose themes because they are topical or timely, they choose us because they are the very stuff of our lives" (cited by Vickroy 114). One would think that three books on the subject of self-disclosure would be sufficient, yet I find myself returning again and again to the self-disclosing classroom. I teach a wide variety of courses, all of which I enjoy, but I am drawn most to those courses in which students make a connection between the curriculum and their own lives. To quote Richard Light, the faculty members who often make the greatest impact on their students' lives "are those who helped students make connections between a serious curriculum, on the one hand, and the students' personal lives, values, and experiences, on the other" (110). Most of my students share my enthusiasm for these self-disclosing courses, and they find such an approach affirming. The reader-response diaries students write in my literature-and-psychoanalysis courses take on a life of their own; and their personal essays in my expository writing courses are often memorable.

I am not alone in believing that students' personal writings are of great interest. In his memoir *'Tis*, Frank McCourt describes his astonishment when, as a new and inexperienced teacher at a vocational high school in New York City, he came across in a classroom closet hundreds of pages of decaying student compositions dating back to 1942. As he is about to dump them into the trash, he begins reading them — essays written by the parents of his present students. Some of the writings depict how the students felt about fighting in World War II and avenging the deaths of brothers, friends, and neighbors. Intrigued by the essays, McCourt reads them to his unruly students, who are suddenly transfixed by what they hear:

> I pile the crumbling papers on my desk and begin reading to my classes. They sit up. There are familiar names. Hey, that was my father. He was wounded in Africa. Hey, that was my Uncle Sal that was killed in Guam.
>
> While I read the essays aloud there are tears. Boys run from the room to the toilets and return red-eyed. Girls weep openly and console one another.
>
> Dozens of Staten Island and Brooklyn families are named in these papers so brittle we worry they'll fall apart. We want to save them and the only way is to copy them by hand, the hundreds still stacked in the closets.
>
> No one objects. We are saving the immediate past of immediate families. Everyone has a pen and all through the rest of the term, April till the end of

June, they decipher and write. Tears continue and there are outbursts. This is my father when he was fifteen. This is my aunt and she died when she was having a baby.

They are suddenly interested in compositions with the title "My Life," and I want to say, See what you can learn about your fathers and uncles and aunts? Don't you want to write about your lives for the next generation? (257)

Whereas previously McCourt's bored students wanted neither to read nor write, now they cannot get enough of both activities. McCourt credits the experience of the "crumbling compositions" with his decision to become a literature teacher. In a later section of his memoir, he describes a similar experience in 1968 when he was teaching middle-aged female students at a community college. Their essays were stiff and self-conscious, dry and tedious until he began to invite them to write about whatever they liked. "They looked surprised. Anything? But we don't have anything to write about. We don't have no adventures." In McCourt's bemused words, "They had nothing to write about, nothing but the tensions of their lives, summer riots erupting around them, assassinations, husbands who so often disappeared, children destroyed by drugs, their own daily grind of housework, jobs, school, raising children" (318).

Two of my passions are teaching and writing—and to write about teaching is a third passion. Unlike many English professors, I don't feel a conflict of interest between teaching and research. I don't agree with Charles Sykes's vitriolic portrait of academia in his book *ProfScam*, in which he asserts that "[a]lmost single-handedly, the professors—working steadily and systematically—have destroyed the university as a center of learning and have desolated higher education, which no longer is higher or much of an education" (4). Nor do I agree with *Traveling through the Boondocks*, Terry Caesar's grim assessment of higher education. Caesar takes issue with a recent study entitled *Priorities*, put out by the Planning Commission of the Pennsylvania State System of Higher Education, which concluded that "most American professors devote most of their time and scholarly endeavors to teaching and would prefer to be recognized and rewarded as teacher-scholars, rather than as pioneers on the frontiers of disciplinary knowledge." To which Caesar responds:

I've never met one. Even people who take life back home in the classroom to be capable of just as much adventure as the frontier recognize that there's a difference nonetheless between a settler and a pioneer. Awhile ago I visited a friend who was once a top scientific researcher in his own country. Now he's an exile, lucky to have a position as an assistant professor at a tiny liberal arts school. But he was gloomy anyway: none of his colleagues read anything, he said, and why should they, since all anybody is asked to do is teach. I don't think he would have been consoled had I invited him into the Pennsylvania state system, where he would be reborn, along with everybody else, as a scholar-teacher. (7)

I agree with Caesar that academic institutions offer many more material incentives for research than for teaching, but the classroom offers its own gratifications. I regard myself as neither a pioneer nor a settler but rather as a teacher-scholar who delights in helping students discover truths about their own lives, truths that are far more complex, and at times far more disturbing, than I could imagine outside the classroom.

Empathic Teaching

Empathic Teaching builds upon my recent publications, but the emphasis here is on how classroom self-disclosure can lead to students' heightened awareness of themselves and their classmates. I try to capture both my students' and my own point of view. I cite my students' writings—with their enthusiastic permission as well as with the approval of the university Institutional Review Board, which must approve all human research—so that they can describe in their own words the ways in which they pursue an education for life. My teaching is based on empathy: trying to understand another person's feelings and thoughts without losing sight of the differences between self and other. Making a difference in a student's life means respecting *difference*—hence, guarding against the temptation to make that student into a disciple or protégé. One recalls Nietzsche's warning here: "One repays a teacher badly if one remains only a pupil." Respecting the boundaries between teacher and student is the best way to avoid the narcissistic entanglements that have bedeviled so many educators. Empathic teaching leads to empathic learning: students becoming more sensitive to and connected with their classmates' lives. Empathic teaching also leads to empathic learning for the educator: teacher and student learn more about each other in this relational paradigm. Empathy also leads to the possibility of forgiveness—and self-forgiveness. I can't imagine a better way for teachers to make a difference in their students' lives than by helping them to become more empathic and (self-)forgiving, especially in an age when these two qualities are underappreciated.

In Chapter 1 I discuss several fictional and filmic representations of literature teachers: James Hilton's 1933 novel *Good-bye, Mr. Chips,* Terence Rattigan's 1948 play *The Browning Version,* Evan Hunter's 1954 novel *The Blackboard Jungle,* Bernard Malamud's 1961 novel *A New Life,* May

Sarton's 1961 novel *The Small Room*, Bel Kaufman's 1964 novel *Up the Down Staircase*, John Hughes's 1985 film *The Breakfast Club*, Peter Weir's 1989 film *Dead Poets Society*, and Norman Holland's 1995 novel *Death in a Delphi Seminar*. Some of these teachers exert a formative influence on their students—though not always a positive influence. I have selected these novels and films out of hundreds of others because they all explore the image of the English teacher and, in the process, raise many of the pedagogical questions that arise daily in literature and writing courses. These questions include how teachers affect and are affected by their students, how pedagogical theories and practices ranging from rote memorization to reader-response criticism have changed over the years, how transference and countertransference issues manifest themselves in the classroom, how sincere praise or insincere flattery affects students, how teachers find themselves in trouble as a result of rescue fantasies and boundary violations, and how education can produce for teachers and students alike breakthroughs—or breakdowns.

Teaching has changed dramatically in the last seventy years, and the world of Mr. Chips is far different from our own. So, too, have educational philosophies and pedagogical styles changed, along with curricular changes. The everyday problems of contemporary students are strikingly different from Mr. Chips's students or even those in *Dead Poets Society*. Despite these changes, it is interesting to see how fictional literature teachers have succeeded or failed in helping their students achieve an education for life. I don't claim that one can learn how to be a literature teacher by reading these novels or viewing these films, just as one cannot learn to be an attorney by reading the endless spate of novels written by lawyers about lawyers, but stories and films about education are not only entertaining but often enlightening as well. If novelists and filmmakers are constrained by the formulaic or generic elements of their stories and films, such as the need to end on an uplifting note, they are sometimes more truthful in representing the troubling ironies and ambiguities of teaching than are educational or literary theorists, whose commitment to a particular ideology may prevent them from acknowledging the realities of lived classroom experience. In addition, novelistic and filmic representations of teaching are nearly always more interesting than scholarly studies, including my own. James Hynes's definition of literature in his satirical academic novel *The Lecturer's Tale* is relevant here: "A literary work is any work of imaginative writing—prose, poetry, or drama—that is inherently more *interesting*— rich, complex, mysterious—than anything that can be said *about* it" (24).

It may still seem odd to examine the image of the literature teacher in novels and films since more often than not he or she is an object of satire. This is especially true of the academic novel. As Kenneth Womack notes in *Postwar Academic Fiction*, the ever-growing number of academic novels confronts readers with "characters either satirically proffered as amoral, self-serving human forms or as larger, coldly manipulative, and omnipresent institutional machines" (2). This criticism does not prevent Womack from exploring these novels in terms of ethical criticism. In the same way, Elizabeth Ann Schlender acknowledges in her illuminating master's thesis, "Images of Self as Teacher in Seven Selected Novels," that although novelists usually present teachers "with so many self-defeating and ineffective approaches to teaching and to their lives" (8), there is nevertheless "much to be learned from the study of teachers in fiction" (207). I agree with both Womack and Schlender that we can learn a great deal by studying the successes and failures of fictional and filmic teachers.

In chapter 2 I discuss the pedagogical importance of empathy, trauma, and forgiveness. As I note in *Narcissism and the Novel*, the word "empathy" is the English translation of the German word *Einfühlung,* coined by Theodore Lipps in 1903, and thus only a century old. Without using the word "empathy," nineteenth-century scholars recognized the importance of teachers trying to understand their students' thoughts and feelings. The great American psychologist William James urged teachers to "reproduce sympathetically in their imagination, the mental life of their pupil as the sort of active unity which he himself feels it to be" (3). James knew that the "genius of the interesting teacher consists in sympathetic divination of the sort of material with which the pupil's mind is likely to be already spontaneously engaged, and in the ingenuity which discovers paths of connection from that material to the material to be newly learned" (70). And yet many teachers and students remain surprisingly mistrustful of empathy, believing that it may be appropriate in a therapist's office but not in a classroom. Empathy seems particularly suspect in a postmodern age in which the attempt to understand another person's feelings is viewed as narcissistic, solipsistic, or voyeuristic. Although empathy has a "dark" side, I believe that empathic understanding is a teacher's most important quality, one that can be developed, like other skills. Empathy allows us to understand trauma—a subject that has now become part of our everyday life. We live in an increasingly traumatized age, and an awareness of trauma reminds us of the value of forgiveness. In chapters 3 and 4 I describe how a series of writing assignments on the family has affected my students' lives and, in some cases, their families' lives. In chapter 5 I show how students bear witness to depression in a course devoted to literature and the healing arts. And in chapter 6 I demonstrate how empathic teaching produces extreme reactions in educators who believe that anyone who encourages students to write about their lives must be a "pervert," a "predator," or a "natural therapist."

Throughout *Empathic Teaching* I cite my students' own words to describe their experiences in my courses. They give me permission twice: first, by allowing me to use their writings, and second, by reading the chapter in which their writings appear and approving of my contextualization of their words. The overwhelming majority of my students report positive experiences, but a few are negative, and I make every effort to quote (with permission, of course) these negative experiences.

The knowledge that a teacher has made a difference in a student's life is both gratifying and humbling: gratifying because it affirms the value and influence of one's work, and humbling because it reminds us of our solemn responsibilities as educators. These responsibilities carry their own reward. Just as parents live on through their children, so do teachers live on through their students, creating an intergenerational continuity linking past, present, and future. Teachers never know when students like Ben will suddenly reappear from the past, offering a "gift in gratitude for the ways, major and minor, intended or unintended," in which they received an education for life. After reading Ben's writings, having dinner with him, and becoming reacquainted with his life, I feel the pleasure that comes from making a new friend with whom one has a great deal in common. And I am so glad that nearly two decades earlier I invited him to a reception hosted by the New York State Writers Institute, listened carefully to his prophetic dream, and then introduced him to Saul Bellow. A statement from the Talmud quoted in an essay by Susan Handelman characterizes my feelings toward Ben: "Much have I learned from my teachers, even more from my colleagues, but from my students, most of all" (127).

CHAPTER 1

"Schoolmastering's So Different, So Important"

FICTIONAL AND FILMIC LITERATURE TEACHERS

Mr. Chips: "An Amalgam Very Gentle and Wise"

No fictional teacher has been more beloved by his students and readers than the venerable pedagogue in James Hilton's best-selling 1933 novel *Good-bye, Mr. Chips*. A classics teacher, the inexperienced twenty-two-year-old Mr. Chipping walks into his first class at Brookfield academy in 1870 and immediately encounters a group of unruly students who challenge his authority. He wins the first round by telling one of the young troublemakers to translate a hundred lines of Latin; thenceforth, "Mr. Chips," as he is affectionately called, has no problem maintaining classroom discipline. In the beginning, he is hardly distinguishable from the other teachers: "he had been, in his early twenties, as ambitious as most other young men at such an age. His dream had been to get a headship eventually, or at any rate a senior mastership in a really first-class school; it was only gradually, after repeated trials and failures, that he realized the inadequacy of his qualifications" (13). Brookfield, the grammar school at which he teaches, was established during the reign of Queen Elizabeth, but it is no Harrow. Nevertheless, it is a "good school of the second rank"— the "sort of school," Hilton adds, with mild sarcasm, "which, when mentioned, would sometimes make snobbish people confess that they rather thought they had heard of it" (12–13).

Chips is politically and temperamentally conservative, and before he meets the person who changes his life, "he did not, he would have said, care for women; he never felt at home or at ease with them; and that monstrous Creature beginning to be talked about, the New Woman of the nineties, filled him with horror" (24). Nor does he like "modern" writers like George Bernard Shaw and Ibsen, whose views are too daring for his taste. By the time he reaches forty-eight, Chips seems thoroughly set in his ways. But when he does meet a "New Woman" with radical socialist ideas, Katherine Bridges, his life changes dramatically. Opposites in almost every way, they are instantly attracted to each other despite the wide difference in their ages. Hilton invests their first meeting with irony, for they meet while mountain climbing in the Lake District of England, and while Chips believes that he is rescuing her, she is the more experienced climber and safely leads him down the mountain after he sprains an ankle. They marry, and Katherine has a profound impact on his life and teaching. Although he remains a Conservative in politics, he absorbs her youthful idealism, which "worked upon his maturity to produce an amalgam very gentle and wise" (39). He has always been a devoted teacher, but now he realizes that teaching can have a transformative impact on his students' lives. "Oh, Chips, I'm so glad you are what you are," she tells him. "I was afraid you were a solicitor or a stockbroker or a dentist or a man with a big cotton business in Manchester. When I first met you, I mean. Schoolmastering's so different, so important, don't you think? To be influencing those who are going to grow up and matter to the world" (32).

The idealized marriage tragically ends two years later when Katherine dies while giving birth to a stillborn child. Unlike Hemingway's Frederic Henry, whose wife Catherine also dies giving birth to a stillborn child at the end of *A Farewell to Arms*, Chips bears the double loss with characteristic equanimity. He never allows himself to succumb to self-pity, bitterness, or cynicism, and Katherine's idealism lives on within him, to the benefit of his grateful students. As he grows older, his eccentricities become more pronounced, but the only person who voices an objection is the ambitious new headmaster, Ralston, eager to raise Brookfield's reputation. "For some time past, you have n't been pulling your weight here. Your methods of teaching are slack and old-fashioned; your personal habits are slovenly; and you ignore my instructions in a way which, in a younger man, I should regard as rank insubordination" (75). Ralston is less interested in promoting a culture of learning than he is in promoting himself. Chips refuses to retire and fortunately has friends in high places, in this case, a former student who, now the school's chairman of the governors, rushes to his defense. This is the first and only time that Chips has an adversarial relationship with the administration; henceforth, everyone at Brookfield—administrators, faculty, students, and parents—reveres him as a legend and seeks his counsel.

What accounts for Chips's extraordinary appeal as a teacher and human being? He is neither intellectually outstanding nor charismatic, and many of his aspirations remain unfulfilled. One of his disappointments in life is that he never writes the book of which he dreams. "[W]riting tired him, both mentally and physically. Somehow, too, his recollections lost much of their flavor when they were written down" (52). His faith in a "sense of proportion"—words that Virginia Woolf satirizes in the portrait of the menacing nerve doctor, Sir William Bradshaw, in *Mrs. Dalloway*—is hardly the stuff of personal or professional distinction. Chips believes in genuine friendliness between teacher and student—"less pomposity on the one side, less unctuousness on the other" (113), but he disapproves of dispensing with certain formalities that his younger colleagues are beginning to challenge. "One of the new masters, fresh from Oxford, even let the Sixth call him by his Christian name. Chips did n't hold with that; indeed, he was just a little bit shocked" (113). Nor does his approach to Latin seem unusual. In fact, he not only resists educational change but also takes pride in the fact that his Latin and Greek lessons are the same as they were decades earlier. How, then, do we explain his enormous charm?

One is tempted to say that Chips's appeal lies not in his educational philosophy but in his endearing personal qualities, but his character embodies his pedagogical approach. His compassion is evident everywhere. He is capable of disciplining his students, sometimes with physical punishment, but more typically he affirms them through his quiet dignity and generosity. At the beginning of his career at Brookfield, Chips had aimed to be "loved, honored, and obeyed—but obeyed, at any rate"; he slowly realizes that love is more important than obedience. "Obedience he had secured, and honor had been granted to him; but only now came love, the sudden love of boys for a man who was kind without being soft, who understood them well enough, but not too much, and whose private happiness linked them with their own" (37–38). There is nothing egotistical, exploitative, or transgressive about this love, and both the teacher and his students are enriched by it. By the time he retires in 1913, at the age of sixty-five, Chips has fulfilled his deceased wife's belief that schoolmasters can make a difference in their students' lives.

Chips unexpectedly comes out of retirement during the Great War to assume the duties of headmaster. The crisis brings out the best in him, and he grows in stature. As he announces the names of former students who have perished in the war, he makes no attempt to conceal his grief. "On Sundays in Chapel it was he who now read out the tragic list, and sometimes it was seen and heard that he was in tears over it. Well, why not, the School said; he was an old man; they might have despised anyone else for the weakness" (101). Chips's tears reveal his love for his students and the institution to which he has dedicated his life. If his short-lived marriage has transformed him into a "New Man" who is worthy of his wife's idealism, Brookfield has enabled him to devote himself to students who help him remain forever young in spirit. He is more than their teacher, as the ending of the story implies. Lying on his deathbed, he overhears two colleagues talking about him. "Pity he never had any children," one of them says, to which Chips responds, in what prove to be his final words: "'Yes—umph—I have,' he added, with quavering merriment. 'Thousands of 'em . . . thousands of 'em . . . and all boys'" (131).

Chips makes a difference by earning his students' trust and by maintaining his commitment to teaching. He lives *for* his students but not *through* them. It matters little that some of them never grasp the ablative absolute or the distinction between a gerund and a gerundive; what matters is that he embodies enthusiasm, dignity, kindness, and good will. He receives as much from his students as he gives; after his wife's death, teaching "filled up an emptiness in his mind and heart" (57). He empathizes with his students' disappointments and rejoices in their successes. By reading the names of the Brookfield students who have perished in the Great War, he not only memorializes the fallen but also helps the living grieve. As the story's title implies, Mr. Chips remains with both the living and the dead.

An interwar novel, *Good-bye, Mr. Chips* was written in an age when school spirit reflected patriotic fervor. The Anglo-Saxon names of Brookfield's students reveal a homogeneous society, devoid of racial, ethnic, gender, or religious diversity. But there is a hint that society is changing. Katherine introduces the "revolutionary" suggestion to invite a group of underprivileged boys from the mission school to play Brookfield's soccer team, and although the entire staff is opposed to the idea, Chips agrees with his wife, and the experiment is spectacularly successful. Notwithstanding Katherine's radical ideas, the novel's social-political vision is evolutionary, not revolutionary, and World War I does not have the shattering impact on society that it has in other interwar novels. The Brookfield community is solidly united during both war and peace; Chips stands at the center of this intergenerational continuity, teaching three generations of students. Brookfield's tranquil community reflects its students' harmonious families. Nostalgia permeates *Good-bye, Mr. Chips*, but what prevents the story from slipping into sentimentality or bathos is Chips's self-effacing humor, poignantly captured in the 1939 film starring Robert Donat, who won an academy award for his performance. (The novel was remade into an unsuccessful musical in 1969.) Chips ages, but his students never grow old; one of the most memorable passages in the novel occurs when he delivers his 1913 farewell speech. "I have thousands of faces in my mind—the faces of boys. If you come and see me again in years to come— as I hope you all will—I shall try to remember those older faces of yours, but it's just possible I shan't be able to—and then some day you'll see me somewhere and I shan't recognize you and you'll say to yourself, 'The old boy does n't remember me.' [Laughter] But I *do* remember you—as you are *now*. That's the point. In my mind you never grow up at all. Never'" (89).

The Browning Version: "God from Afar Looks Graciously upon a Gentle Master"

Unlike Mr. Chips, the retiring schoolmaster in Terence Rattigan's somber one-act play *The Browning Version*, produced in 1948 and later made into a film starring Michael Redgrave, awakens little enthusiasm from his students. The play opens in the sitting room of schoolmaster Andrew Crocker-Harris and his wife, Millie, in an all-boy's school in the south of England. John Taplow, a "plain, moon-faced boy of about sixteen, with glasses" (5), waits anxiously for his teacher's arrival. The term is nearly over, and unlike the other boys who are happily playing outside, Taplow has been scheduled for "extra work." It is also the end for Crocker-Harris, who has reluctantly resigned from his position because of a heart ailment and is about to depart to a less rigorous "crammer's" school for "backward boys" (17). Both student and teacher are living in a state of uncertainty: Taplow doesn't know whether he has passed the grade, and Crocker-Harris doesn't know whether the school's governors will grant him a much-needed pension because of his premature retirement. Taplow bitterly confides to Frank Hunter, a young, self-confident housemaster, the results of an inconclusive conversation with the "Crock": "(*Mimicking a very gentle, rather throaty voice.*) 'My dear Taplow, I have given you exactly what you deserve. No less; and certainly no more.'" In Taplow's view, Crocker-Harris is "barely human" (8). It's not that the teacher is a sadist; rather, "He's all shriveled up inside like a nut and he seems to hate people to like him. It's funny, that. I don't know any other master who doesn't like being liked" (9). And yet Taplow concedes that in spite of everything, he likes the teacher. "I can't help it. And sometimes I think he sees it and that seems to shrivel him up even more" (9).

Like *Good-bye, Mr. Chips, The Browning Version* explores a teacher's impact on his students, but the play takes a dim view of popularity. Hunter realizes that it is inappropriate for him to curry favor with Taplow by encouraging him to criticize a colleague. "My God," he tells Millie, "how easy it is to be popular. I've only been a master three years but I've already slipped into an act and a vernacular that I just can't get out of. Why can't anyone ever be natural with the little blighters?" (13). Crocker-Harris is far too reserved to be familiar with his students; he has never wanted them to regard him as a friend, equal, or confidant. But he has cared for his students and tried his best to be a thoughtful, fair teacher. Thus he is stunned when his replacement, Peter Gilbert, indiscreetly reveals to him that headmaster Dr. Frobisher has called Crocker-Harris the "Himmler of the lower fifth." The remark is so wounding that Crocker-Harris uncharacteristically discloses his feelings about his teaching career. In the beginning, he tells Gilbert, he attempted to convey to his students his enthusiasm for learning. "For two or three years I tried very hard to communicate to the boys some of my own joy in the great literature of the past. Of course, I failed, as you will fail, nine hundred and ninety-nine times out of a thousand. But a single success can atone and more than atone for all the failures in the world. And sometimes—very rarely, it is true—but sometimes I had that success. That was in the early years" (31). During those years he had acquired "many little mannerisms and tricks of speech," and he encouraged his boys' laughter by playing up to it. "They didn't like me as a man, but they found me funny as a character, and you can teach more things by laughter than by earnestness" (31).

Sadly, Crocker-Harris has lost whatever passion he had for teaching and has also lost, it seems, his students' interest and respect. "I knew, of course, that I was not only not liked, but now positively disliked. I had realized, too, that the boys—for many long years now—had ceased to laugh at me. I don't know why they no longer found me a joke" (31). His first explanation is that the students no longer laughed because they knew about his heart condition, but he immediately suspects that the explanation lies deeper than that, a heart problem of a different magnitude. "Not a sickness of the body, but a sickness of the soul. At all events it didn't take much discernment on my part to realize I had become an utter failure as a schoolmaster. Still, stupidly enough, I hadn't realized that I was also feared. The Himmler of the lower fifth! I suppose that will become my epitaph" (32). He has lost his wife's and colleagues' respect as well. Millie has been having an affair with Hunter, and the headmaster coldly informs Crocker-Harris that the school's governors have denied the pension. As if this isn't hurtful enough, Dr. Frobisher then asks him to deliver his farewell speech not at the end of the prize-giving ceremony, as custom dictates, but before the headmaster introduces a popular cricket teacher, whose speech will evoke a tremendous demonstration of gratitude from the students. Crocker-Harris defers to the request, remarking tersely, "I wouldn't wish to provide an anti-climax" (26).

Crocker-Harris is no Himmler, and the play invests him with a quiet dignity and gentleness of character that explain Taplow's genuine affection for him. Although Taplow's imaginative translations of Aeschylus's *Agamemnon* are not faithful enough for the precise Crocker-Harris, the student never doubts his teacher's devotion to literature. In the central scene of the play, Taplow gives Crocker-Harris a used copy of Robert Browning's verse translation of the Agamemnon. The teacher is deeply moved when he realizes that the book is a gift, and he is so overcome by emotion when he reads Taplow's inscription on the flyleaf that he requests the student to bring the bottle containing heart medication. The inscription, which Crocker-Harris knows by heart, comes from Agamemnon's speech to Clytemnestra: "God from afar looks graciously upon a gentle master" (36). Hunter, who has walked into the room, responds with the words, "Very pleasant and very apt," to which Crocker-Harris, still emotionally wrought, objects: "Very pleasant. But perhaps not, after all, so very apt" (36). Taplow then leaves, wishing his teacher the best of luck in the future, while Hunter looks on with a mixture of embarrassment and sympathy.

Crocker-Harris's pleasure and heartfelt gratitude are short-lived, however, because of his wife's mean-spirited suggestion that Taplow's gift is nothing but an attempt to bribe his teacher into passing him. Crocker-Harris too easily accepts this cynical interpretation, believing that his wife never lies to him, and after she leaves, he reveals to Hunter that he has long known about Millie's affair with him, having been told about it by Millie herself. Appalled by her cruelty and ashamed of his behavior, Hunter tries to convince his colleague to leave her, stating that he has never asked to marry her contrary to what she told her husband. Crocker-Harris rejects the offer of sympathy, claiming that their marital situation is "[m]erely the problem of an unsatisfied wife and a henpecked husband. You'll find it all over the world. It is usually, I believe, a subject for farce" (45). But it is clear that Terence Rattigan feels more sympathy for Crocker-Harris than the teacher feels for himself, and the two colleagues agree to see each other again. Before leaving, Hunter asks if he can tell Taplow whether he passed, and Crocker-Harris responds, "It is highly irregular. Yes, you may" (46). The play ends with a telephone call from the headmaster, who is now told by the no longer passive Crocker-Harris that he is unwilling to forego the privilege of being the last speaker at the prize-giving ceremony. Saying that he sees the matter in a different light, Crocker-Harris now states with quiet dignity that "occasionally an anti-climax can be surprisingly effective" (48).

Crocker-Harris's vulnerability makes him an affecting stage character. Part of the vulnerability derives from the fact that he has not realized his potential as a teacher or scholar despite being the most brilliant classicist in his school's history. Years earlier, he wrote a free translation of the *Agamemnon* that he cannot now find. Instead of urging students like Taplow to create their own free translations, he insists pedantically on repetitive parsing and scansion. Crocker-Harris has lost his passion for teaching and his commitment to scholarship, and while he is still conscientious about his work, he does not seek to convey the timeless beauty and power of classical literature. Nor does he embolden his students to adapt the classics to their own lives. He has been afraid to be daring in the classroom, perhaps fearing that experimentation will be mistaken for pandering. Emotionally and perhaps sexually repressed, he is ashamed of self-expression. The moment after Taplow leaves the room to bring the heart medicine, Crocker-Harris breaks down and sobs uncontrollably, and when the student returns, the teacher apologizes, unaware that his vulnerability reveals his humanness: "You must forgive this exhibition of weakness, Taplow. The truth is I have been going through rather a strain lately" (36). Nor can he confide in his wife, whose self-absorption renders her blind to his feelings. In a profession notorious for its lack of material rewards, she robs him of the knowledge that he has enriched Taplow's life. Crocker-Harris may regret his "shameful exhibition of emotion" to Taplow (45), but *The Browning Version* reveals the importance of the affective dimension in teaching. Praise is essential for meaningful learning, and the play dramatizes that praise is essential also for meaningful teaching.

According to Michael Darlow and Gillian Hodson, Rattigan acknowledged that Taplow was modeled on his own experience at Harrow; Crocker-Harris was based upon Rattigan's Greek master Coke Norris, who was in reality a harsher teacher than we see in the play. "The *Agamemnon* had been Rattigan's favourite play at school, and he ascribed a large part of his determination to become a dramatist to having read it in translation in the Harrow school library after his discovery, despite Coke Norris's dry-as-dust teaching methods, that it was a living play and not a dead text" (156). Taplow is a portrait of the artist as a young man, a student whose talent for dramatic art is greater than his proficiency in Greek. Despite the many ambiguities surrounding Crocker-Harris's character, he exerts a formative influence on his student's life and career as a playwright, an influence that the disillusioned teacher can neither acknowledge or appreciate.

The Blackboard Jungle: "I've Broken Through"

Nothing in *Good-bye, Mr. Chips* or *The Browning Version* prepares a reader for the brutal teaching conditions in Evan Hunter's semiautobiographical novel *The Blackboard Jungle*. Although Hilton's Brookfield Academy, Rattigan's private academy in the South of England, and Hunter's Manual Trades High School in New York City are all-boys' schools, they could not be more different. "Boys" may seem euphemistic, for the cynical teacher Solly Klein describes the young delinquents in Manual Trades High School as "garbage," and the teachers are nothing more than "combinations of garbage men and cops, that's all" (76). Klein greets the novel's protagonist, Richard Dadier, with the words, "Welcome to the Forbidden City" (72), and it's not clear until the end of the novel whether "Daddy-oh," as he is disrespectfully called by his students, will survive the test. Survival in this blackboard jungle involves not merely learning how to be a good teacher, or even remaining in the profession, but struggling to stay alive in a school where students routinely rape their teachers, throw them out of windows, and stab them in the classroom.

Published in 1954, *The Blackboard Jungle* immediately became a sensation, and the 1955 film version, starring Glenn Ford as the inexperienced Rick Dadier; Vic Morrow as the vicious Artie West, who challenges his teacher at every point and finally succeeds in stabbing him in the classroom; and a strikingly young Sidney Poitier, who portrays Gregory Miller, the suspicious student whom Rick finally wins to his side, brought further attention to the story. (Directed by Richard Brooks, *The Blackboard Jungle* was the first film to feature rock music, Bill Haley's "Rock around the Clock," which appears during the opening credits.) The novel has been reprinted many times; the 1999 cloth edition contains the following emotionally charged quote from the *New York Times Book Review*: "Shocking . . . arresting. . . . His book seems to have been torn raw and bleeding out of his personal experience. . . . Like *The Jungle* and *The Grapes of Wrath*, this is a book which shouts that SOMETHING OUGHT TO BE DONE." The comparison is apt, for *The Blackboard Jungle* is less interesting to contemporary readers for its literary value than for its depiction of a historical era in which a Darwinian survival-of-the-fittest code of behavior governed the teaching profession. Except for one moment at the end, when Rick achieves in his English literature class a "breakthrough" with his students, there is no real teaching at Manual Trades High School. Rick struggles the rest of the time, with singular lack of success, to maintain discipline and order. He also struggles with an unsympathetic administration that steadfastly denies there is a discipline problem in the vocational school. And he must struggle to avoid succumbing to the temptations of an attractive teacher, Lois Hammond, who poses a constant danger to him.

Rick has discipline problems of which Mr. Chips and Crocker-Harris never dream. Nothing in his professional training at Hunter College has prepared him for the thugs in his class. The principal, Mr. Short, warns the teachers at the opening organizational meeting that they must be tough. "The teacher is boss, and I want them to know that, because we are not running any goddamn nursery school but we are running a school that will teach these kids to be useful citizens of a goddamn fine community, and pardon my French, ladies, but that's exactly the way I feel about it" (41). The battle-hardened teachers support this confrontational approach to discipline, but their message is grimmer: unlike the principal, they do not believe that they can educate or even civilize their students. "If you want to be a success at Manual Trades, or any other goddamn vocational high school," Solly Klein cautions the neophytes, "you've got to live by two simple truths. One: Forget any preconceived notions you may have had about adolescents wanting to learn. There's no truth in that when you apply it to the vocational high school. Two: Remember that self-preservation is the first law of life. Period. Amen" (79). Klein has been teaching at Manual Trades for twelve years, and his three favorite metaphors to describe his students are garbage, criminals, and rotten apples. "Look, Dadier, learn to accept these kids as a big rotten whole. Like an apple with worms in it. The apple is rotten to the core, and it's the worms that make it rotten, but if you take out the worms you're still left with the rotten apple" (169). Klein would lock up the students and throw away the key, but Lou Savaldi, who teaches electrical wiring, has a better idea. "Someday I'm going to rig an electric chair and bring it to class with me. I'm going to tell the kids it's a circuit tester, and then I'm going to lead the little bastards in one by one and throw the switch on them. That's my ambition" (77).

Rick does not share this ambition, but his instincts compel him to assert his authority immediately. The horror stories he hears about the students at Manual Trades convince him of the need for toughness. Delinquents enjoy celebrity status, like notorious gunslingers of the Wild West. Juan Garza, "a little bastard of a troublemaker" (39), had once thrown an inkwell through the principal's window and then nearly threw the principal after it. Bob Canning, who had graduated from Hunter College a semester before Rick, made the mistake of allowing his students to call him by his first name. "The boys had all just loved good old 'Bob.' The boys loved good old 'Bob' so much that they waited for him on his way to the subway one night, and rolled him and stabbed him down the length of his left arm. Good old bleeding 'Bob'" (59). A navy veteran, Rick vows not to make these mistakes; he is not afraid to act like a "little Caesar" to his students. "If you started with a mailed fist, you could later open that fist to reveal a velvet palm. If you let them step all over you at the beginning, there was no gaining control later. So, whereas being a little Caesar was contrary to his usual somewhat easy-going manner, he recognized it as a necessity, and he felt no guilt" (63–64). Although he is frustrated by his students' insolence, he congratulates himself on his early classroom successes. "He had made a few mistakes, true, but on the whole he had done well. He had shown a tough exterior to the kids, and whereas tough teachers were not always loved, they were always respected. He was not particularly interested in being loved. Mr. Chips was a nice enough old man, but Rick was not ready to say good-bye yet" (69).

Indeed, Rick is no Mr. Chips, and he makes a serious error of judgment when he decides on the opening day of the school year to single out Gregory Miller for a "man-to-man talk." He tells Miller that he has checked the students' records and noticed that he has the makings of a leader. "You're bright and quick, and the other boys like you" (89). The narrator leaves no doubt that Rick is lying shamelessly, for he has not yet checked his students' academic records. The teacher not only lies to the student but also acts patronizingly toward him, praising him with the words, "That's my boy." The comment puzzles Miller, and after he leaves, the narrator gives us the teacher's thoughts. "He had been smooth there, all right. Brother, he had pulled the wool clear down over Miller's eyes, clear down over his shoelaces, too. Once he put Miller in his pocket, he'd get West, too. And once he got the two troublemakers, the clowns, the class was his. He'd used flattery, the oldest of weapons, and Miller had taken the hook without once suspecting any trickery. A leader, indeed! *Rickie*, he told himself, *you are a bloody goddamned genius!*" (89–90; emphasis in original). There are two ironies here: first, it does not take Miller long to realize that his teacher has attempted to con him, and the strategy backfires—Miller becomes more disruptive in class, to the teacher's chagrin. Second, Miller *is* superior in intelligence to all his classmates, as the teacher discovers when he looks at their records and sees that Miller has an IQ of 113, far higher than any of his classmate's. Rick learns that it is not enough to praise students; praise must be genuine to have a positive effect on the recipient.

What is the difference between praise and flattery? In *You're Too Kind: A Brief History of Flattery*, Richard Stengel offers the following distinction: "Flattery is strategic praise, praise with a purpose. It may be inflated or exaggerated or it may be accurate and truthful, but it is praise that seeks some result, whether it be increased liking or an office with a window. It is a kind of manipulation of reality that uses the enhancement of another for our own self-advantage. It can even be genuine praise" (14–15). Stengel's definition implies a quantitative rather than qualitative difference between praise and flattery: the latter is less sincere and more manipulative than the former. In his taxonomy of flattery, Stengel cites several recommendations made by sociologist Edward Jones, including "Don't give a compliment and ask for a favor at the same time," "Flatter people behind their back," "Make the compliment plausible," and "Don't flatter the obvious" (224).

Naive about the art of flattery, Rick wishes to be a good teacher though events conspire against him. He knows that cruel teachers are poor educators, but he is not prepared for the level of violence that he encounters. As he is leaving school after trying to enlist Miller as an ally, he comes across a seventeen-year-old student who is trying to rape Lois Hammond on a deserted staircase, and after he subdues the youth with excessive violence, he finds himself elevated to a hero in the eyes of the administration and faculty. To his students he is nothing but a traitor, since they blame him for the would-be rapist's imprisonment. And so despite or perhaps because of his sudden heroism, Rick has new problems in the classroom. He also has a problem of a different kind with Lois Hammond, who relentlessly pursues him.

She is so relentless, in fact, that her aggressive sexuality highlights the novel's troubling depiction of women. If *The Blackboard Jungle* consciously calls attention to the need for reform in public secondary education, it unconsciously exposes the need for a new attitude toward women. Nearly every character, male and female alike, reveals stereotypical attitudes toward women. The opening description of Lois, reflected through Solly Klein's eyes at an organizational meeting prior to the first day of school, portrays her as a temptress: "She was big-breasted and narrow-waisted, and she wore a thin nylon blouse through which the delicate lace of her slip and the slender straps of her brassière could be clearly seen. Solly wondered if she would wear that blouse on Monday, because if she did, there would surely be a rape. Either from the students or the teachers or maybe both" (38). Lois wears a more appropriate outfit on the first day of school, but it does not matter because she is still nearly raped. Rick cannot get the image of her exposed breast out of his mind, and the novel seems to be as fixated on her mammary glands as he is. On two separate occasions she moved in a way that accentuated her chest, "seemingly completely unaware of what her breasts did whenever she went through such a simple maneuver" (174). Rick's pregnant wife, Anne, insists that Lois has provoked the attempted rape, and "even after Rick explained that Miss Hammond hadn't been dressed flashily at all, Anne still held to the theory that no woman gets raped or nearly raped unless she's looking for it" (100).

Rick silently agrees with his wife's criticisms of Lois even though he also believes, with the narrator's approval, that the "psychology of the pregnant woman" renders all females intensely jealous. Anne concedes that Rick had performed nobly in protecting his colleague from harm, but the narrator cannot resist directing the reader's attention to Anne's changing body: "that a slender, attractive, rape-provoking woman had been the cause of his gallantry—well, this did not sit too happily in her lactating breast" (100). The novel's other characters also subscribe to a misogynistic psychology, including Lois, who later tells Rick, whom she has been trying to seduce, that "the first day of school [was] the only true piece of excitement we've had since I've been here"; and when the startled Rick utters the words, "You mean . . ." she completes his sentence: "Yes, I mean. I mean the time that stupid slob tried to rape me, Rick. That's exactly what I mean. My God, sometimes I wish he'd succeeded" (275).

The male teachers share her wish, and their coarse sexual bantering closely parallels their students' behavior. One teacher, ironically named Alan Manners, jokingly asks Rick whether Lois had tried to rape both him and Douglas Miller. "'Some guys have all the luck,' Manners said, wagging his head. 'I'd have known how to take care of that situation, all right.'" Rick responds, smilingly, "That's because you're a Lover Boy," to which Manners replies: "Now is the time to gather in the lady's gratitude" (101–2). Rick does not joke about the near-rape, but many of his spoken and unspoken remarks reveal a preoccupation with locker room sexuality, as when he is being beaten by a group of students: "He couldn't swing because his arms were pinned to his sides, but he could sure as hell struggle, even though he was bleeding like a whore on her legitimate day off" (130). The more Rick resists Lois's advances, the more she insinuates that he is a "eunuch" (279), and she thus emerges as an emasculator whom he must avoid at all cost.

The Blackboard Jungle abounds in macho observations, and there can be little doubt that they coincide with the authorial point of view. Published before the rebirth of the women's movement in the 1960s, the novel is awash in antifeminist ruminations. "No woman enjoys the sight of sagging breasts and a bulging stomach, no matter how maternal her urge. A woman's good looks are a woman's good looks, and there is little good-looking about a pregnant woman," Rick thinks (100). Ashamed of his body after he is beaten, he feels "like a pregnant woman wearing the badge of a bulging body, the badge that proclaims to the world at large, 'I've been layed'" (141). But it is not just his aversion to pregnancy that is startling: Anne too despises the way she looks, and her swelling body reflects her sexual insecurities. Standing in front of a mirror, placing one hand on her hip, the other at the back of her head, she feels "like a prostitute lounging in a dimly-lit doorway"; notwithstanding this moment of "mock lewdness" (196), she plays the role of the innocent Madonna to the whorish Lois Hammond. Not all the male teachers are as lewd as Alan Manners, who desires a transfer to an all-girls' school so that he can seduce (or be seduced by) all the females he wants; but they seem scarcely less vulgar than the students they purport to instruct.

Nor is the novel's judgment of female teachers and secretaries more enlightened. Miss Brady, the principal's secretary, turns out to be a "spinsterish sort of person with mouse-brown hair pulled into a tight bun at the back of her thin neck" (28). A math teacher named Martha Riley rushes to Lois Hammond's aid after the attack and begins to comfort her by "putting her fat arm around her and clucking like a mother hen" (92–93). And in one of the novel's most sympathetic passages, the narrator informs us of Rick's belief that teaching is a challenging profession for men, requiring an act of creativity that will enable them to sculpt young minds and shape young lives. Rick does not believe, however, that teaching should be a challenging profession for women, since they did not need the same kind of creative professional outlet. Creation had been given to a woman "as a gift," and she was "self-sufficient within her own creative shell. A man needed more, which perhaps was one reason why a woman could never understand a man's concern for the job he had to do" (154–55).

Rick fails many times in the classroom before he learns to tap into his own creativity. Apart from the mistake of wielding a mailed fist, he speaks satirically to his students despite the knowledge that sarcasm is a "bad weapon to use against a class" (86). He inadvertently humiliates a grinning student, Santini, by asking him, "What's so funny?" upon which Miller replies: "He the smilinest cat in this whole school. . . . He smile all the time. Thass 'cause he an idiot." Rick looks more closely at Santini's face and "felt suddenly embarrassed for having brought the smile to the attention of the class" (87). Rick gives an in-class grammar exercise and then calls on students to correct the errors; Miller, still angry at the insincere praise given to him on the opening day, deliberately gives the wrong answer, and his classmates follow his lead, thus infuriating Rick. Following these classroom defeats, he and Joshua Edwards are savagely beaten up outside a bar at night. Though unable to recognize the assailants, Rick knows from the mocking words "Hello, Daddy-oh" that the hoodlums are in his class. For the next few days he displays a sullen, unapproachable attitude in class, but that strategy is no more successful than his earlier ones, and he decides to change tactics. He asks the students to write a composition on the topic of "something lost" and gives as an example a student losing a fountain pen. The results are appalling, for not only are the essays poorly written, as he expected, but they all involve a lost fountain pen. "Rick stared at the compositions, feeling completely defeated, wondering how this thing could have happened. Hadn't he made it clear? Didn't they know he wasn't asking for a simple repetition of what he'd given them? God Almighty, didn't they know that? Could they be that stupid?" (148).

Rick's nadir occurs when he realizes that all the formulas for establishing classroom discipline have failed. He satirizes these formulas as "Clobbering," "Slobbering," "Slumbering," "Rumbling," and "Fumbling." The urge to "Clobber the bastards" is always present, he notes, but he rejects this temptation because it is incompatible with the aims of education. "Slobbering," which he says is used most efficiently by female teachers, appeals to the sympathy of boys; the Slobberer whines to her students, "After all I've done for you. . . . You give me this treatment." Rick theorizes that the Slobberer appeals to boys' "innate chivalry, their desire to come to the rescue of the damsel in distress" (221). Male Slobberers can also use this tactic by saying, "Come on, fellows, give me a break. I'm just a poor slob trying to do a job, that's all" (221). Rick rejects Slobbering because it is degrading, "like sucking up to an officer to get a weekend liberty, except that these kids weren't even officers" (223). The Slumberer, like Solly Klein, treats discipline as a nonexistent problem. "He taught, and if no one heard what he was teaching, it was just tough. He taught like a man talking in his sleep. He rattled on and on, and the noises and sounds of the outside world meant nothing to him" (223). The Slumberer's philosophy, Rick concludes, is simple: *Let the bastards kill themselves. So long as I'm not hurt*" (223; emphasis in original). The Rumbler is exactly like the Slumberer except for one difference: "The Slumberer knew there was no discipline in his classes, but he slept soundly at night as well as during the day. The Rumbler, on the other hand, did exactly what the Slumberer did all day long, but then he went home and complained to his wife about the lack of discipline, or he complained to his Department Chairman, or even to the principal" (223). Finally, there is the Fumbler, who simply doesn't know what to do. "The Fumbler kept trying. He tried this way, and he tried that way, and he hoped that some day he would hit upon the miraculous cure-all for the disciplinary problem" (224). Rick characterizes himself as a Fumbler, and he seems ready to conclude in despair that vocational students simply do not want to learn.

Around this time Rick's friend Joshua Edwards suddenly quits. Described as small and meek looking, Josh had dreamed all his life about becoming a teacher, but like Rick, he is now bitterly disillusioned. The two new teachers spend time together in a bar, each confiding his disappointments to the other, and when Rick asks him why he is depressed, the sodden Josh replies, "The things we learned in school. The Ed courses. What a bunch of horse manure" (123). Leaving the bar, the two teachers are attacked by a gang of Rick's students, and not long afterward, Josh brings his cherished record collection to school, only to see his students shatter them and then smash his eyeglasses. Devastated, Josh breaks down. "He was ashamed of the tears, but he couldn't stop them, and they streamed down his face together with the blood, and Rick put his arm around Josh's shoulders and held him in a firm grip, and Josh kept crying and saying, 'Why'd they want to do that, Rick?'" (192). Rick wants to cry himself but doesn't. Josh's decision to leave teaching reflects nothing less than the destruction of his self-worth. "I'm no goddamned good," he confesses to Rick (241), and his departure from the story represents a loss to education.

Rick also grapples with the fear of rejection but receives no help from the administration. He finds himself in trouble with the principal, Mr. Small, after an unfortunate incident with Miller. Rick becomes so exasperated with Miller, who, he believes, has sabotaged his class, that he almost lets slip a racial epithet; he immediately apologizes and then engages in painful introspection after the African American youth's angry departure. Rick is no racist, and during the next class he tries to sensitize his students to prejudice. When one Italian calls a classmate a "wop," Rick insists that such name-calling is harmful, even when spoken in jest. Pointing to the students who come from different racial and ethnic backgrounds, the teacher uses words like "wop," "kike," "spic," "kraut," "mick," and "nigger" to show how hurtful racial epithets are. "You shouldn't use vicious expressions, whether you're joking or serious. Look, my parents are French. Do you know how many times I've been called a frog? Do you think I like it? Well, no, I don't" (216). Miller smiles at Rick's lecture, recognizing that it represents a veiled apology that he now accepts. Unbeknownst to Rick, however, Artie West tells the principal that his teacher has been using racist language, and Mr. Small believes the malicious lie. Only after an explosive confrontation with Rick does the principal finally realize the truth.

The teacher's relationship with Miller remains the most complex one in the novel, and each must work through his misunderstanding and mistrust of the other. Rick discovers that Miller is indeed the most intelligent and resourceful student in the class, a natural leader; the insincere flattery he had bestowed upon the youth in the beginning of the novel gives way to sincere praise at the end. Additionally, Rick learns that Miller has many different sides to his personality and conflicting loyalties: the student who works so hard for Rick for the school Christmas assembly—Miller's idea of having six of his black friends play angels proves to be a resounding success—is the same student who can be so troublesome in class. Rick gradually accepts the fact that Miller's loyalty to his classmates compels him to be sarcastic and difficult to his teachers; but unlike Artie West, who becomes increasingly violent, Miller draws a line of misconduct over which he will not step. Rick learns to accept the "good Miller and the bad Miller, and he felt something like a psychoanalyst treating a schizophrenic" (270). For his part, Miller gradually learns to respect and trust his teacher. Rick disagrees with Miller's belief that Manual Trades is nothing but a "dump heap," and he urges him not to take the easy road, as the other students are doing, but the hard road, using his intelligence to better himself. To his credit, Evan Hunter does not sentimentalize their relationship: every hard-won victory that Rick achieves is followed by a defeat.

Rick's "breakthrough" as a teacher occurs late in the novel when he reads to one of his English classes what he thinks is a war story called "The Fifty-first Dragoon." The story, which he has never seen before, is really a fairy tale called "The Fifty-first Dragon" by the American writer Heywood Broun. First published in 1921, the tale is about a young, timid knight named Gawaine le Coeur-Hardy, a student enrolled in a knight school. Gawaine's lack of enthusiasm for jousting prompts the headmaster and assistant professor of pleasaunce to devise a plan that will motivate him to slay dragons. They teach the reluctant warrior the requisite skills and watch as he progresses from fighting paper dragons to papier-mâché dragons to wooden dragons. After he demonstrates proficiency in lopping off the dummy dragon heads, they give him a diploma and announce his next challenge. "'It's time to get out there and meet Life,' the Headmaster said, in effect, 'and Life, as far as you're concerned, is dragons'" (291). To help the anxious youth fulfill his mission, the headmaster gives him a secret word—"Rumplesnitz"—and tells him that the repetition of the magical word will enable him to kill the fiercest dragon without injury to himself. The headmaster's word has its desired effect, and Gawaine effortlessly slays one dragon after another, growing increasingly self-confident. After a night of revelry, he meets his fiftieth dragon, but before he can slice off its head, as he has done with the forty-nine previous dragons, he realizes that he has forgotten the word. The dragon prepares to eat him, but just as he charges forward, Gawaine remembers the word yet has no time to say it. To his astonishment, he manages to kill the surprised dragon. The next day Gawaine returns to knight school and asks the headmaster for an explanation. In Rick's words, "The Headmaster admitted the truth. Rumplesnitz was not a magic word, it was Gawaine all along who was killing the dragons. The word just gave him confidence, that's all, and wasn't Gawaine glad that he finally knew the truth?" (292). Far from being glad, Gawaine becomes depressed and is dragged out of bed the next day and forced into the forest to confront the fifty-first dragon. The dragon is small but nevertheless prevails and devours the knight, leaving nothing except the medals the knight has always worn in battle. Rick concludes the story by saying that Gawaine's secret was never revealed and that his heroic record of killing fifty dragons remains unequaled.

The teacher doesn't know how to proceed after reading the story, partly because he has no lesson plan on it, and partly because he fears that his students will not understand the allegory. And so he proceeds slowly and tentatively, asking questions about its various levels of meaning and whether "Rumplesnitz" is really a magical word. The story excites all the students, to Rick's delight, and they debate whether the word was truly magical or whether Gawaine just thought it was. Some students have difficulty grasping the implications of the word, believing that it enabled Gawaine to "cheat," but others realize that its power arises from the knight's belief in it. Rick can hardly contain his excitement, "feeling that something was happening out there, something he'd never experienced before" (294). He asks them one question after another, including "What does Gawaine need?" and when a student triumphantly responds with the word "Confidence," the teacher validates him: "Ah-ha, that's it." He then asks them to give real-life examples of magical words. One student admits to saying three "Hail-Mary's" whenever he feels scared; a second refers to his brother-in-law, a "big bull artist" who's "always talkin' about his big deals, but he ain't really got no big deals" (296); a third describes a player on his baseball team who "got to chew gum or else he can't pitch. He don't need the gum. He's a good pitcher anyway" (296); a fourth mentions a boy who can't do anything without his mother saying "okay." Finally a student defines the story's relevance: "It tells about fake words, and how you don't need them. If you're strong and quick, what you need the phony crutch for? You got it all in you anyway. You can kill dragons, not really, but you could maybe be a good mechanic, like that, you know?" (297).

The students' response to "The Fifty-first Dragon" stuns Rick, and the words "breakthrough" and "I've broken through" appear like a magical refrain. Heywood Broun's story has a transformative effect on students and teacher alike. Indeed, Broun's words allow Rick to slay—or rather tame—his own dragons, his students, and to fulfill his calling as a gifted teacher. Just as Rick has broken through to his students, demonstrating how words can affect every aspect of a person's life, the students also break through to him, allowing him to see himself as an effective teacher and not a quitter, like his friend Josh Edwards. Although *The Blackboard Jungle* does not end with this epiphanic classroom scene—Rick's wife goes into labor later that day and delivers a stillborn baby, and the teacher must first overcome his bitterness and then defeat the knife-wielding Artie West in the novel's climax, in the process winning the loyalty of the other students—his discussion of "The Fifty-first Dragon" remains the most important scene in the novel.

Without using the word "empathy," *The Blackboard Jungle* dramatizes a teacher's ability to motivate students to identify with a fictional character and, in doing so, to understand themselves better. Rick's responses like "Ah-ha, that's it" and "Yes . . . exactly" validate his students' interpretations, and when he is not affirming them, he is echoing and summarizing their words, demonstrating that he is listening attentively, allowing them to frame the story. He is both a good English teacher and a good psychologist in this scene, encouraging his students to pursue their own interpretations and make connections between literature and life. His interest in "The Fifty-first Dragon" arouses their interest; his passion generates their passion. Thirteen different students volunteer to speak during the discussion, and although some of them don't "get" the story, Rick never humiliates or belittles them: he never uses sarcasm or irony. *His* words prove as magical to them as the headmaster's word proves to Gawaine. Whereas earlier in the story he believes that education is something that is "done" to a student, "like administering a shot of penicillin to a squirming, protesting three-year-old" (70), at the end Rick learns that teachers cannot simply shoot the needle of education into their students. Rather, teachers must guide students to their own discoveries. Viewed from Paulo Freire's perspective in *Pedagogy of the Oppressed*, Rick rejects the "banking" concept of education, in which students are empty vessels who receive "deposits" from the teacher, and embraces a more egalitarian approach, in which the teacher "is no longer merely the-one-who-teaches, but one who is himself taught in dialogue with the students, who in turn while being taught also teach" (67). The teacher's challenge, as the classroom discussion of "The Fifty-first Dragon" suggests, is to involve as many students as possible, mainly by asking thought-provoking questions and by stressing multiple levels of meaning in a story. Rick knows that he may not be able to reach all of them, but if he can help a few, like Miller, that will be enough.

We should note, however, that Heywood Broun's "The Fifty-first Dragon" is considerably more complex than Hunter implies. First, Gawaine's downfall in Broun's story is a result of hubris as well as loss of self-confidence. Slaying dragons becomes so easy for him that he begins to say "Rumplesnitz" in a "mocking sneer," and as the knight's reputation grows, the headmaster "found it impossible to keep him completely in hand" (Broun 31). Rick devotes only a sentence or two to Gawaine's revelry, but Broun emphasizes the knight's debauchery and pomposity. It is surprising that Hunter omits this aspect from the story, since it could have given Rick the opportunity to point out that overconfidence is as dangerous as underconfidence—a lesson that his students might well remember. It is even more surprising that the film version of *The Blackboard Jungle* omits any reference to "The Fifty-first Dragon," replacing it with a less apt cartoon of "Jack and the Beanstalk" that Rick's students watch on television, and from which the teacher draws the lesson of the need for tolerance of those whom we fear. Second, "The Fifty-first Dragon" demonstrates that self-confidence can be both gained and lost, and passing the test today—be it of strength, heroism, character, or intelligence—doesn't mean that one will pass it tomorrow. One's belief in words may easily change to disbelief, and one may lose faith in oneself and others without constant validation and support. Had the headmaster and assistant professor of pleasaunce talked to the frightened Gawaine, instead of dragging him out of bed toward the forest, he might have regained his self-confidence. Rick will need to remember this if he is to avoid becoming like the cynical, burned-out teachers and administrators at Manual Trades High School. Self-confidence must be internalized to become real, and it must be shored up from time to time in both students and teachers.

Rick begins his teaching career as a con artist, attempting to manipulate Miller through flattery, and he learns to become a genuine confidence man through many pedagogical mistakes, urging his students to educate themselves and make a positive contribution to society. *The Blackboard Jungle* ends with the image of Rick as an empowering teacher, but as "The Fifty-first Dragon" darkly suggests, the headmaster and assistant professor of pleasaunce are responsible for Gawaine's heroism *and* death. Heroism is more ambiguous than the novel implies. Both the headmaster and assistant professor of pleasaunce agree not to inform the school how Gawaine achieved his extraordinary record of success, or how he came to die, fearing that "it might have a bad effect on school spirit" (Broun 35). And so they mythologize him into the school's greatest hero, ignoring the ironies that make him flawed but human.

Hunter concludes *The Blackboard Jungle* by having his protagonist achieve heroic status while remaining "just a teacher." Like Hemingway, whose thematic and stylistic influence is palpable, Hunter has it both ways: his protagonist modestly disclaims heroism while others proclaim his extraordinary feats of courage. "He stops rapes and knifings," affirms Alan Manners on the penultimate page of the story. "I'm just a teacher," Rick self-effacingly maintains, and the novel ends with Rick and his colleagues returning to their classes, "back to the salt mines," to quote the last words of the novel. Will Rick be a temporary hero like Gawaine, who loses self-confidence and succumbs to the demons surrounding him, or will he continue to believe in himself, his students, and his profession, transforming a blackboard jungle into a place of learning? Will he remain a teacher? Hunter wants us to speculate on these questions. As we learn from the biographical notes on the book jacket of the 1954 edition and from the introduction to a 1999 reprint of the novel, *The Blackboard Jungle* is based on Evan Hunter's own teaching experience at a New York City vocational high school. Hunter soon left teaching, preferring instead to devote the rest of his life to writing.

A New Life: "Sometimes, between a Comma and Semicolon, He Reformed the World"

Like *The Blackboard Jungle*, Bernard Malamud's 1961 novel *A New Life* is loosely based on an author's own teaching experience, though the world of Cascadia College in the Pacific Northwest is about as far from New York City as one can imagine. Indeed, the novel's stumbling hero, Seymour Levin, is trying to escape from Manhattan, where he has lived his entire life, and re-create himself into a new man. The blunt opening sentences establish the protagonist's quest to forge a new existence in an unknown place. "S. Levin, formerly a drunkard, after a long and tiring transcontinental journey, got off the train at Marathon, Cascadia, toward evening of the last Sunday in August, 1950. Bearded, fatigued, lonely, Levin set down a valise and suitcase and looked around in a strange land for welcome" (3). Levin is running away from an old life, filled with shameful failures and disappointments, and searching for a new one in which he can find "order, value, accomplishment, love" (189). Whether he succeeds remains an open question.

Only gradually do we learn why the thirty-year-old Levin is fleeing from the past. "The emotion of my youth was humiliation," he tells Pauline Gilley, the unfulfilled wife of the director of composition, Gerald Gilley, Levin's immediate superior and eventual adversary. "That wasn't only because we were poor. My father was continuously a thief. Always thieving, always caught, he finally died in prison. My mother went crazy and killed herself. One night I came home and found her sitting on the kitchen floor looking at a bloody bread knife" (200). Amidst this background, Levin becomes a drunk, the only fate that satisfies him. For two years he lives in self-hatred, brooding over suicide. Struggling to resurrect his soul, Levin finds relief in literature, which is instrumental to his rebirth:

> My only occasional relief was in reading. I had a small dark room in a rooming house overrun by roaches and bugs. Once a week I burned the bedbugs with a candle through the bedsprings; they popped as they died. One Sunday night after a not otherwise memorable day, as I was reading in this room, I had the feeling I was about to remember everything I had read in my life. The book felt like a slab of marble in my hands. I strained to see if it could possibly be a compendium of every book ever written, describing all experience. I felt I had somewhere read something I must remember. Sensing an affirmation, I jumped up. That I was a free man lit in my mind even as I denied it. I suddenly knew, as though I were discovering it for the first time, that the source of freedom is the human spirit. This had been passed down to me but I had somehow forgotten. (201–2)

Sensing that his destiny is tied to literature and education, Levin enrolls at New York University and receives his B.A. in 1940. He is twenty-six when he realizes that he wants to teach and spends two years working in a high school—presumably not the vocational institution we see in *The Blackboard Jungle*. After receiving his M.A. from NYU in 1950, he applies for and unexpectedly receives an offer from Cascadia College, mainly because of Pauline's intervention; she reads his letter of application and feels drawn to him because his photograph reminds her of a Jewish man who had befriended her in college.

Levin's main interest is in literature, but he is hired to teach composition and remedial grammar, and much of the conflict in the novel arises over his efforts to reform the college curriculum as a prelude to reforming himself and the world. "[I]f you stay on here," Gerald Gilley advises him, "comp is what you'll be teaching till you get your doctorate—that's your union card if you want to stay in college teaching. After that you'll be given a lit class or two" (21). When Levin expresses disappointment that he cannot teach literature, Gilley responds, "I personally prefer teaching comp to lit. More satisfaction, I've found. You can just see these kids improving their writing from one term to the next, and even from one paper to the next. It isn't easy to notice much of a development of literary taste in a year" (21). Levin reluctantly agrees, but he is silently mortified when Gilley informs him that Cascadia College has lost its liberal arts program to its sister institution, Cascadia University at Gettysburg, located a hundred miles away in the state capital. To Levin's impassioned statement that the college should try to regain its liberal arts program—"Democracy owes its existence to the liberal arts. Shouldn't there be—er—some sort of protest"—Gilley replies: "You might keep in mind that education for an agrarian society, which is what we are—the majority of our state legislators come from rural areas—is basically a 'how to work' education. And if you've been keeping up on your reading on the subject, more and more liberal arts colleges in America are going in for more and more vocational subjects" (27–29). The young instructor tries to rationalize the situation, biding his time until he receives a better offer.

Levin finds himself unable to remain silent, however, about an approach to composition that he finds so unappealing. The authoritarian chair of the English Department, Orville Fairchild, is the author of *The Elements of Grammar*, the "bible" of composition teachers. "*The Elements*," as it is reverently called, is in its twenty-eighth year, thirteenth edition, and twelve hundred and sixth adoption. Indeed, it is not a single book but an entire approach to writing, as Gilley enthusiastically declaims. "What with *The Elements* and *Elements Workbooks*, Forms A, B, C, for regular, and D for remedial classes, in use, all we really have to worry about is a new freshman reader once in a while" (36). All Levin needs to do, adds Gilley, is to follow *The Elements* and the workbooks "according to our syllabus, keeping an eye out for the d.o. That's the departmental objective final we always give the comp freshmen at the end of each term" (38). Fairchild is enamored of *The Elements* because he believes it has a transformative effect on his students. "'Tell your students the book will be very useful to them.' 'Funny thing,' the professor chuckled, 'they may hate it in the beginning but they'll love it in the end. More than one of my former students have returned to tell me that mastering English grammar was the turning point of their lives'" (53).

Long before the tensions between literature and composition faculty erupted into fierce academic conflicts, Malamud records in *A New Life* the hierarchical nature of English Departments, where tenured professors teach literature and untenured adjuncts, or those without Ph.D.s, teach writing. Malamud describes the comp program at Cascadia College from an insider's point of view, beginning with the "comp room" where graded student essays are kept. "This was the boss's idea," Gilley tells Levin. "Once we collect them, the students can't pass them around for their friends to copy. I suppose you've heard about fraternity files?" (33). Dismayed by the college catalogue, with its "glut of composition, bonehead grammar, and remedial reading, over about a dozen skimpy literature courses" (39), Levin listens disconsolately as Professor Fairchild, who is nearing retirement, affirms that he has "fought the good fight" (53). Malamud sustains the comic tension between the aging patriarch and the young radical instructor. Early in the novel Fairchild lectures Levin on the two types of people he deplores in the teaching profession. "One is the misfit who sneaks in to escape his inadequacy elsewhere and who ought to be booted out—and isn't very often; and the other is the aggressive pest whose one purpose is to upset other people's applecarts, and the more apples, the better. We've had both types here, to our sorrow, and what's worse, sometimes in one and the same person" (41). Fairchild's comments characterize not only Levin's predecessor and doppelgänger, Leo Duffy, who had an affair with Pauline Gilley, for which he was fired, but also Levin himself. Only later does Levin learn from Pauline that Duffy committed suicide, further establishing the kinship between the two instructors. Nor does Levin feel reassured when Fairchild tells him that "you happen to remind me of my poor father, who at one time of his life—I make no secret of it—was an incurable drunkard" (50).

Many of Levin's difficulties arise from the politically and educationally hostile institution in which he finds himself. He is horrified by Fairchild's political views: "His subject usually was creeping socialism, where it crept, the tyranny of the New Deal . . . and the evils of federal aid to education" (100). In one of the novel's most memorable scenes, Fairchild admonishes Levin to be humble and good and then suffers a heart attack. Levin attends faithfully to his dying words, hoping they will contain a final revelation about the meaning of life:

> The old man smiled with wet eyes. His face was smaller now. His lips twitched as he tried to speak. Levin leaned very close.
>   "Try to rest."
>   "The mys-mystery—of the in-fin—in-fin—in-fin—"
>   "Infinite."
>   "In-fin-i-tive. Have—you con-sidered—its possi-bil-i-ties? To be—"

He paused, gazed intently at Levin, and muttered, "Poor papa." His mouth shut sternly. He died. (304)

Malamud sympathizes with Levin's struggle to achieve a new life, but he knows that Levin is his own worst enemy. The young instructor understands what he must do to succeed professionally but nevertheless sabotages his career at every opportunity. He is unable, for example, to follow Fairchild's sensible advice to "refrain from dating students, no matter what the provocation" (49). Levin's affair with an undergraduate leads predictably to disaster. Nor can he refrain from having an affair with the director of composition's wife. His decision to marry Pauline at the end of the novel spells the end of his college teaching career, since the only way that Gerald Gilley will allow her to have custody of their children is if Levin renounces college teaching—a form of blackmail to which he reluctantly agrees. His decision seems both courageous and foolish, consistent with so many of his earlier actions.

Yet if Malamud's attitude toward Levin remains ambivalent to the end, there is little question about the novelist's feelings about Cascadia's English Department. Neither Levin nor Malamud can conceive of a literature or writing course that does not have human experience as its basis. Both believe that literature can change a student's life, though sometimes the novelist cannot resist poking fun at his clueless character. Malamud always has greater insight into Levin's character than Levin himself, as when the new instructor tells his students at the end of the first class of the semester: "If they worked conscientiously in college, he said, they would come in time to a better understanding of who they were and what their lives might yield, education being revelation. At this they laughed, though he wasn't sure why. Still if they could be so good-humored early in the morning it was all right with him" (89). As he walks out of class, he discovers why his students are convulsed with laughter: his fly is open.

Literature, however, is no laughing matter for either Levin or Malamud. They are not against discussions of grammar, only against courses that focus exclusively on grammar. Even if Fairchild's observation to Levin is correct—"Our main function, as I always tell everyone we employ here, is to satisfy the needs of the professional schools on the campus with respect to written communication. In science and technology men must be taught to communicate with the strictest accuracy, therefore we teach more composition than anything else in this department" (40)—innovative teachers can encourage their students to write about their lives as farmers, foresters, engineers, and agronomists. Such writing can indeed be transformative. A writing course without content, however, leads not to a new life but to a dead end, as Levin realizes: "I sometimes feel I'm engaged in a great irrelevancy, teaching people how to write who don't know what to write. I can give them subjects, but not subject matter. I worry I'm not teaching how to keep civilization from destroying itself" (115). Levin stakes his life on the seriousness of literature and does whatever he can to sneak a novel or poem into the comp course. "Sometimes Levin interrupted drill in Workbook Form B, to speak of a good novel or read aloud a poem, the only poem some of them would hear in college, possibly in their lives. Sometimes, between a comma and semicolon, he reformed the world" (166).

Levin's belief that democracy owes its existence to the liberal arts reflects the novel's point of view. This is especially true of the historical period in which the story is set, the Cold War, when the specter of McCarthyism looms over the campus, threatening free speech. Malamud supports not only Levin's eloquent defense of literature but also his uncompromising opposition to censorship. Levin is distressed when both Gilley and Fairchild cave in to a parent protesting the inclusion of Hemingway's short story "Ten Indians" because of its frank treatment of miscegenation. Observes Levin, "A college is no place to show contempt for art or intellect. If you drop the book, you'll be making cowards of us all" (226). Malamud satirizes Levin's messianic fantasies but not his devotion to the liberal arts. "They teach what's for sale in a commercial society, and what had better not be. That democracy is a moral philosophy and can't be defended by lopping off its head. A man can find an ideal worth living for in the liberal arts. It might inspire him to work for a better society. It takes only one good man to make the world a little better" (275).

In an influential essay on *A New Life*, Leslie Fiedler has complained that he can believe in Levin only as long as he remains an "absurd anti-hero," but once he begins to have an affair with a colleague's wife, the novel slips into "what may well be the least rewarding of all American fictional sub-genres, the Academic Novel":

> In this kind of book, some sensitive representative of the liberal tradition finds himself embattled in a world controlled by mindless, callous bureaucrats: Deans and Department Chairmen in the Academic Novel proper, though Big Business or Madison Avenue or Hollywood or the Armed Forces can be substituted for the university without making any essential difference. When he seems at the point of defeat, however, he revenges himself on his persecutors by screwing or running off with the wife of one of them, then retreating to write the very novel the reader holds in his hands. (155)

Fiedler's observation strikes me as too cynical for *A New Life*, though it does apply to a spate of contemporary academic novels that are far more formulaic. Malamud maintains a healthy irony throughout the novel, and in the end Levin's victories are small but significant. Although his life is so out of control that he cannot remain devoted to progressive reform, he nevertheless remains a humane educator, one who believes that "a good teacher is a liberator" (177). For lack of evidence, he refuses to participate in the prosecution of a student whom he suspects of plagiarism, and everyone recognizes his dedication to teaching. He never ceases to question his life, goals, motivations, and principles; he is always harder on himself than on others. Under Levin's leadership the textbook committee unanimously recommends the use of *The Elements* only in the Grammar for Teachers course and the adoption of a more suitable freshman reader for the other courses. In addition, Levin proposes a Great Books program for the faculty, a suggestion that the dean unexpectedly accepts. Unfortunately, Levin will not be around to lead it, for he has been unceremoniously fired by the president. His efforts to defeat Gerald Gilley as the new department chairperson are also thwarted. Levin believes in the end that he has failed the college, and when Pauline reminds him that he has managed to dislodge *The Elements*, he responds glumly: "A hell of a revolution" (366). Nevertheless, it is a beginning for progressive reform at Cascadia College, and if Levin cannot continue teaching in college, he can always return to high school teaching, where he can try to make a difference in his students' lives.

The Small Room: "No Wonder Teaching Was Called an Art"

Published the same year as *A New Life*, May Sarton's *The Small Room* also describes a young instructor's first teaching experience, not at a large Pacific Northwestern university but at an elite New England woman's college. The novel is fascinating in several ways. First, it explores the student-teacher relationship, including the complex and often unruly transference-countertransference dynamics that are rarely acknowledged by educators. Second, *The Small Room* focuses on the personal aspects of teaching, especially the elusive qualities that contribute to the art of teaching. Third, the novel analyzes the different roles teachers play, particularly the role of therapist, for which they are seldom trained or prepared. Fourth, the novel is a cautionary tale about the benefits and risks of teacher interventions in students' lives. And finally, *The Small Room* dramatizes many of the similarities between teaching and psychotherapy, both of which have far more in common with each other than teachers or therapists would like to admit.

Appearing shortly before the resurgence of the women's movement, *The Small Room* contains several minor details—and one major detail—that reveal how different higher education is today. Appleton, which resembles

Wellesley College, is an institution that prides itself on teaching, and for Lucy Winter, who has just received her Ph.D. in English from Harvard University, Appleton represents her initiation into the profession. Lucy had entered a doctoral program so that she could be near her fiancé, a student at Harvard Medical School, but when she abruptly breaks off the engagement, she decides reluctantly to look for a teaching position. Neither Lucy nor Sarton could predict that the 1960s would be one of the few buyer's markets for professors. To anyone in the humanities who has been unlucky enough to be on the job market in the last thirty years, the ease with which Lucy lands a job at Appleton, considered the "pristine well, the essence of female institutions of learning" (12), must seem a fantasy— especially since the twenty-seven-year-old assistant professor, with no publications or burning desire to write, is promised tenure and promotion "in a year or so." Another detail that strikes contemporary academics as strange is the question that she is asked during her on-campus interview: "You are not planning to marry in the immediate future?" (12)—a query that violates current antidiscrimination laws. Unlike today's students, who wear jeans and sweatshirts to classes, for Appleton students the "unrequired but almost universal uniform [is] . . . short pleated skirts and blazers" (30). Neither students nor teachers think twice before lighting up cigarettes during conferences. Teachers drink more alcohol than do their students, a detail that today's students would find archaic.

But what most separates us from the world of Appleton is that the college does not yet have a resident psychiatrist to counsel its students. This is the emotionally charged question that drives the novel's plot, for when Lucy discovers that one of the college's most brilliant students, Jane Seaman, has plagiarized an essay, the campus is polarized around the issue of whether to expel her, as college regulations demand, or recommend that she see an off-campus psychiatrist who will help her uncover the unconscious motives behind the self-destructive act. Adamantly opposing the hire of a psychiatrist are Jane's mentor, Professor Carryl Cope, an internationally famous medieval historian, and Carryl's closest friend and lover, Olive Hunt, an eccentric member of Appleton's board of trustees who has threatened to change her will leaving a multimillion dollar donation to the college, which desperately needs the money to insure its survival.

Why the fierce opposition to psychiatry? Both Carryl Cope and Olive Hunt offer what they regard as irrefutable reasons why Appleton's students would be harmed by a mental health professional. To begin with, the opposition is a generational issue: as the college president explains, Olive Hunt "comes of the old-fashioned school which thinks you pull yourself up by your own bootstraps"; a moment later he elaborates that this is pre-cisely what she did years ago when she was in a crisis: "I suspect that she may have had some sort of breakdown herself, after her father's death, and that she pulled herself out of it on sheer guts" (57). Olive has no use either for therapists or students who need their services: "what the girls need," she states imperiously, "is not more 'help'—ugh, how I loathe that word!—but greater demands on their intellects and souls" (78–79). When Lucy tells her about a freshman, Pippa Brentwood, who is grieving her father's recent death and spending a great deal of time crying, Olive Hunt replies unempathically:

> So did I when I was her age. . . . I suspect that I rather enjoyed it. I got out of it, not because I had a professor who took a personal interest in me, but be-cause I did have (thank God!) a professor who made me take an interest in a subject. It happened to be Greek. Give her psychiatric attention—for I pre-sume what you are saying is that you would be glad to turn this weeper over to someone else and take her back when she combs her hair and stops crying—give her *that*, and she'll just wallow in *self*. (79–80)

Whereas Olive Hunt believes that the appointment of a resident psychia-trist will discourage professors from making challenging demands on their students' intellects and souls, Carryl Cope asserts that there are people such as Pippa who shouldn't be in college because of psychological prob-lems. Carryl is less opinionated than Olive Hunt but no less psychologi-cally obtuse, at least until the end of the novel, when she undergoes a change of heart. Unlike Lucy, who tries to teach all her students, Carryl is devoted only to the most extraordinary. "I teach for the singular, for the exceptional," she maintains; "I teach for the one in a hundred, one in a thousand maybe" (75). Believing that the price of excellence is "eccen-tricity, maladjustment if you will, isolation of one sort or another, strange-ness, narrowness" (69), Carryl is devastated by the seemingly inexplicable behavior of her star student, Jane Seaman, whom she has been grooming as a disciple. Carryl's solution is to hush up the plagiarism so that her protégée's career will not be destroyed; she cannot imagine that Jane com-mitted plagiarism as an unconscious rebellion against the authority figure who has worked so hard to educate her. Carryl is so invested emotionally in Jane that she threatens to resign if the college recommends psychiatric help for her student—thus ironically demonstrating that the faculty might also need psychological counseling.

Lucy Winter, the novel's sympathetic heroine, intuits the reasons be-hind Jane Seaman's plagiarism, Olive Hunt's and Carryl Cope's implacable opposition to psychiatry, Pippa Brentwood's mourning, and the complex dynamics of the student-teacher relationship. Lucy doesn't need to make the case for a liberal arts education, as does Malamud's Levin, nor is she pigeonholed into teaching either literature or composition. Like Levin, she believes that literature can transform students' lives, but she has much greater self-awareness than he does, and she never sabotages her career by becoming involved romantically with her students or her colleagues' spouses. Levin is by temperament a troublemaker; by contrast, Lucy is a peacemaker, and her psychological and pedagogical insights identify her with the authorial point of view.

Lucy recognizes that Jane's paper on *The Iliad* is plagiarized from an essay by Simone Weil published in an English publication, and she asks Jane to explain why she resorted to intellectual theft. "I just got tired of being pushed so hard, tired of the whole racket, tired of having a brain, tired of coming up to the jump and taking it again and again. Lost my nerve" (102). Lucy listens nonjudgmentally to her student's explanation and, without using the word "transference," helps Jane see that her anger toward the increasing demands placed upon her by Carryl Cope is a repetition of her disappointment with her divorced parents, who have apparently neglected her. In Lucy's view, Jane has sought love and approval through intellectual achievement, but when that fails to fulfill her deeper longings, she sabotages herself by committing a crime that she knows will lead to eventual discovery and expulsion. Lucy thus interprets Jane's plagiarism as a psychological cry for help, and she urges her to seek professional treatment to expand her self-awareness. At first Jane angrily rejects her teacher's words, concluding that "You're just like everyone else who has read a little Freud and thinks he can paste a label on things and solve them with a label" (161), but she gradually overcomes the fear of exploring her unconscious motivation and agrees to go with Lucy to New York City to visit a psychoanalyst with whom she begins treatment.

Lucy also helps Carryl Cope explore countertransference issues, namely, how and why the intense demands that she has placed on her young protégée have been damaging to both of them. Lucy again functions as a psychoanalyst, suggesting tactfully that what Jane needs most from her professor is not more intellectual knowledge, as Carryl believes, but understanding of a different kind. Carryl initially rejects this interpretation, denying that she has pressured her student. Nor does she realize that her effort to cover up the plagiarism will make the situation worse. Only gradually does she recognize that she has "refused to recognize the whole person in Jane Seaman" (232). As the novel closes, Carryl admits that she has been more involved than she should have been in her student's success and failure; she also discovers that teachers must preserve a delicate balance between involvement and detachment. "Part of the art of teaching," her colleague Hallie Summerson observes, "lies in how this pseudo-intimacy is handled" (40–41), a pseudointimacy that is as problematic in the student-teacher relationship as it is in the patient-analyst relationship.

Contemporary readers may believe, as I do, that Lucy's psychoanalytic interpretation of Jane Seaman's plagiarism is too neat. Plagiarism is now so common that few teachers seek to discover the underlying psychological motivations behind it; moreover, the problem of how to respond to plagiarism would still remain even if that motivation could be determined. Another problem with *The Small Room* is that few assistant professors have the courage—or foolishness—to confront a senior professor's lifelong pattern of relating to students. Nor is it credible that Olive Hunt, so contemptuous of psychology, should agree with Lucy that Carryl Cope sees Jane as a younger version of herself. "I think Carryl saw in that girl . . . the image of herself when she was young; Jane does have a sort of primary intensity, hunger for work, whatever it is, that one doesn't find every day" (204). Both Carryl and Olive accept many of Lucy's psychoanalytic interpretations at the end of the novel, further straining credibility.

Lucy's attitude toward her "weeper," Pippa Brentwood, is also puzzling. She recoils in horror when Pippa tells her, after their first class, that her father has died recently; Lucy is unnerved by what she regards as her student's inappropriate "plea for sympathy" (38). She dreads to see Pippa in conference because her student "is clearly incapacitated by some private woe" (79). Lucy conveys her discomfort with the personal aspect of teaching to Hallie Summerson: "What depressed me, I think, was that I tried to say something about learning and teaching, and the only result was that a girl wanted to tell me about her father's death" (39). Hallie's response indicates that she too is critical of the student's tears. "Pippa Brentwood . . . does tend to dramatize . . . and I'm afraid her father's death, sudden and tragic as it was, has given her rather a chance to indulge herself" (39). The judgment of grief as a form of self-indulgence seems to reflect the authorial point of view, for a few pages later Lucy scolds Pippa when she asks for help:

"I know this is hard for you, Pippa, but I think the less you dramatize—" How harsh it sounded!

"It's real suffering," Pippa wailed, and the tears poured down her cheeks like summer rain. "You can't say it's not real!"

Face this, Lucy admonished herself. Be kind. After all, she's only a child.

"Of course it's real. The loss of one's father at any age . . . " But where to go from here? "Is your mother finding it very hard?" She heard the tone of her voice, cool, sympathetic, yet withholding. It was hateful to be in this position where it was kindness to appear a little less than human. The question only produced loud sobs. Lucy talked on at random, saying all the commonplaces about death, about time, waiting for the girl to regain command of herself. (49).

Pippa's tears strike at the heart of the novel, for they signify what Lucy calls the "old universal wound" (49). Lucy knows all about this wound because of disappointment with her own father, a successful surgeon who seemed to derive more pleasure from his career and hobbies than from his family. Pippa's tears penetrate Lucy's defenses, awakening her deepest psychological conflicts. Throughout the novel Lucy struggles to empathize with her students without being overwhelmed by their problems; at times she prefers to relate to Pippa only as a student, while at other times she speaks more personally, acknowledging her own vulnerability. "She found herself speaking quite gently now about the load of guilt children always do carry around about their parents, and how self-blame can, after a point, become self-indulgence. 'It's the human condition, Pippa'" (49). Lucy's words soothe Pippa: "It was touching to see the immense relief in the face of innocence before her, relief like some clear dawn taking the place of disintegration and darkness." Pippa thanks her teacher, but Lucy still fears personal involvement, and Pippa remains needy: "You won't refuse to see me?"—a question that sets up the following dialogue:

"On professional matters, Pippa, I'll always be here. This has been an excursion outside them."

"I'm a terrible nuisance, I guess," Pippa said hopefully.

"No," Lucy summoned dispassion to her side as if it were a guardian angel. "But you are, perhaps, confusing me with someone else, an imaginary someone, let us say, 'a father confessor and friend.' I don't see myself in that role, I'm afraid." Lucy got up and stood with her back to the window. It was meant to be a dismissal.

"You sound so hard," Pippa said in an accusing voice.

"I'm not hard," she shot back, fatally on the defensive. "I'm too vulnerable. I have never been a teacher before. And I don't believe in college teachers being amateur psychoanalysts." She recovered herself firmly. "There must be a subject between us, Pippa, an impersonal subject," she said, facing the girl squarely.

"Well," Pippa, accepting defeat, gathered her books together as slowly as possible, "but if I could just see you when I get desperate? I'll try not to, I really will," she added eagerly.

"I'm not a monster, after all," Lucy said, and left it at that. (50–51).

Lucy certainly is not a monster, though she does strike me as surprisingly fearful of empathizing with her student's distress. Lucy's youth and professional inexperience heighten her vulnerability, making empathy dangerous, but what most surprises me is May Sarton's portrayal of Pippa's grief as a form of self-indulgence. There's something comical about the number of times Pippa "wails" in her teacher's presence. She has every right to cry over her father's recent death, yet the novel depicts her tears as excessive. Later Pippa again cries in Lucy's office, this time because of the accurate perception that Carryl Cope is playing favorites by trying to conceal Jane's plagiarism, but now the narrator tells us that "Pippa's tears, this time, could not be pushed aside as self-indulgent" (133). "It takes some courage to face out the self-righteous indignation of your peers," Lucy observes. Once Lucy acknowledges her own confusion and self-doubt, she senses that the "intimacy which this painful interview was establishing between her and Pippa, far from feeding a 'crush' as she had feared it would, was rooted now in mutual respect" (135–36). Both feel better after their discussion, and the chapter closes with Lucy wondering "whether crisis may be one of the climates where education flourishes—a climate that forces honesty out, breaks down the walls of what ough[t] to be, and reveals what *is*, instead" (138).

May Sarton provides readers of *The Small Room* with a degree of closure at the end without resolving the pedagogical questions raised by the novel. Lucy receives an appreciative note from Jane indicating her progress at the sanitarium where she is being treated: "They say I shall get well, and I am trying" (210). Pippa is also doing well: she turns in a thoughtful essay on Emerson and Thoreau, and she seems to be in control of her grief. "You've taught me a lot," she gratefully tells Lucy, who is pleased with her academic progress. Yet Lucy is still troubled by the degree to which her student's academic growth depends upon personal feelings toward the teacher. "Oh Pippa. . . . Do it for the thing itself, not for me," to which Pippa responds firmly, "For you as well. . . . Teaching is more than just a subject, you know. It's a person, too. You can't get away from that, even if you want to" (212). Lucy clearly *wants* to escape from the personal element in teaching, fearful that it will result in a loss of boundaries in the student-teacher relationship. Her final realization is that teaching is always personal but must never be the main focus of education. "There was no avoiding the issue: the most detached teacher in the world infused her detachment, and if one student or another received this as a personal message, well, maybe one had to accept that that was one way of learning.

No wonder teaching was called an art, the most difficult kind of art in which the final expression depends upon a delicate and dangerous balance between two people and a subject. Eliminate the subject and the whole center collapses" (212–13).

The Small Room raises intriguing pedagogical questions that are as important today as they were when the novel was published. It remains one of the most authentic fictional studies of the student-teacher relationship. Carryl Cope speaks for all of her colleagues when she observes that the "relation between student and teacher must be about the most complex and ill-defined there is" (83). Sometimes this complexity is gently satirized, as when Lucy tells her students on the first day of the semester, "You will discover . . . that you appreciate teachers rather a long time after you have suffered from them" (34). The narrator is well aware that "teaching is first of all teaching a person" (104), an insight that affirms teaching the whole person. Teachers can never predict when a story will speak to its readers, but sometimes it is only when a student is experiencing a crisis. Thus it occurs to Lucy that "it was perhaps only at points of conflict that some door in the lazy attention was finally forced open, and people became educable—at least if the conflict were not too intense or deeply buried" (131).

Lucy learns a great deal about teaching, and as the novel closes, she makes the kind of difference in her students' lives that her own teachers have made in hers. Indeed, during her first day of class she tells her students about the "great teachers" who have had a transformative effect upon her. She knows that "there are as many kinds of good teachers as there are of artists" (110). Despite differences in teaching styles and subjects, they were all humble and respectful. One teacher was "devastatingly honest, with a kind of honesty that forced him to ask questions rather than to make statements, and to question himself as seriously as he did us" (35). Another teacher failed Lucy on a midterm but told her that her paper contained an original idea that many of the A exams lacked. And a third teacher "wore his learning so lightly that he forced you to wear yours with at least an attempt at a sense of proportion" (37).

It may not be surprising that all these teachers are male, but how do we explain the fact that fathers seem to have a stronger influence on their daughters' growth and development in *The Small Room* than do their mothers? One learns a good deal about Lucy's, Pippa's, and Carryl's fathers but almost nothing about their mothers. Significantly, the novel's major father-daughter relationship is highly conflicted, a detail that may have been shaped by biographical forces. Just as Lucy had "suffered from being the only child of a man too absorbed in his own work to be a father" (13–14), so did Sarton have a strained relationship with her own father. According to biographer Margot Peters, Sarton's father, an eminent historian of science, failed to give his daughter the support and approval she needed.

May Sarton has indicated that *The Small Room* was based on her own college teaching experiences. Although she never attended college, she taught composition at Harvard from 1950 to 1953 and creative writing at Wellesley College from 1959 to 1964. She wrote to a friend in 1961 that *The Small Room* "was a kind of love letter to the profession of teaching . . . but I was anxious both not to be snide (as so many novelists have been when dealing with college life) nor sentimental" (*Selected Letters, 1955–1995* 92). Mark Fulk notes that her "advocacy here—revolutionary at the time—for the use of professional counselors on campus ties in with her own commitment to become more candid, honest, and open with herself, and to model that openness for others" (84). Sarton stated in an interview that she loved teaching but decided to leave the profession when she was fifty-five because "it takes exactly out of you what writing does" (Ingersoll 47).

Curiously, Sarton's attitude toward psychoanalysis in *The Small Room* is more positive than her statements elsewhere suggest. In a letter written in 1947, she complained that "Freudianism . . . excuses everything one may do or be" (*Selected Letters, 1916–1954* 274)—a statement that echoes Pippa's sentiments in the novel. Sarton also objected to the psychoanalytic bias against homosexuality. "I would be an anti-Freudian in that I never believed that a homosexual was a cripple" (Ingersoll 71). In her next novel, *Mrs. Stevens Hears the Mermaid Singing,* published in 1965, Sarton disclosed her own lesbianism.

The world has changed profoundly in the last forty years, and nowhere is this change better seen than in the fact that today's students seek help at college counseling centers in record numbers. The question today is not whether a college should appoint a resident psychiatrist but whether it has the resources to hire enough mental health professionals to treat all the students who seek counseling. Few novelists could have predicted in the early 1960s how many future college students would suffer from clinical depression, suicidal ideation, anxiety and panic attacks, eating disorders, and drug and alcohol addiction. Pippa's grief over her father's death anticipates the anguish of countless students whose families have been shattered by divorce and who may have lost contact with one or both of their biological parents. If psychological counseling is essential to a student like Jane Seaman, what about the students sitting in our classrooms who are in more desperate situations? *The Small Room* demonstrates that although teachers cannot replace mental health professionals, they can help students to understand and cope with problems of living. Lucy recognizes finally that Appleton is not primarily a college for scholars but for the "total human being," where students "learn to think about feeling as well as about everything else" (235).

Up the Down Staircase: "The Teacher-Pupil Relationship Is a Kind of Tightrope to Be Walked"

Bel Kaufman's 1964 novel *Up the Down Staircase* describes a young teacher's tempestuous initiation into a once-genteel profession. Like *The Small Room*, it is a lively and affectionate account of a young English teacher's baptism by fire, and again like Sarton's novel, it focuses on the tension between a teacher's involvement with and detachment from her students. The teaching conditions at Calvin Coolidge High School in New York City are not as brutal as in *The Blackboard Jungle*, but they are bad enough: a decaying school building, inadequate supplies, overcrowded classrooms, insolent students, and callous administrators. Sylvia Barrett, the novel's embattled heroine, is an attractive and idealistic woman who discovers that nothing she learned in her courses on Anglo-Saxon literature, pedagogy, or in her master's thesis on Chaucer has prepared her for the vicissitudes of everyday teaching. Calvin Coolidge seems more like a medium-security prison than a high school, and Sylvia confronts obstacles that would defeat a less committed educator. Her workload is staggering: she teaches 201 students in her English classes and supervises—or rather polices—another 42 in homeroom. The school's administrators add to her problems, harassing the teachers at every opportunity. The principal and his underlings (especially J. J. McHabe, who signs himself "Adm. Asst.,"and whom Sylvia refers to as "Admiral Ass") are portrayed as bureaucratic, mindless, and humorless, placing a premium on conformity and, thus, mediocrity. Sylvia's only friend among the staff is Bea Schachter, a savvy veteran who helps her decipher the avalanche of mind-numbing memos that bury the teachers in paperwork. Explains Bea, "The clerical work is par for the course. 'Keep on file in numerical order' means throw in a wastebasket. You'll soon learn the language. 'Let it be a challenge to you' means you're stuck with it; 'interpersonal relationships' is a fight between kids; 'ancillary civic agencies for supportive discipline' means call the cops; 'Language Arts Dept.' is the English office; 'literature based on child's reading level and experimental background' means that's all they've got in the

Book Room; 'non-academic minded' is a delinquent; and 'It has come to my attention' means you're in trouble" (14).

Up the Down Staircase alternates between absurdity and despair, and Sylvia and Bea are the only teachers who can appreciate the craziness of the educational system, including the unintentional humor of the school memos. "How can I take seriously," she asks Bea, "such mimeographed absurdities as 'Lateness due to absence,' 'High under-achiever,' and 'Polio Consent slips'"? (151). Teachers have keys but no locks, blackboards but no chalk, students but no seats. Students cannot use the library—though few have the desire to read—nor are they allowed to purchase paperback editions of Shakespeare or other authors because they would be exposed to insufficiently edited or unexpurgated editions. These details give the novel its comic authenticity and help establish the reader's identification with the protagonist's rites of passage from an inexperienced teacher to a battle-hardened professional. Sylvia never loses her humor or compassion amidst this hostile environment, and although she is tempted to resign to take a position at an affluent private school where she can teach her beloved Chaucer to a class of eight students, she decides to remain at Calvin Coolidge, where she is needed and finally accepted by her students.

The novel is narrated largely through a series of letters that Sylvia writes to Bea and a friend; the epistolary technique, which is omitted from the 1967 film starring Sandy Dennis, is juxtaposed with brief classroom writings, which indicate the students' increasing respect for their teacher. Sylvia's imaginative writing assignments encourage her students to make connections between the stories and myths discussed in class and their own lives. One assignment asks her students to describe what they have learned from their English courses; a second asks them to write about a best friend; a third asks them to write about why they wish to drop out of school. In addition, the teacher creates a suggestion box and challenges them to imagine how they would improve their education. Many of the student writings reveal both the sadness and humor of their lives, as in Frank McCourt's memoir *'Tis*, and the tragicomic tone is sustained throughout the novel. Some of Sylvia's letters end with a disturbing postscript about the reality of education in New York City, including such observations that out of every hundred children who start school, only fifteen go on to receive a college diploma, and that 90 percent of dropouts are Negroes and Puerto Ricans.

Up the Down Staircase is one of the few novels or films that actually shows a literature teacher reading and commenting on student essays, and we see the consequences of the commentary. Alice Blake, a sixteen-year old, "pale with love, lost in a dream of True Romances" (69), is infatuated with Sylvia's fellow English teacher, Paul Barringer, who is the "Glamor boy" of the English Department. An unpublished poet who drinks too much and who attempts to woo Sylvia with his rhymes, Barringer is a heartthrob to all his female students; Sylvia is also interested in him but recognizes his irresponsibility and superficiality. Dismayed by the rejection slips he receives from publishers to whom he has submitted his poetry, he cultivates an attitude of superiority that distances him from students and teachers alike. He also arrives late to school every day, though one of his admirers, a school clerk, regularly punches in his time clock. Barringer receives a love letter from Alice Blake revealing her unhealthy obsession with him; it does not take clinical training to recognize that the letter is a cry for help, especially when she writes, "If I could die for you! . . . Like the Lady of Shalot you read to us, floating dead on the river under his window, and Lancelot never knowing" (228). Barringer responds only by correcting her grammar, punctuation, and spelling. "You might look up the spelling of the Lady in Tennyson's 'Idylls of the King'" (232), he writes at the end of his brief comment. He remains silent over the desperate content of the letter and later, after she jumps out of the window of the classroom in which he was supposed to be sitting, denies any responsibility for his failure to notice the signs of her instability. "I am the villain of the melodrama," he tells Sylvia in a defensive note. "Was I supposed to *encourage* a neurotic adolescent? . . . She left me a note full of dots and renunciation. It had to do with a love letter she had sent me, which I handled in the only way possible" (238–39). The student's fall is broken by the ledge below the window, and she survives the suicide attempt, though not without incurring serious and perhaps permanent injuries. Barringer never acknowledges his role in her suicide attempt and never changes his attitude of amused detachment.

How should the English teacher have responded to his student's letter? The novel never answers the question directly, but the authorial Sylvia realizes that a teacher's responsibility extends beyond grammatical corrections. Writing to her friend, Sylvia observes: "Paul asks how *I* would have handled a love letter from a student. I don't know—by talking, maybe, by listening. I don't know. How sad that we don't hear each other—any of us" (240–41). Sylvia is herself a good listener and an empathic reader of her students' writings. She responds compassionately to an angry, bitter letter from the school's "problem-child," Joe Ferone, who announces that he is quitting school at the end of the term because he believes no one cares about his existence, including those who, like Miss Barrett, pretend otherwise. "But you're even phonier than the others because you put on this act—being a dame you know how—and you stand there pretending that you give a damn. Who you kidding?" He invites her to fail him on the essay because of his vocabulary; he is beyond caring, he adds, and is prepared to join the "dogs eating dogs eating other dogs in the great big lousy world you're all educating us for." He is sure that she will not miss him: "Don't worry, you'll find plenty of others willing to play your game of baah, baah, little lost lambs, come back to school." Sylvia senses in Ferone a rebelliousness similar to her own, and she proves she cares by responding to both the form and content of his essay:

> Joe—Though your vocabulary is colorful, certain words would be more effective if used sparingly. You express yourself vividly and well, and your metaphors—from dogs to lambs—are apt. I would tend to give you a considerably higher mark than you give yourself, and I am not speaking of English.
> There is some truth in what you say, but you are far too intelligent to cling to a view as narrow as yours. As for your indictment of me—in this country one is innocent until proved guilty. Why not give me the chance any suspect gets? I think we should have a talk. Can you see me after school today?
> S. Barrett (82–83)

Sylvia knows instinctively how to correct her students' essays—and part of the knowledge is her humility, which reminds her that there are no easy pedagogical formulas for responding to writings filled with so much anger and despair. To this extent, she resembles Lucy Winter, who also responds sensitively to her students' writings. Reading essays on the topic "My Best Friend," Sylvia wonders: "How do I correct them? What do I correct? Spelling? Punctuation? The inarticulate loneliness between the lines? I don't know where to start, or whether to laugh or cry. Perhaps the two are the same" (131). Again like Lucy, she realizes that empathy requires understanding her students' points of view without losing her own, and that maintaining the proper distance is sometimes tricky. "There is a need for closeness, yet we can't get too close. The teacher-pupil relationship is a kind of tightrope to be walked. I know how carefully I must choose a word, a gesture. I understand the delicate balance between friendliness and familiarity, dignity and aloofness. I am especially aware of this in trying to reclaim Ferone. I don't know why it's so important to me. Perhaps because he, too, is a rebel. Perhaps because he's been so damaged. He's too bright and too troubled to be lost in the shuffle" (90).

Sylvia finally cannot reclaim Joe Ferone: she can make a difference in many of her students' lives but not in his. And it is this failure that marks the novel's realism. In the most dramatic scene in *Up the Down Staircase*, Ferone accepts his teacher's invitation to speak with him after school, but he mistakes her compassion for sexual desire and is confused when she doesn't respond to his advances. She is herself confused: she reaches out and touches his face in an effort to express tenderness and support, as if he were a child, but she knows that he is a grown man who is eager to exploit her weakness. It is not her empathy that heightens her vulnerability but her need to be loved, which momentarily clouds her judgment and results in a near-loss of boundaries. The film version of *Up the Down Staircase* depicts this scene more like an attempted rape than does the novel, in which Sylvia blames herself for creating the dangerous situation: "Ferone taught me. Our roles became reversed. *He* had reached *me*; I was the one who needed *him*, to make me feel" (304). In both versions, however, Sylvia knows that she cannot transgress boundaries without injuring both her student and herself. Ferone leaves but not before uttering, "Damn you to hell" (303), and Sylvia then breaks down in tears, realizing that he had detected and exploited a need within her that cannot be acted upon in a teacher-student relationship without incurring a terrible price.

Up the Down Staircase contains many of the characteristics of the high school novel—a sympathetic teacher battling unenlightened administrators and a society that spends insufficient money on education—but what allows the story to transcend the limitations of the genre are the many touching selections from student essays. The writings reveal the difficulty of growing up in a dangerous world, and some of the selections are insightful and original, as when a student in Bea's creative writing class writes a paragraph on "life reflected in the television eye": "I see the television eye. It does not see me albeit I scream jump laugh weep rant rage stick out my tongue at it. Within the television eye, among the shadows and the horizontal streaks the little people live and love and eat and die interupted by commercials. While I, yes I, possess the power to turn them off whenever I feel like it. Just so to God are we as they, for Lo! He can stop our mouths while in the middle of a sentence and snap our hearts in twain. His Eye sees us albeit we do not see Him. What is God?—God is the Universal Antenna" (146). Sylvia Barrett is an engaging heroine, and Kaufman's willingness to describe her young teacher's vulnerability makes her more appealing. The novel shows that teachers can make a difference in their students' lives, even if that difference is less dramatic than one hopes. The novel also warns teachers about having too lofty expectations and accepting too much responsibility for students' failures. "You're not God," Bea gently reproaches Sylvia, "Nothing is your fault, except, perhaps, poor teaching" (166). The reader never doubts Sylvia's decision to remain at Calvin Coolidge High School, and the novel finally affirms the possibility that teachers can cut through pedagogical red tape and challenge their students intellectually while helping them to develop emotionally. *Up the Down Staircase* begins with a student calling Sylvia Barrett "teach" and ends with her responding in kind: "Hi, pupe!" (340). In the process, the story endorses an observation made by Aristotle: "Those who educate children well are more to be honored than parents, for these only gave life, those the art of living well" (138).

The Breakfast Club: "We Think You're Crazy for Making Us Write an Essay Telling You Who We Think We Are"

The urban environment of *Up the Down Staircase* differs from the suburban setting in the 1985 film *The Breakfast Club*, written and directed by John Hughes, but the educational system seems no more conducive to learning. Five suburban high school students—Andrew Clark, a wrestling "jock" (played by Emilio Estevez); John Bender, a sardonic "hood" (Judd Nelson); Claire Standish, a self-absorbed "princess" (Molly Ringwald); Allison Reynolds, an antisocial "weirdo" (Ally Sheedy); and Brian Johnson, a "nerd" struggling for social approval (Anthony Michael Hall)—are assigned detention for unspecified transgressions and forced to spend a Saturday together in the high school library under the supervision of teacher-disciplinarian Richard Vernon (Paul Gleason). At first Vernon seems to be reasonably professional in his treatment of the students, telling them that they must write an essay describing who they are, but it doesn't take long before Bender locates his weaknesses, raising insolent questions like "Does Barry Manilow know you raid his wardrobe?" and exhorting the others to "show Dick some respect." The five students take turns humiliating each other, but their hatred of the common enemy drives them together. The bond strengthens as each discloses something secret about his or her life: a weakness, fear, or vulnerability that they have not revealed to their closest friends. Andrew's father lives vicariously through him; John's father brutalizes the entire family; Claire's friends pressure her to remain the most popular girl in school; Brian is failing shop and considering suicide; Alison is desperately lonely and seeks attention through compulsive lying.

The problem with these self-disclosures, and with the film in general, is that the characters never probe their vulnerability or connect it to other parts of their lives. *The Breakfast Club* offers amusing one liners, as when the attractive Claire denies she's fat, to which John cruelly responds, "Well, not at present, but I can see you're really pushing maximum density," but it does not describe the impact of the self-disclosures on the group. Claire's makeover of Allison at the end of the film is as improbable as the new love relationships between Claire and John, Allison and Andrew. "In an ordinary social relationship," Sidney Jourard argues, "disclosure is a reciprocal phenomenon" (66), but it is impossible to believe that students will reveal themselves in a hostile setting: people disclose secrets only when they believe they will not be betrayed. Self-disclosure flourishes only in a trusting, empathic environment, for hostility begets hostility. Moreover, it is difficult to believe that a single self-disclosure will change a person's life, particularly if that self-disclosure is not accompanied by rigorous self-examination.

The hostility implicit in the film's self-disclosures recalls the nightmarish vision of psychotherapy in Ken Kesey's 1962 counterculture novel *One Flew over the Cuckoo's Nest*. The benumbed patients in the psychiatric ward, terrorized by an emasculating nurse aptly named Miss Ratched, are reduced to a flock of angry chickens who tear each other to pieces. The novel's antisocial hero, McMurphy, describes the therapeutic "pecking party" in the following way: "The flock gets sight of a spot of blood on some chicken and they all go to *peckin'* at it, see, till they rip the chicken to shreds, blood and bones and feathers. But usually a couple of the *flock* get spotted in the fracas, then it's their turn. And a few more get spots and gets pecked to death, and more and more. Oh, a peckin' party can wipe out the whole flock in a matter of a few hours, buddy, I seen it. A mighty awesome sight. The only way to prevent it—with chickens—is to clip blinders on them. So's they can't see" (55). Although the students in *The Breakfast Club* are not the victims of a matriarchy, as are the lobotomized, drugged, and electroshocked inmates of the psychiatric ward in *One Flew over the Cuckoo's Nest*, they share Kesey's belief that institutions stifle individuality and creativity.

The main weakness with John Hughes's film is that we do not see the students reaching any insights from their experience with "the breakfast club." Instead of each person writing the essay required by his or her teacher, or at least contributing to the essay through collaborative group work, they delegate Brian to speak for all of them, and his one paragraph cannot reveal anything significant about their experience together. "Dear Mr. Vernon: We accept the fact that we had to sacrifice a whole Saturday in detention for whatever it is we did wrong, but we think you're crazy for making us write an essay telling you who we think we are. You see us as you want to see us: in the simplest terms, in the most convenient definitions. But what we found out is that each one of us is a brain, an athlete, and a basket case, a princess, and a criminal. Does that answer your question? Sincerely yours, The Breakfast Club."

Dead Poets Society: "Words and Ideas Can Change the World"

"Make your lives extraordinary," exclaims John Keating to his adoring students in the 1989 movie *Dead Poets Society*. Though the film appeared four years after *The Breakfast Club,* its spirit is far closer to the world of *Good-bye, Mr. Chips*. Directed by Peter Weir, *Dead Poets Society* was enormously popular and received an Oscar for Tom Schulman's screenplay. Keating, played by Robin Williams, is a charismatic, inspirational teacher who believes not only in educating his students but also in helping them to transform their lives. His unconventional pedagogical methods awaken his students' passion for literature, but in the process he is accused of being responsible for the suicide of one of his disciples and consequently loses his job. Although the film is simplistic in its portrayal of teachers, hopelessly dependent upon stereotypical characters, and melodramatic in its depiction of suicide, it is an instructive cautionary tale for any teacher who believes that education can help students to achieve breakthroughs.

Keating is an English teacher at Welton Academy, an exclusive New England academy which is, in the boastful words of headmaster Dr. Nolan, "the best preparatory school in the United States." Welton is an American version of Brookfield though more snobbish: Fully 75 percent of its graduates go on to Ivy League colleges. Nolan becomes, not surprisingly, Keating's chief antagonist despite the fact that Keating is himself an honor graduate of Welton, aptly dubbed "Hellton" by one of his students. It is never clear why the free-spirited Keating returns to such an educationally unfriendly institution or how he was able to flourish there as a student. The school's slogan—Tradition! Honor! Discipline! Excellence!—masks intellectual rigidity and conformity, prompting the students to offer their own counterslogan: Travesty! Horror! Decadence! Excrement! Keating enters the story whistling Tchaikovsky's 1812 Overture and seems ready to wage war against the dissonant forces of Welton's administrators and faculty, though always with an angelic smile on his face and with self-mocking humor. He is the only teacher who is joyful about his work and who takes a personal interest in his students. Nor are his interests narrowly limited to education; a student finds an old yearbook which describes Keating as "Captain of the soccer team, Editor of the school annual, Cambridge bound, Thigh man, and Dead Poets Society." Keating remains, in short, too good to be true, though his colleagues perceive him at the end as antithetical to everything in which they believe.

Keating explains the Dead Poets Society as a secret organization in which past students devoted themselves to the magic of literature. "The Dead Poets was dedicated to 'sucking the marrow out of life,'" he declaims. "That's a phrase from Thoreau we would invoke at the beginning of every meeting. You see, we would gather at the old Indian cave and take turns reading from Thoreau, Whitman, Shelley—the biggies—even some of our own verse. And in the enchantment of the moment, we'd let poetry work its magic." His favorite poets are the Romantics, as his Keatsian-sounding name suggests, and his favorite theme is "Carpe diem": seize the day. Thus he reads Robert Herrick's "To the Virgins, to Make Much of Time" to his students, urging them to "Gather ye rosebuds while you may"—a theme his testosterone-driven males are eager to pursue. Keating himself is nonsexual: there is no hint of anything licentious about his personal life. Without being morbid, he reminds his students of the inevitability of death, declaring that we are "food for worms." He invites them to write poetry, presumably in the Romantic tradition that he espouses, and he never loses faith in the power of language. "No matter what anybody tells you, words and ideas can change the world."

Keating has no use for the Realists, however, and he demonizes any approach to literature other than his own. He ridicules the editor of the school's poetry anthology, one "Dr. J. Evans Pritchard, Ph.D.," whose need to call attention to his doctoral degree aligns him with the pompous Dr. Nolan. Pritchard's introductory essay, "Understanding Poetry"—perhaps an allusion to Cleanth Brooks's and Robert Penn Warren's influential 1950 New Critical anthology of the same title—offers an easy mathematical formula for determining a poem's greatness. "If the poem's score for perfection is plotted on the horizontal of a graph and its importance is plotted on the vertical, then calculating the total area of the poem yields the measure of its greatness." Keating is so incensed by this reductive approach that he orders his students to rip out the entire essay from their textbooks, an act which the film portrays as liberatory. "Armies of academics going forward, measuring poetry. No! We'll not have that here. No more." There is no suggestion that Keating's mutilation of the anthology is a form of censorship that is more dangerous than Pritchard's chilling formulaic approach.

Dead Poets Society portrays all authority other than Keating's as tyrannical. The benevolent patriarchal society in *Good-bye, Mr. Chips* is nowhere to be seen here: all the father figures are controlling, harsh, and punitive. The one mother in the film appears weak and ineffectual. Keating has no trouble winning over his students' hearts and minds because he is essentially an older, uncorrupted version of themselves. Indeed, he is one of them, a fact that makes Welton's other teachers and administrators uneasy. Fiercely antiauthoritarian, he embodies a tradition of proud individuality and iconoclasm, exhorting his students to be free thinkers. He recites Walt Whitman's "O Captain! My Captain!" and invites his students to call him either Mr. Keating or, if they are more daring, "O Captain! My Captain." Robin Williams plays Keating's role so deftly that we are rarely disturbed by the grandiose and, at times, messianic implications of his character.

What are Keating's unorthodox pedagogical methods? How does he magically unleash his students' creativity? Why are they irresistibly drawn to this Pied Piper? These questions expose the film's greatest flaws. Keating is depicted as being infinitely wise, playful, patient, empathic, and forgiving, but we don't see him teach his students how to read a poem. As every teacher knows, education is a slow, laborious process, and real breakthroughs—whether they be intellectual or emotional—are generally preceded and followed by periods of prolonged, uneventful activity. To his credit, Keating never humiliates his students, though he does gently poke fun at them when they refuse to participate in the challenges he poses to them, such as writing an original poem or, in an obvious allusion to Thoreau, marching to their own drummer. He encourages his students to find their own voice but does not disguise his preference for writers who challenge the status quo. A master of ventriloquism, he expertly impersonates Marlon Brando and John Wayne performing Shakespeare, but he does not disclose how he has honed his comic art.

Keating's assumption that creativity arises from rebellion against authority undergirds the film, though he does not anticipate Harold Bloom's Oedipal theory of the anxiety of influence, in which originality and creativity arise from a poet's misreading of an earlier writer. Keating's educational philosophy rests on the belief that the unfettered—and untutored—imagination will create its own gods. "Now, we all have a great need for acceptance. But you must trust that your beliefs are unique, your own, even though others may think them odd or unpopular, even though the herd may go, 'that's bad.'" Despite the fact that the film takes place in 1959, Keating seems to be more influenced by his reading of Nietzsche's *Thus Spake Zarathustra*, with its vision of the herd mentality, than by Holden Caulfield's alienation in *The Catcher in the Rye*, published in 1954. Keating's pedagogical methods would probably excite Holden, though one suspects that if Salinger were writing the screenplay for *Dead Poets Society*, he would portray Keating as a phony or suggest, as he does about

Holden's favorite teacher, Mr. Antolini, that there is something sexually improper about his feelings toward male students.

Keating insists on the importance of looking at life from different perspectives. "Just when you think you know something, you have to look at it in another way. Even though it may seem silly or wrong, you must try! Now, when you read, don't just consider what the author thinks. Consider what you think." But this is no reader-response approach, which seeks to explain the diversity and divergence of readers' responses to literary texts. Nor do we see a thoughtful exchange of different world visions. Keating believes, solipsistically, that any interpretation that feels right must be right. We never see different interpretations of the same poem or learn about competing theories of the creative process. Except for one moment when a student under duress utters lines that may indicate the emergence of a poem, there is no awareness that the revisionary process is as important as a sudden burst of creativity. Nor do we have insight into Keating's character or the motivation behind his liberatory pedagogy. In short, he remains a mystery, a teacher who is so committed to his students that he has no personal life.

Dead Poets Society would have been a more authentic film had it explored the interpretive differences that inevitably arise when reading any text, literary or otherwise. The film could have investigated different teaching styles, suggesting that there is more than one way to cultivate students' love for poetry. And it could have foreshadowed the movement toward diversity that was to begin only a few years later. Not only is there no hint of the importance of race, class, gender, and religion in this exclusive all-white, all-male, prep school, but the one student whose family is not rich—Neil Perry—is shown to live in a house with elegant wood paneling, tasteful furniture, and an impressive library. Nor are there significant social or economic differences between faculty and students. Keating's presence inspires one student, Charles Dalton, to insist, in an unauthorized article published in the school newspaper, that female students should be admitted into Welton Academy, but we never see any serious criticisms of its privileged world.

The only student who seems conflicted over his career and identity is Neil Perry, who reconvenes the Dead Poets Society without Keating's knowledge. Torn between his father's demand that he become a physician and his own passion for acting, Neil follows his dream and tries out for the role of Puck in *A Midsummer Night's Dream*. Mr. Perry is furious when he finds out and orders his son to withdraw from the play. The contrast between Neil's good surrogate father, Keating, and his bad biological father could not be more striking. Throughout the film, Keating walks a fine line between emboldening his students to follow their passion and cautioning them to act responsibly. He gently scolds Dalton for getting into trouble with Dr. Nolan: "Sucking the marrow out of life doesn't mean choking on the bone. Sure there's a time for daring and there's a time for caution, and a wise man understands what is called for." Though he comes close to sounding like a psychologist when he exhorts his students not to let the fear of failure inhibit their creativity, Keating never transgresses professional boundaries. Nor does he act inappropriately toward Neil. He urges the troubled youth to talk to his father and thus cannot be held accountable for Mr. Perry's close-mindedness nor the disastrous events that follow. Neil gives a star performance as Puck, but his success is short lived when his disapproving father shows up in the audience. Later that evening, after he has been told that he must withdraw from Welton and enroll in a military academy, Neil shoots himself, an act that the film comes dangerously close to romanticizing. Suicide is always more complex and multi-determined than *Dead Poets Society* implies.

The suicide roils Welton Academy and culminates in the search for a scapegoat. Keating makes no effort to defend himself against the false accusations of Mr. Perry and Dr. Nolan, and he is victimized by one of his students, Cameron, who tells the authorities that "Mr. Keating put us all up to this crap." The teacher feels no anger, indignation, or ill will toward his accusers, only pain and sadness over Neil's death. If Keating does not quite seem a Christ figure at the end of the story, he is nevertheless a martyr who is betrayed by one of his disciples. Keating's future remains uncertain; will he remain an idealistic, committed teacher, devoted to his students, or will he go on to lead a life of quiet desperation? His expulsion from Welton perhaps prevents him from becoming as stodgy as the other teachers. At the end of the film, after his abrupt dismissal of the iconoclastic teacher, Dr. Nolan demands that Keating's students recite Pritchard's infallible formula for aesthetic success, but the students, with their fired mentor looking on approvingly, defy the headmaster by standing on their desks, prepared to risk expulsion rather than endure the horrors of repressive education. Keating's last words—"Thank you, boys. Thank you"— suggest that his mission is now complete.

Dead Poets Society remains one of the most popular examples of a nurturing teacher who is prepared to take appropriate risks on behalf of his students. If his unorthodox teaching methods are incompletely dramatized, and if he remains, to cite E. M. Forster's distinction, a flat rather than a round character, we can nevertheless search for pedagogical strategies to empower our students with the knowledge that will help them transform themselves and their world. We can learn from Keating's mistakes, escaping from the binaries that constrict the film's vision: imagination versus reason, romantic versus realistic, freedom versus discipline, innovation versus tradition, release versus restraint. If we frame these issues not as either/or but as either/and, then we can avoid many of the problems that bedevil Keating. We can also suggest how contemporary teachers may use some of Keating's pedagogical strategies to achieve results that would please both Keating and Dr. Nolan. And we can raise a question that Keating himself never asks: What would happen if a teacher encouraged students like Neil Perry to write about their problems and share their essays with teachers and classmates? Might tragedies like adolescent suicide be averted if students were encouraged to express their conflicts and discover, through their teachers' and classmates' nonjudgmental responses, that their situation is not as bleak as it seems to be?

Death in a Delphi Seminar: "Real People Reading Books"

Pedagogical risks of an entirely different kind appear in the 1995 novel *Death in a Delphi Seminar*. "Inside every critic is a frustrated writer" (48), observes psychoanalytic literary critic "Norman N. Holland." The quotation marks surrounding the English professor's name suggest that he is fictional, like the other characters in this fascinating murder mystery set in the mid 1980s at the State University of New York at Buffalo. And yet anyone who is familiar with Norman Holland's distinguished academic career—he is the dean of American psychoanalytic literary critics and the author of more than a dozen scholarly books—will recognize his kinship to the fictional professor. An early proponent of reader-response criticism, Holland has written a detective novel that ingeniously dramatizes the major ideas he has developed in the past thirty years. Although *Death in a Delphi Seminar* is both a mystery and a roman à clef, it reads like nonfiction, and some readers may believe that Holland is describing an actual murder that took place in one of his literary seminars. Holland has constructed a suspenseful plot that holds the reader's interest from beginning to end. In searching for the solution to a puzzling crime, the reader is initiated into the often arcane world of contemporary literary theory, a world strongly influenced by Freudian and poststructural ideas.

As *Death in a Delphi Seminar* opens, we learn that a female student in Holland's graduate seminar on reader-response criticism has been poisoned, presumably by another member of the class. The narrative arises out of the conflicting texts surrounding Patricia Hassler's death: transcripts of police interviews, student essays, department memos, newspaper accounts, the professor's private journal, and the inner musings of Lt. Norman "Justin" Rhodes, who is in charge of solving the murder. All eight members of the Delphi seminar are suspects—the seven students plus an untenured assistant professor who is sitting in on the course to learn more about Holland's psychoanalytic approach to literature. Holland himself is a suspect, for he has, along with the others, the motive, means, and opportunity to do away with the obnoxious Hassler, whose disruptive behavior alienates everyone in the seminar. Before her murder is solved, a second corpse appears, that of an ominous interloper who has been secretly disrupting the seminar by writing hate letters to the other students. Lieutenant Rhodes's task is to solve these two perplexing crimes. Rhodes succeeds, largely by enlisting the help of Holland's controversial theory of reading.

To appreciate the intellectual force of the novel, the reader needs to understand both the workings of the actual Delphi seminar that Holland pioneered in the 1970s and the significance of his contributions to psychoanalytic literary criticism. *Death in a Delphi Seminar* may be considered a "theoretical thriller" in that it dramatizes the challenges to traditional humanistic scholarship posed in different ways by Holland, the deconstructive philosopher Jacques Derrida, and the French psychoanalyst Jacques Lacan. Although the fierce theoretical disputes of the academy may not be of much interest to those outside its ivory towers—the reason academic politics is often vicious, Henry Kissinger, a former academic, has observed wryly, is because so little is at stake—Holland's story reveals that these battles have far-reaching consequences.

In 1975 Holland published an essay in *College English*, cowritten with his friend and colleague Murray Schwartz, called "The Delphi Seminar." Focusing on the Delphic oracle's injunction, Know thyself, the seminar used psychoanalytic techniques to enable students to analyze their personal styles of reading and writing. In the first half of the course, students write about their free associations to various poems and stories. These free associations, which the students then circulate to their classmates, resemble those of a patient in psychoanalysis. The students analyze their own reading styles in the second half of the course, and by doing so, they reflect on their own identities. Each person, in Holland's view, has a unique "identity theme." The term comes from the psychoanalyst Heinz Lichtenstein, who argues that Freud's repetition compulsion principle affirms the continuity of human identity. "Identity, in man," writes Lichtenstein, "requires a 'repetitive doing' in order to safeguard the 'sameness within change' which I believe to be a fundamental aspect of identity in man" (103). This identity theme remains remarkably constant over time but is capable of variations, thus allowing for change. As Holland observes in *The I*, "[I]f we imagine a human life as a dialectic between sameness and difference, we can think of the sameness, the continuity of personal style, as a theme; we can think of the changes as variations on that theme" (35). Expanding upon Lichtenstein's theory, Holland has sought to show how each reader has a characteristic identity theme that is the product of his or her drives, defenses, and fantasies.

During the second half of the semester the fictional Delphi seminar becomes problematic. Each week a different student is "it," as in hide-and-seek: the student receives interpretations of his or her identity theme from classmates and must react to these responses. Although Holland tells his students to censor highly personal material—they are to disclose themes in their lives, not actual events—some students may become angry or defensive. Self-disclosure is often difficult and fraught with peril; psychoanalysis, as Freud well knew, brings out the worst in people. It is not clear whether many of Holland's real Delphi seminars in Buffalo, where he taught for close to twenty years, or at the University of Florida in Gainesville, where he has now taught for over a decade, were or are emotionally explosive.

In the novel, however, a fatal problem arises because of the volatility of two students: Hassler, who is victimized by her own murderous rage, and Christian Aval, a young Frenchman who first met Hassler at Yale, where they studied literature together and came under the influence of Yale's famous English Department, with its French poststructuralist approach to literature. Following the breakup of a stormy love affair with Hassler, in which each accused the other of plagiarizing an honor's essay, Aval followed her to Buffalo, where they both enrolled in Holland's seminar, despite the fact that their Franco-American views on literature are in sharp opposition to his Anglo-American ones. Ironically, the students' instability accurately reflects their deconstructive belief that everything in language is built along a series of linguistic differences and that, consequently, every text reveals internal inconsistencies. Taking deconstruction to its most nihilistic conclusion, Hassler and Aval assert that nothing exists outside of language, which they claim is inherently duplicitous. In the novel's brief account of postmodernism, Nietzsche argued that the subject is only a fiction or construction; Foucault came along and proclaimed that the author is merely a projection of how we think about literary texts; then Roland

Barthes followed with the claim that the reader is a composition of other texts of linguistic codes. Neither writers nor readers exist in such a post-modern world, only language. Gone, too, is the human self.

In his critique of the more radical assumptions of postmodernism, Holland insists that any totalistic philosophical system that abrogates human identity, autonomy, and free will is dangerous. When asked to identify himself by Lieutenant Rhodes and acknowledge that he is being tape re-corded, Aval responds in a way that highlights his absurd credo: "I would make the claim that I cannot be recorded in the mode you indicate. That is, language flees, leaving behind only traces of disparate and destabilized meanings. No effort to fix it can succeed" (22). Aval is right, in one sense, when he says that he is always a "shifter." His shifty complicity in two deaths and his subsequent disappearance and probable suicide suggest the bankruptcy of any philosophy antithetical to humanistic values.

Holland agrees, however, with the postmodernist premise that there is no real, true, or objective reality. It is for this reason that each character in Holland's fictional Delphi seminar sees Patricia Hassler differently: there are as many interpretations as there are interpreters. The difference between Holland and other postmodern literary theorists is that whereas many of them privilege language over readers, he insists that readers create interpre-tation, based on their own characteristic identity theme. And whereas many theorists seem dismissive of actual experience, Holland seeks to examine real readers by studying their interpretive responses to literary texts. He would certainly agree with Freud and Charcot that theory is good but it doesn't prevent facts from existing—facts which each reader perceives differently.

Unlike Lacan, Holland maintains that we control our language more than it controls us. He also believes that the ego can reconcile the compet-ing claims of the id and superego. Holland is in the tradition of Heinz Hartmann and Ernst Kris, who emphasized the adaptive, integrative func-tions of the ego. In further contrast to Lacan, Holland has created a psy-choanalytic model of identity consistent with the findings of cognitive psy-chology and neurophysiological research into the functioning of the brain—a psychoanalytic model that is as scientific as possible. Holland argues in all his writings that psychoanalysis must be based upon empiri-cal observation and scientific testing if it is to progress, discarding those elements of its theory that are not verifiable.

Although some readers will take issue with Holland's faith in the future of psychoanalysis, others will enjoy his satirical attack on the New Cryptics, whose willfully obscure language has produced so many unreadable academic texts. Whether one agrees or disagrees with Holland's ideas, he is never guilty of linguistic mystification. (He would be dismayed by the fashionable belief that clarity is merely an ideological position.) Literary and psychoanalytic theory come alive in *Death in a Delphi Seminar* in ways that they seldom do in textbooks or in the classroom. I suspect that an increasing number of graduate students and professors would secretly agree with the statement of one of the members of the Delphi seminar, who, exasperated by the dominance of theory in the academy, yearns for a return to the study of imaginative literature: "What I didn't anticipate was that the study of literature wouldn't be the study of literature. It would be this dreary 'theory.' That's why I'm taking this seminar. It has to do with real people reading books" (223). *Death in a Delphi Seminar* does not ring the death knell for theory, but it reminds us of the enduring power of literature, which can never be reduced to ideology.

This is not to say that *Death in a Delphi Seminar* is a great novel. It is not, nor does it pretend to be. The characters for the most part embody theoretical positions, and Holland's psychoanalytic profiles of his seminarians are formulaic. Like most novels of ideas, *Death in a Delphi Seminar* does not contain psychologically complex characterization. Holland's persona in the novel closely resembles the one he has portrayed throughout his scholarly writings—that of a man who is erudite, affable, witty, and passionately devoted to literature and psychoanalysis. Liberal in his social and political views and conservative in his lifestyle, he is totally committed to the life of the mind. If there is a darker side to his character, he keeps it carefully hidden. In one of the most autobiographically revealing statements in the novel, Norman Holland observes about his own identity theme: "I think my own motivation is, if I go deep enough, that I'd like to know what makes people tick, but I don't want to get close enough to find out" (140). Perhaps this explains why the novel's intellectual force is greater than its emotional power. Despite references to the "emotionally charged" texts written by the students, *Death in a Delphi Seminar* contains a cerebral quality that prevents it from being entirely fulfilling. The novel's limitations may derive not only from Holland's identity theme but also from his understandable need to defend his students from the volatile emotions that are often released from self-disclosure. As his fictional persona notes, "[T]he students are pretty protective both of the person being studied and of themselves. After all, if you're responding to a story by some long-dead author, you can say anything you want, and no one's the worse for it. So associations and evaluations go all over the place. But if you're writing about somebody who's sitting right there in front of you, you're going to be a lot more careful, more rational, more to the point, more tactful" (44). In limiting class discussions to authors' cognitive styles, Holland remains distant from his students' emotional lives.

Significantly, neither the real nor the fictional Norman Holland reveals much interest in empathy, a word that is conspicuously absent from the story. Might empathy have defused some of Patricia Hassler's suicidal fury or at least helped her to understand it? The professor acknowledges dreading her tirades against him, and it is surprising that he never requests a conference to discuss her disruptive class behavior. "She was an absolutely maddening person. Maddening! I wanted to kick her out. But then I'd stop myself. 'No, that isn't professional. That isn't what you do in a Delphi seminar. Whatever she says, you have to let it come out, and you have to face it and discuss it rationally'" (46–47). But is it professional for a teacher to allow himself to be terrorized by a student in a course built on self-disclosure, which flourishes only in an atmosphere of safety and trust? The students find her behavior as offensive as the professor does. "She was a pretty horrible person. She made a mess of this seminar, taunting Norm and arguing with him, and she was hard on the rest of us. Very hard" (32).

Death in a Delphi Seminar dramatizes what Deborah Tannen calls the "culture of critique," in which verbal assault masquerades as the pursuit of truth. Although it would have been inappropriate for Holland to confront Hassler in class—such a confrontation might not have been productive— it certainly would have been appropriate, even necessary, for the teacher to speak to her outside of class. Or one might use what Dawn Skorczewski calls a "freeze frame" technique in which the teacher and students discuss how their unconscious tensions impede class discussion. Perhaps the reason Holland doesn't engage Hassler in a discussion of transference-countertransference issues is because he believes that she is not finally in control of her behavior. "There were times when she seemed to me what the psychiatrists call a borderline personality," he tells Rhodes, "someone whose boundaries between self and others are very shaky and often tangled up with uncontrollable anger. Do you remember Alex in the movie *Fatal Attraction*? That anger-mixed-with-sexuality? Trish is like that" (116). Hassler wants her teacher and classmates to hate her, and they do. "We couldn't help it," exclaims one student, "and she played on that. I think she felt that if we hated her, then she was justified in hating us and being as nasty to us as she was" (41). In such a situation, where transference and countertransference issues are so deadly, it might have been necessary for the professor to ask the student to drop the course. But before resorting to this extreme, the professor might have tried an empathic approach. Empathy may have no place in a detective novel, but it is essential to any course that depends on self-disclosure. Empathy might also have made the characters' self-disclosures more revealing. The students in the novel are constantly self-disclosing, but they are rarely affected by each other's revelations. We never see how the students' lives have been changed by their experience in the Delphi seminar.

Like *Death in a Tenured Position* by Amanda Cross (Carolyn Heilbrun) and, more recently, *Murder at the MLA* by D. J. H. Jones and *Cold and Pure and Very Dead* by Joanne Dobson, *Death in a Delphi Seminar* is an academic mystery novel that will appeal mainly to academics. But it will also interest readers who wish to learn more about the pedagogy of self-disclosure. In the final analysis, Holland remains a more forceful literary theorist than a novelist; as his fictional counterpart wryly observes, "I'm pretty good at reading identities, but I'm not sure I could write a novel or a play" (72). Holland does indeed write the novel, an intriguing "postmodern mystery" that explores but does not resolve the mystery of identity.

Empowering Teachers

What conclusions can we draw from these novels and films about teachers who make a difference in their students' lives? What are the temperamental qualities that make one teacher empowering and another disempowering? And what are the pedagogical strategies that succeed or fail in the classroom?

To begin with the obvious, teachers who respect themselves respect their students; the corollary is also true. Empowering teachers are compassionate and attentive, and though their educational philosophy and pedagogical styles may vary, they affirm their students' curiosity for knowledge and self-worth. They demonstrate their commitment by reading carefully their students' essays and expressing concern when they sense that someone is in a crisis, as we can see with Lucy Winter in *The Small Room* and Sylvia Barrett in *Up the Down Staircase*. They know how to bestow sincere praise on their students and avoid the insincere flattery that appears in *The Blackboard Jungle*. Empowering teachers help their students gain self-confidence, motivating them toward personal development and academic success. Empowering teachers are inspirational, like Lucy, Sylvia, and Keating in *Dead Poets Society*. They are not afraid to acknowledge affection for their students, though they realize the need to maintain appropriate boundaries in order to avoid exploiting their students' vulnerability or having their own vulnerability exploited. They trust their students and are in turn trusted by them.

Empowering teachers like Mr. Chips tend to be idealistic and hopeful, while disempowering teachers like nearly all those found in *The Blackboard Jungle* and *The Breakfast Club* are cynical and pessimistic. Some teachers, like Crocker-Harris, begin their teaching careers idealistically but end bitter and disillusioned. Teachers seem particularly susceptible to burnout, perhaps because of the large number of students they teach and the modest salaries and relatively low social status of their profession. Mr. Chips and Crocker-Harris form an instructive contrast here. Both are childless, but whereas Mr. Chips comes to see his students as his offspring, feeling deeply fulfilled by the thousands of young boys he has taught during his long career, Crocker-Harris has lost his passion for teaching and also his self-respect. From the point of view of Erik Erikson's influential taxonomy of human development, "Eight Stages of Man," Mr. Chips and Crocker-Harris conclude their careers on opposite ends of the spectrum: Mr. Chips affirms "generativity," "concern in establishing and guiding the next generation," while Crocker-Harris displays "stagnation," associated with despair and human impoverishment (267).

The fictional and filmic literature teachers who make a difference in their students' lives reveal many of the characteristics that Ben describes in his writings in the introduction. They instill confidence in their students and help them to personalize knowledge. They take an interest in their students and know how to respond to their problems. Unlike Crocker-Harris and Carryl Cope, they are interested in teaching *all* their students, not simply the one in a thousand who may be academically exceptional. They come across as real people rather than aloof authoritarians. Chips's tears, while reading the names of the Brookfield students who have perished in the Great War, reveal compassion that is evident to everyone. Rick Dadier's only moment of success in the classroom occurs when he encourages his students to connect "The Fifty-first Dragon" with their lives. At the end of *The Small Room* and *Up the Down Staircase*, Lucy and Sylvia, respectively, have acquired the knowledge and experience to maintain the delicate tightrope between involvement and detachment. So, too, does Keating inspire his students through his passion for poetry and his effort to reach all his students, not just the brightest. And Norman Holland succeeds pedagogically with a theory of reading that aims to help students discover their own identity themes and, by implication, their characteristic ways of looking at the world and themselves.

With the exception of Lucy Winter, the literature instructors who make the greatest difference in their students' lives teach in high school rather than in college. One reason may be the perception that high school students are more impressionable than college students and therefore more easily influenced by their teachers. A second reason is that many fictional college professors are drawn to transformative educational experiences of a different kind: romantic entanglements with their students. Most "professors of desire," to cite the title of Philip Roth's 1977 novel, are men, and their objects of study are college coeds. Levin's affair with an undergraduate leads to disaster in *A New Life*; but even when professors marry their students, as in John Barth's existential novel *The End of the Road*, the union is "terminal"—the last word of the novel. "Fiction feeds on unhappiness," notes a professor in David Lodge's novel *Thinks*; "It needs conflict, disappointment, transgression. And since novels are mainly about the personal, emotional life, about relationships, it's not surprising that most of them are about adultery" (211). In Meg Wolitzer's *The Wife*, a professor of desire marries a student who ghostwrites his prize-winning novels, but that doesn't prevent him from having sexual affairs, which he then narrates to his wife, who dutifully transmutes them into "fictional" stories. And a third reason may be that authors of academic novels, many of whom are academics themselves or former academics, simply do not believe that a story about a teacher making a difference in a student's life will be of sufficient interest or complexity to readers, who may prefer to see breakdowns rather than breakthroughs.

To make a difference in a college student's life *and* to maintain appropriate boundaries remains a challenge for teacher and student alike, and few novels or films have portrayed this situation. Nor have many novels or films shown how teachers can help their students to achieve breakthroughs in their self-understanding. Norman Holland is interested in this question in *Death in a Delphi Seminar*, yet the reader-response criticism he espouses leads to the worst imaginable scenario, with students exploiting each other's self-disclosures. In its theoretical sophistication, *Death in a Delphi Seminar* could not be more different from *The Breakfast Club*, but both describe self-disclosure gone awry. We rarely see in any of the teacher novels or films students being encouraged to confront traumatic knowledge or to pursue an education for life. How, then, can high school or college literature teachers embrace a pedagogy of self-disclosure that does not wound or murder their students? The question takes on added significance when we consider that in many ways today's teachers and students differ markedly from those of the past.

Life in the Contemporary Classroom

I am neither as idealistic as Mr. Chips or John Keating nor as cynical as Crocker-Harris or Rick Dadier. I teach at a university that is worlds apart from the privileged worlds of Brookfield, Welton Academy, or Appleton. I have never suffered the humiliations of the students in *The Blackboard Jungle, Up the Down Staircase,* or *The Breakfast Club.* Although I make plenty of mistakes in the classroom, my philosophy of teaching is not built on Clobbering, Slobbering, Slumbering, Rumbling, and Fumbling. My pedagogical strategy is based on Affirming and Confirming, both of which produce better academic outcomes than Rick's in *The Blackboard Jungle.* I would rather be teaching now than fifty or a hundred years ago, yet in many ways the problems of the past pale before those of the new millennium. Adolescent suicide has tripled since the 1950s; binge drinking has reached epidemic proportions; eating disorders are rampant; sexual abuse is ubiquitous; and university counseling centers are treating depressed students in record numbers. Mid-twentieth-century students worried about the Cold War and Vietnam, but contemporary students worry about a problem much closer to home: AIDS. However violent Manual Trades High School is in *The Blackboard Jungle,* students do not need to pass through a metal detector, as today's students do. Past students worried about being drafted to fight overseas' wars, but today's students worry about terrorism both abroad and at home.

Unlike Mr. Chips's students, many of mine cannot write a simple declarative sentence, much less decline a Latin noun. They hold part-time or even full-time jobs while attending college, and rather than "seizing the day," as Keating urges his students to do, many of mine cannot make it through the day without falling asleep at their desks. As a tenured university professor, I have far more freedom than Mr. Chips or Keating, but I have pressures that escape them: teaching increasingly large classes, educating students who are sometimes the first in their family to attend college, and ordering books that some of my students cannot afford to buy. I'm twice Keating's age (though not yet Chips's age) and have less energy—and certainly less comic wit—than he does. I admire the Romantic poets as much as he does but identify myself more with the Realists, who lived longer and generally knew how to stay out of trouble.

My teaching methods combine traditional and nontraditional approaches. Unlike John Keating, I spend a great deal of time commenting on my students' writings. My students tell me that I write far more comments on their essays, particularly of a technical nature, than do their other teachers. To this extent, I resemble Levin's antagonists in *A New Life*, Professors Fairchild and Gilley. Unlike Fairchild's dying affirmation of the "mystery" of the "in-fin-i-tive," grammar fails to arouse my deepest passion, but I do tell my students that I find semicolons "sexy" when used correctly. Like Sylvia Barrett, I can intuit the "inarticulate loneliness between the lines" of my students' essays, but unlike Sylvia, I don't believe there is a contradiction between commenting on the often moving content of these essays and correcting grammatical, spelling, and typographical errors. I have found that students come to expect if not welcome these criticisms. Their writing improves noticeably and, in some cases, dramatically. To this extent, I am a traditionalist. But I also encourage my students to write personal essays in expository writing courses and reader-response diaries in literature courses. I agree with Lucy Winter that teaching depends upon a "delicate and dangerous balance between two people and a subject," but unlike her, I believe that this subject may be the students' own lives. I have never been a participant in Holland's Delphi seminar, but I am committed to reader-response criticism. If I had to define my pedagogical identity theme, I would characterize myself as a teacher who tries to bring out the best in his students by paradoxically helping them to express their worst feelings about themselves. My students' self-disclosures are far more revelatory—both disturbing and affirming—than any in *The Breakfast Club* or in *Death in a Delphi Seminar*.

Unlike Keating or Chips, I call my students by their first name or nickname and, since I believe in reciprocity, invite them to call me by my first name. I prefer the informality of first names, though I realize that a majority of my colleagues do not feel this way. Cultural and intergenerational forces shape the ways in which we address others, and both parties must agree on forms of address. A few students call me "Jeff" but most feel more comfortable with "Professor Berman." Sometimes they begin with the latter and end with the former, particularly when they write letters to me after the semester has ended. I'm not sure if teachers and students who call each other by first names feel greater empathy for each other, but they may feel heightened connection. I've never believed that students who call me by my first name feel less respect.

I rely extensively on students' signed and unsigned writings so that I can have greater understanding of their lives and their reactions to my courses. I would never presume to say, "I know how you feel" because no one can know *completely* how another person feels. I doubt whether anyone can truly know himself or herself; the best we can do is to know how we feel at the moment, but even then we may not be in touch with our unconscious selves. Complete self-knowledge is impossible. Whether we accept the modernist notion of the self or the postmodernist notion of subjectivity, I believe, with D. H. Lawrence, that self-knowledge is at best imperfect. "The soul of man is a dark vast forest, with wild life in it," Lawrence declares in *Studies in Classic American Literature,* and even as we try, like the practical Benjamin Franklin, to tame the psyche into a "neat back garden," it can never be entirely fathomed or domesticated (10–11).

If, then, we cannot know ourselves, how can we know others? The answer, I believe, is that we can begin the search for knowledge by reading each other's writings. Writing heightens self-awareness, as E. M. Forster affirms in his famous question, "How do I know what I think till I see what I say?" I know more about my students' lives by reading their writing than if I did not read their writing, and I use their diaries and essays so that I don't have to put words into their mouths. I show my students how I intend to use and contextualize their words. Additionally, I ask them, months or years after the semester has ended, to describe the impact of the course on their lives. I am particularly interested in how they feel about rereading their diaries and essays long after they have written them. In rereading their own and their classmates' words, students reach new conclusions about themselves and others. We thus can see their expanding knowledge, including their recognition of contradictions and ambiguities. I don't claim that my students' words, written over an extended period of time, evoke a full portrait of their lives, but they do offer a striking and memorable snapshot, one that helps us to understand contemporary American college students.

Unlike Dick Vernon, I strive to create an empathic, nonjudgmental atmosphere in which students can write safely on a wide range of topics that most teachers would deem too dangerous to discuss in the classroom: family conflicts, divorce, eating disorders, drug and alcohol addiction, sexual abuse, depression, and suicide. I affirm my students' willingness to write on painful and shameful subjects, and these comments complement my grammatical and stylistic criticisms of their writing. They know from my technical criticisms that I take their writing seriously and that I am helping them to improve their power of expression. They also know that I am listening attentively to their words and not judging their lives. I encourage everyone in the classroom to remain attuned to classmates' words. Many of my students feel at the end of the semester a connection with each other reminiscent of that in the *Breakfast Club.* The difference, however, is that my students have not hurt each other. They feel a bond that arises from an upsurge of empathy, a subject to which we now turn.

CHAPTER 2

Empathy, Trauma, and Forgiveness
CLASSROOM IMPLICATIONS

Empathy is essential to self-disclosure, but before I discuss the strategies to create a safe classroom atmosphere, I should state that I am not talking about superhuman understanding of others. Once, when explaining my teaching style to a skeptical colleague, I was told that I must be an "empath." The comment puzzled me. I had never seen the word in the scores of books and articles that I had read on the subject, and the tone of the remark struck me as patronizing. Only later, when I related this incident to a friend, did I learn that "empath" is apparently an allusion to a *Star Trek* episode. I became angry upon realizing that I was compared with an extraterrestrial being, thus disproving my colleague's comment. His lack of empathy weakened my own, and I reacted defensively rather than trying to understand why the concept was so threatening to him.

As my friends and colleagues will confirm, I am not blessed with extraordinary empathic powers. But I have learned from more than thirty years of classroom experience the importance of listening attentively to my students and encouraging them to listen attentively to each other. Heinz Kohut, who wrote more extensively on the subject than anyone else, observes that empathy is an investigative tool that allows us to increase our understanding of other people. Empathy enables us to glimpse others' thoughts and feelings and create strong relationships. Any discussion of empathy must include Kohut, for he affirmed its importance not only in psychotherapy but also in everyday life.

Heinz Kohut and Self-Psychology

Unlike Freud, who advises colleagues in his 1912 essay "Recommendations to Physicians Practicing Psycho-Analysis" to model themselves on the surgeon, "who puts aside all his feelings, even his human sympathy" (115–16)—a recommendation that Freud never followed in practice—Kohut urges the use of empathy, which he calls in *The Search for the Self* the "power that counteracts man's tendency toward seeing meaninglessness and feeling despair" (2:713). Kohut's first major statement about the importance of empathy appears in his seminal 1959 essay "Introspection, Empathy, and Psychoanalysis," where he discusses the "empathic-intro-spective" stance and recommends a new paradigm for therapeutic cure. Kohut was constantly broadening and expanding his definition of empa-thy; in his posthumous 1984 book *How Does Analysis Cure?* he contrasts his early "terse scientific definition" of empathy as "vicarious introspec-tion" with his "best definition" of empathy as the "capacity to think and feel oneself into the inner life of another person" (82). A similar definition appears in his 1985 book *Self Psychology and the Humanities:* "Through empathy we aim at discerning, in one single act of certain recognition, complex psychological configurations which we could either define only through the laborious presentation of a host of details or which it may even be beyond our ability to define" (115). In Kohut's view, empathy is an essential psychological nutriment that sustains life. Empathy is an act of imagination that enables us to apprehend each other. As David Klugman notes, "Kohut's recognition of the role of empathy in the analytic process parallels the Romantic recognition of the role of imagination in percep-tion and experience" (700).

Kohut affirms empathy as the "operation that defines the field of psy-choanalysis," a "value-neutral tool of observation" that "(a) can lead to correct or incorrect results, (b) can be used in the service of either com-passionate, inimical, or dispassionate-neutral purposes, and (c) can be employed either rapidly and outside awareness or slowly and deliberately, with focused conscious attention" (*How Does Analysis Cure?* 174–75). He elevates empathy to central importance in his emerging psychoanalytic approach, which he calls self psychology, while at the same time trying not to mythologize empathy. "Although self psychology must not claim that it has provided psychoanalysis with a new kind of empathy, it can claim that it has supplied analysis with new theories which broaden and deepen the field of empathic perception" (*How Does Analysis Cure?* 175).

Kohut does not equate empathy with love or compassion since empathy "can be used decisively for hateful purposes" (*Self Psychology* 222), an observation with which most theorists would agree. Nevertheless, nearly all his references to empathy are positive, and while he concedes that it is "dreadful" to use empathy to plunge a dagger into another person's weak spot, he insists that it is more dreadful to grow up in an nonempathic environment. Kohut believes that empathy is the best response to "thwarted narcissistic aspirations," by which he means "hurts to one's pride, injuries to one's prestige needs, interferences with conscious, preconscious, or unconscious fantasies concerning one's greatness, power, and specialness" (163). He uses a literary example, a short episode in Tolstoy's *Anna Karenina*, to illustrate the consequences of narcissistic rage:

> a man . . . had written a scientific treatise and was now anxiously waiting for the reviews. Finally the first review came; it gave the book a tremendous panning, but cleverly and wittily, although everything was subtly distorted. The author wondered why in the world this man used his considerable intelligence and wit to distort so cleverly what he had written, in order to pan him. And then he remembered that two years ago he had met the man in a social gathering and had corrected *one* word the man had used. Now everything became clear to him. He had shamed this man in public by correcting him; and now, two years later, the opportunity for revenge arose and the man used it with glee. He knew there was nothing to be done. (*Self Psychology* 162–63)

In *How Does Analysis Cure?* Kohut observes that empathy "is not God's gift bestowed only on an elect few. For the average individual, training and learning make the difference, rather than the fact of endowment" (83). As he grew older, he became less afraid to challenge many of Freud's statements that had become gospel truths in psychoanalytic institutes, and he remained a "patient-friendly" analyst: "If there is one lesson that I have learned during my life as an analyst, it is the lesson that what my patients tell me is likely to be true—that many times when I believed that I was right and my patients were wrong, it turned out, though often only after a prolonged search, that *my* rightness was superficial whereas *their* rightness was profound" (93–94; emphasis in original).

Charles Strozier states in his biography that empathy came to have four crucial meanings to Kohut: "First, empathy is the oxygen of psychological life. We cannot breathe without it. . . . Second, therapists who seriously employ empathy not only see things differently but change the world they encounter. . . . Third, the capacity for empathy is not gender-related. Both sexes have an equal capacity for (or blockage against) empathy. . . . Fourth, since empathy is such a powerful bond between people—and is a much more uniting force than sex—it serves to counteract 'man's destructiveness against his fellows.' Empathy is the hope of peace" (347). Contrary to Kohut's assertion, most studies demonstrate that women tend to be more empathic than men, but his other claims about the value of empathy have been accepted by many psychologists.

Strozier views Kohut's revision of mainstream psychoanalysis as "the pivotal event in the transformation of the field into what is generally termed 'relational psychoanalysis'" (x). He adds that Kohut's new approach "was almost immediately recognized by feminists as the first important psychoanalytic theory that validated the experience of women" (262). Louis Agosta argues that empathy is the foundation of intersubjectivity, largely because "empathy furnishes a way of access to the other person's emotional life and of disclosing how our lives overlap or diverge" (60).

Part of Kohut's revolutionary impact on psychoanalysis lies in his undying optimism about empathy's transformative power. It is not death we fear, he wrote shortly before his own death, but the loss of empathic support in the final phase of our lives (cited by Lichtenberg, *Reflections on Self Psychology* xvii). In his last essay, "Introspection, Empathy, and the Semicircle of Mental Health," he makes a statement that he knows critics will attribute to the "suspension of abandoning scientific sobriety and of entering the land of mysticism or of sentimentality." The statement, which hardly seems challengeable, is that "empathy per se, the mere presence of empathy, has also a beneficial, in a broad sense, a therapeutic effect— both in the clinical setting and in human life, in general" (85).

Carl Rogers and the Person-Centered Approach

No less than Heinz Kohut, Carl Rogers elevates empathy to the highest importance in psychotherapy—and in education as well. Rogers defines his approach to psychology and education in many ways—nondirective counseling, client-centered therapy, student-centered teaching, and group-centered leadership—but he seems most comfortable with the term "person-centered approach." He believes that three conditions must be present for a growth-promoting educational climate. The first he calls realness or genuineness in the facilitator. "When the facilitator is a real person, being what he or she is, entering into relationships with the learners without presenting a front or a facade, the facilitator is much more likely to be effective. This means that the feelings that the facilitator is experiencing are available to his or her awareness, that he or she is able to live these feelings, to be them, and able to communicate them if appropriate" (*A Way of Being* 271). The second is "'prizing,' 'acceptance,' or 'trust,'" which "shows up in a variety of observable ways. The facilitator who has a considerable degree of this attitude can be fully acceptant of the fear and hesitation of the students as they approach new problems as well as acceptant of the pupils' satisfaction in achievement. . . . The facilitator's prizing or acceptance of the learners is an operational expression of his or her essential confidence and trust in the capacity of the human organism" (271–72). And the third growth-promoting quality is empathic understanding. "When the teacher has the ability to understand each student's reactions from the inside, has a sensitive awareness of how the process of education and learning seems *to the student*, then, again, the likelihood that significant learning will take place is increased" (272; emphasis in original). Significantly, these growth-promoting qualities may be seen in several of the fictional literature teachers, including Mr. Chips, Lucy Winter, Sylvia Barrett, John Keating, and Norman Holland.

Rogers was a tireless advocate for empathy, even (or especially) when he realized that his statements ran counter to the conventional wisdom of the age. "This attitude of standing in the other's shoes," he wrote in his 1969 book *Freedom to Learn*, "of viewing the world through the student's eyes, is almost unheard of in the classroom. One could listen to thousands of ordinary classroom interactions without coming across one instance of clearly communicated, sensitively accurate, empathic understanding. But it has a tremendously releasing effect when it occurs" (112). To this extent he resembled Kohut, who also incurred the opprobrium of many colleagues in the professional organizations to which he belonged. Rogers was one of the first psychologists to demonstrate that a "high degree of empathy in a relationship is possibly *the* most potent factor in bringing about change and learning" (139). His essay "Empathic: An Unappreciated Way of Being," first published in 1975 and then reprinted in his 1980 book *A Way of Being*, remains probably the most incisive paper on the subject. He presents several research findings, all or most of which can be applied to education as well as to psychotherapy: "The ideal therapist is, first of all, empathic"; "Empathy is correlated with self-exploration and process movement"; "Empathy early in the relationship predicts later success"; "In successful cases, the client comes to perceive more empathy"; "Empathic understanding is provided freely by the therapist, not drawn from him or her"; "The more experienced the therapist is, the more likely he or she is to be empathic"; "Empathy is a special quality in a relationship, and therapists offer definitely more of it than even helpful friends"; "The better integrated the therapist is, the higher the degree of empathy he or she exhibits"; "Experienced therapists often fall short of being empathic"; "Clients are better judges of the degree of empathy than are therapists"; "Brilliance and diagnostic perceptiveness are unrelated to empathy"; and "An empathic way of being can be learned from empathic persons" (146–50). Elsewhere in *A Way of Being* Rogers offers one of the most striking metaphors of empathic listening:

Almost always, when a person realizes he has been deeply heard, his eyes moisten. I think in some real sense he is weeping for joy. It is as though he were saying, "Thank God, somebody heard me. Someone knows what it's like to be me." In such moments I have had the fantasy of a prisoner in a dungeon, tapping out day after day a Morse code message, "Does anybody hear me? Is anybody there?" And finally one day he hears some faint tappings which spell out "Yes." By that one simple response he is released from his loneliness; he has become a human being again. There are many, many people living in private dungeons today, people who give no evidence of it whatsoever on the outside, where you have to listen very sharply to hear the faint messages from the dungeon. (10).

Rogers marshaled a great deal of evidence to demonstrate the educational benefits of a person-centered approach. The most effective teachers, he argued, are those who exhibit a high level of facilitative qualities. These teachers "have more positive self-concepts than low-level teachers," "are more self-disclosing to their students," "respond more to students' feelings," "give more praise," "are more responsive to students' ideas," and "lecture less often" (A Way of Being 310). Rogers's optimism, which he shared with Kohut, extended to both psychotherapy and education, and in his view, the main role of the therapist and teacher was to create the climate that fosters therapeutic and educational growth. "I have come to trust the capacity of persons to explore and understand themselves and their troubles, and to resolve those problems, in any close, continuing relationship where I can provide a climate of real warmth and understanding" (38). To enact educational reform, Rogers proposed that empathic facilitators lead three-week group sessions with cognitive and experiential elements. "Many educators might be fearful that personal damage would result from these intensive group experiences," Rogers concedes, but he cites research indicating that damage would result only when the leader is "confronting, challenging, attacking, or intrusive" (282).

Emmanuel Levinas and the Other

There are few references to empathy in the opaque theoretical world of Emmanuel Levinas, the early twentieth-century Lithuanian-born Jew who spent most of his adult life teaching continental philosophy in France, but his influential ideas on ethics and alterity are crucial for anyone who seeks to learn more about the other. Levinas constructed an ethical philosophy where one's duty to the other is a transcendent responsibility. "[M]an is responsible for the other man," he observes in an interview in Is It Righteous to Be? "and he is responsible for him even when the other does not concern him, because the other always concerns him. The other's face always regards me. And this is *de jure* limitless. At no moment can you leave the other to his own destiny. I sometimes call this *expiation*, extending all the way to substitution for the other. I am thinking of the talmudic statement, 'Do not judge the other without putting yourself in his place'" (99). So important is this duty to the other that Levinas often quoted a sentence from Dostoevsky's *The Brothers Karamazov*: "Each of us is guilty before everyone and for everything, and I more than all the others" (*Righteous* 56).

Levinas defines ethics as a "comportment in which the other, who is strange and indifferent to you, who belongs neither to the order of your interest nor to your affections, at the same time matters to you. His alterity concerns you" (*Righteous* 48). Like Martin Buber, Levinas sees a dialogical relationship between self and other, but whereas the former envisions the I-Thou relationship as reciprocal, the latter maintains that it is asymmetrical. In Levinas's world, assuming responsibility for the suffering of others reveals mercy, which he sees as part of the phenomenon of love; the origin of love lies in sympathy for the other's suffering. "The only absolute value," he concludes, is the "human possibility of giving the other priority over oneself" (170)—a value that demonstrates holiness. "I apologize for always speaking of holiness," Levinas remarks in an interview. "But it is the ideal of holiness which renders possible the love of the neighbor. The man who is affirmed in his humanity can still be considered a rational animal, but he is not a complete man. The recognition of the unique, the recognition of the other, the priority of the other is, in a certain sense, unreasonable. One may even be astonished that men would manifest goodness, each on the part of the other. There is no grace as astonishing as this peace" (*Righteous* 111).

One need not share Levinas's vision of a transcendent morality or belief in asymmetrical self-other relationships to recognize one's responsibility to diminish suffering. Nor does one need to follow the tortuous intricacies of Levinas's metaphysics to recognize the value of ethics in an age that privileges epistemology over morality and justice. Levinas "challenges the hegemony of knowledge," writes Richard Cohen in his book *Ethics, Exegesis, and Philosophy*. "Knowledge, by itself, as has become nearly transparent today, is incapable of determining worth, value, or purpose. It knows, to be sure, but it cannot rank importance. Its object is 'difference' not excellence" (5). The question for Levinas is not Hamlet's "To be or not to be" but rather one's "right to be" (*The Levinas Reader* 86). Deeply affected by the Holocaust, Levinas came to believe, as Cohen points out, that "the only sense that can be made of suffering, that is to say, of evil, is to make one's own suffering into a suffering for the suffering of others. Or, to put this in one word: the only ethical meaning of suffering, indeed, 'the only meaning to which suffering is susceptible' is *compassion* (276–77; emphasis in original). This compassion arises through empathy, Levinas declares in his study of Husserl's phenomenology, "which is an act that reveals the conscious life of others" (cited by Cohen 87). Empathy also makes possible, Levinas observes in his book *Discovering Existence with Husserl*, intersubjectivity (30).

Levinas's belief in taking responsibility for the other implies the need to affirm and be affirmed by the other. In *A Sense of Self: The Work of Affirmation*, Thomas Cottle explores the relational aspects of affirmation. He summarizes what psychologists have called the "Michelangelo phenomenon": "Predicated on interpersonal relationships, the Michelangelo phenomenon represents an attempt by social scientists to describe how the individual self is formed by the perceptions of it of some significant other, as well as by the behavior of this significant other. The essence of this phenomenon rests on the notion that the more the self is affirmed by the perceptions and behavior of the other, the more the individual self 'moves' toward its own conception of an ideal form" (24). Cottle's recognition that affirmation underlies the concept of empathy has important educational implications, suggesting that teachers who affirm their students not only heighten their students' sense of self but also increase their understanding of classmates. Mark Bracher makes a similar observation when he suggests that in cases "where the subject matter is threatening to students—because either its content or its difficulty threatens students' identities—teachers will find it useful to employ techniques similar to those used in supportive and expressive therapy," including "reassuring students of their intelligence, ability, human worth, and eventual success as they are struggling with intellectually or emotionally difficult material" (117).

Most people use the words "empathy" and "sympathy" interchangeably, and psychotherapists, philosophers, and experimental psychologists have long debated the differences between the two. Most researchers conclude that they are similar but not identical. Lauren Wispé conjectures that in empathy, the "self is the vehicle for understanding, and it never loses its identity. Sympathy, on the other hand, is concerned with communion rather than accuracy, and self-awareness is reduced rather than enhanced. In empathy one person reaches out for the other person, whereas in sympathy the sympathizer is moved by the other person" (79). Candace Clark implies that sympathy has a moral dimension that empathy lacks. "Sympathy giving begins with cognitive, emotional, or physical empathy, that is, in one way or another taking the role of the other. Empathy allows one to grasp the outlines or the details of the other's situation. The resulting image may lead one no further, or it may lead one to experience emotions antagonistic to the other's—glee at the other's misfortune or satisfaction that the other deserved what he or she got. In either case no sympathy exists" (78).

The philosopher Martha Nussbaum also distinguishes between empathy and sympathy: "a malevolent person who imagines the situation of another and takes pleasure in her distress may be empathetic, but will surely not be judged sympathetic. Sympathy, like compassion, includes a judgment that the other person's distress is bad" (*Upheavals of Thought* 302). She further distinguishes empathy from compassion in that the former "is like the mental preparation of a skilled (Method) actor: it involves a participatory enactment of the situation of the sufferer, but is always combined with the awareness that one is not oneself the sufferer. This awareness of one's separate life is quite important if empathy is to be closely related to compassion: for if it is to be for *another*, and not for oneself, that one feels compassion, one must be aware both of the bad lot of the sufferer and of the fact that it is, right now, not one's own" (327). Nussbaum ranks compassion and sympathy as higher than empathy in moral philosophy, but she also believes that art and literature should be mainly concerned not with erudition but with "empathy and the extension of concern" (432).

Nearly everyone agrees that empathy has a dark side, for not only can it be used to exploit another person's weakness, but it can also lead to empathic distress. This can be seen in William Blake's 1789 poem "On Another's Sorrow," in which the apprehension of suffering leads to suffering:

> *Can I see another's woe,*
> *And not be in sorrow too?*
> *Can I see another's grief,*
> *And not seek for kind relief?*
>
> *Can I see a falling tear,*
> *And not feel my sorrow's share?*
> *Can a father see his child*
> *Weep, nor be with sorrow fill'd?* (122)

In *The Altruism Question* C. Daniel Batson writes that "if empathy-induced altruism is an antidote for meaninglessness and tension, then this antidote comes with a warning label on the bottle. Just as too much of almost any medicine will do you harm, too much selfless concern for others may lead to what has recently been labeled 'compassion fatigue.' It appears that the most concerned doctors, social workers, hospice workers, and therapists, those who take on an especially heavy load of other people's burnouts, are vulnerable to a form of burnout in which they feel they have run dry and have nothing more to give. One cause of this syndrome may be that there is a limit to the number of times in a given period that we can take another person's perspective and become empathically aroused" (223). Empathy is a virtue that "few dispute and fewer seem to practice," David Morris suggests, adding that a "bioethics based on empathy tends to over-look our remarkable powers to turn away from suffering, especially when suffering occurs in hospitals or other remote places, like Bosnia" (259).

Empathy is "seldom seamless, nor should it be," Alfred Margulies asserts; it is the "struggle toward empathy and understanding that creates discord and forces clarification and, sometimes, the creation of meaning" (98). Empathy can be inaccurate and, when coming from a therapist, physician, or teacher, lead to what Lorraine Code calls an "asymmetry in the power of its participants. . . . Where there is a difference of power, knowledge, expertise, a claim to 'know just how you feel' can readily expand into a claim that I will tell you how I feel, and *I* will be right, even though you might describe it differently, for your perceptions are ill-informed, and my greater expertise must override them" (84).

Empathy and Feminist Theories of Development

Psychoanalysis and feminism have long had an adversarial relationship, but Kohut's emphasis on empathy has helped shape feminist theories of development. Mary Field Belenky and her associates argue in *Women's Ways of Knowing* that empathy is the basis for connected knowledge. "Connected knowers develop procedures for gaining access to other people's knowledge. At the heart of these procedures is the capacity for empathy. . . . Connected knowers know that they can only approximate other people's experiences and so can gain only limited access to their knowledge. But insofar as possible, they must act as connected rather than separate selves, seeing the other not in their own terms but in the other's terms" (113). Empathy functions as the key element in the "self-in-relation" theory associated with Wellesley College's Stone Center model of development. Judith V. Jordan and her associates offer a definition of empathy in *Women's Growth in Connection* that emphasizes mutuality, which they believe is lacking in Kohut's definition:

Empathy always involves affective surrender and cognitive structuring, and, in order for empathy to occur, ego boundaries must be flexible. Experientially, empathy begins with the basic capacity and motivation for human relatedness that allows perception of the other's affective cues, verbal and nonverbal. This is followed by a surrender to affective arousal in oneself—as if the perceived affective cues were one's own—thus producing a temporary identification with the other's emotional state. Finally, there occurs a resolution period in which one regains a sense of separate self that understands what has just happened. For empathy to be effective, there must be a balance of the affective and cognitive, the subjective and objective. (29)

The Stone Center's self-in-relation theory is based on "empathic attunement" or "mutual intersubjectivity," which is defined as the "attunement to and responsiveness to the subjective, inner experience of the other, at both a cognitive and affective level" (Jordan 287–88). The Stone Center authors argue that women are more empathic than men with the important exception of self-empathy, which occurs when the "observing, often judging, self" makes "empathic contact with some aspect of the self as object" (77). Self-empathy may take the form of "having a memory of oneself in which the inner state at that time has not been fully integrated because it was not acceptable. To be able to observe and tolerate the affect of that state in a context of understanding becomes a kind of intrapsychic empathy, which actually can lead to lasting structural change in relational images and self-representations" (286).

Expanding upon the Stone Center's relational theory, and recalling Kohut's and Rogers's undying optimism in the transformative power of empathy, Jean Baker Miller and Irene Pierce Stiver state in *The Healing Connection* that "[m]utual empathy is the great unsung human gift. We are all born with the possibility of engaging in it. Out of it flows mutual empowerment. It is something very different from one-way empathy; it is a joining together based on the authentic thoughts and feelings of all the participants in a relationship" (29). For the Stone Center psychologists, a relational model of therapy depends upon empathic understanding, and I argue that the same holds for a relational model of education.

Heightened connection is both a cause and effect of trust, and both are conducive to self-disclosure. In *Boundaries of Privacy* Sandra Petronio cites a study suggesting that "secure individuals want, as an interaction goal, to become intimate and emotionally close to others and work to guarantee that they have boundary linkages with others" (97). Petronio also observes that "disclosure contributes to the progression of relational intimacy through building a shared set of private information where there is an expectation of mutual reciprocal responsibility" (87).

A philosopher rather than a psychologist, Nel Noddings has argued for a new theory of ethics and moral education that arises from empathy. In her book *Caring*, she takes an approach that is "rooted in receptivity, relatedness, and responsiveness" (2). Noddings bases her ethics of caring not on a "peculiarly rational, western, masculine" view of empathy, which the *Oxford University Dictionary* defines as the "power of projecting one's personality into, and so fully understanding, the object of contemplation," but on a "feminine" view of empathy that "does not involve projection but reception" (30). (She doesn't comment on the impossibility of "fully understanding" the other.) Regardless of whether empathy involves projection or reception, "pedagogical caring" has important educational implications, beginning with the teacher's relational bond to his or her students. "[T]eaching involves a meeting of one-caring and cared-for. I can lecture to hundreds, and this is neither inconsequential nor unimportant, but this is not teaching. To teach involves a giving of self and a receiving of other" (113). Noddings emphasizes the dialogical nature of the teacher-student relationship, which involves not simply the teaching and learning of a body of knowledge but the encounter between two persons. "When a teacher asks a question in class and a student responds, she receives not just the 'response' but the student. What he says matters, whether it is right or wrong, and she probes gently for clarification, interpretation, contribution" (176).

Attachment Theory

Women's Ways of Knowing, Women's Growth in Connection, The Healing Connection, and *Caring* do not include John Bowlby's work in their extensive bibliographies, but there are important links between a feminist theory of development and attachment theory. Indeed, Bowlby's pioneering research demonstrates that the need for attachment is one of the most important human drives; anything that shatters or weakens this bond threatens a person's well-being. Bowlby's classic three-volume work *Attachment and Loss* describes the behavioral systems that are activated or deactivated by the child's attachment to his or her parents. Bowlby viewed development as a complex interactive process involving both genetic endowment and adaptation to the environment. Attachment behaviors are those actions that result in a child's closeness to the parent, such as cooing in the presence of a parent and crying in the parent's absence. A child's first caregiver is generally the mother but also includes the father and grandparents. Attachment theory postulates that young children develop internalized mental representations of their parents that are based on their experiences with them. These mental representations, or working models, are then incorporated into the child's personality and shape his or her behavior toward other people. Although the parent-child bond remains a crucial factor in influencing future behavior, other attachment bonds become increasingly important, such as with peers and friends. Attachment behaviors change over time, but attachment bonds generally remain stable.

Bowlby believed that adolescents who have strong attachment figures are more likely to experience positive self-esteem and general well-being than those who have weak or ambivalent attachment figures. Many empirical studies of attachment theory have supported Bowlby's belief that children who experience consistently nurturing parents develop a mental representation of others as strong, secure attachment figures, while children who experience inconsistent or unresponsive parents develop a mental representation of others as weak, insecure attachment figures (see Bernstein et. al., and Coleman and Hendry). Strong attachment bonds are linked not only to the capacity to form loving, trusting relationships but also to heightened self-esteem, competence, and general well-being. Strong attachment bonds are especially important for adolescents, since the adolescent years are associated with an increased risk of psychological difficulties, including low self-esteem, anxiety, depression, and suicide. These strong attachment bonds promote empathy and concern for the other. Attachment theorists such as Nancy Weinfield and her associates argue that empathy is the "complement or counterpoint to aggression. Whereas aggression often reflects an alienation from others, empathy reflects an amplified connectedness, and whereas aggression reflects a breakdown or warping of dyadic regulation, empathy reflects heightened affective coordination. In fact, in many ways aggression is dependent upon a lack of empathy or emotional identification with others." Weinfield adds that attachment theory "makes a strong prediction with regard to the development of empathic capacity" (78).

Arielle Berman Albert has used an attachment theory perspective to explore whether parental and peer group bonds can predict late adolescents' psychological adjustment to college. Most of the college freshmen and sophomores in her study selected their mother rather than father as their major attachment figure, which is consistent with the findings of attachment research. Females reported more depression symptoms and lower self-esteem than males, which is also consistent with research. Unexpectedly, no gender differences were found in levels of parental and peer support. Albert's major finding is that both parental and peer support

play significant roles in raising adolescents' self-esteem and lowering depression symptoms. Interestingly, parental and peer support seem to be
equally strong in predicting late adolescents' psychological adjustment to
college: neither is a stronger predictor than the other. The relationship
between parental and peer support and psychological adjustment is strong
for both males and females. Albert concludes her study by noting that her
findings are particularly useful for college counselors and residence advis-
ers, who often interact with students struggling with depression and low
self-esteem. "Such individuals can encourage late adolescents to make use
of their important relationships with family and friends (rather than to feel
uncomfortable or ashamed for relying on them) in order to derive a sense
of increased security and support, and promote their psychological adjustment" ("Parental and Peer Support" 112).

The Teacher as Attachment Figure

Most of the research on attachment theory focuses on the child's and
adolescent's attachments to parents and peers. Bowlby did not consider
teachers as attachment figures, but he did recognize the importance of
attachment figures in an adult's life. As he observes in *The Making and
Breaking of Affectional Bonds*, "[w]hilst attachment behaviour is shown
especially strongly during childhood when it is directed towards parent
figures, it none the less continues to be active during adult life when it is
usually directed towards some active and dominant figure, often a relative
but sometimes an employer or some elder of the community" (87). Bowlby
also affirmed the importance of attachment bonds for a student's success
in college. "When a student feels confident that relationships at home are
secure, supportive, and encouraging he finds no difficulty in making the
most of the new opportunities that college offers" (*Attachment* 350).

Attachment theory has intriguing educational implications, for it suggests that students' success in learning depends upon strong attachment to
their teachers. In one of the few studies on the teacher as an attachment
figure, Carollee Howes and Sharon Ritchie noted the changes in children's
attachment organization when they were taken out of community child
care environments and placed in a therapeutic preschool. The three- to
four-year-old children, who previously demonstrated out-of-control behavior, experienced heightened attachment security. The authors conclude
that sensitive caregivers, such as teachers, can help to strengthen the attachment behavior of students with prior relationship difficulties. "[P]ro-
viding children with teachers who can be trusted to be consistently posi-

tive will help disconfirm the children's expectations that adults will be inconsistent, neglecting or harsh, and lead to more positive teacher-student relationships" (420).

Teachers who make a difference in their students' lives and who are regarded as supportive, dependable, and empathic become attachment figures, and they are the ones whom students regard as instrumental in their personal and professional lives. These teachers help to instill in their students a sense of "basic trust," which Erik Erikson defines as "consistency, continuity, and sameness of experience" (247). Students who experience their teachers as stable and dependable are likely to internalize these qualities and develop internal representations of others as stable and dependable. This attachment is not to be confused with dependence, as Bowlby makes clear. "[D]ependence is not specifically related to maintenance of proximity, it is not directed towards a specific individual, it does not imply an enduring bond, nor is it necessarily associated with strong feeling. No biological function is attributed to it. Furthermore, in the concept of dependence there are value implications the exact opposite of those that the concept of attachment conveys. Whereas to refer to a person as dependent tends to be disparaging, to describe him as attached to someone can well be an expression of approval" (*Making and Breaking of Affectional Bonds* 132). To be an attachment figure, a teacher needs to be caring but not a caregiver. And in a self-disclosing classroom, where safety and trust are essential, the teacher must know how to create and maintain students' bonds with each other. Anything that is likely to strengthen students' attachment to their teacher and classmates is likely to encourage connected learning.

Teachers who are attachment figures are attentive to their students' needs. They look at their students and observe whether they are smiling or frowning, interested or bored, engaged or disengaged. They seek their students' responses and elicit their questions and answers. They listen carefully to their students' words, attentive to their speech and silence. They encourage their students both to agree and disagree with them. They cannot presume to know their students' thoughts and feelings, but they can encourage students to share their thoughts and feelings in signed or unsigned essays and diaries. They enter into dialogical relationships with their students in which they teach and learn from them. Although the teacher-student relationship is asymmetrical in terms of institutional power, attachment teachers affirm reciprocity, mutuality, and intersubjectivity. Attachment teachers know that they can create a secure relationship with their students by establishing an empathic classroom in which no one feels threatened or humiliated. Peter Fonagy's observation about the contemporary view of the psychoanalyst-patient relationship applies equally well to the teacher-student relationship: "The ideal psychoanalyst ceased to be a neutral observer but rather the patient's collaborator engaged in a continuous negotiation about truth and reality—the conversation with the other person being the only way of escaping preconception" (125). Above all, these attachment teachers remain connected to their students, attuned to their emotional as well as intellectual growth inside and outside the classroom.

Many researchers have demonstrated the educational benefits of empathy and, by implication, the value of attachment teachers. In reviewing several academic studies, Arnold Goldstein and Gerald Michaels conclude that despite methodological difficulties, most of the research "underscores the robustness of the empathy-achievement relationship" (148). Teacher empathy is also associated with a "variety of positive, nonachievement outcome criteria," such as harmonious peer relationships and heightened self-esteem (155). Research on empathy and academic outcomes indicates impressive correlations between student scores on measures of empathic understanding and grade point averages, higher reading comprehension, and enhanced critical thinking skills and creative thinking (Cotton 8). Empathy training programs for therapists, teachers, and parents have been shown to be valuable for heightening affective and cognitive empathy. These programs emphasize role-taking, which was pioneered by the anthropologist Margaret Mead as well as by Carl Rogers. Empathy training programs include training in interpersonal perception and empathic responding as well as locating the similarities between oneself and others. Kathleen Cotton points out that "virtually all considerations of the empathic process have noted the close connections between responding empathically to another person and perceiving that person as similar to oneself" (5).

Teachers become attachment figures by promoting empathic learning, which has both cognitive and affective components: intellectual and emotional knowledge. Empathic learning is vitally important in the self-disclosing classroom, where students share their writings with classmates. There are many ways for teachers to encourage students to empathize with classmates, beginning with teachers themselves modeling the behavior they wish their students to follow. Empathic learning implies a willing suspension of disbelief and a suspension of the usual type of critique that occurs in most classrooms. Thus teachers listen to students without offering criticism, commentary, or advice. To empathize does not mean that one approves or agrees with another person, but it does mean that one is trying to understand that person. To withhold judgment or disapproval of another person does not mean self-censorship, but it does mean that we must remain silent if we are to hear others.

Of the five levels of listening described by Stephen Covey, "ignoring, pretend listening, selective listening, attentive listening, and empathic listening," the last is the most developed. "Listening in this manner gets you inside *another's* frame of reference—with the rest of the listening levels you never get outside *your own frame.* You not only learn a lot about the other party by listening empathically. You open yourself up to a host of new ideas" (153–54; emphasis in original). In an age in which people understandably tune out the barrage of sound bytes to which they are exposed, empathic listening allows people to tell their own stories and, in the process, to reach their own interpretations. The writers' classmates also reach their own conclusions about the stories they have read or heard. Complete understanding of the other or even of oneself is impossible, but empathy allows us to *begin* to understand other people's feelings and thoughts. The more we understand others, the more we become aware of their vulnerability—hence, the more we need to make sure that we do not take advantage of that vulnerability.

"What is central to the empathic mode of listening," J. Brooks Bouson suggests, "is the analyst's ability both to step inside the patient's subjective world and to reflect on what he or she has heard and experienced. In a parallel sense, the critic/reader must both enter into and reflect on the experiential world proffered by the text" (169). Empathic listening allows speakers to speak and writers to write without the fear of interruption, interrogation, or disapproval. Empathic listening implies neither boredom nor lack of interest; on the contrary, it shows the highest respect, for it demonstrates that nothing is more important than hearing the other, to whom we grant permission to speak or write on any subject. Empathic listening promotes reciprocity: we listen carefully and sensitively to others so that they will listen carefully and sensitively to us. Empathic listening is not easy in an "argument culture," in which everything is contested and often litigated, but it is essential if we are to learn more about others and ourselves.

The injunction to remain empathic and nonjudgmental, respecting people's feelings without challenging them, does not imply the adoption of a speech code or the stifling of free speech. I mention this because of the controversy arising from the "guidelines for classroom discussion" that are part of the syllabus for a popular women's studies graduate course at the University of South Carolina at Columbia. In "Guidelines for Discussion, or Thought Control?" appearing in the September 27, 2002, issue of the *Chronicle of Higher Education,* Thomas Bartlett describes the fierce debate that has erupted over Lynn Weber's guidelines, which she wrote eighteen years ago and published in a feminist journal in 2000. In an effort to "create a safe atmosphere for open discussion," Professor Weber asks her students to "acknowledge that racism, classism, sexism, heterosexism and other institutionalized forms of oppression exist" and to "assume that people—both the groups we study and the members of the class—always do the best they can." Bartlett reports that conservative critics see the guidelines "as an ideological litmus test that some students can't pass and [that] no student should be asked to follow." The conflict, adds Bartlett, "has generated a surprising amount of attention—Ms. Weber recently declined an invitation to discuss her guidelines on the national television program *The O'Reilly Factor.* And while some critics are worried about violations of the Constitution, supporters wonder what could be so harmful about a set of guidelines that Ms. Weber says are created to encourage more sensitive and respectful discussions."

I'm sympathetic to Professor Weber's pedagogical goals, but while I share her social and political assumptions, I'm uncomfortable with her guidelines, with which many conservative students would not agree. Asking students to remain empathic and nonjudgmental while listening to a classmate's personal essay is different from asking them to endorse a series of highly ideological social and political assumptions. Empathic listening allows us to hear a classmate's essay about an abortion without making a judgment about abortion. The essay can teach both prolife and prochoice readers what the experience was like and how the writer now feels about it. Empathic listening does not force students to subscribe to a speech code. Rather, empathic listening allows a writer to narrate a story, which may be filled with pain or shame, without the fear that a classmate will criticize that story for being "self-pitying" or "self-indulgent." Sometimes a student makes a statement that is inadvertently wounding to a classmate, and when such empathic failures occur, it is the teacher's challenge to help the student realize why the comment was offensive.

The Resistance to Empathy

Empathic education is not easy to achieve. Many who have written on the subject acknowledge the strong resistance to it. Clinicians from a wide variety of disciplines who consider empathy important concede that their professional training or institutional practices often work against this approach. To offer only one example, in the introduction to *Empathy and the Practice of Medicine,* Howard Spiro, a noted gastroenterologist and director of the Program for Humanities in Medicine at the Yale University School of Medicine, writes:

> As studies repeatedly show, most people still go to physicians looking for help for existential pains, for the suffering of living in this world, for ailments that no technology can correct. That is where the patient's story comes in, for it can reveal what is important in the images the doctor obtains. The physician's first and foremost task is to decide what is going on, what tests must be done, if any. At the same time, doctors must listen to what the patient tells them, remaining open to be moved by the story even, for that will often clear the path to diagnosis. Listening goes straight to the heart and helps to create empathy. Empathy opens our eyes to let us see what the CT scan has missed. The ear is as important as the eye in medical practice. Is it too much to claim that the physician must be the mediator between the images and the patient? (4)

Spiro then admits, however, that medical training seldom encourages students to remain empathic. Physicians are not rewarded financially for being empathic toward their patients. According to Spiro, only when physicians fall ill do they recognize the importance of empathy. "Most sick doctors ignore their problems, deny their very real disability, and then come to lament their isolation from their imperturbable colleagues. Moreover, physicians still healthy are glad not to confront the sickness of a colleague, for it signals their own mortality. One reason why 'No Visitors' signs appear so automatically when doctors are admitted to the hospital may be to permit their colleagues to pass by without feeling guilt, the one emotion doctors still allow" (5).

Academics also tend to be suspicious of empathy, believing that it is a sentimental, inauthentic, and "touchy-feely" concept. Empathy is seldom discussed in undergraduate or graduate literature courses, and relatively few articles and books have been published on the subject, especially in composition studies. For example, there is not a single reference to the word "empathy" in *Cross-Talk in Comp Theory: A Reader,* edited by Victor Villanueva Jr., published by the National Council of Teachers of English — despite the fact that the anthology contains 786 pages, including a 23-page index with more than 20,000 entries. Nor do any of the 41 essays refer to empathy. Few if any composition scholars would find this omission surprising or disturbing. The one essay that might be expected to discuss empathy, Joel Hoefner's "Democracy, Pedagogy, and the Personal

Essay," takes a dim view of personal writing and so ignores the subject: "students may find some topics that speak directly to them, but the personal essay often remains alien, a species of discourse imposed by the institution" (516).

Nor is empathy widely theorized. None of the "master" theorists whose work is so influential in the academy—Marx, Lacan, Foucault, and Derrida—had much to say about the subject. Freud commented briefly on empathy but did not make it an important part of his theory; moreover, he was distinctly *un*empathic to many of his patients, such as Dora. The lack of interest in empathy may help to explain why so many colleges and universities have become such contentious places in the last thirty years. And English departments seem to generate the most divisiveness.

In my own department, for example, the anger and mistrust among colleagues have been so intense at times that one feels the need to wear a bulletproof vest to meetings. I'm not referring simply to contentious personnel meetings, where hiring and tenure issues affect people's lives, or to the well-publicized "canon wars" over curricular issues, but to other issues such as office space. Perhaps most demoralizing of all are the "memo wars" in which a faculty member writes an angry letter to a colleague and then distributes copies to everyone else in the department, including graduate students. Gone are the days, it seems, when professors expressed their anger in private to colleagues in an effort to resolve disagreements or misunderstandings. Academic conflicts, which have been widely satirized in such novels as Alison Lurie's *The War between the Tates*, David Lodge's *Changing Places, Small World,* and *Thinks,* Jane Smiley's *Moo,* Richard Russo's *Straight Man,* and Lennard Davis's *The Sonnets,* would be funny were they not so destructive to collegiality and teaching. I was on a committee that spent more than an hour debating whether to accept or reject the preceding meeting's minutes. The members of the committee, all tenured professors, began shouting at each other, and the acting chair, who had been appointed by the administration to heal the wounds of a bitter departmental civil war, abruptly ended the meeting, unable to restore order. Fortunately, the end of the academic year arrived, and the committee was dissolved: Imagine trying to agree on the minutes of a preceding meeting that could not agree on the minutes! It is hard to remain empathic in such an explosive atmosphere, where so many political and ideological tensions mask unaddressed personal animosities.

Empathy may not be a reliable antidote to internecine academic wars, but I am convinced that it is a powerful tool in the classroom. Empathy helps us to understand not only what our students are thinking and feeling but also our impact on them and their impact on us. Empathy enables us to understand the traumas that so many students have experienced and the ways in which they have responded to these wrenching experiences. Awareness of trauma theory, a body of knowledge that is by no means limited to cataclysmic historical events, may be useful for teachers, who often find themselves witnessing their students' troubled lives.

Trauma

It may seem odd to discuss trauma in a book on empathic teaching, for how often do traumatic events occur to students? Trauma is an appropriate subject for mental health professionals, whose patients suffer from a variety of psychological illnesses, and it has become an increasingly important subject for literary theorists and historians, who investigate the extent to which language can represent such unrepresentable events as the Holocaust. But how does trauma manifest itself in the classroom? It is true that one student commits suicide in *Dead Poets Society* and that another contemplates suicide in *The Breakfast Club*, but these are fictional suicides, which have become formulaic in their literary and filmic representations. There are also rapes, beatings, and murders in many of the other stories and films I discuss.

The day after I typed the preceding words into my word processor, the United States suffered the worst terrorist attack in its history, killing thousands of people and traumatizing a nation. The image of a hijacked jetliner crashing into the World Trade Center and bursting into a huge fireball, replayed again and again on television, is now indelibly etched into our national psyche. Everyone stared with shock, horror, fear, and disbelief at the images of the collapsing World Trade Center twin towers and the fire-ravaged Pentagon. "Surreal" was the word used by the witnesses, and the events of the day looked like they came from a disaster or war film. Newspaper headlines proclaimed "America under Attack," inaugurating us into a new and frightening era. Those of my generation, born at the end of World War II, can recall precisely where we were and what we were doing when John F. Kennedy was shot on November 22, 1963, just as our parents can recall where they were when they heard about the Pearl Harbor bombing on December 7, 1941. The same will be true of the September 11, 2001, attack. No one can predict how this apocalyptic event will change American life, but rather than speculate on the future, I want to give a brief summary of the history of trauma including its ever-widening definition and impact on society. This summary will help us to under-

stand many of the traumatic events about which students write, events
that have now become an everyday reality for so many people.

Before doing so, however, I acknowledge the difficulty of finding the
right words to describe trauma. "A curious fact about language," Terrence
des Pres states at the beginning of his 1976 book *The Survivor*, "which
Tolstoy and then Hemingway used to advantage, is that to write about terrible things in a neutral tone or with descriptions barren of subjective response tends to generate an irony so virulent as to end in either cynicism
or despair. On the other hand, to allow feeling much play when speaking
of atrocity is to border on hysteria and reduce the agony of millions to a
moment of self-indulgence" (vi). To write on trauma is to acknowledge
unbearable suffering, and one searches for a vocabulary and tone that will
be attentive and respectful to suffering while avoiding clinical detachment,
on the one hand, and emotional excess, on the other. Also, describing trauma
may traumatize the reader, who thus becomes implicated in another's suffering. Readers may feel "empathic unsettlement," which Dominick LaCapra
defines as "[b]eing responsive to the traumatic experiences of others, notably of victims, [but without] the appropriation of their experiences" (*Writing History, Writing Trauma* 41).

"Trauma" means "wound," and the word first entered the public consciousness in the nineteenth century, when railway accidents produced
severe physical injuries that prevented employees from returning to work.
Trauma was a contested medical and legal subject from the beginning,
with railway owners and employees disputing the extent and duration of
the injury. Freud was the key figure in the transition from physical to psychic trauma, and he created psychoanalysis to understand the link between the two. Freud and his coauthor Josef Breuer asserted in *Studies on
Hysteria* (1893–95) that the symptoms of hysteria could be traced back to
a patient's sexual life. In their famous formulation, "*Hysterics suffer mainly
from reminiscences*" (7; emphasis in original). Based on the stories told
him in analysis, Freud believed that his female patients were seduced by
their male relatives, but he soon found it inconceivable that so many of
them, who came from respectable Viennese families, could have been
telling the truth. In a letter to his close friend and confidant Wilhelm
Fliess, Freud wrote on September 21, 1897: "I no longer believe in my
neurotica": it was "hardly credible" to him that "perverted acts against children were so general" (*Origins of Psychoanalysis* 215–16). Freud's crisis of
doubt led to two of his most momentous theories, the Oedipus complex
and the distinction between psychic and historical reality. "Only one idea
of general value has occurred to me," he confided to Fliess on October 15,

1897. "I have found love of the mother and jealously of the father in my own case too, and now believe it to be a general phenomenon of early childhood, even if it does not always occur so early as in children who have been made hysterics" (223).

Freud's breakthrough, however, led to the unintended and unfortunate devaluation of historical reality. Although psychoanalysis is itself a historical process, attempting to reconstruct in painstaking detail a patient's past, Freud's early followers assumed too quickly that their patients' stories of sexual trauma revealed fantasies and wishes instead of actual events. Thus a patient who had a dream or nightmare about incest was expressing an unconscious desire rather than reliving a historical event. Sometimes this was true, but other times it was not. I don't believe it was intellectual cowardice that led Freud to abandon his "seduction" theory, as Jeffrey Masson claims in his 1984 book *The Assault on Truth*; Freud never shrank from the role of being disturber of the world's sleep. Rather, he simply could not imagine that sexual trauma was so widespread. Nor did any of his contemporaries realize this.

Freud exerted such a strong influence on his disciples that, fifty years after the birth of psychoanalysis, they still did not question his judgment that incest was a fantasized rather than real event. In Otto Fenichel's encyclopedic *The Psychoanalytic Theory of Neurosis*, for example, first published in 1945 and reprinted in 1972, there is not a single reference to real as opposed to fantasized sexual trauma. Nor is there an entry for "rape" in the Index, which covers thirty-eight pages. If one looks for the word "incest," one is referred to the long entry for "Oedipus complex," which gives thirty-one different subjects (including "castration complex," "Don Juan," and "homosexuality"), but nothing remotely having to do with incest, child sexual abuse, or rape. The omission of any reference to sexual trauma is striking. Sidney Furst's 1967 psychoanalytic volume *Psychic Trauma* does speak about incest but in a way that a contemporary reader finds astonishing. "A recent survey of cases of incest by Irving has similarly revealed that pubertal and prepubertal girls who have been involved in sexual relations with their fathers rarely experience guilt and show little evidence of psychologic disturbance. A common finding of these as well as of other studies has been that the children involved in many instances welcomed, provoked, or even solicited the sexual contact with their elders" (21). Although contemporary psychoanalysts such as Jody Messler Davies and Mary Gail Frawley concede Freud's error in ignoring real childhood events, this has been a relatively recent development.

We now know that *actual* trauma is far more widespread than anyone had imagined. The statistics on child sexual abuse are chilling. Diana Russell states in her groundbreaking 1986 book *The Secret Trauma* that "16 percent of the sample of 930 women reported at least one experience of incestuous abuse before the age of eighteen years" and that "31 percent of the sample of 930 women reported at least one experience of sexual abuse by a nonrelative before reaching the age of eighteen years" (60–61). Additionally, Russell's survey indicates that "both incestuous abuse before eighteen and extrafamilial child sexual abuse before fourteen have quadrupled between the early 1900s and 1973" (81). She speculates that the factors contributing to the increase in child sexual abuse include pornography and the sexualization of children, the sexual revolution, the backlash against sexual equality, untreated child sexual abuse, and the growth of stepfamilies. One of Russell's most disturbing conclusions is that "women who were raised by a stepfather were over seven times more likely to be sexually abused by him than women who were raised by a biological father" (234).

Nearly all researchers agree that child sexual abuse has both short-term and long-term consequences. "Like other victims, abused children experience significant psychological distress and dysfunction," notes John Briere. "Unlike adults, however, they are traumatized during the most critical period of their lives: when assumptions about self, others, and the world are being formed; when their relations to their own internal states are being established; and when coping and affiliative skills are first acquired" (17). Many researchers have documented the immediate and delayed symptoms of child sexual abuse. Citing several studies, Anna Salter reports that "depression appears to be found more often in adult survivors of child sexual abuse than any other symptom"—in more than 90 percent of victims (165). Judith Herman, who has written extensively on this subject, concludes in her book *Father-Daughter Incest* that patients' accounts of childhood sexual abuse can be corroborated in a majority of cases.

The increasing reports of the prevalence of child sexual abuse have led some to question the reliability of these memories, especially when they emerge late in life. One of the major controversies in contemporary psychological research is the accuracy of "repressed" or "recovered" memories of child sexual abuse. Researchers have acknowledged that in some instances the truth may never be known. Stephen Ceci and his associates at Cornell University have conducted some of the most intriguing research on children's memories. Ceci has found that children tend to *forget* false information given to them by other children, but they *remember* false information given to them by their parents. Under certain conditions, then, children's memories are highly susceptible to false information. Many mental health professionals believe that adults remember at least part of the story of their sexual abuse. "People who say that their accusers are completely fabricating may be missing the essence of how traumatic memories manifest themselves," psychologist Lenore Terr remarks in *Unchained Memories*. "Parts are true—often the gists. Parts are false—sometimes details in the descriptions of the perpetrators" (203).

Child sexual abuse is such an explosive subject that sometimes the researchers themselves have had their objectivity and privacy called into question. A case in point is Jennifer Freyd. In her book *Betrayal Trauma* Freyd suggests that under certain conditions, "betrayals necessitate a 'betrayal blindness' in which the betrayed person does not have conscious awareness, or memory, of the betrayal" (9). She contends that betrayal results in the experience of trauma cognitively encoded in a person's consciousness or memory; sometimes it is too dangerous to acknowledge betrayal, especially when the betrayer is a relative whose trust is necessary for one's well-being. Freyd discloses at the end of her closely argued book that eight months after she presented her research findings at a professional conference, her parents formed the False Memory Syndrome Foundation—presumably to discredit her own claim of sexual abuse, which she had published under a pseudonym. The disclosure is stunning, and though the reader does not have enough information to judge the reliability of Freyd's point of view, it is impossible to disagree with her conclusion: "My own history does not argue for or against betrayal trauma theory. The theory must stand or fall on its own evidence and logic" (199).

Apart from sexual abuse, there are many other forms of trauma, including the trauma of war, which gave rise to one of Freud's most provocative books, *Beyond the Pleasure Principle*. Freud speculates, on the basis of his knowledge of shell-shocked soldiers of the Great War who would relive their nightmarish battle experiences, that there is a "death instinct" superseding the principle of wish fulfillment. "At this point we cannot escape a suspicion that we may have come upon the track of a universal attribute of instincts and perhaps of organic life in general which has not hitherto been clearly recognized or at least not explicitly stressed. *It seems, then, that an instinct is an urge inherent in organic life to restore an earlier state of things* which the living entity has been obliged to abandon under the pressure of external disturbing forces; that is, it is a kind of organic elasticity, or, to put it another way, the expression of the inertia inherent in organic life" (36; emphasis in original). There has been little clinical or empirical evidence to support Freud's theory of a death instinct, and it has been widely discredited. But Freud's postulation of the repetition-compulsion principle has generated enormous interest. His discussion of watching a one-and-a-half-year-old boy (his grandson) playing with a wooden reel with a string tied around it has come to be known as the *fort-da* game. "What he did was to hold the reel by the string and very skilfully throw it over the edge of his curtained cot, so that it disappeared into it, at the same time uttering his expressive 'o-o-o-o.' He then pulled the reel out of the cot again by the string and hailed its reappearance with a joyful '*da*' [there]. This, then, was the complete game — disappearance and return" (15). Admitting the difficulty of interpreting a child's motivation, Freud nevertheless makes a persuasive argument that the child is in a *passive* situation in the beginning but takes on an *active* role by repeating the unpleasurable action role. The compulsion to repeat, then, implies the need for mastery: one repeats traumatic experiences in order to overcome them.

Post-Traumatic Stress Disorder

The term "shell shock," used by Freud and his contemporaries to describe traumatized World War I soldiers, was the precursor to "post–traumatic stress disorder" (PTSD), which became an officially sanctioned diagnosis in 1980, when the American Psychiatric Association included it in the third edition of the *Diagnostic and Statistical Manual of Mental Disorders* (*DSM-III*). "The essential feature of this disorder is the development of characteristic symptoms following a psychologically distressing event that is outside the range of usual human experience (i.e., outside the range of such common experiences as simple bereavement, chronic illness, business losses, and marital conflict)" (247). The traumatic event is reexperienced in at least one of the following ways: (1) "recurrent and intrusive distressing recollections of the event (in young children, repetitive play in which themes or aspects of the trauma are expressed)"; (2) "recurrent distressing dreams of the event"; (3) "sudden acting or feeling as if the traumatic event were recurring (includes a sense of reliving the experience, illusions, hallucinations, and dissociative [flashback] episodes, even those that occur upon awakening or when intoxicated)" and (4) "intense psychological distress at exposure to events that symbolize or resemble an aspect of the traumatic event, including anniversaries of the trauma" (250). According to the *DSM-III*, the traumatic stressors lie "outside the range of usual human experience," such as war, kidnaping, or torture, but in later editions the stressors have become far more common and include "violent personal assault, serious accident, or serious injury experienced by a family member or a close friend; learning about the sudden, unexpected death of a family member or a close friend; or learning that one's child has a life-threatening disease" (*DSM-IV* 424).

The *DSM-III* does not quantify the prevalence of PTSD, but the *DSM-IV* cites figures ranging from 1 percent to 14 percent in the general population and 3 percent to 58 percent among at-risk individuals such as combat veterans. Bessel van der Kolk, one of the leading proponents of the expanded classification of PTSD, cites studies indicating that one out of five of the 23 percent of American adolescents who have been the victims of physical or sexual abuse or witnesses of violence against others developed PTSD ("Black Hole" 5). In another study, about 10 percent of the 76 percent of American adults exposed to extreme stress developed PTSD. "The majority of psychiatric inpatients have consistently been found to have histories of severe (usually intrafamilial) trauma, and at least 15 % meet diagnostic criteria for PTSD itself" ("Black Hole" 5). Rates of PTSD among persons with severe and persistent mental illness are even higher. David Albert has found that the rate of PTSD in this population exceeded 20 percent; moreover, PTSD among persons with severe mental illness is largely undetected in clinical settings. Van der Kolk speculates that one reason victims are "addicted to trauma"—that is, voluntarily reexpose themselves to situations reminiscent of the original trauma—is because of the release of endorphins, which have a temporarily calming effect. He cites as filmic examples of this addiction to trauma *The Pawnbroker*, the Russian roulette scene in *The Deer Hunter*, and the opening scenes of *Apocalypse Now* (*Psychological Trauma* 73). Most people exposed to traumatic stressors are able to resume their lives, but a small percentage remain haunted by intrusive memories and flashbacks and are unable to function.

Paradox and mystery surround PTSD, and it remains one of the least understood psychiatric disorders. "On the one hand, traumatized people remember too much; on the other hand, they remember too little. They seem to have lost authority over their memories. The memories intrude when they are not wanted, in the form of nightmares, flashbacks, and behavioral reenactments. Yet the memories may not be accessible when they are wanted" (Herman, "Crime and Memory 5). Literary theorist Cathy Caruth points out that the "trauma of the nightmare does not simply consist in the experience *within* the dream, but in *the experience of waking from it*. . . . What is enigmatically suggested, that is, is that the trauma consists not only in having confronted death, but in *having survived precisely, without knowing it*" (34; emphasis in original). Lilian Furst suggests in her study of psychosomatic disorders in medical and imaginative literature that PTSD partakes of conversions from the mind into the body: "The mutism, profuse sweating, violent heart beating, and other exaggerated responses . . . are idioms of distress that devolve from and obliquely refer back to the originating traumatic event" (175). Many of the ambiguities over the accuracy of recovered memories inhere in PTSD. Alexander McFarlane and Giovanni de Girolamo point out that since "some common stressful events" are related more closely to PTSD symptoms than "more extraordinary stressful events," there is a temptation to widen the list of stressors, but as the diagnosis of PTSD widens, some fear that a "culture of victimization" will also widen, discouraging people from accepting responsibility for their actions (138).

PTSD raises crucial questions about the functioning and malfunctioning of memory and thus about identity itself. "Memory implies identity," suggest Paul Antze and Michael Lambek, "the self caught between its roles as subject and object of memory, the telling and the told" (xix). We are what we remember, and if our memory is unstable and unreliable, so is our identity. Even as we struggle to create and maintain unified memories, we encounter not only the usual forgetfulness associated with advancing age but also the unusual forgetfulness associated with unexpected traumatic events. These traumatic events may leave gaping holes in our memory or create dissociated, sealed off memories that may be inaccessible to consciousness. Contemporary research suggests that memory is "anything but a photographic record of experience; it is a roadway full of potholes, badly in need of repair, worked on day and night by revisionist crews. What is registered is highly selective and thoroughly transformed by interpretation and semantic encoding at the moment of experience" (Kirmayer 176).

Controversies surround trauma research. Philosophers and cultural historians have challenged not only the prevalence of PTSD but also whether it actually exists as a distinct psychiatric illness. The subtitle of Allan Young's 1995 book *The Harmony of Illusions: Inventing Post–Traumatic Stress Disorder* conveys his belief that the history of the illness reveals a psychiatric construction rather than the discovery of a new scientifically verifiable phenomenon. Deconstructing the ambiguities of psychiatric case studies, Young states that "PTSD is no longer a distinctive nosological category: the syndrome would now be indistinguishable from combinations of already established psychiatric disorders, such as depression, generalized anxiety disorder, and panic disorder" (116). Young suggests elsewhere that people "'choose' PTSD . . . to reorganize their life-worlds, because it is a widely known and ready-made construct, [because] it is sanctioned by the highest medical authority, [because] it is said to originate in external circumstances rather than personal flaws or weakness, [and because] (in some situations) it earns compensation" ("Bodily Memory and Traumatic Memory" 98). Ruth Leys takes a similar approach, arguing in *Trauma: A Genealogy* that the history of trauma research is not a "continuous narrative" but a series of "irruptive events" that alternate between what she calls a "mimetic" approach, in which trauma is understood as an "experience of hypnotic imitation or identification," and its opposite, an "antimimetic" approach (8–10). Ian Hacking has challenged the diagnoses of both PTSD and multiple personality disorder. Basing his "memoro-politics" approach to psychiatric classification on Michel Foucault's "anatomo-politics" approach to sexuality, Hacking asserts that the "new sciences of memory . . . emerged as surrogate sciences of the soul, empirical sciences, positive science that would provide new kinds of knowledge in terms of which to cure, help, and control the one aspect of human beings that had hitherto been resistant to positivist science" ("Memory Sciences, Memory Politics" 70). In *Rewriting the Soul* and *The Social Construction of What?* Hacking suggests that the concept (rather than the actual practice) of child abuse is also socially constructed; he defines constructionism in the latter book as the "various sociological, historical, and philosophical projects that aim at displaying or analyzing actual, historically situated, social interactions or causal routes that led to, or were involved in, the coming into being or establishing of some present entity or fact" (48).

Working Through

It is not likely that the debates between the neurobiologists, on the one hand, who argue that PTSD changes the biochemistry of the brain, and the cultural historians and philosophers of science, on the other, who insist that PTSD is largely a constellation of unrelated symptoms that has been organized into a unified but misleading diagnosis, will soon be resolved. Notwithstanding these debates, the compulsion to repeat trauma implicit in both Freud's repetition-compulsion principle and in post–traumatic stress disorder has intriguing narrative implications. One of the reasons we tell stories is to understand and come to terms with their themes and contents. We tell painful or shameful stories to work through painful or shameful experiences. In *Shattered Subjects* Suzette A. Henke uses the word "scriptotherapy" to describe how female writers have used autobiography to heal themselves from traumatic illnesses and injuries. Storytelling and storywriting have both therapeutic and aesthetic value in that we search for endings that will revise, reinterpret, or resolve difficult experiences.

Cognitive psychologist Jerome Bruner has suggested that we "*become* the autobiographical narratives by which we 'tell about' our stories" (15). And Dominick LaCapra argues that working through traumatic historical events such as the Holocaust has significant ethical and political implications that have not yet been fully appreciated. "Working-through implies the possibility of judgment that is not apodictic or ad hominem but argumentative, self-questioning, and related in mediated ways to action" (*Representing the Holocaust* 210). We may not be able to change the past, but we make possible a more empowering present and future by working through our interpretation of the past.

Writing, reading, and revising all contribute to the working through of psychic conflict. Although repetition characterizes both acting out and working through, the difference is that the former occurs without insight and the possibility of change whereas the latter involves constant self-discovery and self-transformation. Both the "talking cure" and the "writing cure" are parallel efforts toward reparation and recovery. Both are coping mechanisms for difficult experiences, as Ronnie Janoff-Bulman states in *Shattered Assumptions*:

> There are three major strategies used by survivors. One involves appraisals based on comparisons with others; more specifically, survivors compare their experiences with the real or imagined outcomes of others, particularly other victims. A second strategy entails interpretations of one's own role in the victimization and involves instances of self-blame. A third process focuses on reevaluations of the traumatic experience in terms of benefits and purpose, reflecting attempts at "meaning-making" by survivors. By engaging in one or more of these reappraisal processes, survivors ultimately facilitate the assimilation of their victimization. Survivors' reappraisals locate and create evidence of benevolence, meaning, and self-worth in the very events that first challenged and shattered these illusions. (118)

Posttraumatic Growth

Richard Tedeschi and his associates have coined the term "posttraumatic growth" to signify the positive changes that may arise from a crisis. The antithesis of post–traumatic stress disorder, posttraumatic growth implies that people have the ability to re-create their lives following a devastating loss and grow in new and unexpected ways. Growth includes changes in perception of self, interpersonal relationships, and meaning of life. Tedeschi, Park, and Calhoun note in *Posttraumatic Growth* that one of the most important examples of a change in perception of self is to see oneself as a survivor rather than a victim; other examples include heightened self-reliance — "if I can survive this, I can survive anything" — and heightened awareness of the fragility of life, leading to a greater appreciation of life. Examples of interpersonal growth are heightened self-disclosure and emotional expressiveness. Howard Tennen and Glenn Affleck cite research suggesting that the process of "devictimization" helps trauma survivors by "mitigating feelings of stigmatization and restoring their self-esteem" (80). In another essay in *Posttraumatic Growth*, Park observes that "[p]erceiving benefits in difficult situations is one important way that individuals can reframe difficult experiences, find ways to assimilate them into their worldviews, and, perhaps, to accept and recover from them" (156). In the concluding essay of the volume, Calhoun and Tedeschi discuss how survivors' active construction of traumatic events can lead to revisions of their life story:

> For some persons, the trauma may produce the first conscious examination of the life story. Given that there was a great loss, and a memorable struggle with psychological distress, and that previously held higher order goals and beliefs may have undergone substantial changes, it is readily apparent that the trauma was a crucial event in the person's life history. Reflections on how the trauma was handled and what was learned can become important evidence to individuals for what kind of persons they are, and had been before the trauma. In this way, the critical event and its aftermath may come to occupy a significant place in that narrative, with the individual seeing the event as a point where a radical change occurred, and where life took a sharp turn. For persons experiencing PTG, the turn is viewed as a turn for the better, at least in certain ways, with a more meaningful and fulfilling life subsequent to the trauma. (232)

Posttraumatic growth may be seen in many of the student writings that appear in this book, beginning with Ben's letters to me, in which he describes his efforts to reconstruct his life after the wreckage of the 1990s, to the students who write about their shattered family life and frightening experiences with mental illness. In reconstructing the traumatic events of the past, they are regaining control of their lives. Many are also bearing witness and writing about aspects of their lives that they have never disclosed previously.

Traumatic Witnessing

How does one bear witness to traumatic stories? And how does one bear witness in a "post-traumatic culture," to cite the title of Kirby Farrell's study of injury and interpretation in the 1990s? In their book *Testimony* Shoshana Felman and Dori Laub discuss the hazards of listening. The "listener to trauma," Laub writes, "comes to be a participant and a co-owner of the traumatic event: through his very listening, he comes to partially experience trauma in himself. The relation of the victim to the event of the trauma, therefore, impacts on the relation of the listener to it, and the latter comes to feel the bewilderment, injury, confusion, dread and conflicts that the trauma victim feels. He has to address all these, if he is to carry out his function as a listener, and if trauma is to emerge, so that its henceforth impossible witnessing can indeed take place" (57–58). Laura Tanner makes a related observation in *Intimate Violence*, a study of reading rape and torture narratives in twentieth-century fiction. "The intimacy of the reading experience often allows us to come close to characters and experiences that we might otherwise never encounter; by the same token, however, it can force our intimacy by subtly pushing us into imaginative landscapes of violation from which it is difficult to extricate ourselves" (ix).

Witnessing can thus be painful, even traumatic. In *Worlds of Hurt* Kali Tal argues that *"the personal myths of the reader are never 'tragically shattered'* by reading. Only trauma can accomplish that kind of destruction" (122; emphasis in original). Tal does not consider, however, the "Werther" effect. Immediately following the publication in 1774 of Goethe's autobiographical novel about a young man who, rejected by his lover, commits suicide at the end of the story, dozens of readers imitated the act, some of them wearing the same clothes worn by Goethe's self-tormented hero. As I demonstrate in *Surviving Literary Suicide* and *Risky Writing*, reading painful literature can trigger symptoms of anxiety, depression, or suicidal ideation in readers that may last for weeks. Recent social science research provides additional evidence that "listening to traumatic accounts leads to stressful consequences for the confidant" (Petronio 119). Readers who identify closely with a story or film are especially susceptible to these symptoms.

"If we take pedagogy to mean the inculcation or the transmission of a body of knowledge or the creation of new knowledge," state Michael Bernard-Donals and Richard Glejzer in *Between Witness and Testimony*, "then we have to recognize the possibility that whatever knowledge is transmitted or created bears only an oblique relation to the events that form its source" (xii–xiii). Nowhere is this more true than the Holocaust, an event that tests the limits both of representation and understanding. Even as the witness is rendered both "speechless and terrified," he or she feels a "compulsion to speak" to bear testimony. What is needed, then, Bernard-Donals and Glejzer add, is a "pedagogy of trauma, in which the teacher recognizes that the students themselves are also witnesses to a witnessing; they are witnesses to testimonies that are shot through with a kernel of the event" (xii–xiii).

Trauma in the Classroom

Shoshana Felman offers a classroom example of traumatic witnessing that itself bears witnessing. In chapter 1 of *Testimony*, "Education and Crisis, or the Vicissitudes of Teaching," Felman recalls a graduate seminar she taught at Yale in 1984 entitled Literature and Testimony. The thirty students read texts by Albert Camus, Fyodor Dostoevsky, Sigmund Freud, Stéphane Mallarmé, and Paul Celan, and they saw two autobiographical accounts of the Holocaust borrowed from the Video Archive for Holocaust Testimonies at Yale. The teacher wanted to conclude the course with examples of the *"liberating, vital function of the testimony"* (47; emphasis in original), but to her surprise, the "eloquence of life—coupled with the eloquence of literature," had an unintended consequence: "The class itself broke out into a crisis" (47). Felman reports that the students looked shaken and subdued after they finished the screening of the videotapes. "What was unusual was that the experience did not *end* in silence, but instead, fermented into endless and relentless talking in the days and weeks to come; a talking which could not take place, however, within the confines of the classroom but which somehow had to *break the very framework of the class* (and thus emerge outside it), in much the same way as the writers we examined somehow all *broke through the framework* of what they had initially set out to write" (47–48; emphasis in original).

Felman's students began calling her at her home at odd hours to talk about their distress. Friends and roommates of her students wrote her letters expressing interest in the course. They were, as one letter put it, the "coerced listeners." The students and their acquaintances had suddenly become, in Felman's word, "obsessed," and they kept turning to their teacher and classmates for support. "They felt alone, suddenly deprived of their bonding to the world and to one another. As I listened to their outpour, I realized the class was entirely at a loss, disoriented and uprooted" (48). Worried by their response to the videotape, Felman turned to Dori Laub, the psychoanalyst who had interviewed the Holocaust survivors on videotape and whom she later invited to coauthor the book in which she tells the present story. Laub advised her to "reassume authority as the teacher of the class" and, in her words, "bring the students back into significance" (48). She then prepared a thirty-minute lecture as an introduction to a second screening of the film. She articulated to them *"an integrated view* of the literary texts and of the videotapes" (49; emphasis in original), in which she reviewed the students' responses to the first screening, described their *"anxiety of fragmentation,"* and commented on their recognition of the impossibility of language to express the inexpressible. She then offered them a linguistic reassurance based in part on the language of Celan's 1958 Bremen speech that the class had read earlier: "This, the language, was not lost but remained, yes, in spite of everything. But it had to *pass through its own answerlessness,* pass through a frightful falling-mute, pass through the thousand darknesses of death-bringing speech. It passed through and yielded no words for what was happening—but it *went through those happenings.* Went through and could come into the light of day again, 'enriched' by all that" (50–51; emphasis in original).

Following these words, Felman invited her students to write a paper about the experience of witnessing the Holocaust testimonies and their feelings about the course. "I admit," she told them, "that it would be a *precocious testimony*: I know you feel you are not ready. But perhaps the testimony *has* to be precocious, perhaps there is no other way" (52; emphasis in original). Reading their essays, she inferred that her students successfully worked through their crisis. "Looking back at the experience of that class, I therefore think that my job as teacher, paradoxical as it may sound, was that of creating in the class the highest state of crisis that it could withstand, without 'driving the students crazy'—without compromising the students' bounds" (53). In an epilogue she quotes brief excerpts from two papers in which students comment on how the course has emotionally affected them.

I am sympathetic to Felman's approach to testimony, but I find many of her characterizations troubling. I don't doubt that several of her students were disturbed, even horrified by the videotapes, but she speaks of them as a collective body rather than as a group of individuals: her use of the second person plural pronoun intimates that all experienced the same crisis. I have never shown Holocaust videotapes to my students, but in my literature courses I often read aloud wrenching accounts of personal tragedies, and in my writing courses students read aloud personal essays about their own traumatic experiences. Not everyone witnesses suffering in the same way. It is likely, for example, that relatives of Holocaust survivors would react differently to the videotapes than nonrelatives. Felman remains silent about the differences in her students' responses, and she never discusses their *personal* issues with the Holocaust. She admits that she was worried about *their* crisis of witnessing but never reveals whether *she* experienced *"anxiety of fragmentation."* I agree with her that verbal and pictorial accounts of an event as horrific as the Holocaust may create shock; I also believe, as she may not, that verbal and pictorial accounts of everyday tragedies may be shocking to read or view. I don't understand, however, why she is stunned that her students' responses had to *"break the very framework of the class"* (48). Surely the boundaries between the classroom and the rest of life are not as rigid and fixed as she intimates. Nor is it clear to me how her students could work through their shock, grief, and horror by means of her abstract, often bewildering linguistic theory. She does not analyze, for instance, how the Holocaust testimonies affected her students' relationship to her or to each other; nor does she analyze her students' empathic distress or her own feelings toward the class.

What is perhaps most unsettling is the way in which Felman brings everything back to—and, in my view, reduces everything to—language. Like Lacan, she takes a performative approach to working through: her discussion of Holocaust testimonies highlights the suffering of *language* rather than of *people*. To this extent she reflects the linguistic theory of her mentor, Paul de Man, who viewed language as a reenactment of traumatic loss, dispossession, and mourning. Felman's breathless, apocalyptic prose suggests that language has a life and death of its own, and rather than believing, as I do, that people gain or lose control of their words, she implies that language gains or loses control of people.

Felman admits that she has "never been as stupefied by the inadvertent lesson and the unforeseeable effects of teaching" (6–7) as she was in 1984 when she taught Literature and Testimony. She has never taught the course again with the same series of texts. Was the experience too dangerous for the teacher or for the students? If the course was as valuable for her students as she claims—and I have no reason to dispute this—then the decision not to teach it again suggests her fear of being retraumatized. If so, one wonders how other teachers present traumatic readings and testimonies to their students without being stupefied in the process.

The Holocaust is the most sinister and systematically planned trauma in history, and it remains a unique event, similar to but different from other horrific examples of mass genocide. Michael Rothberg uses the term "traumatic realism" to describe efforts to represent the "peculiar combination of ordinary and extreme elements that seems to characterize the Nazi genocide" during the Holocaust (6). Without widening the definition of trauma to the degree where it loses all meaning, we can say that trauma has now become ubiquitous. Although few teachers show Holocaust videotapes to their students, probably every teacher encounters students on a daily basis who bear traumatic scars silently or not. Many of these wounds arise from their parents' conflicted or divorced marriages, which shatter the security of the nuclear family and often leave the children feeling as if they have been rejected or abandoned. Other scars may be symptomatic of sexual abuse, eating disorders, or depression. In dealing with these conflicts, students must decide whether to forgive those responsible for inflicting pain upon them, however unintentionally, and they must also decide whether to forgive themselves for injuring others. A discussion of trauma, therefore, inevitably leads to the question of mourning and forgiveness.

Mourning

To confront trauma is to confront one's losses and to grieve. Freud's classic 1917 essay "Mourning and Melancholia" analyzes the symptoms common to both "normal" grief or sadness and depression. "The distinguishing mental features of melancholia are a profoundly painful dejection, cessation of interest in the outside world, loss of the capacity to love, inhibition of all activity, and a lowering of the self-regarding feelings to a degree that finds utterance in self-reproaches and self-revilings, and culminates in a delusional expectation of punishment. This picture becomes a little more intelligible when we consider that, with one exception, the same traits are met with in mourning" (244). Freud believed that both mourning and depression involve an identification with a lost object (which is usually a person) and that, in a famous formulation, the "shadow of the object fell upon the ego" (249).

In *Black Sun* Julia Kristeva elaborates on the relationship between loss and depression, discovering "antecedents to my current breakdown in a loss, death, or grief over someone or something that I once loved. The disappearance of that essential being continues to deprive me of what is most worthwhile in me; I live it as a wound or deprivation, discovering just the same that my grief is but the deferment of the hatred or desire for ascendency that I nurture with respect to the one who betrayed or abandoned me. My depression points to my not knowing how to lose—I have perhaps been unable to find a valid compensation for the loss? It follows that any loss entails the loss of my being—and of Being itself. The depressed person is a radical, sullen atheist" (5). As Avivah Gottlieb Zornberg observes in *The Particulars of Rapture*, "In Kristeva's discussion, depression is the condition of those who are 'painfully riveted' to the object of their loss; fascinated by that object, they disavow its loss" (438).

We generally think of education as the acquisition of knowledge, but the gain in understanding often reminds us of the inherent losses in life and the inevitability of death. But it is not only death with which we must come to terms but also the fact that new knowledge implies the giving up or even destruction of old knowledge. Teaching may thus be viewed as a kind of mourning, a working through of grief and sorrow, and nowhere is this better seen than in the literature and composition classroom, where students read and write essays on life, death, and suffering.

This indeed is the suggestive thesis of Marshall Alcorn's essay "Ideological Death and Grief in the Classroom: Mourning as a Prerequisite to Learning." Alcorn remarks in the beginning of the essay that contrary to the optimistic predictions of a decade ago, there is no evidence to suggest that students view their writing teachers more as collaborators than as adversaries. Nor have students readily embraced social and political change. Why so much resistance? Alcorn's answer is that poststructural theories of subjectivity, which view the self simply as an effect of language, underestimated the tenacity of identity. Though sympathetic in general to Jacques Lacan and Louis Althusser, Alcorn believes that the former's theory of the mirror stage and the latter's theory of interpellation misleadingly imply that subjectivity can be easily changed. Another reason for student resistance to change involves the nature of education, which might be better conceptualized "not as the transmission of some content knowledge, nor as the social construction of some object knowledge, but as a labor of mourning that works upon a dead or dying body that we might call a body of knowledge or a body of ideology." In Alcorn's view, teachers should not underestimate the student's difficulty of "managing the grief, pain and anxiety that is released by undoing attachments to old, comfortable ideas" (172).

If, as Alcorn maintains, all significant changes in important beliefs and attitudes require mourning, then what are the properties of "grief work"? He lists three. First, "[g]rief work is not accomplished by simple acts of thought." Rather, "[m]ourning is complicated and difficult because acts of thought that involve mourning require massive and painful adjustments in the entire apparatus involved in thinking the thought" (176). This is especially true when we mourn the death of a loved one, who may continue to live in the unconscious. Mourning the loss of a person requires not simply the recognition that he or she is gone forever from the external world but also the realization that there is a "persistently painful wound or emptiness located within the self" (178). Second, "[s]ignificant pain is required for the modification of important internal representations." In Alcorn's words, mourning is painful because "memories and hopes must be abandoned. Grief, then, is not a thought to be thought; it is a feeling to be felt" (178). Mourning involves emotional as well as intellectual work;

we mourn with our hearts as well as with our minds. Third, mourning requires time to heal "tears in the fabric of self." "Mourning presents a situation where 'accepting' changes requires an unusually difficult change in self-experience. It begins with denial, moves to anxiety, and finally requires the recognition of a painful internal wound or emptiness in the self" (179).

Alcorn's suggestion that there is a parallel between our attachments to people in real life and our attachments to explanatory and value systems that support our identity has far-reaching pedagogical implications, many of which he explores in his book *Changing the Subject in English Class*. We cling to deeply held beliefs and values with the same tenacity that we cling to important people, and for better or worse, we do not easily abandon the past. Invoking John Bowlby's theory of attachment and loss, Alcorn suggests that mourning is a long and arduous process, one to which teachers as well as clinicians must be sensitive. Although he places greater emphasis on the mourning required in abandoning "dead" ideology—this is where the originality of his recent work lies—Alcorn reminds us of the centrality of mourning in our daily lives. Literature is filled with countless examples of characters trying to make sense of suffering and death. As David Aberbach suggests in *Surviving Trauma*, writing memorializes loss and helps the writer achieve a victory over death, "the love and care lavished upon the work of art serving as a permanent testimony to the artist's attachment to the lost person" (23). John Fowles makes a similar observation in the foreword to the revised edition of *The Magus*: "loss is essential for the novelist, immensely fertile for his books, however painful to his private being" (9).

Teachers can encourage their students, in a wide variety of liberal arts courses, to write about the significant losses in their lives, either the deaths or disappearances of loved ones, such as parents, or the demise of explanatory systems, such as the belief in God. Students can work through these losses by writing about them and sharing their writings with classmates, whose empathic identification aids the mourning process. Teachers can assist the mourning process through the creation of a safe, empathic classroom in which students write about painful losses without the fear of being critiqued or attacked. To apply D. W. Winnicott's clinical term to an educational setting, a safe classroom is a "facilitating environment" (*The Maturational Processes* 239). Teachers can do this by remaining teachers, not therapists or counselors. For a great many of our students, the central mourning issue will involve the breakup of their families, which affects every aspect of their lives, including their interpretation of the past, their understanding of the present, and their expectations of the future.

Forgiveness

It is hard to imagine a student's pedagogical transformation that does not involve a change of heart as well as a change of mind, but forgiveness has not sparked much academic interest or debate until recently. Despite the fact that countless novelists have explored the dynamics of crime and punishment, literary critics have not turned their attention to forgiveness, perhaps because it has long been identified with theology. Nor have many psychoanalysts explored forgiveness. A glance at the general subject index in volume 24 of the *Standard Edition of the Complete Psychological Works of Sigmund Freud* indicates that there are dozens of references to anger, revenge, and punishment but not a single reference to forgiveness. Political scientists have been largely silent on forgiveness, perhaps because the twentieth century has been the most violent and unforgiving period in recorded history. Few philosophers have challenged Nietzsche's observation in *The Genealogy of Morals*: "An inability to take seriously for any length of time their enemies, their disasters, their *misdeeds*—that is the sign of the full strong natures who possess a superfluity of moulding plastic force, that heals completely and produces forgetfulness. . . . Such a man indeed shakes off with a shrug many a worm which would have buried itself in another; it is only in characters like these that we see the possibility (supposing, of course, that there is such a possibility in the world) of the real '*love* of one's enemies'" (650). In language that is less cryptic than usual but no less paradoxical, Maurice Blanchot asserts in *The Writing of the Disaster*: "Do not forgive. Forgiveness accuses before it forgives. By accusing, by stating the injury, it makes the wrong irredeemable. It carries the blow all the way to culpability. Thus, all becomes irreparable; giving and forgiving cease to be possible. Forgive nothing save innocence" (53).

There are few men or women who have the full strong natures to avoid being injured physically or psychologically by wrongdoers. All of us at one time or another will find ourselves in the role of victim *and* wrongdoer, and consequently, all of us will need to confront the question of forgiveness. As Jeffrie Murphy states, "[e]ach of us, if honest, will admit two things about ourselves: (1) We will within the course of our lives wrong others— even others about whom we care deeply; and (2) because we care so deeply about these others and our relationships with them, we will want to be forgiven by them for our wrongdoings. In this sense we do all need and desire forgiveness and would not want to live in a world where the disposition to forgive was not present and regarded as a healing and restoring virtue" (32).

In the last two decades, academic scholars from a variety of disciplines have started to write about forgiveness. Most of this research has been done in developmental psychology, counseling psychology, clinical psychology, and social psychology. William Ickes and Jeffrey Simpson begin their essay "Managing Empathic Accuracy in Close Relationships" by citing two proverbs, both of which represent the thesis and antithesis of their argument: "*To understand all is to forgive all*'—French Proverb; *'To understand all is to forgive nothing*'—English Epigram" (218; emphasis in original). One of the most comprehensive books on the subject is *Forgiveness: Theory, Research, and Practice*, edited by Michael McCullough et al. The editors offer a history and overview of the subject, raise questions for further study, and discuss the benefits and risks of forgiveness. Acknowledging that the lack of consensus in definition is "one of the most pernicious problems in the field today" (7), the editors propose their own definition: forgiveness is "intraindividual, prosocial change toward a perceived transgressor that is situated within a specific interpersonal context" (9). The definition emphasizes the dual nature of forgiveness: a personal act that has social consequences. Jean Hampton's definition is simpler: "Forgiveness is a change of heart towards the wrongdoer in which one drops any emotions of hatred or resentment towards him and his deed, takes a pro-attitude towards him and is disposed (under most conditions) to make the offer of reconciliation" (157).

Researchers are quick to point out that forgiveness is always risky. "Inevitably," writes Joram Graf Haber, forgiveness "entails placing trust in another's good-will when such trust has previously been violated. Certainly, to forgive a wrongdoer for a wrong she has done is to leave oneself open to further misconduct" (110). Haber quotes a statement made by Descartes: "It is prudent never to trust wholly those things which have once deceived us"—a statement, Haber adds, that applies as much to people as to the senses (110). The people who most hurt us are often those who are closest to us. Jeffrie Murphy quotes a passage from Francis Bacon's 1597 essay "Of Revenge" in which the Duke of Florence quips: "You shall read that we are commanded to forgive our enemies; but you never read that we are commanded to forgive our friends" (17).

To forgive is not to forget. Indeed, one must remember to forgive, as Desmond Tutu affirms in *No Future without Tears*, a memoir about his involvement with the Truth and Reconciliation Commission in South Africa. "In forgiving, people are not being asked to forget. On the contrary, it is important to remember, so that we should not let such atrocities happen again. Forgiveness does not mean condoning what has been done. It means taking what happened seriously and not minimizing it; drawing out the sting in the memory that threatens to poison our entire existence. It involves trying to understand the perpetrators and so have empathy, to try and stand in their shoes and appreciate the sort of pressures and influences that might have conditioned them" (271). Lest Tutu's statement about forgiveness be seen as relevant only to Christians, Michael Henderson quotes a statement made by the Jewish philosopher Hannah Arendt: "The discoverer of the role of forgiveness in the realm of human affairs was Jesus of Nazareth. The fact that he made this discovery in a religious context and articulated it in religious language is no reason to take it any less seriously in a strictly secular sense" (70). Arendt's observation comes from her 1958 book *The Human Condition*, in which she argues that the faculty of forgiving, which she believes is related to the faculty to make and keep promises, is necessary for the possible redemption from the predicament of irreversibility:

> Without being forgiven, released from the consequences of what we have done, our capacity to act would, as it were, be confined to one single deed from which we could never recover; we would remain the victims of its consequences forever, not unlike the sorcerer's apprentice who lacked the magic formula to break the spell. Without being bound to the fulfillment of promises, we would never be able to keep our identities; we would be condemned to wander helplessly and without direction in the darkness of each man's lonely heart, caught in its contradictions and equivocalities—a darkness which only the light shed over the public realm through the presence of others, who confirm the identity between the one who promises and the one who fulfills, can dispel. Both faculties, therefore, depend on plurality, on the presence and acting of others, for no one can forgive himself and no one can feel bound by a promise made only to himself; forgiving and promising enacted in solitude or isolation remain without reality and can signify no more than a role played before one's self. (237)

Both Tutu's and Arendt's statements remind us of the link between empathy and forgiveness. To try to understand others, to "stand in their shoes," is to understand why people hurt us, often involuntarily and without any awareness of their wrongdoing. Several scholars have suggested that empathy and forgiveness "are intimately, maybe even causally, linked" (Malcolm and Greenberg 180). Whether empathy is a cause or effect of forgiveness may be unanswerable, like the chicken-and-egg debate, but there is little question that it is easier to forgive one's wrongdoers if one understands why they have acted in the way they have, especially if they have not consciously intended wrongdoing. Forgiveness generally results in increased empathy for the victim and wrongdoer alike. In addition, "forgiveness, or at least nonretaliation observed by others, may have the curious quality of generating empathy and warm feelings for the injured victim from observers who were usually in no way involved in the initial fight or confrontation" (Newberg et al., 97).

Forgiveness may be partial or complete, temporary or permanent. One may forgive minor wrongdoings or major crimes. For many people, the Holocaust was so horrific a crime that forgiveness is impossible. Forgiveness may occur with or without the wrongdoer's knowledge or admission of wrongdoing. Although forgiveness may lead to reconciliation, the two are not identical: "Forgiveness is one person's response to injury. Reconciliation involves two people coming together again" (Enright et al. 49). Forgiveness may be genuine or not. "Forgiveness must be separated from 'pseudo-,' or false, forgiveness, which is a ploy to exercise superiority over the one who has ostensibly been forgiven" (Elder 151). For some people, such as Jeffrie Murphy, forgiveness is acceptable "only in cases where it is consistent with self-respect, respect for others as responsible moral agents, and allegiance to the rules of morality (Murphy 19); if these conditions are not met, Murphy adds, forgiveness is not warranted, and revenge may be the appropriate response. For others, such as Jean Hampton, forgiveness is a gift, an act of mercy, that is offered freely and unconditionally.

One of the many benefits of forgiveness is self-forgiveness: studies have suggested that self-forgiveness "may be a major factor in the reduction of anger, guilt, and depression, as well as the enhancement of health" (Thoresen et al. 256). The authors hypothesize that forgiveness "may foster more perceived security and/or greater positive self-evaluative and optimistic thoughts that strengthen 'host resistance' to taking offense"; "may foster stronger perceived competence or self-efficacy to take needed steps to reduce disease-enhancing or pathogenics 'agents'"; "may provide higher levels of perceived social and emotional support, especially from more intimate close relationships"; and "may encourage a greater sense of a transcendent consciousness (or moving 'beyond the ego') and more inner experiences of communion with God, a Higher Power or an Infinite/Universal Energy, especially among more spiritually or religiously oriented persons" (259–60).

The forgiveness process implies the "construction of a new narrative of self and other," one that entails a shift in one's perspective (Malcolm and Greenberg 180). This shift involves a new story about the experience of violation and its impact on the victim, the forgiver, and the wrongdoer, the forgiven. Forgiveness involves what Joanna North has called a process of reframing, which she defines as "not just a way of putting the wrong-doer and his action *in context* but . . . also a way of *separating* the wrong-doer from the wrong which has been committed":

> When we are deeply hurt by another person we tend to think of him as a "bad person," as if his crime "shoots through," or defines, his whole personality. The son regards his father's whole being as devoid of love; the husband sees his wife as an adulteress. . . . But, in most cases, people are not wholly bad, and their actions result from a multiplicity of background factors. Reframing does not do away with the wrong self, nor does it deny the wrongdoer's responsibility for it, but it allows us to regard the wrongdoer in a more complete, more detailed, more rounded way—in a way, that is, which does justice to the complexity of the wrongdoer's personality. (26; emphasis in original)

"Forgiveness studies" is not yet an academic growth industry, but it is a topic that commands increasing scholarly respect and attention. Indeed, in an article in *USA Today* about the burgeoning "positive psychology" movement, forgiveness is the trait "most strongly linked to happiness" (December 9, 2002). Nor is forgiveness limited to psychotherapy; as McCullough et al. conclude: "Education for forgiveness has the potential to prevent or mitigate some of the long-term pain that follows a trauma. Forgiveness could become a topic of discussion, if not training, in primary, secondary, and higher education within secular as well as religious institutional settings" (315). Martha Nussbaum makes a similar recommendation in her essay "Compassion and Terror," urging that an "education in common human weakness and vulnerability should be a very profound part of the education of all children." In Nussbaum's view, one of the best ways to achieve this "education in common human weakness"—or what I call an "education for life"—is through "stories and dramas," in which students learn to "decode the sufferings of others" (24). And one of the best settings for discussions of empathy, compassion, and forgiveness is the college classroom, where students may be encouraged to explore vexing real-life issues, including perhaps the most vexing and traumatic subject of all: the family.

CHAPTER 3

Family Snapshots 1
LETTERS TO AND FROM PARENTS

*Children begin by loving their parents. After a time they judge them.
Rarely if ever do they forgive them.*
   OSCAR WILDE

Oscar Wilde's aphorism must have scandalized readers a century ago, when
the Victorian family was still considered sacrosanct; it would have also
scandalized readers of *Good-bye, Mr. Chips* in 1933. Contemporary readers, however, many of whom come from shattered families, will be less
shocked. Divorce is so common that it rarely makes the news. And yet for
many students, divorce remains the central issue of their lives, the event
that influences their daily existence. They may rarely speak or write about
their parents' broken marriages, but the subject is never far from their
thoughts, producing pain, sadness, anger, and confusion. They may still
love their parents, but as Wilde suggests, they may come to judge them
and, in some cases, fail to forgive them. This is especially true for the
nearly 40 percent of young Americans who do not have their biological
fathers at home. "Most of these youngsters," observes psychiatrist Richard
Fitzgibbons, "have great difficulty in understanding and forgiving their
fathers for the pain of betrayal with which they struggle daily" (65). The
lack of forgiveness has far-reaching consequences.

The Culture of Divorce

The American family in which I grew up in the 1950s is strikingly different from the one in which my students grew up in the 1980s and 1990s.
These differences manifest themselves in family relationships and structures, economic resources, and gender roles. The security that I took for
granted and assumed would be the norm for generations to come is now
an artifact of history. As Andrew Cherlin declares, the divorce rate began
to increase during the early 1960s, doubled between 1966 and 1976, and
then leveled off during the 1980s, where it has remained near its historical
high. The lifetime level of divorce for the parents of baby boomers was
unusually low, while the lifetime level of divorce for the baby boomers

138

themselves is unusually high (Cherlin 25). Because most divorced men and women remarry, and because more second marriages end in divorce than first marriages, many children experience multiple parental divorces. These children must cope with the situation of living with biological parents and stepparents, a living arrangement that can be both stressful and bewildering. An article in *USA Today* reports, "Divorcing before age 30 is becoming so common that it is creating a demographic phenomenon: the starter marriage" (January 31, 2002), a term that captures the instability and low-commitment level of many marriages. An article published in the British medical journal the *Lancet* indicates that "children growing up in single-parent families are twice as likely as their counterparts in two-parent families to develop serious psychiatric illnesses and addictions later in life." The study, "unprecedented in scale and follow-up," tracked a million children for a decade, into their middle twenties. "The scientists found that children with single parents were twice as likely as the others to develop a psychiatric illness like severe depression or schizophrenia, to commit suicide or try to, and to develop an alcohol-related disease" ("One Parent Children Are Found at Risk," *New York Times*, January 24, 2003).

The high divorce rate and the rising number of children born out of wedlock have created a new phenomenon: the absent father. As David Popenoe points out in his 1996 book *Life without Father*,

> Fathers in America today are living apart from their biological children more than ever before in our history. Close to 40 percent of all children do not live with their biological fathers, a percentage that is steadily climbing. Of children born in the past decade, the chances that by age seventeen they will not be living with both biological parents stand at over 50 percent. Many studies have shown that the typical nonresident father neither supports nor even sees his children on a regular basis. And, to make matters worse, many men who *do* live with their children are often removed from the day-to-day upbringing of those children. The new, nurturing fathers certainly exist, but in overall numbers they remain in short supply. (19)

Popenoe refers to many studies attesting to the father's striking importance to children's welfare and development, including a twenty-six-year longitudinal research project that examined the relationship between parental behavior in early childhood and empathic concern in adults. In Popenoe's words, "The researchers' main finding was 'quite astonishing': the most important childhood factor of all is 'paternal involvement in child care.' Fathers who spent time alone with their children more than twice a week, giving meals, baths, and other basic care, reared the most compassionate adults" (149).

To understand students' lives, we must acknowledge the disturbing state of most American families. Judith Wallerstein, the author of several groundbreaking books on the short- and long-range consequences of divorce, has written about the cataclysmic changes for parents and children. In *Surviving the Breakup* Wallerstein points out that "[o]ne major legacy of divorce is discontinuity in many parent-child relationships, in which the changes of separation, divorce, and its extended aftermath are reflected in unexpected and far-reaching alternations in the child's relationship with both parents" (99). In *The Unexpected Legacy of Divorce* Wallerstein notes that "we've created a new kind of society never before seen in human culture":

> Silently and unconsciously, we have created a culture of divorce. It's hard to grasp what it means when we say that first marriages stand a 45 percent chance of breaking up and that second marriages have a 60 percent chance of ending in divorce. What are the consequences for all of us when 25 percent of people today between the ages of eighteen and forty-four have parents who are divorced? What does it mean to a society when people wonder aloud if the family is about to disappear? What can we do when we learn that married couples with children represent a mere 26 percent of households in the 1990s and that the most common living arrangement nowadays is a household of unmarried people with no children? These numbers are terrifying. (295–96)

Mental health professionals representing a spectrum of theoretical approaches agree that we are influenced profoundly by our parents or parent surrogates. Creative writers have long shared the same assumption; as William Wordsworth writes in his 1807 poem "My Heart Leaps Up," "The child is father of the man" (160). Parental influence is both positive and negative, and it is rare to find a person who does not feel ambivalence toward one or both parents. Those who love their parents may find themselves struggling to separate themselves from them, while those who hate their parents may discover, to their dismay, that they have internalized precisely those parental qualities they most dislike.

In a study aptly entitled *A Generation at Risk*, Paul Amato and Alan Booth use a life course perspective, which emphasizes the interdependence of lives over time, to investigate changing family structures. Like Wallerstein and other researchers, they argue that "the disruptive effects of divorce on parent-child relationships persist well into adulthood" (69). They also suggest that in the last three decades "declines in economic resources, changes in gender relations, and increases in marital discord and divorce . . . have resulted in a net *decrease* in ties of affection, contact, and support between the generations" (83). Amato and Booth indicate a glaring conflict in the divorced father's role toward his children: "as the public is increasingly embracing the idea that fathers should take on a greater share of child-rearing responsibility, changes in family structure mean that many fathers are less involved with children today than were fathers in previous generations" (20). The researchers draw a gloomy conclusion from the fact that marital discord among parents predicts marital discord among their offspring. "If marriages are as happy now as they were a generation or two ago, then there is little reason for concern. But if happy marriages have become more difficult to attain, and if, as our study strongly suggests, marital happiness is transmitted across generations, then we can expect the cohort of children currently reaching adulthood to face additional obstacles to achieving satisfying and stable intimate relationships" (119).

Amato and Booth are careful to remind us that although parental divorce is associated with a number of difficulties among children, including low self-esteem, behavior problems, and psychological distress, parental divorce does not have a uniformly negative impact on children. One of their major findings is that the consequences of marital dissolution are related to predivorce marital quality. "For offspring residing with parents in poor quality marriages, divorce does not appear to have negative long-term consequences for well-being. In contrast, offspring whose parents' marriages are not highly conflicted appear to suffer when the marriage ends. It is precisely under these conditions that children are most likely to view marital disruption as an unexpected and unwelcome event" (204). Divorce seems to be helpful for the children whose parents have highly conflicted marriages; the researchers estimate that between one-fourth and one-third of marriages ending in divorce fall into this category. Divorce is harmful, however, for the children whose parents had relatively low-conflict marriages that end in divorce. Amato and Booth conclude that the "worst situation for children to be in is either a high-conflict marriage that does not end in divorce or a low-conflict marriage that does end in divorce" (238).

What can be done to minimize divorce's harmful impact on children? Amato and Booth affirm the power of education. Although acknowledging that divorce generally lowers children's educational and occupational attainments, the researchers point hopefully to the fact that the educational levels of American men and women have been rising for decades. "Because educational attainment is, to a certain extent, transmitted from parents to children, improvements in education in one generation are likely to increase the likelihood that a high level of education is maintained in the next generation" (179). The rising educational status of women is particularly noteworthy for this reason. Amato and Booth make several recommendations for policy changes, including strengthening the government's commitment to education and improving family-friendly workplaces. They argue, additionally, that "marriage and family counselors have an obligation to make sure that parents have a full understanding of the consequences of divorce for offspring" (238).

Apart from these changes, students can increase their own understanding of the consequences of divorce by writing about their experiences and sharing them with classmates. I can't imagine a more significant topic in higher education than the family. Indeed, the family is perhaps *the* central topic in a wide range of liberal arts disciplines including literature, history, psychology, sociology, anthropology, and economics. Encouraging students to relate their personal lives to scholarly readings allows them to connect the private and public sides of life and to engage the full complexity of family issues both emotionally and intellectually.

Several studies indicate that children acquire empathy from their parents and other caregivers. (For an overview of the clinical literature, see Cotton.) Empathy has intergenerational implications: a child who has a loving and secure relationship to a parent is more likely to be empathic than another child who has a conflicted relationship to a parent. But children who grow up in conflicted families can become more empathic: like other interpersonal qualities, empathy can be developed. Children of all ages who are able to increase their empathic understanding of their parents are likely to experience increased empathy toward others as well. This has important educational implications, for if teachers can help students to develop empathic understanding of their family through reading and writing assignments, they may become more empathic toward nonfamily members. The reverse is also true: heightened empathic awareness of other families may lead to greater understanding of one's own family.

To see our parents clearly and accurately, including their strengths and weaknesses, is to see ourselves clearly and accurately; knowledge of other generally leads to self-knowledge. This is particularly true when we can acknowledge the ambivalence we feel toward the people who have contributed the most to our development. Sometimes this ambivalence can be overwhelming or even paralyzing, causing us to split our feelings into the "good" and "bad" parent rather than recognizing that we are talking about different sides of the same parent. "The test of a first rate intelligence," F. Scott Fitzgerald writes in the autobiographical *The Crack-Up*, is the ability "to hold two opposed ideas in the mind at the same time and still retain the ability to function" (69). Many otherwise "first rate intelligences" cannot untangle their convoluted feelings about their parents.

How can a teacher encourage students to become more empathic? It is not enough simply to discuss the many benefits of empathy, for such a discussion may lead to intellectual but not emotional intelligence. A better way, in my view, is to encourage students to write about the most important people in their lives—their parents—and to imagine how their parents might respond. The teacher can then encourage students to share their writings with classmates so that each person will have insight into as many different families as possible.

Minimizing Risk

Teachers who encourage classroom self-disclosure should be aware of the potential dangers and establish protocols so that students do not become at risk. In *Risky Writing* I discuss in detail the protocols that I regularly put into place. I use the word "protocol" rather than "safeguard" because there is no infallible way to eliminate risk, but there are many ways to minimize risk. Students have the option not to write on any topic they deem too personal or threatening, and they can remain anonymous when sharing an essay with classmates. (I read aloud anonymous essays, and there is no class discussion of them.) I grade personal essays pass/fail so that students do not feel they are being evaluated by the degree of their self-disclosure. We avoid harmful critique by agreeing in advance to remain as empathic and nonjudgmental as possible. Students will self-disclose only when they trust their teacher and classmates. Self-disclosure begets self-disclosure: even students who describe themselves as low self-disclosers will share their writings with classmates who have revealed aspects of their own lives. The key to self-disclosure is an empathic classroom, and the teacher's challenge is to create and maintain a trusting atmosphere in which students are willing to write about painful or shameful issues that they would not otherwise disclose to a group of strangers.

The portrait of my students' family life that emerges in the following pages is strikingly different from that seen in *Good-bye, Mr. Chips,* and it differs sharply from that described by psychiatrist Daniel Offer in his two books on adolescent life. Offer and his associates designed a detailed self-esteem questionnaire in which they asked teenagers to evaluate how they felt about themselves and their families. They found in *The Adolescent* that "eighteen out of nineteen items strongly indicate that the adolescents have positive feelings toward their families. At least seven out of ten normal [that is, those who were not 'juvenile delinquents'] adolescents indicate that they experience good feelings toward their parents and toward their own role in their families" (67). These teenagers describe the family as a "harmonious and well-functioning social system" (71). Offer found only minor differences between 1960s and 1970s adolescents. In a 1988 international study, Offer found that the "overwhelming majority of teen-agers in all ten countries disclaimed negative attributes toward their fami-lies" (*Teenage World* 63). Eighty-two percent of the respondents agreed with the question, "Most of the time my parents get along well with each other" (64). I did not give the students in my expository writing class a questionnaire about their feelings toward their parents, but based on their classroom writings, I doubt their answers would have resembled those of Daniel Offer's respondents. It may be that American society has changed dramatically in the last twenty years; or it may also be that in-depth per-sonal essays portray a different picture from the one that comes from multiple-choice survey questionnaires.

The Therapy Generation

Have college students changed significantly in the last three or four de-cades? Their lives have almost certainly grown more anxious, as I indi-cated in my discussion of May Sarton's *The Small Room*. College students throughout the country are visiting campus mental health services in unprecedented numbers. According to the *New York Times*, Columbia University's counseling service reports a 40 percent increase in use since the 1994–95 academic year, reflecting trends elsewhere. The large num-bers of college students seeking counseling have strained campus resources, resulting in long waiting periods for all but emergency cases. Consequently, many universities have expanded their mental health services. A Harvard Medical School researcher has estimated that 37 percent of Americans aged fifteen to twenty-four, many of whom are college students, have a diagnosable mental illness (cited in "Treating Mental Illness in Students: A New Strategy," *Chronicle of Higher Education*, June 16, 2000). The grow-ing use of campus counseling services reflects complex cultural forces. "College does not exist independently of society," observes Vivian Boyd, director of the counseling center at the College Park campus of the Uni-versity of Maryland and president of the International Association of Coun-seling Services. "The whole notion of the divorce rate among parents, the economic shifts that are occurring, the disappearing of whole classes of jobs that people used to count on going into, the fact that the degrees of freedom making choices in your life are growing shorter and shorter be-cause the cost of being wrong comes at a higher price—there are societal pressures that exist independent of the college environment to which young people are responding" (*New York Times*, January 13, 2002). Students study the family in many of their courses, but seldom do they have an opportunity to study their *own* families. To examine one's own family is to examine one's past and, given the complex role of nature and nurture, one's future. Most are born into a family, though many never know members of their immediate family. It is impossible to imagine a subject more crucial to one's identity than one's family, yet it is the one subject that an increasing number of people try hardest to forget.

English 300: Expository Writing

In what follows, I describe an expository writing class that I taught in the spring of 2001. I believe that the class will be of interest to teachers, students, and anyone who wishes to learn more about an empathic approach to education. The cast of characters includes nineteen college juniors and seniors who were taking the course mainly to fulfill a writing requirement. I write from the point of view of the "participant-observer," the term that Mary Belenky and her associates use to describe "connected teachers [who] try to discern the truth inside the students" (223). Harry Stack Sullivan used the same term, concluding that the "data of psychiatry arise only in participant observation" (3). Or to use Kurt Spellmeyer's term, I write as a "student of experience," a scholar-teacher "committed to discovering how people actually *feel*" (143). The students read my 1994 book *Diaries to an English Professor*, on which many of the writing assignments were based. The setting is a college classroom—unremarkable in every way, with antiseptic walls, uncomfortable seats, an unused blackboard, and tiny windows overlooking a parking lot. The plot of the story was set into motion by a series of writing topics on the family—topics that encouraged them to explore previously unexplored aspects of their lives, which they then shared with their classmates and teacher.

Everything that happens in the following pages is true: that is, I reproduce to the best of my ability my own point of view as well as my students'. Their point of view derives from their writings, which they allowed me to use for this book, and from interviews that I conducted with many of them six to twenty-four months after the semester ended. I have not changed or edited a single word of the essays that appear here except to disguise the writers' names and identities. (They supplied their own pseudonyms.) Many of the essays contain grammatical and stylistic errors that I commented on in class but that appear here unedited. I have not fictionalized or imagined anything, though by deciding what to include and exclude, I am shaping the material into a story, making it as coherent and compressed as possible.

There are no heroes, heroines, or villains in the story I am about to tell, nothing as dramatic as what we have seen in the literature teacher novels and films. We had an explicit agreement at the beginning of the semester that we would try to remain as empathic and nonjudgmental as possible, and for the most part we were successful. Nevertheless, there were two moments when this agreement was unintentionally violated, leading to tension, misunderstanding, and anger. These transgressions produced two emotionally charged experiences for the students and teacher, experiences that could have led either to breakthroughs or breakdowns.

The most efficient way to run a writing workshop is for students to read their classmates' essays *before* class rather than *during* class. But efficiency comes at a price, for readers cannot hear the writer's voice, which helps to establish the connection between the writer and the work. The writer's voice is especially important in risky essays describing painful or shameful feelings, since the writer's voice reveals the difficulty of writing about wrenching experiences. Sometimes the writer's voice falters, and once or twice a semester a student may be unable to continue and will ask me to complete the reading. A risky essay generally heightens the empathic bond between writer and audience. Classmates can usually tell when a writer is having trouble reading an essay: they generally do not look then at the writer until after he or she has completed the reading. Students have the option *not* to read their essays aloud; if they wish, I read their essays aloud anonymously, and the writer then becomes another member of the audience. Writers of anonymous essays who hear their words spoken aloud by another person experience a detachment that might not otherwise be possible; their point of view expands, and they see themselves as both a participant and observer.

Two Writing Assignments

I write extensive comments on every essay, including grammatical and stylistic corrections, before I hand it back to the author. Students come to expect these comments, and one of the gratifications of teaching is to see their writing improve throughout the semester. We spend at least a third of every class discussing grammar, diction, and tone. Each week I select one or two poorly written sentences from every essay submitted the previous week. I type the sentences onto a sheet, which I then photocopy and distribute to everyone in the next class. I divide students into groups of three, assign each group several sentences to revise, give them a few minutes for group work, and then we reconvene. Each student reads a revised sentence aloud to the entire class. A sentence may contain a single error, such as mistaking "effect" for "affect," or many errors, such as dangling or misplaced modifiers, comma splices, colloquialisms, or convoluted syntax. Since no one knows the author of the sentence he or she revises, no one feels embarrassed. (The author's identity may be revealed later in that class, when he or she reads aloud an essay containing a sentence subsequently revised by a classmate, but sufficient time has passed so that the author generally does not feel embarrassment.) I have never received an essay in which I had difficulty finding a sentence that needs revision.

Why the emphasis on grammar, diction, and tone? Because my students desperately need to improve their writing skills. Nor is the need for improvement limited to my students. One of the findings of a study issued by the National Commission on Writing in America's Schools and Colleges, as reported in the *New York Times*, is that "[w]riting, always time-consuming for student and teacher, is today hard-pressed in the American classroom. . . . Of the three R's, writing is clearly the most neglected" (April 26, 2003). In an article provocatively entitled "Why Johnny Can't Write, Even Though He Went to Princeton," appearing in the January 3, 2003, issue of the *Chronicle of Higher Education*, Thomas Bartlett discusses the failure of writing courses at prestigious colleges and universities. Officials at Princeton, Duke, Columbia, Brown, and Bowdoin all agree that "their college has not been doing a good job of teaching students how to write" (A3). Bartlett offers several explanations for this failure: writing instructors do not receive much respect in academia; students do not take seriously writing requirements; graduate students, who often are assigned to teach writing classes, have insufficient training and experience; and programs such as "writing across the disciplines" often work better in theory than in practice. Another explanation, not cited by Bartlett, is that many professors, particularly those outside English departments, prefer to comment on content rather than form. Nor do many English professors believe it is their responsibility to help students with deficient writing skills.

Another article in the same issue of the *Chronicle of Higher Education*, "Of Grammatophobia" by Rodney Huddleston and Geoffrey Pullum, authors of the new *Cambridge Grammar of the English Language*, ponders the consequences of this widespread neglect. "Faculty members commonly complain that today's high school graduates are not acquainted with even the most basic concepts of grammar, such as tense, case, or even parts of speech. We encounter students working toward the Ph.D. who are not familiar with grammatical concepts like clause or participle." The authors add that "English-literature departments have long since turned from syntactic construction to semiotic deconstruction" (B20).

One laments the widespread decline in writing and that writing programs have not addressed this problem. Bartlett points out, for example, that two years ago an internal review committee at Columbia determined that nearly everyone disliked the freshman writing requirement, which contained a number of "absurdities," including a ban on assigned writings. "The policy was intended to place the emphasis on writing, but it backfired: Students didn't have anything to write about" (A4). The committee recommended a number of actions, including lifting the ban.

There is no contradiction between encouraging students to write about the most important subjects in the world—their own lives—while helping them simultaneously to improve their writing skills. Indeed, students who write on personal issues want to express themselves clearly and cogently, and an emphasis on the mechanics of writing teaches them how to do this. Discussions of grammar are not only essential in the writing classroom but are also an excellent way to avoid the danger that may arise from classroom discussions of personal writing, namely, that students may find themselves giving unwelcome or inappropriate advice to classmates. Students need to be supportive of each other in a writing class, but the writing class is not a support group: the emphasis should be on how to improve a writer's essay. Paradoxically, if students confine themselves to improving a classmate's writing, they will improve their classmate's life, for all will come to realize that, regardless of each other's social or political agenda, and regardless of differences in race, class, gender, and religion, only the student's writing skills will be exposed to scrutiny and constructive criticism, not his or her feelings and value judgments.

My emphasis on grammar in writing courses is different from the "bonehead English" courses satirized by Bernard Malamud in *A New Life,* where composition courses do not allow students to write about their experiences. It also differs from the "back to basics" approach championed by conservative academics such as Allan Bloom, E. D. Hirsch, and Dinesh D'Souza, as well as by Lynne Cheney and Robert Bennett, former heads of the National Endowment for the Humanities, all of whom advocate a return to traditional culture and education. None of these people would be sympathetic to autobiographical writing since they believe it fosters self-absorption and self-indulgence. Roger Rosenblatt's pronouncement is typical of this point of view: "I don't think anyone ought to teach memoir writing to undergraduates, because they don't have enough to remember" (cited in the *New York Times*, June 18, 1997). Nor have those on the political left, which is closer to my own point of view, expressed interest in personal writing. As Sandra Gilbert and Susan Gubar observe in their "academic melodrama" *Masterpiece Theatre*, both the conservative "Back to Basics" academics and the radical "Forward into Instability" academics — a group that includes feminists, Marxists, deconstructivists, and cultural critics — engage in "canon wars" while remaining, "for the most part, blind to the real needs and problems of real students, that is, to the crisis in literacy that means the very processes of reading and writing are probably more important at this point than the culture war's questions about what is to be read and what is to be written" (xix–xx). Sometimes the most dangerous place to be is in the middle, caught between opposing ideologies and personalities. Nevertheless, experience — which is the word we use to describe our failures, as Oscar Wilde observed wryly — teaches me that we can best help our students by encouraging them to write about subjects that are of the greatest importance to them while at the same time helping them to improve their language.

Getting to Know Each Other

Whenever I teach a writing course, I begin with assignments that help students get to know each other. The first two assignments involve each student's writing two classmates' biographies. In the first assignment, which I describe in detail in *Risky Writing*, each student is asked to draw up a chronology of the ten most important events in his or her life, ranging from birth to the present. For each event, the student writes a paragraph describing its significance. Each student exchanges the autobiographical chronology with a classmate, interviews the classmate, and then writes a biographical essay based on the paragraphs and the interview. In the second assignment, a student is paired with a different classmate and writes a biography based on one of the chronological paragraphs, which is expanded into an entire essay. Each student is thus paired with two different classmates and collaborates with them in writing two different biographical essays.

The biographical assignments are valuable for several reasons. First, they encourage students to reflect upon their lives, identifying the most important events and their significance. Some of these events are painful, even traumatic. Second, students share their life stories with classmates whom, as a consequence of the assignments, they begin to understand and trust. Third, students begin to think about themselves as writers and storytellers. Our discussions focus on language: for each essay read in class, we identify the most and least effective sentences. We also ask clarifying questions designed to help the writer develop the essay further. It is seldom difficult, even in a poorly written essay, to find good sentences; nor is it difficult, in an excellently written essay, to find sentences that need revision.

Once they complete the biographical essays, students are ready for the next two assignments, which are designed to encourage them to write about their families. The first assignment asks students to read the chapter "Sins of the Fathers" in *Diaries to an English Professor* and discuss whether they were surprised by the ways in which parental divorce affects children and adolescents:

> Which of the seven students in the chapter did you most sympathize and/or identify with? Why? If you wish, discuss how parental divorce has affected your own life. Did reading this chapter awaken strong emotions in you, such as love, hate, sadness, anger, guilt? Did you learn anything from this chapter that might help you understand better the complex effects of divorce on children?

I knew this was a challenging assignment, since the student diarists in "Sins of the Fathers" write about the wrenching consequences of divorce. It was not easy for the students to write these diaries, nor is it easy to read them. Many of the students' writings reveal "father hunger," the term psychoanalyst James Herzog uses to describe the yearning boys and girls feel for a father who is either physically or emotionally absent from their lives as a consequence of divorce. Judith Wallerstein and other researchers report that the impact of divorce lasts for decades and has disturbing intergenerational consequences. "Contrary to what we have long thought," observes Wallerstein, "the major impact of divorce does not occur during childhood or adolescence. Rather, it rises in adulthood as serious romantic relationships move center stage" (Wallerstein et al. xxix). Few extended families have remained untouched by the culture of divorce. After asking students to write about divorced families, I thought they would be ready for the next assignment, which was due a week later:

A Letter to a Parent and His or Her Letter to You
    Please write a letter to one or both of your parents in which you describe your feelings about their marriage and the way in which they raised you. Include in the beginning of your letter your reactions to reading the chapter

"Sins of the Fathers" in *Diaries to an English Professor,* and discuss briefly how your classmates' essays on this subject affected you. If your parents are divorced and you no longer see one of them, you might wish to express how you feel about him or her. Or you might wish to describe your feelings toward a stepfather or stepmother. If one of your parents has died, you might wish to write a letter explaining your feelings toward him or her. If you are a parent, you might wish to write a letter to your child.

After writing this letter, imagine how your parent would respond in a letter to you. Try to capture your parent's voice and point of view. These two letters should be spontaneous and informal, as letters usually are, but try to make them interesting, articulate, and free from grammatical errors. Remember that you are writing these two letters for a writing class: try to give enough information so that the reader can understand your two letters. Showing is better than telling.

If this assignment is too personal for you, you may write on another topic: for example, an essay discussing any aspect of the parent-child relationship, including how best to raise children.

The two assignments encouraged students to reflect on the ways in which they have been raised and to identify problematic aspects of their lives. They were also encouraged to analyze their lives in relation to the people who created them. Additionally, the assignments required them to imagine a parent's point of view—one that might be different from or, in some cases, in opposition to their own viewpoint. I asked them not only to "take the role of the other person," as the influential American social psychologist George Mead suggested (366), but also to "think like a parent"—a daunting challenge. The assignments encouraged multiple perspectives as well as self-analysis. The students were not required to show their essays to their parents, but I was curious to see whether the assignments would enable the writers to begin a dialogue with parents whom, in some cases, they hadn't seen for years.

Would the self-disclosing assignments increase the students' empathy toward each other? That is, would the students become more aware of each other's lives, more attentive to the painful and shameful issues that many of their classmates confront on a daily basis? If so, how would this heightened empathic awareness be revealed? Would the students feel a stronger connection with their classmates and teacher? Would they reach new insights about themselves and others? How would students from loving, intact families respond to classmates from shattered homes? Would empathic awareness create any unforeseen problems in the classroom, and if so, how would the teacher respond? I was also curious whether increased student empathy would lead to heightened forgiveness of their parents and, for those who could not think about their parents without feeling angry, hurt, confused, or guilty, forgiveness of themselves.

I should note before presenting these essays to you that at no time in the semester did I discuss forgiveness. I never offered advice to a student about a personal issue, nor did they, with one conspicuous exception, offer advice to a classmate about a personal issue. I believe in forgiveness, but I don't believe that I should advise students to forgive those who have hurt them. Only when I looked carefully at all the student writings after the semester was over did I realize the importance of forgiveness—and self-forgiveness—for so many people in the class. For these students, to forgive or not to forgive a parent was the *central* question in their lives. The question of forgiveness was particularly important to those who describe domestic traumas which, however ordinary and commonplace, are nevertheless painful to endure.

My discussion begins with four students—Cory, Danielle, Lydia, and Nat—who wrote about conflicted relationships with one or both of their biological parents. I quote their two assignments and then comment briefly on them. (To avoid confusion, I indent the fictional parents' letters.) Cory, Lydia, and Nat each read one essay aloud, while Danielle asked me to read one of hers anonymously. Cory and Danielle described their families as intact but troubled; Lydia and Nat wrote about parents who had been married and divorced two or three times. All four students expressed painful feelings in both assignments, and while three of the four did not anticipate that they would send the letters, they wanted their parents to read the letters. All four wrote about rejection, either rejecting or being rejected by one or both of their parents. All felt saddened and angered about their relationships with their parents, and they sought either reconciliation with their parents or at least an end to warfare. Although the four students were writing for their classmates and teacher, they were also writing for themselves: writing to untangle their feelings and to see whether they could narrow the distance between themselves and their families. Not all four students believed that they could improve their relationships with their parents, but each sought greater understanding. They did not want to make their parents' mistakes. In offering snapshots of their family life, the four students freeze time, allowing them to look more closely at their past, present, and future.

"Happy families are all alike; every unhappy family is unhappy in its own way." Thus begins Leo Tolstoy's celebrated novel *Anna Karenina*. But there are at least two problems with this generalization. First, happy families are *not* all alike; and second, unhappy families resemble each other in *many* ways. These unhappy commonalities are particularly striking in the writings that follow.

Cory: "I Am Powerless against My Silence"

One of the characteristics of conflicted families is the difficulty of communication, as can be seen in Cory's writings. His parents' inability to speak with each other is reflected in his own silence. He opens by observing that his father discovered recently that his computer at work has been disconnected, foreshadowing the termination of his job. Cory's writings reveal the multiple disconnections in his life, including estrangement from his parents:

Last night I called home to wish my father a happy birthday. He told me that he was just fired from his job. Earlier in the week my father went into work and found that his computer had been disconnected. As he looked at his computer, trying to understand why it was disconnected, two men walked into his office behind him. One man was a worker that my father had recognized from personnel. The other man was someone that my father had not yet met. By their nervous and sad demeanor, my father knew what was happening.

They lead my father to a nearby office and told him that the company decided that it was in their best interest to terminate him. They said that they needed to move the company forward.

"Move the company forward? But the company grew during the past two years that I worked here. I thought I have been helping the company move forward."

The man who my father had not yet met then introduced himself. He was from the company's head office in California. He flew to New York to see to it that my father's termination went smoothly. He told my father that "the decision has been made and it is irreversible." He added that he wanted to work with my father to make sure he is taken care of during his time of transition.

"Am I being fired, or is my position getting terminated?"

My father's new friend answered, "we already started looking for a replacement."

They gave my father one half hour to pack his things and leave.

Over the past ten years my father has worked for six companies. That's an average of less than one job for every two years. When my father told me that he was fired I was not worried about the financial future of my family. I have been through enough terminations to know that his unemployment was not terminal. I knew that he would spend the next few months engulfed in an intense job search. He would relentlessly sign cover letters, network with every connection he ever met, and become an avid reader of the help wanted section of the newspaper. The one thing that his career has taught him was an expertise in job-hunting.

This sensitivity to my Father's feelings is newfound. Until recently, my father has been an alien. He was a man who I lived with since birth. Nothing more than that. I don't know why this is. He never hit me. He never discouraged me. He never said no to me. All that he ever did was support me, giving me all of his heart. All that he ever wanted was to be my friend. In return, I rejected him. I never gave him any of my time or any of my heart.

I remember the first time that I connected with my father on a human level. A few months ago I received a call from my Dad late at night. He sounded sad. It was a sadness that was painfully familiar. Hearing his voice was like looking into a mirror. It was four in the morning and he was awake, staring at his overdue bill and calculating his credit card debt. I knew these were things that overwhelmed him. I also knew that these were just sad distractions from what was really hurting him. He felt alone. Just like me. Just like everyone in this world.

We talked for about an hour. I still can't describe the feeling I had once we hung up. I don't know if I felt better, or worse. For the first time I saw my father as a human being, as myself. I felt an over-powering sense of kinship to my Dad. I knew that we both felt the same world.

Now that my father was human, I saw my past differently. I was able to see the relationships in my family in a clearer perspective. I began to understand why I never let my father into my life.

I asked myself why can't I open myself up to a man who has never done anything but love me. I then realized that it wasn't the way he treated me that hurt, but it was the way he treated my Mother. My Father has never hit my Mother. My Father has also never loved my Mother.

My Father has never been there for my Mother. Throughout his various jobs he has always worked extremely late hours. When my family would complain, he would dodge responsibility, saying that it wasn't his choice. He claimed that whatever boss he had at the time demanded unreasonable hours from him. By his fifth job in nine years my family had realized that it was not his job that was keeping him from being home. Five consecutive unfair bosses was too great of a coincidence. It wasn't his job that was keeping him from being home, but his wife that was keeping him from coming home.

This notion is acted out every time I go home. When I'm home my father will call every day from work. He'll ask what my plans are for the evening, with hopes of having dinner, or catching a movie with me. If I tell him that I'll be home at dinner time he'll leave work "early" and come home. If I tell him that I'm not going to be around, he'll come home after dinner.

While my father desperately attempts to spend time with me, my mother basks in her solitude. My mother is beautiful. She is a nurse and spends time with ill children. Her dedication to her work and to her family is what makes her beautiful.

After a stressful day of work my mother returns home, only to share her time with Loneliness. Loneliness is her husband. When I was younger it didn't matter as much that my father was not home. She had her children to fill her life with. She would cook for us, talk with us, and fight with us. Now her children have all grown up. When she comes home from work she is alone. Now she fills her life by cleaning the already clean house everyday.

A few weeks ago I was home visiting when my Father called home, to see if I would be around for dinner. Knowing that he would call, I had made plans to go out with my friends. "No Dad, I'm not going to be home." I looked at my Mom sitting on the couch, alone. "You know, MOM'S HOME! She's home if you want to come home for dinner. I'm not going to be here, but MOM'S HOME!"

My Mom overheard and both her and my Father grew awkward. They both knew what I was implying. My Mother told me that it made her feel good to know that I understood. She told me that she was proud of my sensitivity but she didn't want to be pitied by her own son.

This was the first and only time that I ever expressed my awareness and discontent with their relationship. I should rephrase that. That was the first time I verbally expressed such feelings. I have been expressing my feelings through intense resentment my entire life. My resentment lead me to punish my Father the only way I knew how; by closing myself off from him.

This understanding of how my parents' relationship affects me is new. Although I may be angry, I don't think it is fair to punish my father. He is a man of beautiful intention. If people were judged solely by their intentions, then my Father would be the greatest human that ever lived. He never meant to hurt my mother nor me. The attack should not be on him, but on his inability to communicate. He needs to learn to confront his feelings of why he doesn't share his life with my Mom.

I feel that by recognizing why I shut my Father out, I am already vastly improving our relationship. Last year I came across a phrase that will always be a part of me; "The Good Fight." "The Good Fight" is the fight for good. It's the recognition of all of the loneliness and hurt in this world, and the perseverance against it. "The Good Fight" is a war against all that is bad. "The Good Fight" is the unification of all that is beautiful. My parents' relationship may have problems. But I sincerely believe that somehow their relationship as well as the rest of my family, are part of the "Good Fight."

Though Cory doesn't use the word, the phone call seems to be the first time in his life that he empathizes with his father. Now that he sees his father as a fellow human being, a fellow sufferer, he begins to see his own past differently. Asking himself why he has never let his father into his life, Cory reaches an important conclusion: his anger and resentment spring from his father's treatment of his mother, a conclusion that he elaborates in abundant detail. The more Cory "opens up" in his writing, the more insight he reaches into his family life. Whereas in the past he expressed his resentment through silence, now he discovers, in part as a result of writing the essay, that he should "attack" not his father but rather his father's—and his own—"inability to communicate." Cory realizes at the end of his essay that he must be able to express his feelings toward his parents if he is to improve his family situation, and he proceeds to do that in the following letter:

Dear Mom and Dad,

I remember seeing Mom right before I left the house to meet some friends. I remember seeing her at the top of the stairs, looking at me as I scrambled to find my keys, my hat, and whatever else I needed to grab before I escaped. I remember her looking at me and asking, "Isn't there anything you can tell me about yourself? Anything? Just something about who you are?" I thought about my car warming up in the driveway. She looked so sad. She desperately wanted to meet her twenty-year-old son. "Uh, sorry but not really. I'm fine though Mom." And with that said, the door closed behind me.

Things have been this way for as long as I can remember. I have never had the ability to let you guys into my life. I don't know why this is. You have always given me your trust, your love, and your support. All that I have been able to give in return is my cold silence. I want to apologize. But I won't. The reason that I don't share my life with you is not by my choice. This may seem like my usual dodge of responsibility. However, I promise you that it is not. I am powerless against my silence. I want to let you guys in. I want to be able to sit down at the dinner table and open up. I want to be able to look you guys in the eyes and let all my thoughts and experiences rain. I want to tell you about my friends. I want to tell you about how happy I am sometimes, just to be alive. I want to tell you how sad I become, just because I'm alive. I want to tell you about how I'm going to one day be President and cure everything that needs a cure. I want to tell you everything. But I can't. When I try my tongue begins to swell. My eyes shut. My ears throb. And my head explodes.

So I write my thoughts in this imaginary letter. Imaginary in that you will never read it. But also very real in that I am truly writing it. As I look at this letter, I realize that it is a good representative of life. That is, the part of life that is unspoken. It makes me think about all of the times that I play things out in my head. When I relive a memory but change it, to make it fit better in my mind. There are so many times when people are rude or act condescending to me. I usually freeze and back down. But as soon as I leave the situation I go back in time. I play the situation over, but in my version I don't back down. I tell the person about how I think he's an asshole who needs to treat people poorly in order to feel important. There are so many times in my life that I say the most idiotic things to girls who I really like. Or even worse, times when I don't say anything at all. When I play these instances over in my head I have a new sense of confidence. The girl responds to my confidence and is interested in what I have to say. She's interested in me. After doing the math I would venture that half of my entire life is imaginary. If you added up all the time that I spend wishing that the world were different, it would be equal to the time I spend thinking about how the world is. This letter is just one example of this imaginary world that I sometimes live in.

Now that I'm in imaginary mode I'm free to talk to you guys. My tongue no longer swells. My eyes are wide open and the gag is lifted from my mouth. I want to use this opportunity to let you guys into my life. I want to tell you about all of the pain that I've seen you cause each other as well as the rest of the family. More importantly, I want to tell you about the overwhelming sense of love and gratitude that I have for you guys.

I have learned so much about relationships during the past few years. I have learned that what I once thought were outside factors, are really internal factors when it comes to relationships. What I mean is that it is not what happens to you, but how you handle what happens to you. You have no control over a lot of the forces that hit you, but you can control how you want it to effect you. I think that this applies to relationships. You can't control how a person acts or treats you, but you can control how you will cope with it.

There are certain things about both of you that are miserable. However most of these things are part of who you are. I have known both of you for twenty years and by now I realize that these things are never going to change. Accept it. Stop hating each other for being yourselves. Mom, Dad is always going to be a malcontent. He is never going to be an enthusiastic, easygoing person. He will always keep a close count on his money. He will always scrutinize the check at restaurants. He will always be unhappy with the car he is driving; the sunroof will make a noise, or the door handle will be on a slight tilt. He will always work late. He will always get mad when he has to throw out stale food because someone bought duplicate boxes of Ritz crackers. He will always throw a fit when the vacuum bag explodes because no one took the initiative to change it. He will always gag when he smells may-onnaise. Accept it.

Dad, Mom will always do laundry obsessively. She will keep putting in loads until all the hampers are empty or she runs out of soap. She will never like to travel. She will never become spontaneous. She will always compli-ment her own cooking. She will always tell the same stories to entertain her friends. Mom will always be scared of snow, elevators, subways, and air-planes. She will never stop making excuses for herself when she feels backed into a corner. Accept it.

You guys could fight and hate each other as much as you want but in the end it doesn't matter. All of these things that I just mentioned will always be true. What you need to do is decide if it is worth it. Stop blaming each other for being who you are. Until you learn to accept these things about each other, they will continue to eat away at you. Your marriage will continue to be empty. Our house will continue to be empty.

If you guys decide that you can't accept these things, fine. I understand. But end it. Don't live together. Don't be married. I don't need to see it any-more. It's a burden on the entire family.

You raised me in a silent house. Not once have I seen you have a conversa-tion about how each other's days were. About each other's feelings. I've never even seen you talk about the things you don't like about each other. At this point I rather see you fight then not talk. At least with fighting, there's hope.

I sit here and wonder why I feel so crippled when I try to let you guys into my life. Meanwhile, this letter is helping me to realize that I'm a product of a silent house. As I close this letter, I am left with an image. I see myself at my computer typing this letter. I see Mom at work, sitting at her desk filing records. And I see Dad in his car, driving home, daydreaming. All of our mouths are shut. It's like watching an accident happen.

Love,
Cory

Dearest Cory,
     Your father and I just read your letter.
I can't explain how painful it was for us to examine ourselves as your letter forced us to do. I want to make promises that things will change. But as I know you will understand, father and I can not vouch for what the future will bring.
     Your letter forced us to see things that we were both afraid to see. You did not tell us anything that we did not already know. Your letter allowed us to look inward and see how we feel. What you said about the importance of accepting each other was on target. However, I feel that your letter over simplified things. I am willing to accept your father's disdain for mayo, but I am not willing to

accept his disdain for me. I am willing to accept most things about him, but there are some things that hurt too much to accept. Your father needs a partner who will go places with him. He needs a partner, who will share his view of the world with him. Maybe I'm that person. I know I was at one point. Things have changed though. We have both grown over the years. We need to figure out if we can find a way to grow back together.

We both love you so much that it hurts. Your letter was a beautiful and courageous effort. And we both thank you for it. Hopefully we too will have the courage to do what is right.

We love you,
Mom and Dad

Cory states that he is tongue-tied in the presence of his parents, rendered speechless by "cold silence," but his "tongue no longer swells" in his letter to them. The "imaginary mode" of writing enables him to "lift" the "gag" from his mouth and summon his parents back into his life. He asks them to accept their differences and begin a dialogue that will reanimate their silent house. In terms of speech act theory formulated by J. L. Austin in *How to Do Things with Words*, Cory's letter is a performative utterance: one in which the "issuing of the utterance is the performing of an action" (6). For Austin, words do not merely *describe* but also *do*. As Sandy Petrey observes: "Words and things, speaking and doing are one and the same when language performs" (6). Austin subdivides performative utterances into several types, including "behabitives," which are utterances that are concerned with "reactions to behaviour and with behaviour towards others and designed to exhibit attitudes and feelings" (83). Austin's example of a behabitive is "I apologize": "it is the happiness of the performative 'I apologize' which makes it the fact that I am apologizing: and my success in apologizing depends on the happiness of the performative utterance 'I apologize'" (47). The paradox of Cory's letter is that he apologizes even as he says he cannot and thus takes the first step toward improved communication with his parents.

Cory is under no illusions that a simple letter will change his parents' marriage. Indeed, he knows that his words will hurt them. He demonstrates that dialogue will not be easy by having his mother speak for her husband. Cory's mother does not disagree with any of her son's observations, but she does believe that he has oversimplified—an admission that comes from Cory himself since he is imagining his mother's response. His words portray her as thoughtful, articulate, and dignified. Distressed by her son's sadness, she wonders whether she and her husband will have the courage to repair their marriage. Cory endows her with a memorable line:

"I am willing to accept your father's disdain for mayo, but I am not willing to accept his disdain for me." Despite the differences between them, she and her husband love their son. Nowhere does the word "forgiveness" appear in either letter, but the spirit of forgiveness animates Cory's writing, including the search for understanding, acceptance, and reconciliation. Cory closes the letter to his parents on a note of cautious optimism: he is sitting at his computer, completing a writing assignment that he hopes will avert a terrible accident.

Danielle: "You Climbed into a Bottle and You Haven't Left That Safe Haven Since"

Danielle's opening essay illustrates the adage that one should be careful about one's wishes, for they may come true. Her innocent childhood desire to have divorced parents so that she could be like her friends nearly came true—with a vengeance. Reading Tracey's diary entry in "Sins of the Fathers" triggered Danielle's own anguished memories of her parents' warfare, and she describes how she is implicated in their battles:

I came home from kindergarten one afternoon at lunchtime. My mother was sitting in our dinning room with the collapsible ironing board lowered to her seat. As she ironed my father's khaki pants, her brow was wrinkled as she scrutinized her work. It was early in the school year and I had just begun to make what were then, astounding discoveries about my new classmates. "Mom?" I asked. "Who was your first husband?" My mother dropped the leg of the pants in confusion. A smile then spread across her face as she surveyed the curious five-year-old who looked on in a manner of accusation. "Your father is my first husband," she answered. "Nah uh!" I returned placing my tiny hand on the side of my waist, further determined to get to the bottom of my parents illicit doings. "Where is this coming from?" my mother asked with a giggle. "Sandy told me that her mom has two other husbands and six half brothers and sisters. Chris also has a new daddy," I announced. My mother calmly sipped her cup of tea and started to explain divorce to me. Although I remember listening, the dominant idea playing out in my five-year-old mind was a fear of being different from my "sophisticated" friends. When my mother had finished her explanation, I sat silent for thirty seconds. When I interpreted my newfound information I had decidedly announced, "I think you and daddy should probably get a divorce now." Although I wanted to be like my friends, I would later fear that my parents' would actually get a divorce and I would silently berate myself for this former conversation.

Reading the chapter "Sins of the Fathers" in Diaries to an English Profes-

sor was not surprising to me. Growing up I had a number of my friends who had suffered through the divorce of their parents. Each of them carried scars and emotional problems with them into adulthood. Reading each of the essays in this book reminded me of some of my friends and their parents. Tracey's diary entry had awoken memories in me that had been dormant for several years. Like Tracey's parent's, my parents had a mother child relationship. The one sentence that spoke to me in Tracey's entry was, "My father was an overgrown child who has never been able to face his responsibilities to his family." Unfortunately, it is that sentence that most accurately describes my own father.

My mother and father lived a Peter Pan and Wendy existence. My father would travel to a multitude of destinations during the week where his work would be one adventure after another. My mother was the actual parent to my brother and me. Bills were paid, food was prepared, the house was kept clean, and the kids were washed and dressed all by the freckled hands of my mother. On Friday nights, my father would return home from the drive to both children bandaged from the wounds of the week. This lifestyle continued until I was twelve. Although my father would still return on Friday nights to tell us his adventures, my mother no longer stayed in the room to listen. Instead, she would busy herself in the kitchen or pretend to fold laundry that had already been folded.

I would lay in bed in the room with my young brother Paul. The screams and the accusations that would fill the downstairs would force Paul out of his bed. I was afraid, but I never let him see. I had to be fearless for him as he nestled his tiny body into the cradle of my arm. The day after, my mother would look worn but my father would be beaming and ready for a day of fun and adventure. Promises of no more fights and apologies became a commonplace for Saturday mornings. Saturday nights, the moon would shine through my window, illuminating my brother's bed. I would leave my own bed, equipped with extra blankets to place at the crack underneath the doorway. It was for Paul that I would try to buffer the sounds of breaking glass and screams, but to no avail. Sunday morning, I would awake to the tiny body clinging to me.

I guess I had understood my mother and her emotions more than I had my father. I was angry that he would sweep through the door on Friday nights and virtually upset the steady balance that my mother had created during the week. My father would switch jobs because he couldn't get along with this one or with that one. He would run up phone bills that reached into the hundreds, always in search of that ideal job. Monday morning would come again with my mother picking up the broken glass, paying telephone bills and making sure the kids were clothed, fed and sent safely to school. Eventually my mother grew weary of being parent to three kids instead of two. As I got older, I became her sounding board, her confidant. Her regrets and fears were filtered through her older child. My role at twelve had enlarged to include mother to my mother. My judgment of my father had become aggressively critical. I would witness my mother straining to keep our family afloat both financially and emotionally. My father would continue to return home on Fridays to reap the spoils of that hard work.

My father came home a week after Thanksgiving that year. Screams of breaking glass followed. Paul struggled to get to my bed without being hit by the words that flew like artillery. The next morning I came downstairs at eight o'clock. My parents had not gone to bed yet, but sat at opposite ends of the couch in an apparent cease-fire. My mothers swollen eyes glanced up at me. The shattered remains of the antique mirror were scattered around the stairway like ashes of the dead. I knew immediately something had happened. The mirror had been a symbol to me of my parents love. It was the first purchase they had ever made together and they proudly displayed it on our mantle piece. Now it was smashed on the floor, lifeless. My mother seemed to gain courage with the sight of her child surveying the wreckage from the stairs. Without fanfare, without ceremony, my mother announced it. "Your father is moving out." My father stayed there that night to prepare for his move. I hid myself on the landing when the screams erupted. I had discerned from their agitated and halting speech that my father had made a discovery while on one of his adventures. Her name was Laura. I crept back to my room with my new secret. I was devastated. My father had met someone else. I didn't sleep that night. I cried, I looked out the window, I thought of running downstairs and telling my dad that he can't love Laura, he loves mom. I talked myself out of it. I sat by the window on Sunday and watched him carry his bags to his green Jeep. He left that night and he did not come back that weekend or the weekend after that.

Dad called. He was good with the phone, as history had proven. Mom had deteriorated. Most of the time she slept. When she would awake, she usually did with tears. I was left to make sure that Paul got dressed, fed and safely to school. I was now my mother and I hated my father for abandoning us. I also hated my mother for being weak. I hated everything and everybody. But on the surface, we all looked fine. I took care of my brother and my mom. We were fantastic at disguising our pain from everybody. When my friends would ask about my father, I would tell them that he was working away from home for an unexpected amount of time. That was easy, he was never around anyway. When he was, he would crack a joke and make my friends believe I had the funniest dad in the world.

Nobody knew about my parent's separation until the night of my thirteenth birthday. I had invited a friend to dinner, shopping and a movie. My mom was just starting to recover her old self and take her role back. She was trying to compensate for my father's absence and planned for my birthday diligently. It was a Thursday and my mother's car was not in the school parking lot as was planned. My friend and I waited for two hours. My mom never came. I waited, horrified, explaining to my friend, making elaborate excuses for my mother's neglect. Tears would begin to form, but I pushed them away. A friend of our families pulled alongside the curb where we waited. My friend aggravated, me silent. He made an excuse for my mother stating that there was a family emergency.

After my friend was driven home, I entered my dark, skeleton of a house. My mother sat on the couch destroyed with a pink package resting on her lap. As I passed into the living room, tears and apologies escaped her eyes and lips. I had no pity. My mother tried to pass me the gift. The once compliant daughter now seethed with hatred and dropped the box to the floor. I smashed its pink purity into the floor with my heel. I didn't care that my mother had spoken to my father today. I didn't care that he kept telling her how happy he was. I didn't care that Laura wanted to meet his kids over vacation. I didn't care. I ripped through the house destroying everything in my path. My mother stood silent as I reached for the phone and dialed my father's line. I screamed into the receiver. I would scream at my father and then turn to target my mother. I hated them both for making me old.

Two years after my parent's separation I got to experience what most of those student diary entries had wished for. When I was fifteen my parents got back together again. I honestly don't know how they reconciled. I either don't remember or I didn't care enough to pay attention. I know my father moved his stuff back into the clothing closet and the dresser draws. I know my mother had repossessed her role as caregiver with renewed rigor. I know Paul would stay up late with my father talking about Dad's adventures in Wonderland. I know I crept in and out of the house ignoring both my father and mother. Their authority over me had dwindled. I did not fear them anymore because I saw their weaknesses. I hated them for letting me see. They had already made me into an adult and they were not going to fucking treat me like a child again.

I love my parent's. I really do. I feel disloyal in writing about them this way, especially my father. I didn't think that I would be able to write anything comparable to the entries in "Sins of the Fathers," never having experienced actual divorce. When I read Tracey's entry, I was compelled to write *this. Anytime I remember the events of those two years I brush them aside. Tracey's entry let me feel less shameful about hiding my parent's behavior. I guess it helped to know that other people have similar problems.*

What I have learned from reading about divorce and its effects was that divorce does leave a lasting mark on you. It can impair you. Even though my parents have reunited, I still live with that two-year period as one of the most scarring ones to date. My images of my parents's were destroyed and much of my fears in life are a direct result to this time period. I know we have recovered from this. I know I have forgiven my Parents and they have forgiven me but I don't think any of us will ever forget or ever completely heal.

Contrary to her fear that nothing she writes can compare to the entries in *Diaries to an English Professor*, Danielle produces a haunting essay, a tribute, perhaps, to her identification with Tracey's diary entry. The most notable line for me—"The shattered remains of the antique mirror were scattered around the stairway like ashes of the dead"—conjures up the image of an irretrievably smashed family life in which words "flew like artillery." Although she sides with her mother, she admits to seething with rage as a result of being forced to abandon her childhood and become the family's caretaker. Throughout the essay Danielle contrasts her present self—highly reflective, mature, and compassionate—with her younger self, an adolescent who was angry and bitter at the world. To write about the hatred she felt toward her parents requires courage and strength, especially since her past actions are so painful to recall. She never softens or rationalizes her past actions that she now regrets so deeply. She probably would not have written about these experiences were it not for Tracey's entry, which allows her to feel "less shameful" about hiding her family's behavior. She ends the essay by noting that although she and her parents have forgiven each other, they have not completely healed. Significantly, she mentions her father's infidelity, but it is not until the letter to her father that she mentions a more serious problem—alcoholism—one that endangers boh his marriage and his life:

Dear Dad,

Recently I read a series of essays in the book, Diaries to an English Professor. *I read a chapter entitled, "Sins of the Fathers." This chapter was devoted to the feelings that students had about the divorce of their parents. My professor asked us to write our own response to the letters and our own feelings about the topic. Although you and mom are not divorced, I found that I had a great deal to say on the topic. After I described that period of time when you and mom separated, I discovered that I had unresolved issues with you that I would like to address in this letter. The essay that I related to the most was written by a girl named Tracey. Tracey described her father as not being able to uphold his responsibilities to his family. Unfortunately this is the statement that made me reflect on my own childhood.*

We sat in the darkened bedroom of our old green house. Mom lay on your bed, staring off into the distance. A look of concern playing out, on her then youthful face. Paul and I sat in a semi-circle of blankets and pillows. A make-shift shrine to you as you stood in the center. Your booming voice bounced off the shadowed walls as you told your stories. Your face flushed from the bottle of rum. Mouths agape, eyes transfixed, we were your faithful worshippers, await-ing your next words eagerly. The candle light plastered your enormous shadow on the wall as you moved around the room, using your body to enhance the story. The story was about your boarding school in Ireland. You had seen a ghost with your classmates. The details of the translucent figure gliding to and fro in the courtyard terrorized us. Your face was mischievous, but I'm not con-vinced that you created that image simply for our entertainment. That night was filled with your stories. You would only pause to reach for your drink.

I reflect on that night often. Your figure so powerful, so large and encom-passing. You always dominated a room. It is funny to me now that although you are still a large and majestic personage, you have always stood at just five feet, eight inches. It is also funny to me that you were able to convince us that the absence of lighting was an effect to add to the power of your story. Not a result of your failure to pay the electric bill. I knew that then, but when I was younger it was always much easier to believe in your fiction than it was to believe in naked reality.

You had lost your job again. You couldn't get along with somebody or your boss told you that the job would be ending. It was always someone elses fault. It wasn't the drinking that made you late for work or nasty to your co-workers. It wasn't your chronic depression that forced you to the liquor store everyday. Along with your drinking came a blur of promises, mostly unful-filled, but I always believed in them. I always clung to them as a small child would cling to a security blanket. "Everything will be okay. I got a line on this fantastic job. We'll start all over again. We'll have more money, a better life. I'll stop drinking then." Those promises kept us hopeful, eager for this new life to begin. Those promises were always accompanied by another rum and coke.

You still can't cope with reality. You still make promises but you no longer have a faithful band of worshippers creating your shrine. I guess I stopped believing in your fiction when mom got sick. That is when I discovered your weaknesses. Mom was confined to a wheelchair. This once active woman *had a life filled with raising children, cleaning the house, and caring for you. Her life had been reduced to being dependant upon the rest of us. She could no longer cook dinner, clean the house and most importantly, she couldn't take care of you. When mom began to fail, I had to pick up the slack. Your life wasn't altered on the surface. Mom made sure, even as her legs became motionless and heavy, that you didn't have to worry about anything. I was left to do the worrying. Trips to the hospital and making sure that mom could reach the bathroom was paralleled with your phone calls to catch that dream job. Your voice on the phone was light hearted and airy. No suggestions that your family's source of strength couldn't even climb the stairs. Your evenings were spent in a drunken stupor and the promises of a better job and life were slurred in the dark living room.*

You abandoned me. You left me alone to care for our family, prioritizing rum and the phone over explaining to bill collector's our situation. You fell apart. I had to call the electric company and explain, "My mother is in the hospital and my father just recently lost his job. Can you please wait before you turn off the electricity, maybe we can arrange something. All of our income is going to hospital bills." I did it alone. You climbed into a bottle and you haven't left that safe haven since. I tried to shield Paul from your weakness. He could smell the rum on your breathe. He could see your eyes lit from the pungent serum. Mom could too. I would walk into the hospital room. I would watch as she lay in bed. Her hair was matted to the plastic pillow from the tears that fell from her face. Hoses and tubes entering and exiting her every orifice. Pain contorted her face, pain from your irresponsibility, from your failure. I saw it in her glassy, hazel eyes, the years of promises, the years of drinking, the years of pain. Mom should have been worried about recovering, not about your sobriety.

I didn't understand it then, I don't understand it now. Alcohol continues to be your life force, your passion, your love. I know we have talked about this forever but why cant you see? We all have. Mom still takes care of you but Paul doesn't really talk to you. I don't. We all stopped trying. That should be an indication of sorts to you that you have a problem. I have even held a mirror to your face. The reflection showed a yellow and emaciated face. Bloodshot eyes, aged skin, yellow, yellow, yellow. Your not eating, you haven't for awhile. Your slowly dying. It is as if the liquor acts like a formaldihide in your system. It keeps you preserved, but your dead inside. Your killing mom, too. Her face is listless, sunken and pale. I see her sometimes and I know this is not the life that she imagined as a young woman. I guess it is not the life that you had imagined as a young man either.

Dad, I love you! I see you killing yourself and no matter what I say, it falls on deaf ears. I don't know what I can do. Please tell me what I can do. I'll do anything.

In the dark room you sit, the candle light reflects your emaciated figure on the wall. No longer a shrine. Worshippers gone. But promises still echo off the aged walls.

Love,
Danielle

Dear Danielle,

Your father has read this but he has asked me to respond instead. Your letter was extremely difficult for him. He doesn't deny his failures or weaknesses. He doesn't try to justify them either. Your letter is just another confrontation that he is not ready for. Instead of responding, he internalizes everything. That is where the drinking comes in. Dad numbs himself when he is forced to deal with a difficult situation. I guess he does it to numb himself from life in general. I'm not writing this to excuse his behavior toward you or the family. I would just like a chance to explain it.

When your father was eight-years-old, his own parents sent him away. Dad grew up in a boarding school in Ireland alone. His sisters and brothers were allowed to stay at home, but he had no choice but to go. Although he made friends, he was neglected by your grandparents. During the Holidays, he was sent to a relative's house in another city. When he was attending school, he created a life for himself in books. His only friends in the world were fictitious characters from The Wind in the Willows. *It was those characters who cared for him when he was sick. Soothed him when he was lonely and sad. The trust he created with those characters was unparalleled in reality. He couldn't trust anyone, because they would eventually leave him.*

Dad has never repaired his relationship with his own parents. You've been witness to that during holidays and vacations. They have tried to approach him and attone for the pain that they caused him, but you can see that the damage is permanent. Phone calls have been filled with tension. Christmas cards have been written with the carefulness of walking on egg shells. Years have been spent trying to overcome the past, but to no avail. Dad will always feel like that eight-year-old child, alone and pawned off to distant relatives.

When I met your father I immediately fell in love with his humor and charm. Unfortunately, he always kept me at a distance. I convinced myself that I could care for him, that I could eliminate his pain. He always had another way to diminish the pain though. His drinking was typical of a twenty-year-old boy with an Irish background. Both of us having been raised with an emphasis on our Irish heritage, the drinking had not been a suprise to me. Funerals, weddings and family functions always consisted of high balls and whiskey sours. Celebrations of any kind required a large assortment of liquor bottles. It had been a large part of our childhoods. The drinking only started to be a problem when he moved back into the house after our separation.

The figure you describe at the beginning of your letter is the man that I see. Your father has always been the center of any room. His stories would dominate the audience. He has a way of becoming the focal point of every room, whether it be a large crowd assembled for a party or just me. The presence of your father has always been consuming. It has now completely consumed me and I am drained. I was always your father's biggest defender, but he failed me just like he failed you. When I got sick, I only had you to rely on. Paul was still in school and I was trying to protect him. You had already become the only other person I could get help from and unfortunately I had to lean on you. Dad had lost yet another job right around the time of my illness. By that time it had become a pattern. As you cited in your letter, dad could never get along with anyone he worked with. He always had dreams of a better job, the one that would make us rich. I never wanted to be rich. I wanted stability. At that point, your father had not even been able to provide that. I was in no position to put my foot down. I couldn't even walk let alone fight with your father. It would have been futile to convince him that, after years of dreaming, to suddenly stop it. So I got sick and you were the only other person who could help me. I still reflect on that time with disgust. I was disgusted with your father and disgusted with the fact that the only way I could take a shower was with your assistance.

Dad really did crawl into a bottle. He is still there. I have talked with him about how he left the responsibility to you and he knows that I resent him for it. However, he beats himself up enough for me to constantly remind him of his failure. That is what the alcohol is. He pours drink after drink as if he will find all the answers to his problems at the bottom of the bottle. When he discovers that there is nothing at the base of the bottle, he opens a new one and his journey resumes. I cant get him to stop drinking and I don't think that he can even stop himself. Nor do I think he wants to stop drinking. The only explanation I can give for his absence during my sickness is that he could not cope with it. I have always filled a variety of roles for him. I have been his wife, mother, father, and friend. When he was faced with the reality that that person who he relied on might not be around, he withdrew and lived in a world of inebriated denial. He tried to stop by pursuing that dream job with added gusto. It was a way for him to alleviate his guilt by attempting to provide for his faultering family. When attempt after attempt would fail, he punished himself with the rum. I was forced to rely on you because he also abandoned me. I am still very bitter but it is counter productive to remind him of that period of time. It becomes just another excuse for him to drink.

I guess that is the effect that this letter has had on me. He cannot address it, but he knows that you feel this way. We are all blue in the face after telling him that he is going to die if he doesn't stop drinking. I have come to terms with the fact that he may die. I see that he is yellow and I see that he is gaunt. I hear his promises everyday of this better life. I stopped hoping for this better life a long time ago. Now I just hope that he will eat one meal.

I apologize to you Danielle. I apologize for myself and for your father. I wish he didn't hate himself so much. I wish he didn't drink so much. I wish he would be responsible for his family. I never imagined this life for my children or myself. I never imagined this life for him. What you don't know is that I still see that twenty year-old boy that I fell in love with. He still shines, he still has humor, charm, and a love for story telling. Your father is not an evil man who meant to do these things to us. He is a very sad man who believes he is only doing these things to himself.

I'm sorry.
Love, Mom

Danielle's Dickensian portrait of the family is filled with wrenching details that never become sentimental, including holding a mirror to her father's face to convince him that he will soon die unless he stops drinking. Her letter is another version of a mirror, contrasting her former image of her father as a larger than life figure with the present image of a man bent on self-destruction. The comparison of liquor to formaldehyde captures the way in which the daughter sees her father, preserved in a death-in-life state. Anger gives way to sorrow and helplessness as she closes the letter, the light slowly being extinguished from her father's life.

Although the letter is addressed to her father, Danielle imagines her mother speaking for the two of them, perhaps because the father can no longer speak for himself. The letter sounds so authentic that we almost forget that the daughter writes it. Danielle anticipates that her words will wound her father, "another confrontation that he is not ready for." She offers a compelling explanation—not justification—for her father's alcoholism, an intergenerational theory of the "sins of the fathers" in which parents neglect their children who in turn abandon their own children. Danielle captures her mother's conflicting feelings: love, anger, sadness, pain. Remarkably, Danielle is able to imagine her mother still in love with the young man whom his children have known only briefly, a man whose humor and charm have slowly vanished over time. It would be hard to imagine a more heartbreaking letter, for Danielle realizes that her father will experience her words, written in love and anguish, as one more reminder of his failure. She demonstrates that an alcoholic can never forgive himself. Danielle's mother can only apologize to her daughter for the family situation and ask for understanding if not forgiveness. The wish seems to have been granted: Danielle's understanding of her mother's situation is extraordinary. The letter closes with the statement that "What you don't know is that I still see that twenty year-old boy that I fell in love with." The two letters demonstrate that both mother and daughter still love the man whose life had once held such promise. Danielle was not the only student in the class to write about the destructive consequences of alcoholism—another student described how her father's life was destroyed by drinking—but I have never read a more heartrending description of a daughter's helplessness in watching a beloved father deteriorate in front of her eyes.

Lydia: "I Know You Love Me, but Most of the Time I Don't Feel It"

In her opening essay, Lydia observes that she has spent her entire adolescence "consumed by the fights" with her mother, adding that "[o]ur weapons were our words." These verbal battles created lacerating wounds that continue to fester. Lydia's essay explores in painstaking detail the scars she has incurred from her parents' multiple divorces, and only in the last paragraph does she suggest that she will benefit from their mistakes:

Unlike most of the women whose diaries appear in "Sins of the Fathers" I have always blamed my mother for the divorce. I spent my entire adolescence consumed by the fights between us. Our home was like a battleground. Our weapons were our words. The wounds we suffered are deep and still throbbing with pain. Although I acknowledge that the extreme feelings of anger and hatred I have felt towards her are paralleled by feelings of love, I still seem unable to forgive her for an event that occurred before I can even remember.

My parents have been divorced since I was three years old. My only memory of them in the same room together is from when I was eight years old and the three of us were in therapy. I have never seen their wedding pictures or any pictures of them as a couple. I can't conceive how two people that hate each other so much could have ever been married or been in love. My father's explanation for the divorce has always been, "Your mother and I couldn't get along and eventually we stopped loving each other." My mother's explanation has always been, "I never loved your father. The only reason I went through with it was because I was afraid I would never be married, and I was too embarrassed to give all the gifts back." Well I think those are the stupidest reasons to get married. I still can't believe that she actually gave that to me as an explanation. She wouldn't even allow me to have the childhood dream that at some point my parents loved each other a little. I faced the harsh reality of my parents divorce when I was three years old and I still face it every day.

Until I was sixteen my dad was always in my thoughts and represented my ideal of the perfect man. He was my hero and the embodiment of perfection. I never took into account that his distance from me, and the mere three phone calls I received from him every two months, hardly qualified him to win a father of the year award. My mom on the other hand has always been there for me. She came to every school play, on every school trip, washed my laundry, cooked me dinner every night and appeared, on the surface, to be a perfect mom. However, the mere mention of my father's name would be enough to send her on a rampage. In an instant the woman who claimed to love me more than anyone in the world became so consumed by her own anger and hatred that she could forget I was her daughter. Mentioning my father was met with the same repercussions that the church would impose upon a catholic for committing a deadly sin. My association with him trans- formed me from her daughter into the devil's spawn. She almost never hit me, and it was only when I got older that she started saying I was a bitch. What she did do was scream at me, "You're just like your father!"

In "Sins of the Fathers" Ron talks about his mother using this same phrase to describe him. His father is successful, logical and selfish. I have begun to witness these same qualities in myself. But I didn't learn them from my father. I learned them from my mother. My mother has always placed herself on the opposite end of the spectrum. Completely selfless. She has spent half her life sacrificing and struggling for her children, and the other half regretting al- most every decision she has ever made. She resents my father for living his life after the divorce. He has been free to travel, take vacations, and buy a new car. But my mother has been stuck in the same house, in the same city she grew up in, surrounded by the same people. Although this has been her choice, she claims that the demands of motherhood have placed drastic limitations on her options. This also comes from a woman that has never worked a full-time job in her life. It's difficult to take exotic vacations and hire babysitters when there isn't enough income to maintain the house you live in.

What my mother has never quite understood is that the only reason this man, whom she detests, is in my life is because of her. This is why I think it is essential for adults to spend some time being married, making sure that they are willing to remain together, before they decide to have children. Ac- cording to my mother, she already knew marrying my father was a mistake, so who's brilliant idea was it to have a kid?!

Ron's statement, "If [my father] wasn't happy how could he make the rest of us happy?" greatly disturbed me. This is simply a way to justify his father's selfish behavior, making it seem reasonable and necessary. In my opinion, it's bullshit! Children need security. They need a loving home that remains in tact, even when everything else in their lives is falling apart. They need to know that their parents are strong and will be there to support them and love them. What they don't need is a couple of parents that are so preoccupied with their own fucking happiness, that they forget their children have needs that may conflict with their own. Having a child is a sacrifice. Naturally when you have a child your individual needs are put on hold because now, you are responsible for meeting the needs of another individual: an individual that you decided to create and bring into this world. Once two people decide to have a child, the sacrifices they make and the time they spend, and the money they spend is their obligation. Children owe their parents nothing. Anything and everything they do for their children, is their job; It's part of the job description. All these are reasons why selfish people should not have children.

I also differ from the other women in the chapter because I do not feel it is my job to become my mother's caretaker. She has been depressed for years, and I have spent years trying to understand why. I know why. It's because she spent her life living for other people, her parents, her children and husbands. I will not allow myself to make the same mistake. I am selfish and plan on being selfish for a long time. I want to travel and I want to have a career and I want to live in a house I can pay on my own, without worrying about finding a man to help me. Then when I have finally done what I feel I need to do to make me happy, then and only then will I have children. If I never find happiness within myself I won't have children. I may not ever be perfectly sure that I marry the right man, but I know that when I do get married and if I decide to have children, we are going to do whatever is necessary to make it work. I will never put my children through the trauma I have gone through.

Both of my parents have made mistakes, and I blame them both for the divorce. I think I have always been harder on my mother because I spent more time with her. Legally, the divorce provided a separation. But emotionally my parents are forever bound because of their careless decision to have a child. Luckily I have benefited greatly from their separation. I matured quickly and already have a clear picture of the type of parent I hope to be. I'm thankful I can benefit from their mistakes.

Lydia's essay reads as a cautionary tale for future parents, warning them not to make the errors of judgment that her mother has made. The worst mistake a parent can make, in her view, is to attack a spouse and make a child feel guilty for having been born. Lydia cannot forgive her mother for this; "the mere mention of my father's name would be enough to send her on a rampage." The mother's statement, or rather accusation—"You're just like your father!"—is the ultimate injury. Lydia describes two kinds of selflessness: the healthy sacrifices parents make for their children, providing them with love, security, and support; and the unhealthy self-sacrificial martyrdom that she identifies with her depressed mother. She vows at the end of the essay never to put her children—should she have them—through the trauma she has experienced. Lydia's anger spills over into the letter to her mother, which is filled with confessions that she knows her mother will experience as betrayals:

Dear Mom,

I have a confession to make. Over the break while I was home, I went into the basement to do laundry. I was so bored that I decided to look around and see if I could find anything of mine that I packed and put into storage, forgetting about after I went away to school. I never found anything interesting of my own. What I did find was a box of your things. I opened it and instantly the smell of stale paper invaded my nostrils. Maybe I should have ignored it and accepted that I had no business snooping, but for some reason I couldn't. I thought that maybe the reasons you are so depressed and so resentful of me, might be in the box. I found diaries and personal documents, photographs and old greeting cards. Quickly catching my attention was a card with a huge heart, drawn in red crayon, made from construction paper, with the words, "I Love You Mommy" printed on the front. It surprised me that you kept this. It occurred to me then that it must still be important to you. Maybe it's the only evidence you have that I was once your naive, loving daughter, who viewed you as, "the best mom in the whole world."

There was one photograph of you, possibly from the prom, that made my eyes fill with tears. You were so beautiful. And what I noticed even more than that, was how happy you looked. I think I would give anything to see that kind of happiness appear on your face again. The next thing that caught my attention was a yellow, manila folder with the words, "Show and Tell Lydia" printed on the front, in pencil. I had to see what was in it. Inside were all the letters my father had ever written to you, copies of child support checks and finally legal documentation of your divorce. I'm assuming that since the envelope had my name on it you eventually intended to show this to me, possibly waiting for me to be old enough to understand what it contained. But I have to say, I don't know if any child is ever old enough, or if it is ever necessary, to see that.

I'm taking an expository writing class in school and unfortunately one of the topics we have been discussing for the past few classes is divorce. Yes the dreaded, talked to death subject divorce. I have spent years of my life blaming you and blaming Dad for getting this terrible divorce, that I had been convinced, has ruined my life. It leads me to believe that some of the problems I've experienced in regard to our relationship and my own feelings about relationships and marriage in general, stem from the poor examples I've watched as a child.

What does a successful marriage actually look like? This is something I may never know. I never saw what your relationship with my father was like, but from what I hear it was a torturous experience for both of you. At least when I've asked him about it, he admits to loving you, but being unable to make it work. Whenever I've asked you, you told me you never loved him and married him out of your own worst fears of never being married, and because you felt foolish giving back the wedding gifts. I don't even think you can imagine how horrible a thought that was for me when I was younger, to think that you never loved my dad. Then why did you have me? Why would you ever want to have a child with a man you hated?

I've always had so many questions about your separation that were never answered. I wanted to know why. I knew that there must have been something specific that triggered these intense feelings of hatred in both of you. Finally I found out. Mom, you had an affair. You won't admit this to me and I don't know why and we've had this conversation before. But please don't lie and insult us both. I know the truth. Our whole family knows the truth.

I can still remember you telling me, whenever I had my heart broken by some stupid boy, that I should just get over it and move on. Move on like you do? Hop from one man to the next, thinking about nothing else but my next prospect? Someday get married and have children and if my marriage fails, move on without giving a second thought to my children and how it will affect them? Mom, I've grown up and have watched my parents get divorced twice. Twice. Now I have the joy of hearing you bitch and complain about my father and my ex-stepfather. I get to watch my family get torn apart and I get to make the choice, who's side am I on.

Did you know that I have never experienced a healthy relationship? Have you paid attention? First there was Murray who I lost my virginity to while he had a girlfriend. You forbade us from seeing each other so I never had the luxury of actually being with the guy I shared one of my most cherished moments. Then there was Ed, an alcoholic that was so into drugs that we hardly did anything else but fight. You loved him of course. Then there was Mitch. Ahhh yes Mitch. You hated him, but funnily enough he treated me better than anyone ever had, that was until I found out he had been sleeping with his ex-girlfriend the whole time we were together. Since then there have been countless amounts of meaningless relationships, pretend relationships I've had with guys who are just my friends and want nothing more, all in hopes that I will someday find a healthy relationship, to prove that they do in fact exist!

Well at this point I'm pretty close to giving up. And believe me I'm not just saying it's all because of you. I haven't forgotten that Dad is on his third marriage, a marriage that works so well because his wife is flexible enough to go along with whatever he wants to do. Is that a healthy relationship? I wouldn't know, but from watching other people, I'm inclined to say no. Anyway, I like to think there are more important things in life than having a man. Do you remember what happened last summer? Well if you don't I'll remind you. I came home from the beach and found you passed out completely drunk, on the bathroom floor. I thought you were dead. That was right after a guy had left. You had been crying all week, and telling me to take care of my sisters in case something were to happen to you. You wanted to kill yourself over a guy. Over some fucking guy! You told me that day that I didn't need you anymore. But that's just the thing. I need you in a way now, and I always have in a way that you can't be there for me.

All my life I've wanted the love and attention that you have given to these men. These insignificant men that have caused you to tear yourself apart. These men that are so important that you allow them to make you depressed. I know you love me, but most of the time I don't feel it. I feel like you hate me because all I am is a reminder of a failed relationship. Maybe having a child kept you from finding the knight in shining armor. Why can't you tell me how you really feel? I'm not a child anymore. I'm a woman that's about to enter the real world and is scared to death of spending the rest of her life alone, never finding love and happiness because I've stopped believing in them. No matter what, we will always have each other and I think it's time we stop fighting each other and start supporting each other. I love you so much, more than you may ever know. I just want you to wake up and see that jumping from relationship to relationship in the hopes of finding true happiness is a waste of your time. You want someone to need you? Well I'm telling you right now, I need a mother! I'm tired of being one.

Your daughter,
Lydia

Lydia,

I can't begin to tell you how hurt I feel. Not only have you made some hurtful accusations, but you have also violated my privacy. You had absolutely no right going through my things. I hope at least you were finally able to see the kind of man your father is, and what I've had to deal with these years. I had saved that file for you so that maybe, someday, you would send a little blame his way.

If this is truly how you feel about me than I feel sorry for you. I have spent my life sacrificing for you and trying to be the best mother I know how to be. Nothing I've done has ever been good enough for you. I have been here for you through everything, and where was your father?! Your father has continued doing what he's always done, taking care of himself and considering you as an afterthought.

Don't you dare make me feel guilty for wanting a relationship. I love the man I am living with just as I have loved many people in my life. I'm happy and I refuse to regret any of the decisions I've made. Any mistakes I've made are my own and are no concern of yours. You're in college now and you're never home, so it is none of your business who I am living with or how I live my life.

I have tried to raise you the best I could and keep you from making mistakes. And you insisted on making them anyway. What you do from this point on is up to you; I've told you that already. I no longer have control over anything you do. I refuse to take responsibility for your failed relationships. Our entire family has made some shitty relationships choices, not just me. At least I am determined to get it right this time around.

You'll see. Someday you'll be all grown up and have children of your own. Maybe then you'll understand how difficult it is to be a mother and a wife and a woman all at the same time. Until then, save your judgments.

I love you Lydia, with all my heart, and nothing you do will ever change that. However, I will not allow myself to be the subject of this verbal abuse. You say we need to talk . . . fine. But I will not have any type of serious exchange with you through letters. That is your father's way, not mine. You know where to reach me if you need me.

Mom

Unlike Cory and Danielle, whose letters to and from their parents demonstrate the desire for greater closeness, Lydia fears that the letter to her mother will only widen the distance between them. She spends the greater part of the letter detailing the ways in which she has felt abandoned by her mother, whose unsuccessful marriages have destroyed any possibility of a stable family life. She ends the letter with a plea for her mother's love and approval, one that apparently has little effect on her mother.

In the fictional letter, the mother is stung by Lydia's criticisms and clings to her interpretation of reality, namely, that despite sacrificing her life for her daughter, she has never received any gratitude or respect. The mother's tone is angry and accusatory, and although she ends the letter by expressing love, she makes it clear that she equates her daughter's letter with "verbal abuse," which she will never tolerate. In portraying her mother as unforgiving, Lydia does not see much hope for a reconciliation. Her mother may acknowledge making mistakes but will never concede that these actions have injured her daughter's life. One senses Lydia's fear that words wound more than they heal.

Nat: "To Think of You as My Mother Would Violate the Life Affirming Peace I Have Enjoyed"

Nat has not communicated with his mother for two years. Nor has time softened his anger. Though sympathetic to women's issues, he perceives his mother's "brand of feminism" as male bashing, for which he cannot forgive her:

It's not so much the divorce, that matters. This might actually be the good part of it all. When my parents finally signed their divorce seven years had already passed since they split. They were legally seperated weeks after my mom left which was right around my tenth birthday. After my mom cooled off I was asked to spend time with both parents equally. I didn't know how to divide my needs in two so instead I chose independence. As soon as I began to see them seperately my unconscious need for "them" was supposed to become a conscious desire for one of them at a time. The problem initially with this was that it had nothing to do with me. My parents decided when I would shuffle back and forth and how often; what was good for their schedules became the deciding factor. Most kids just lie down and take this kind of crap. Not me though. My parents' split and the resulting change in priorities, namely that I wasn't one, became a never ending source of anger for me. This anger fueled my early rebellion and need to be independent. It's a good thing I had it otherwise I would have gotten obliterated by their unified selfishness, which was the only thing left intact. Eventually though, my internalized anger had to be dealt with.

Up until this point I had the strongest physical bond with my mother. That is, when I was sick as a child, her presence comforted me in a mystical way. That feeling waned after the divorce.

Most of the people in the "Sins of the Fathers" chapter identified and aligned with their same sex parent and all of them felt truly connected to one or the other. My case was different since neither of my parents had done something so bad to cause the divorce that I shouldn't get to see them. My mother did run away, but only to her friend's house; who was also getting divorced. They created an organization called "Bash and Blame," and al-

though my mother still said I was her son, as a male I wouldn't be welcome there. Suddenly the two supposed former hippies would transform into old shrews who claimed to know everything that was worth knowing about the opposite sex.

My parents' marriage was different, as were my parents. My dad was older than my mom when they had me. They came from two different generations and neither related to my experience. My upbringing included morals from the great depression and the women's movement which awarded no prizes to a boy in the eighties. The gender roles were less defined with my parents as my father took part in cooking and cleaning and my mother fixed things when they broke. To understand my parents' marriage one must first understand my mother's first marriage. She married at twenty-one to an aggressive workaholic, assuming a relatively domestic position in the relationship while he became emotionally abusive and slept with other women. She divorced him after being awakened by the women's movement in the 70s and its message about financial and emotional independence.

Between marriages she raised my half brother for a while as she worked. By the time she met my dad a metamorphosis had ocurred. She had become resentful of dominating men, and would only deal with passive types; apparently they only came in two varieties. My dad fit this role well, he was so passive that when he was furious he would say, "I'm very dissatisfied with you," as if saying, "Pass the ketchup please."

My father didn't have a lack of aggression, he had a lack of emotion. He wasn't sensitive, he was silent. Suddenly after twelve years and one more kid my mother realized she had gotten something she hadn't bargained for. Her second marriage had little if any passion and the two shared nothing in common. It wasn't a total loss though. Having a manageable marriage allowed her to work, and this would continue to be her main focus after the marriage ended.

For a little while I didn't know what had caused the split. At first my mom told me straight to my face it was my fault, but listening to her badmouth my dad for years convinced me I had nothing to do with the mess. When she started to say I was just like him, I knew to take it as an insult. Once she even told me she had me for him; she had been satisfied with one kid. And while she tried to destroy my image of my father, he refused to say or hear anything negative about her.

It vexed me as a child that nobody understood the impact of the divorce on me. The stories of divorce in "Sins of the Fathers" illustrate that most divorces are shaped by the patriarchal model the corresponding marriages were a result of. My mom tried to construct her marriage with feminist ideas in mind though she eventually found that impossible. Her brand of feminism convinced her that relationships were about power and if she was the one with it at least she would be happy. After twelve years she decided domination was draining her and began to yearn for freedom again.

I was shifted back and forth between them in the beginning because they had joint custody. I identified with neither as my primary nurturer or caretaker. If I saw anybody as helpless it was my father, he was the one who had been used. Sometimes I would try to show him how she manipulated him, but he stayed under her control until she moved away after I graduated high school. The vacuum created by her departure was a safe space for him to see how he had been mistreated. Once he began that process we got along much better. Before that he was more like a battered spouse with no defense against her relentless onslaught.

He deferred to her on most decisions concerning me because she was the expert in child psychology, or so she had convinced him. She had countless stories of what worked with other parents, and she had raised one child without him. So when she thought I didn't deserve something I wanted like a telescope or a bike it would be easy to bring dad to her cause. He had a phobia of spending money. It wasn't because he was cheap, the depression had taught him to save money if he valued his life. He had few nice clothes as a kid, so when my mom refused to buy me clothes he told me style wasn't important.

She used to say, "Get your father to buy you clothes," or whatever else it was I needed to fit in. "He's the one with all the money. I've got nothing since the divorce," she used to say. But later I found out that she had been lying. After her hold on my dad had been lifted he admitted to giving her more money during the separation and the divorce than was truly hers. While they had joint custody and I lived with him, he paid her huge sums in child support that never went to me. At the lawyers' final meeting, she suprised all of them by asking for more money on the grounds that as a woman she had contributed more to the pot. She not only had a job but had done most of the house work for which she was never repaid. She brazenly used judicial reforms designed for victims of patriarchal family arrangements to obtain money which wasn't hers.

I didn't live in a bubble though. At the time feminism meant little to me and I evaluated my parents' relationship and divorce in terms of other peoples experiences. When I looked at the fathers of my friends I saw men in control of themselves, these guys never let anyone manipulate them. I interpreted my dad's vulnerability as weakness and this gave a whole new twist to the oedipal complex. Instead of trying to take my dad's role in order to have my mother all to myself, I tried to take his place in order to prevent his emasculation.

As I grew older I took on the role of the angry victim. That didn't help much since she had convinced herself that four men were to blame for everything that had gone wrong with her life. Her victimhood made more sense and she didn't have to look at herself in the process. Here's how the story went. Her father had trained her to be weak. Her first husband had made her look like a fool. Her second husband made her feel like an idiot for getting it wrong again, and I made her resentful, reminding her of it all the time.

Even after she moved out and traveled to another part of the country, the hurt kept on. I thought it would stop with her leaving but it just manifested in a new way. After high school I began dating more though it seldom brought me any joy. The women I attracted and was attracted to were independent and beautiful. They had careers in mind and depended on no one, thus when they chose me I knew they really liked me for me. This part was all fine; it's the other qualities that drove me nuts. I repeatedly sought out workaholics with no time for a relationship. And what's worse I sought from these women the emotion my mother had denied me. While a part of me knew that I could never get what I wanted from the women to who I was helplessly attracted, secretly I still hoped. I unconciously attempted to resolve my need for the attention I was denied during my parents' unconventional divorce. In order to do this I unintentionally sought out women who would be sure to reject and leave me and try to make them stay. Everytime a relationship failed I felt the original pain once again. When I met women who stayed however, I lost my attraction. That is to say, when it worked out it stopped being interesting.

Overcoming this has been a complicated task. Some years ago now, I became fed up with how the women in my life treated me and decided to step back and look at everything. Also, I realized that my fear of work descended from memories of my mother absorbed in her work so much she would still be at her desk when I came down for Saturday morning cartoons.

In the end I remember feeling throughout my teens that the divorce was not supposed to have an impact on me. A teacher once said to me the year of my parents initial split, when I came into class without my homework that I had better not use my parents divorce as an excuse. If I even thought of the divorce as putting me in an unfair position, then I would be using it as an excuse. This warning alone was so powerful it almost ruined my life.

In tracing so many of his present issues to his parents' failed marriage, Nat offers an unusually detailed and analytic interpretation of his life. He sees himself reacting against matriarchal influences; the women he dated were all versions of his mother: "I unintentionally sought out women who would be sure to reject and leave me and try to make them stay. Everytime a relationship failed, I felt the original pain once again." Nat felt that the only way he could avoid being hurt by his mother again was to sever completely his relationship with her, and for this reason he did not wish to reopen old wounds:

Dear Bertha,

I've been referring to you for some time with your first name since it gives me the emotional distance I need. To think of you as my mother would violate the life affirming peace I have enjoyed. Though it's been two years I am not writing a letter to you as a way of reconnecting. While we have not communicated at all I still need more distance. Some suggest forgiveness is the only way to move forward; I disagree. In order to forgive you I would have to open myself up to you, which I could never do again. Given our cyclical pattern of conflict, I believe it would be foolish to ever attempt to have a relationship with you again.

This is not a letter of closure for me; the damage has been done. How could I have closure? Everyday I recall a different way in which your psychotic behavior imprinted me with confusion. Having these two years off from your negating onslaught has given me a safe space in which to negotiate the effect you have had on my life. The way I interact with people on every level has been infected by my experience with you. True, I've become familiar with some of the darkest regions of the human psyche through you, and this will help me help other people, but where does it leave me?

I never thought knowing you could mess up my relationships with women. On the outside you're so independent, a great quality. Who wants a woman who doesn't care about herself? Yet it's not that simple. Being the first and most present woman in my life, by default I might add, I came to understand and have expectations of women through you. I learned to expect many things about women; that they would be strong, empowered, beautiful, intelligent. When I unconsciously sought those qualities along with a need for my partner to prioritize me by valuing work and success over emotional connectivity, I continued to be hurt by you, though you were not actually there. Women until recently have been a constant reminder of what you never made up for, and never will since I've now done it for you.

To think that the feminist beliefs you never shared with me would one day free me from your effect is so ironic. By the way, do you really consider yourself a feminist? See, I think you're just angry, and feminism gives you the easy excuses you need to say it's not your fault and that you're justified. I don't want to sidetrack you because that's not what this is about anymore; yet I can't resist since I have such relative clarity from which to speak now.

You resent the failure of two marriages; on one hand believing your marriages were not your fault because you were duped by the patriarchy. Don't fool your self, you bought into that ideal because you were promised benefits by it, and now your angry because you never got your end of the deal. Well nobody did, it wasn't just you. By the way, there is no instruction in feminism for married women to dismiss their children along with their husband, you misinterpreted.

On the other hand, you are constantly beating yourself for the mistakes you've made, and rather than truly learning from them by introspective reasoning, you've determined living in an imagined bubble, protecting yourself in a way that only hurts others. Does keeping my father's last name give you the illusion that you only screwed up once? This can't even be counted since it's continuous.

The lesson of your second marriage should have taught you that avoiding being dominated by dominating is not an answer. Do you honestly think you treated my father fairly? Did you ever give him the kind of chance or respect he afforded you? For all the times you badmouthed him to me, he never spoke negatively about you; god knows I tried to get him to. Your unending belief that you are never wrong and your never-ending manipulation of him into submission over the years is proof that you have no heart.

I hold you totally responsible for yourself. You're too capable a person to blame others as much as you do. Though, these days I know that talk like this is useless. You will never realize anything about yourself, you're so scared to really look in the mirror that you haven't in a long time. I'm not going to tell you that you need therapy; you could never be honest enough with another person about the way you really feel to help you. Rather, you concentrate on the way you would like people to think you feel.

About my cat, you are the only person that will ever really know what happened to her and it's taken me a while to come to terms with that. I didn't want to believe it when it happened, but when I overheard you telling people she was old and sick anyway and why it shouldn't matter, you made me want to vomit in your face. I don't want to hear another acceptance or denial of wrongdoing again, you supplied me with plenty of both.

Remember when I went to rehab weeks after smoking pot with you? On family day I had an opportunity to look you in the face and tell you what I really thought of you. Instead you intimidated me and I just sat there shaking and tearing. Well that Nat has become strong enough to face you, it's a shame it took so long, since now I would have nothing to gain by doing that I've evolved to a point where I don't need you anymore, in any way. I don't want your love or your hate; it's all the same. It used to be hard, looking at other people who are able to be friends with both their parents. That's okay

though because Dad makes up for you, you never realized how compassion-
ate and fun he really is. It's just really amazing how things have gotten
better for me all around since I decided to never see you again.

One thing you told me throughout our "relationship" was that you would
outlive me. I have a few things to say about that. If you died I would never
come to your funeral. If I died you would never be welcome at mine. In the
end it doesn't matter who outlives who, this is not a contest as much as you
might want it to be.

This letter was something new for me, it's been the only time in my life I've
ever been able to speak my mind to you. My thoughts are complete and I
don't need or want a response.

Nat Rosenberg

Dear Nat,

This is not a surprise from you Nat, nothing new. You've been blaming me
since I left your father. Your writing seems to have gotten better though, you're
more to the point, less confused. Still want to be a teacher? I'm sure you'll make
a great one.

You seemed very troubled in your letter, especially about stuff that happened
such a long time ago. At this point in my life I have come to peace about those
events. I have no regrets. Everything has brought me to this wonderful place where
I have a new and better life. I wouldn't recommend picking up and starting over for
anyone, but it really freed me. It's too bad moving out here didn't work for you.

I guess I realized when you weren't at your brother's wedding last summer that
you didn't want to see me. I used to hold grudges like that too. It would have been
nice to see you, still.

I'm surely sore about hearing that you have trouble with women. Didn't you
always? You were always friends with weirdos. It's nice to know that you're not
gay, though. At the same time, don't you think you focus on me a little too
much? This sounds like some superimposed Oedipus complex; has somebody
been teaching you Freud, that chauvinist cocaine addict? Maybe therapy is the
answer Nat, but not that kind. As for me I've been through therapy, it doesn't
really apply to me. I get everything I need from my meditation. Have you had
any dreams about me lately? While in Eckankar I've acquired the ability to visit
other people in their dreams and I've tried to reach you a couple of times but kept
getting a busy signal.

I now teach in a private school and it's great. I wish you luck in pursuit of
your education career. It's tough out there. Try not to let your success go to your
head though, you'll never find a woman in that state.

Though you said some really cold things about seeing me again I know the
day will come when we can talk again. I did the best I could raising you, much

better than most parents, and I never expected you to know how to appreciate
that. I know you think I was some horrible parent because I divorced your father,
but life isn't perfect. I had to think about me since no one else was. I'm truly sorry
you have to feel this way. I'll be waiting for the rest of my life to hear how much
my beloved son really loves his mother.

Bertha Rosenberg

Nat's anger toward his mother is so intense that he calls her by her first name, thus distancing himself from her. Unlike his three classmates, he makes no attempt to open a dialogue with his parent, nor does he seek reconciliation. As he notes, he believes that forgiving his mother would lead only to revictimization. His characterization of her is unrelentingly negative, and he holds her responsible for his unsuccessful relationships. His present happiness, he states, was made possible by the decision to banish her from his life. He ends his letter by observing that this is the first time he has been able to speak his mind to his mother, a victory that is ironically undercut by her unapologetic letter to him.

In the letter to his mother, Nat portrays himself as having moved on with his life, acquiring strength and independence; but in the fictional letter, his mother still sees him as a child, blaming her for everything. Whereas the son's tone in his letter to her is angry and indignant, her reply is sarcastic, as when she tells him that he will make a "great" teacher. There are several contradictions in her letter. She tells him, for example, that she doesn't hold grudges but then makes a cutting reference to her son's "weirdo" friends. Her most hurtful remark is when she calls into question his sexual orientation: "It's nice to know you're not gay." Perhaps her most disturbing sentence is the one that follows: "At the same time, don't you think you focus on me a little too much?" Since the sentence origi-nates from Nat, we cannot be sure whether he believes this may be true. The mother closes her letter with a statement tinged with irony: "I'll be waiting for the rest of my life to hear how much my beloved son really loves his mother."

Response Essays

How did Cory, Danielle, Lydia, Nat, and their classmates feel about the letter to and from a parent assignment? To find out, I asked them in the next week's assignment to respond to as many of the following questions as possible:

1. How did you feel when I gave the assignment? How did you feel when you were writing the assignment? How did you feel after completing the assignment?

2. Was it hard or easy to imagine your parent's response to your letter? Do you think you were successful in imagining how your parent might have responded? Are your parent's voice and point of view different from your own?

3. To what extent did this assignment help you to understand divorce's impact on children? If you have a conflicted relationship with the parent to whom you wrote, do you believe that this assignment might change that relationship in any way? Please explain.

4. Would you consider showing this assignment to the parent to whom you wrote? How do you think your parent would respond to your letters? To what extent did this assignment increase your understanding of your parent?

5. How did you feel when you heard your classmates' letters read in class? Please be as specific as possible. Did hearing your classmates' letters to and from their parents provide insights into your own relationship with your parents?

6. To what extent did this assignment increase your understanding of and empathy for your classmates? Please explain.

7. How would you describe the class's response to the essays that were read in class?

8. Did you find yourself becoming at risk as a result of writing or hearing your classmates' letters? (I define "at risk" as feeling anxious, panicky, depressed, or suicidal—feelings that were serious enough to warrant clinical attention.) If you did experience these feelings, are they continuing?

9. Were you satisfied with my written comments on this assignment?

10. Was this a valuable assignment for you? Explain. Would this be a good assignment to give to a future expository writing class? Would you suggest any changes in the assignment?

Cory: "Another Gut-Wrenching Assignment"

Cory began his response essay by noting that he was not initially excited by the topic. "It was another gut-wrenching assignment that I knew would awaken powerful feelings." It was not difficult for him to write on the topic: the words seemed to pour out of him. "I felt like a transcriber who was mindlessly recording pre-determined ideas. Both my words to my parents and their response flowed effortlessly. I was a muse." He felt relieved when he finished the assignment, but it was not therapeutic relief. "I did not experience any form of healing. I knew that my parents would never see my letter. I would never show them it and the idea of them seeing it worried me. If I did show them it, I don't think that their marriage would be magically remedied. I feel that the only thing that the letter would do is bring them a great deal of pain. They would feel guilty if they knew the way I felt. They would blame each other as well as themselves for hurting me." Cory considered showing his brother and sister the letters but decided against doing so, believing that they would neither understand nor agree with his feelings for his parents. "My brother would look at me and say, 'Where did you come up with this shit? Mom and Dad love each other and I think they did a pretty good damn good job with us. It's too bad you don't think so.' I see my sister reading the letter and crying, not wanting to talk about it."

Cory was initially interested in his classmates' letters, but he was soon exhausted by them. "Most of the letters were not uplifting. I did not want to hear students go on about neglect, infidelity, alcohol abuse, and hurtful parenting any longer. It made me feel sad. It made me not want to be there." One of his fears, he said, was that "if so many students suffered such great pain from their own parents, then what does this say about the world?" He began to wonder whether he or any of his classmates would have a happy marriage. "One day I will be an unsuspecting newlywed. How will I be any less naive than all the other newlyweds that ultimately destructed? When the last essays were read I stopped reading along and started watching the class as they read. I remember looking at the different faces and thinking, 'I wonder if she will one day get divorced. I wonder if he will one day cheat on his loving wife.' It's a sad way to think."

Despite these misgivings, Cory concluded that the assignment was valuable and recommended it for future classes. "I think that the assignment helps students identify their own feelings. Most importantly it created a safe and open forum for students to discuss their past. Although it upset me at times, I think the assignment helped the class develop a sense of camaraderie. The assignment painted the world as a dangerous and painful place. More importantly, it let me know that I'm not in *this place* alone."

Danielle: "A Weight Lifted from My Shoulders"

Danielle wrote a three-page single-spaced response essay in which she discussed in abundant detail her feelings about the assignment. She was apprehensive about the topic because she knew that she would direct her letter to her father. How could she write about her father's alcohol addiction without betraying her family? "As I wrote about my father forgetting to pay the electric bill or falling apart during my mother's illness I was mortified. These are things that my friends didn't even know. Although I felt embarresed while writing this, it was comingled with relief. I have spent the majority of my life supressing what I had written down. I never told my friends that my father is an alcoholic. I never let on that as a result, we were broke. I spent so long trying to hide this information from myself and others that I was exhausted. When I reread my letter, it was as if I had a weight lifted from my shoulders."

Danielle attempted to imagine how her father would respond to her letter, but the question proved daunting. "I tried very hard to imagine how my father would respond to my harsh words. I made several attempts to capture his voice, his point of view. Instead I could only hear my mother's words as I had so many times before, trying to explain that man who had proven to be a mystery to me." And so she decided instead to re-create her mother's voice and point of view. "I think she was fair in her response about my father and my letter. I also believe that her point of view coincides with mine. I know she recognizes my fathers illness but she also understand it's origins. I also know that she feels powerless in the face of his addiction." Danielle said that she couldn't show the letter to her father because it would only hurt him. "My father would read it and then praise the technical aspects of it. However, I would be able to detect the pain in his face as a result of its content. My father would never say anything to me, but I would overhear him late at night talking to my mother. 'Does she hate me? I didn't mean to mess up their lives. I didn't mean to hurt anyone.' He would ignore my pleas of asking him to stop drinking. He would instead, focus on his abandoning me when my mother became ill. I didn't write this with the intention to assault my father for his wrongs."

Danielle felt that her words would not be able to change her father's life, but they were beginning to change her own. "I'm discovering more and more that I wrote this [letter] for myself. Because I had spent such a large part of my life trying to subdue these memories and feelings, I was in someway injuring myself and the relationships in my life. I could never be honest with anyone about my father, not even myself. When I reread my work, I discovered that these feelings and emotions had to come out. They were always inside, but this is the first time I have ever had a vehicle for them."

Danielle found herself "transfixed" by many of her classmates' essays that were read aloud, and she inferred from this that she didn't have to be ashamed of her own family situation. "For myself, I have been influenced by the courage of my fellow classmates. Last semester I could not have conceived that I would write about personal topics let alone have somebody else read or listen to them. Although I have not read aloud anything of a personal nature, I have allowed you to read mine anonymously. For me, that is a tremendous step. What I have learned about each of my classmates, aside from their courage, is that all people have experiences that culminate in the person they eventually become. It is wonderful to understand that our fears and behaviors originate from our experiences and that is what their stories have taught me." Danielle added that she felt anxious only when she sensed that a classmate was having difficulty reading an essay aloud. "This sounds terribly sentimental, but I have to suppress the urge to run over to the discomforted reader and hold their hand. I will also admit to trembling at certain descriptions of their childhoods. There have been a number of times when it took everything in my power not to openly weep. I don't define myself at 'risk' but I could definitely see the potential for it when I hear these accounts."

"I am being one hundred percent honest," Danielle concluded, "when I say that this has been the most valuable assignment I have ever had. I have written throughout this paper that I have spent the majority of my life trying to suppress my fathers illness with alcohol. For the first time in my life, I feel as if a weight has been lifted from my shoulders. I am not ashamed of my experiences as a result of writing the paper. The assignment was a cathartic one that I recommend you use in future courses. I wouldn't recommend any alterations in the assignment."

Lydia: "It Helped Me to Understand the Hurt I've Felt"

Lydia was excited when she received the assignment but soon discovered that she underestimated its difficulty. "I found that because my feelings are so conflicted towards my mother it was difficult to really tell her how I feel because most of the time I'm not sure." She was proud of herself after completing the assignment because she conveyed exactly how she felt. "Although I will never send this letter it helped me to understand the hurt I've felt. Maybe that's the first step to getting over it." She believed that no significant change in the relationship would occur until she had children herself and could then see her mother's point of view. "Maybe then I still won't agree with it but I can understand it."

Lydia's greatest anxiety over the assignment was that her mother would accidentally discover it. "I have contemplated burning this letter for fear that my mother will someday find it. I can't even begin to explain how much she'd hate me for it, especially since I wrote it for a class and shared it with people. My mother believes that sharing family business with other people is close to a mortal sin. She'd probably be humiliated and horrified at the way I've portrayed her. I can't say that I understand *her* more as a result of the assignment. I merely learned that I know her better than I thought. When I was reading her letter aloud in class it felt as if she had really written it to me." After the semester ended, Lydia and I discussed her fear that one day her mother might come across her class writings. She decided to delete her writings from her word processor, and we took special precautions to disguise her identity.

Like many students, Lydia felt a simultaneous need both to reveal and conceal a secret, in this case, anger toward her mother; the desire to express her feelings clashed with the need to repress the truth. The stronger the conflict, the more ambivalent the self-disclosure. Sometimes this conflict results in students asking me to read anonymously an essay and then missing the class during which I read it; other times students do not give me permission to read an essay aloud. These secrets range from angry feelings toward a relative or friend to guilt or shame arising from an eating disorder, sexual abuse, or a suicide attempt. Students may fear that disclosing a secret will hurt themselves or another person; it is not uncommon for them to fear that my feelings toward them will change as a result of a self-disclosure. This rarely happens, largely because I am no longer surprised by my students' disclosures. The Roman poet Terence's observation—"homo sum, humani nihil a me alienum puto": I am human, so nothing that is human is foreign to me—is relevant here; moreover, students are discreet about their disclosures. They have rarely disclosed committing crimes, apart from driving under the influence of alcohol or shoplifting, which they now regret.

People conceal and reveal secrets for many reasons, as Sissela Bok intimates in *Secrets*; "the question whether to leave evil secrets alone or try to defeat them by draining them of their destructive power recurs in many therapeutic and investigating practices" (4). I have never betrayed a disclosure entrusted to me by a student, though like all educators, I would be legally compelled to notify the appropriate authorities if a student expressed the intention to harm another person or him- or herself. The self-disclosing classroom reveals not so much that "all our secrets are the same," but rather that we all have secrets, many of which resemble other people's secrets, and that the disclosure of these secrets is a way to confront our worst fears and, in the process, exorcise them.

Reading the letters aloud in class was painful for Lydia. "I wanted to cry almost the whole time, especially when I was reading my mother's response. I was afraid everyone was going to feel bad for me, and I got nervous that maybe I had been unfair to my mother in my portrayal of her. Some of the incidents I spoke of, like my mom having an affair and my relationship with men were things that I don't often speak about to people other than my close friends. I was afraid of being judged but even more afraid they would judge my mom. It's funny how protective I am of a woman I spend so much time bashing." Lydia felt that her fears of being judged were unfounded because her classmates were gentle in their comments. She also believed that my written comments on her assignment were appropriate. "You made some great observations about places where more detail might have been effective and at the same time acknowledged the strength of the material and your personal response to it. It was fulfilling to know that you walked away from it feeling the way I had intended."

As with Danielle, the major value of the assignment for Lydia was that it helped her to realize she was not the only person in the class with conflicted feelings toward a parent. "Hearing the classes responses first made me realize that I'm not the only one that has mixed feelings towards my parents and feels that they could've done a better job. But even more importantly I learned that there are good parents out there and there are marriages that work. This gives me hope. Even if I can't find the positive examples I long for in my own family, I may be able to find them in someone else's." Lydia felt that the assignment was perhaps most valuable for those who, like herself, have stormy relationships with a parent. "However, I guess it is also effective for those that have a positive relationship with one of their parents because it gives them a chance to say all the wonderful things a parent has done when most often nothing would be said."

Nat: "An Act of Closure or Even Healing"

Nat "gasped" the moment he read the assignment. "It asked me to do something I had not done in over two years, talk to my mother. To make this even more complicated I was asked to respond in her voice, which would require me to actively recall my experiences with her. It's just that I remember so much of my maddingly frustrating years with her multiple personalities already." Nat soon realized, however, that the assignment would allow him to convey his feelings toward her in a more ordered way than he had done before. He was intrigued by the challenge to imagine his mother's voice. "Her lack of impulse control in her own speech created a situation where I never knew what she was going to say next or how she was going to feel. I tried to create a response letter that would show an attempt at manipulation through speech amidst a variety of disorganizations of time, place, and emotion."

Nat did not believe that the assignment could change his relationship with his mother, but he felt that it increased his understanding of her. "Being able to write or say these thoughts in my head, and also to a certain extent reading it to other people who listen without judging, can be an act of closure or even healing." He regretted that his mother was so unapproachable that he could never send the letter or speak to her about its contents. He identified closely with Danielle, whose essay I had read aloud anonymously. "In class a letter about a father who was an alcoholic and never really there for anyone in the family, struck me for some reason. Though the story seemed little like mine it did talk about a parent who was unreachable in a way that is necessary for any child. The kind of regret about that experience, expressed in the letter, was much like my own. Even through all the anger I feel towards my mother, who is really a horrible person in so many ways, I wish that she could have heard me the way I needed."

Unhappy Families *Are* Alike

Cory, Danielle, Lydia, and Nat all wrote about unhappy families, but contrary to Tolstoy's observation, their stories reveal several commonalities. All felt estranged from one or both parents and described serious communication problems in their families. They felt implicated in their parents' unhappy marriages and carried emotional scars that they attributed to their parents' marital wounds. They wanted their parents to take responsibility for their own lives rather than blame their spouses or children. They feared that the "sins" of their fathers or mothers would intergenerationally haunt them in the future. They resented the burden placed upon them at an early age of defending one parent against the other. None of them wanted to feel anger or resentment, but they couldn't wish these feelings away. All realized that their letters would hurt one or both of their parents; Danielle and Lydia felt disloyal in sharing their stories with classmates. They believed that writing helped them clarify their complex and ambivalent ties with their parents, and, except for Nat, they sought a closer relationship with the parent to whom he or she wrote.

The four students wrote letters that seemed, to a stranger, to capture their parents' point of view. Indeed, the parents' letters appear so authentic that it is easy to forget they are fictional. The parents' letters offer perspectives that differ from their children's and that reveal intergenerational disagreements. The parents seem older but not necessarily wiser than their children, and like their sons and daughters, they are still searching for happiness, with or without partners. Life has not turned out as they expected, and they are saddened by the knowledge that their children are unhappy. They want their children to know that they have always loved them and that they have raised them as best they could, but they also know that their love has not always seemed apparent or sufficient to their children. Cory's and Danielle's mothers apologize to their children; Lydia's and Nat's mothers emphatically do *not* apologize. Is it significant that all four students imagine their *mothers'* responses? Why are the fathers silent?

Four students is far too small a sample from which to draw gender implications. Nevertheless, it's interesting that most of the students in the class chose to imagine their mothers' points of view, even when they wrote to their fathers or to both parents. Is it because the students believed that their mothers are the central figure of their families and thus best able to speak for both parents? If so, then the letters reinforce the observations made by Carol Gilligan in *In a Different Voice* and Nancy Chodorow in *The Reproduction of Mothering* that children feel stronger bonds to their mother than to their father, a conclusion that is consistent with attachment theory research. Nat alone does not wish to be reconciled with his mother, yet his letter imagining her point of view implies the difficulty of freeing himself from her influence.

Classmates' Reactions

Cory, Danielle, Lydia, and Nat were not alone in concluding that the two assignments were helpful. Nearly all of their classmates felt the same way. Those who wrote about turbulent parent-child relationships believed that they were able to express important issues that needed to be discussed even if they never showed their letters to their parents. Cory's metaphor of "opening up"—which is also the title of James Pennebaker's influential book about self-disclosure—can be seen in many of his classmates' response essays. Writing is not a substitute for speaking, but sometimes it can be a more effective form of communication, enabling candid conversations to take place in the future, as the following two students observe:

When you first gave the assignment to write a letter to a parent I did not like the idea. I have never written a letter to either of my parents. I usually talked to them face to face or on the phone. But, when I was writing the letter, I found it easier to speak what was on my mind. I started to open up more than I would have if they had been right in front of me. After I had finished writing the assignment, a small weight had been lifted off my shoulders. Even though I had not really talked to my father, I felt like I had.

When I first received the assignment I was thrilled. The idea of expressing emotions toward my father in a controlled atmosphere made me feel comfortable. The anger and frustration I have for him runs much deeper than any words could describe but I felt the experience would be rewarding to me nonetheless. I was also intrigued by the idea of using his voice in a response essay. I feel I know his personality and I presumed that hearing his voice through my own would help me to come to terms with my own insecurities and pains. So, on a Friday afternoon I began writing this piece with overwhelming expectations of my emotions and myself.

I was wrong. I must have had at least ten sessions where I stood at a blank computer screen struggling with my emotions, hoping to pull them from the remotest parts of my unconscious. I thought I knew the words to express my feelings of abandonment and sorrow, but I only got broken fragments of a once angry child. I realized, as I fought to extract hidden memories, that I had lost so much time trying to forget the circumstances of my childhood and blanket the consequences with less painful ones.

I felt a sigh of relieve after completing the assignment. I didn't feel I divulged enough information but what I expressed was heart felt and honest. That's all I wanted to do. I have a long way to go with my father and myself and I think these letters illustrated a faithful attempt on my part to come to terms with them both.

About a third of the students said that they had positive relationships with both parents, and they discovered, sometimes to their surprise, that they had more to say about—and to—their parents than they had first thought. These essays were important to hear, for they suggested that happy marriages and happy families were possible. Contrary to Tolstoy's assertion, not all of the students from happy families were "alike," as the following story demonstrates:

Audrey: "If You and Dad Did Not Adopt Me Where Would I Be?"

Dear Mom,

Remember when I told you about the writing class that I'm taking up at school? Well, my teacher has asked us to write a letter to one or both of our parents. In this letter I have to talk about my feelings about your marriage and the way you and dad raised me. Also, I want to tell you about a book that my professor wrote called Diaries to an English Professor. *In his book, Professor Berman writes about such topics as divorce, eating disorders, suicide, and sex. For our last assignment we had to read the chapter on divorce.*

The first chapter is called "Sins of the Fathers" and is extremely touching and insightful. You and dad have never had a divorce so I obviously don't know what it feels like to go through one. In this chapter I read seven students diary entries about how they viewed their parents divorce. The diaries were emotional and painfully honest. I wrote about how reading this chapter really opened my eyes to divorce. I never truly understood how divorce affects children; I still don't believe I ever will. Other students in my class wrote about their experiences with divorce. A majority of my peers come from single parent homes. While I was listening to stories about wicked stepmothers and absentee fathers it made me think about and appreciate what you and dad have.

Although we never really talk about being me being adopted, I just want you to know that I would not change my life for any other. I love you and dad. I look back at my childhood and cannot think of one bad thing. I was, and am, exceptionally blessed to have you as parents. I want you to know that when I first read the syllabus for this class I thought, "What am I going to write about? My parents are happily married, I've never been raped, I do not have an eating disorder, and I have never attempted suicide." These were my initial thoughts about writing in this class. Now I realize that even though none of the horrible events I mentioned have happened in my life, I can still write about my experiences or the lack thereof. In earlier essays I have written about my adoption. I think being adopted is the biggest and most significant detail of my life. If you and dad did not adopt me where would I be? Would I have a good life? Do you think I would be in college? Would I get along with my parents? Would I have sisters or brothers? These are some questions that used to tug at my mind. I believe that they are better left unknown. I truly am happy with my life as it is. I have never wanted for anything. You and dad have been the most remarkable parents. I admire the way you brought me up without any experience or help. I love the way you love each other. I have never felt the threat of divorce and I am grateful.

As you know I am taking an Educational Psychology course. In this class we talk a lot about raising children. For six hours a day and five days a week a teacher has to act like a parent. I have learned that there is so much pressure in parenting. Children need special amounts of scolding, playing, exploring, and growing. The only aspect of childhood that has no limit is love. A child needs to be loved. He or she requires a sense of security. I have always felt loved. You and dad have always made sure I was happy and secure. I am so impressed with the job that you have done in raising me. If you would have done one simple part wrong in bringing me up I might be a totally different person. If you had told me I was bad too often I might have a serious problem of thinking that I am a bad person. A child's mind is par-

ticularly impressionable; I have to say that I am grateful to you and dad for putting the right ideas and behaviors into mine.

Love always,
Audrey

Dear Audrey,

Of course we remember you telling us about your class. We always love to hear about school. I know you like this writing class a lot and it sounds like the assignments are interesting. The book your teacher wrote sounds a little depressing. I am glad that you feel appreciative of your father and I. We are thankful that you turned out the way you are too. We are so proud that you are in college. I always tell my friends that you go away to school in Albany. We constantly brag about your grades, even if they are not all A's. You already know how your father and I would have loved to have ten kids. Since its only you, we have to smother you with love and pride. I know we never talk about you being adopted, but there are good reasons. I know that you are not my flesh and blood, but you are my daughter. I have never thought of you in any other way. I'm sorry that you have so many unanswered questions. If I knew the answers I would tell you. I am so happy you wrote me this letter. You are a great writer and the letter was beautiful.

Raising a child is a trying and difficult task. Your father and I were scared at first. We have never had such a huge responsibility. There were many details about bringing up a child that I didn't know. Grandma and my friends helped out a great deal. Uncle Morty was always there for you, that's why I bother you so much to call him. He taught you how to ride a bike and how to swim. Your uncle and I toilet trained you; daddy had no clue what to do. I know what you mean when you say teachers have to act like parents. You know I've been teaching for twenty-five years and your dad for thirty. We think of the students as our "kids." Even in high school you have to tell them to sit down, stop talking, etc.

Your father and I tried to give you as much love as humanly possible. We strive to give you good morals and values. You are our only child and we thank God everyday for giving you to us.

Love,
Mom

Audrey captures in the fictional letter the crucial importance of parents' affirming love for their children—an affirmation that her daughter appreciates. Mother and daughter mirror each other's love. Later in the semester Audrey read aloud another essay to the class, on the topic "the most hurtful comment that you have made to another person." The essay, entitled "Why I Called the New York Times," allowed her to honor her mother both as a teacher and a parent:

A couple of days ago my mom called me with great news. Last year the New York Times *had an essay-writing contest. The subject was "who inspires you?"*

A student wrote her essay about my mom and won. My mom received a letter inviting her to a luncheon award reception.

I was so proud of my mom when she told me this. I always knew she was a great teacher. Finally someone was giving her the recognition she deserved. My mom went into school and was congratulated by all her colleagues. She felt a surge of pride and happiness. Yesterday, a man from the New York Times called my mom. His name is Norman. Norman told my mother that they had made a mistake and that she was not, after all, going to receive the award. When I tell you that my mom was crushed by this phone call, I literally mean flattened. She called me up hysterical crying. She didn't know how she could go back into school and tell her friends and fellow teachers that this was a mistake. I tried to calm her down and tell her that she didn't need the award. I told her how everyone already knows what a great teacher she is.

After hanging up with my mother I picked the phone back up and called information. "Can I please have the number for the New York Times," I asked the operator. I called this man named Norman. I told him how heart broken and embarrassed my mother was. I told him how when my mother goes food shopping she buys extra drinks and bags of chips and cookies for "her kids." I am an only child. "Her kids" are her students. I told Mr. Norman about dropping my mom off early at her school before going to mine so she could tutor students before classes began. I also told him that she would take the bus home those days because she would stay after school to help kids who couldn't make it in the morning. My mom is receiving the award and attending the luncheon on April 22.

When I was much younger I said something to my mom that I have regretted my whole life. As you know I am adopted. My mother and I were fighting and I said, "you can't tell me what to do, you're not my real mom." That was the most hurtful comment I believe I have ever made to anyone. I tried to apologize afterwards, but my mom was too upset and wouldn't listen to me. I have never forgotten what I said, and my mother or myself never mentioned it again. When you asked us to write about this topic I knew I would talk about this situation. I had to rewrite the paper and include the New York Times award. You ask, "What would you now like to write to that person?" I don't wish to write a letter to my mom apologizing for my comment all those years ago. When I called her and told her that she was receiving the award and going to the luncheon I felt as if I did my duty as her daughter. She said that what I did was "the sweetest thing anyone has ever done" for her. I told her how proud I am to call her "mom." I don't think I have ever felt so good or needed. I am proud of myself for standing up for my mom. I love her and want her to be happy. Those are the only reasons I had to call the New York Times.

Audrey's essay is significant for several reasons. She demonstrates the importance of affirmation for teachers and parents alike, and the consequences of disaffirmation. She implies that her mother has made a difference in her students' and daughter's lives—teaching and parenting are both nurturing acts. In writing about this story, Audrey reveals the most hurtful comment she has made to another person, a comment that she had *not* disclosed in the earlier, idealized essay about her parents, presumably because she was too ashamed to repeat it. In the earlier essay she stated that "I look back at my childhood and cannot think of one bad thing"; now, however, she qualifies that observation by revealing to her classmates and teacher a remark she has regretted her entire life. Why does she express the secret now rather than earlier? Perhaps because now she trusts the class to empathize with her feelings. Both the disclosure and the telephone call to the *New York Times* may be viewed as acts of reparation leading to self-forgiveness.

Empathic Understanding

Most of the students believed that the two assignments on the family increased their empathic understanding of the painful consequences of divorce. A few stated that they had already shown their letters to one or both of their parents; others were not sure they would ever feel comfortable enough to do so. Many were uncertain whether their relationships with their parents would improve: they were not, as a group, sanguine about this possibility. Nor did they feel that *any* writing assignment could improve a relationship that had been conflicted for years. There was, however, striking agreement that their empathy toward each other had dramatically increased as a result of hearing essays read aloud in class. Indeed, *every* student remarked upon this. They evaluated their family situations in terms of other students' experiences, and the result was a deeper appreciation of their classmates' struggles. Witness, for example, the following comment from a student who wrote about her "Partridge Family":

This assignment created an extreme amount of empathy for my classmates. When I first read "Sins of the Fathers" I was selfish. My reaction to that chapter was naive and inconsiderate. I felt as though there were a group of students feeling sorry for themselves while the rest of the world continued to move around them in an orderly fashion. Maybe it was because those were characters in a book, not real people to me. Or maybe I was simply being insensitive. As the stories unraveled in class about the lives of people I see on a daily basis, I realized the immaturity of my reaction. Divorce is a painful situation. I had no idea how it affected those that were indirectly involved as well as those who are captured in it's grasp. After sitting through class, and hearing painful story after painful story I began to realize that these students aren't feeling sorry for themselves. They are finally given the opportunity to speak openly about the secret that they haven't had the chance to openly discuss amongst their peers. Most of us, as students, carry on with our high speed lives and rarely take the time to really sit and think about the lives and tribulations of those around us. This was their time to take a step back and look at similar people's lives that have felt the pain that they feel. I think it was an excellent assignment for those students, as well as for those of us who have never had the time to listen. My heart goes out to those students that fight this battle every day. My support goes out to their strength.

The students learned about their classmates' lives and found themselves questioning the easy advice they had dispensed in the past. "I definitely felt more empathic about the feelings of others. Prior to this class, or college in general, I would tell people to get over their problems and deal with the cards life has dealt. People would come to me with problems and I would always give great advice, but deep down I wished they would just put it to the side and ride an excuse. I still feel sometimes people put the blame on others so they wont have to deal with the guilt of failure, but I have learned that events affect others more than I knew. I have always been strong with my problems and faced them and overcame them as they came along, but I see that not everyone can do that. Sometimes not even me." Students who knew classmates from a prior course began to see them in a new light. "After hearing Cory's letter I felt sad. The lack of communication between him and his parents brought back memories when I could not share my thoughts and problems with my parents. His letter moved me in a way that the other letters did not. I have been in other classes with Cory before and did not know a single aspect about his life."

One person described how he felt "good" when he heard his classmates' letters but then immediately qualified the word so that no would accuse him of schadenfreude, pleasure in another's pain. "I felt good when I heard my classmates' letters read aloud. Let me clarify. I say I felt good because it helped me put that fifty-one percent divorce rate into perspective. In a class of nineteen students, the overwhelming majority could either relate to my situation, were in my situation, or unfortunately, were in an even worse situation than my own. As feelings of empathy rushed through me, so did feelings of relief." Only one student did not feel strong empathy, but his response seemed to be limited to those letters describing happy families. "It's hard to say how hearing other people's letters made me feel about them. I found myself growing annoyed with all the Beaver Cleaver thank-you-for-being-so-wonderful letters. I suppose that's a case of feeling more envy than empathy. On another level, this assignment has taken yet another step in showing me that I am not the only one that deals with a complex and difficult family life."

Did students find themselves at risk? This is always a crucial question because teachers must know when to recommend a student to the university counseling center. Three people indicated that they were becoming anxious or fearful, though not to the extent that they considered counseling. One man feared that he would cry in front of his classmates while reading his essay. "I honestly did find myself at risk when I was revising my paper. I felt as if some type of emotion would overcome me. Since a young child I was taught not to cry in front of others because it shows weakness. I thought that reading my paper aloud would evoke very strong sentiments that I would not be able to control. None of those feelings would warrant medical attention, but for me to write about family is especially hard, since I care for them so deeply." Another man feared succumbing to dark emotions associated with his family. "I felt I was at risk of experiencing seriously bad emotions since the day this project was assigned, which is why I put it off for so long. I chose the road of less resistance in writing about my mom instead of my dad, but I still had to do battle with some pretty dark feelings during the creative process. I feel much better now, although it will be a while before I tap into those emotions again." And a woman felt herself becoming anxious at the thought of reading her essay aloud. "I felt myself at risk in writing this letter. Although there is a different level of respect in this class than in any other class here, I was too anxious to read my essay. I wasn't depressed about it, but I did consider the issue for quite a while." She decided that she did not want the essay read aloud, even anonymously.

"Do You Regard Me as a Therapist Rather Than as an English Teacher?"

Nearly all the students suggested, either explicitly or implicitly, that the assignment was therapeutic. (Cory was one of the few exceptions.) They may have been saddened by their classmates' stories—recall Audrey's "mother's" observation that "the book your teacher wrote sounds a little depressing"—but there were enough joyful essays to provide a balanced perspective. Regardless of whether they intended to show the letters to their parents, they felt relief by writing about their conflicted feelings. Yet if they found the assignment therapeutic, does that imply that they regarded their teacher as a therapist and the class as a therapy session? I felt that the question was important enough to ask them to explore it in the following in-class exercise, to which they responded anonymously:

> Opponents of personal writing argue that sooner or later teachers and students will find themselves in a dangerous situation: students will come to view their teachers as therapists, and teachers will find themselves dispensing clinical advice for which they are not trained. There are at least two possible adverse results, opponents argue: the first is that students will become psychologically dependent upon their writing teachers; the second is that students will become at risk as a result of their self-disclosures and forced to go into therapy to undo the damage that has been done by their writing teachers. Please spend a few minutes responding to these criticisms of personal writing. Do you feel that professional boundaries have been transgressed in this course? Do you regard me as a therapist rather than as an English professor? Have I been responding to you, either during class or in my comments on your writings, as a therapist? Do you feel vulnerable as a result of the course?

The following responses are representative:

The day I had my conference with you, I was waiting outside your office while you were speaking to another student. The student blurted out suddenly, "Are you a therapist?" At first I laughed at her "silly" comment and responded to myself, "of course not, he's just an English professor!" But then I gave it a little more thought. We do write about very personal issues in our class. I do not feel, however, that this class is a therapy session. We write the assignment, make copies, read it to the class, and analyze the grammatical, stylistic, and punctual errors. We do not suggest what the author of the essay should or should not think about the issue, nor do we give advice on how to help the author through it. I feel very confident and comfortable about reading my writings in class, and the feedback on my technicalities and style is great! I do not depend on you or the class to be my therapists.

I do not feel that any professional boundaries have been crossed in this course. I see you as my English teacher and someone I trust. None of the comments you have given me sound like a therapist. All your feedback has been based on how I wrote the assignment not what I wrote. I don't feel vulnerable as a result of this course. Whatever I revealed, I did because I wanted to. You've always responded empathetically to my writing but have never tried to counsel me. No one is forced to open up. Everyone has control over what they reveal.

This course, I feel, is what lies between two extremes. One is a straightforward English class, and the other is group therapy. Writing about personal issues such as divorce and suicide can be very painful, and many students may not be stable enough to handle those feelings once they surface in these writing assignments. I recall, however, you giving the class a "disclaimer" during the first week. Each person knew that he or she would be writing about issues which may bring up some emotional conflicts. To say that we as students will start relying on you as a therapist seems bizarre to me, because we are all at an age where it seems we have been able to place our feelings in certain places with certain people. Yes, you do read about many personal issues we have, and once read it is privileged knowledge, but you do not play the role of the therapist. If you felt you had to, I'm sure you would step in and help a student (if you felt they were in trouble) but that is what any professor should do. Shouldn't they? When stripped down, this is a writing class, and although the class may overstep these boundaries at times, I feel we are at a comfortable place in this classroom.

I feel you are a therapist, but not in the conventional way. You let us express ourselves and analyze ourselves, but we also come to our own conclusions. All you do is facilitate. I also do not feel vulnerable (except for one assignment). Boundaries haven't been crossed. However, I know there has to be a catch to us writing so many personal essays. I just wish I knew what it was.

I return shortly to the question whether there was a "catch" to the personal writing assignments, as well as to the one time that boundaries were broken, but there was, as several students remarked, a paradox: the course was not a therapy session but was nevertheless therapeutic. It is the same paradox that Hans Strupp and Suzanne Hadley report in their 1979 study, as cited by Andrew Solomon: "Patients undergoing psychotherapy with college professors showed, on average, quantitatively as much improvement as patients treated by experienced professional psychotherapists" (451–52). Curious to see how my students would elaborate on this paradox, I gave them another anonymous in-class exercise a week later:

> Several of you suggested that our writing class is not a therapy session but is nevertheless therapeutic. This distinction might be difficult for nonmembers of the class to understand. Please elaborate on the ways in which you find the class therapeutic. Which assignments have been the most therapeutic for you—and why? What prevents the course from becoming a "therapy session"?

Several conclusions can be drawn from these students' responses. First, writing is therapeutic when it allows the writer to express feelings and thoughts that are seldom verbalized. Nearly all the students imply that writing is a way to release pent up feelings, to "vent," to bring hidden material to the surface, where it can be examined and evaluated. No one feared, in psychoanalytic terms, the "return of the repressed": the process of self-analysis was slow, deliberate, and controlled, the antithesis of an explosive unleashing of energy. Second, the empathic classroom is, as one person suggests, a "safety net for fragile feelings." Students do not fear that their feelings will be invalidated, threatened, or critiqued by their classmates or teacher. They agree that focusing attention on writing helps them to avoid the problems that may arise when their feelings or perceptions are challenged. "We do not discuss our feelings, we merely state them." Third, freedom from worrying about a classmate's or teacher's judgment allows writers to reach their own judgment about the contents of an essay. "We are our own judges of our actions. You just make sure we write them correctly." Freedom from criticism and judgment encourages self-criticism and self-judgment, respectively. Fourth, students develop an empathic connection when hearing their classmates' essays, a connection that helps to counter the fear that others will not be able to understand their sadness, loneliness, shame, or grief. This empathic connection, arising from the students' attachment to their teacher and classmates, makes possible the "connected knowledge" formulated by the Wellesley College Stone Center theorists: gaining access to other people's knowledge. "None of us are alone in our readings, at one point or another," one student remarks, a statement that is similar to a classmate's observation: "Hearing my classmates' essays gave me comfort. I learned that I am not the only one who has had a rocky relationship with my parents, and I also learned it is possible to have a loving relationship with them." Finally, the knowledge that no one in the class will play the role of therapist allows each person to perform this role for himself or herself. The only student who felt the class was not therapeutic nevertheless concludes that "some people may feel better because of being given the chance to express personal feelings, but if that's the case, maybe they're their own therapists"—a conclusion similar to a classmates's statement that "if anything, we are our own therapists."

As the students suggest, classroom writing can be therapeutic without the teacher playing the role of therapist. This is an important conclusion because much of the opposition to personal writing is based on the fear that the teacher will be tempted to play the role of therapist, minister, or healer—a role for which the teacher is not trained. Students neither expect nor desire their teacher to transgress roles or boundaries; indeed, they believe that they have the resources to confront and resolve their own conflicts without relying upon others' prescriptions or proscriptions. What they desire is a safe, empathic classroom in which they can express their thoughts and feelings without fear of criticism or attack.

For all of the differences between therapy and teaching, there are also similarities, including, as Phillip Lopate suggests, the "cultivation of observation and detachment, the attention to language and its subtexts, the necessity for empathy" (80). Lopate adds that psychotherapy was important not only to his writing but also to his teaching:

> In my case, I knew I lacked the *Sitzfleisch* [patience] to sit hour after hour listening to other people's problems. But I often wonder whether I would have made a good therapist. What I did become was a teacher. Even more than helping me with my writing, psychotherapy gave me important tools as a pedagogue. I learned, for instance, that the best thing to do in conference with a student was simply to listen and keep my mouth shut, offering an empathetic grunt. I also learned to monitor my gut responses to a student, checking for the unearned fondness or disgust triggered by physical appearance, tone of voice, or resemblance to someone I knew. Finally, I learned to discount student crushes on me as an inevitable transference. (80–81)

Lopate's comments on teaching suggest an intersubjective model of education in which teachers listen without offering advice or judgment and remain empathically attuned to their students. The teacher's role in this process is not passive but active: teachers observe their reactions to students' writings and guard against the projection or incorporation of inappropriate feelings. Empathy is the key element to this process, and the teacher's greatest challenge is to allow students to disclose painful or shameful experiences without becoming traumatized in the process. Over time, as students disclose their stories and hear their classmates' experiences, an empathic bond develops, allowing students to achieve an understanding of and connection with their classmates that would not otherwise develop.

But an intersubjective model of education implies more than teachers remaining empathically attuned to their students. Intersubjectivity suggests that teachers and students influence each other and that they cocreate and negotiate meaning, whether it is the meaning of a poem, a student's essay, or a teacher's interpretation. Intersubjectivity also implies that one person's subjectivity influences the other person's subjectivity in a dyadic relationship. A branch of phenomenology, intersubjectivity has been embraced by relationally oriented psychoanalysts, who argue that the classical model of the autonomous, objective, detached analyst remains a harmful myth. As Stephen Mitchell observes in *Influence and Autonomy in Psychoanalysis*, "[T]he analyst's point of view, even if arrived at through rational, self- reflective observation, cannot be separated from his forms of participation. Observation is never neutral. Observation is always contextual, based on assumptions, values, constructions of experience" (87). In *Relationality* Mitchell asserts that an "individual human mind is an oxymoron: subjectivity always develops in the context of intersubjectivity; we continually process and organize the enormous complexity of ourselves and our world into recurring patterns" (57). The relational psychoanalyst Thomas Ogden similarly argues that "we must live with the paradox (without attempting to resolve it) that there is no such thing as an analysand apart from the relationship with the analyst, and no such thing as an analyst apart from the relationship with the analysand" (20). Clinical intersubjectivity entails, Joseph Natterson and Raymond Friedman point out, "reciprocal causal relationships of all parts of the human universe with all other parts. All human events are co-created by the participants. Everyone changes, and is changed by, everyone else" (xiii). No less than the therapist and patient, teacher and student work collaboratively in an asymmetrical but nevertheless mutual relationship. In such an inter-subjective paradigm, everyone in the classroom teaches and learns from each other. This is especially true in the empathic classroom, where everyone works hard to understand each other.

CHAPTER 4

Family Snapshots 2

EMPATHY AND ITS VICISSITUDES

What happens when the empathic atmosphere in the classroom is disrupted? How should teachers respond, for example, to a student essay that they know will anger and offend many of the writer's classmates? This situation arose during the middle of the semester when Charlie distributed copies of his essay, written in response to the chapter in *Diaries to an English Professor* on "hunger artists," a discussion of how female college students write about their experiences with anorexia and bulimia:

Charlie: "People Were 'Feeling Sorry for Her.' She Was Loving It"

I am one of those people who does not have an eating disorder, and I do find myself striving to understand and empathize with those that do; to no avail.

Before I even begin to make my case I want to be clear that I have no distaste or disrespect for the people who do have these "disorders." I am just a skeptical person, in all aspects of my life. That is the way I was raised. To take responsibility for my own actions and thoughts, and to always challenge my own actions and thoughts, as well as those of others. I don't believe in psychics, or magic, and I tend not to lend much credit to people who claim themselves unaccountable for their own actions. I despise people who are addicted to cigarettes and complain all day that they want to quit but just don't have the willpower to do so. To me that is just weakness. I was not raised to let some drug, or fear, or anything else incapacitate my life, and as a result of that, I was raised to question those who did.

After reading this chapter I am touched by the sadness and the desperateness in the entries of the students. It troubles me to think that they are, or were, my peers, and that they are going through such trying experiences that I could never imagine. I watch my weight, I work out everyday, some people say I'm skinny and I think I'm fat. But all these things don't make me anorexic or even able to fathom what it would be like. Everyone, I believe, worries about his or her appearance. Especially for teenagers this is a main concern of life.

One of the first reasons that I am inclined to be skeptical of people who claim to have eating disorders is that I knew a girl once who claimed just that. Harsh parents raised her and she didn't have many friends. She didn't get much attention. She was good looking who was thin with a nice body, but one day we found out that she was taking a number of diet pills. She was also not eating and sometimes she would mix all of those circumstances with a couple of drinks and completely pass out. I knew this girl really well because she was my girlfriends friend, so I saw her a good amount. Sooner or later she was getting attention from kids she never knew, and teachers who would never have listened to her before. Teachers gave her extensions on papers and tests and people who never cared about her became her best friends. People were "feeling sorry for her." She was loving it. I'm not saying this to be mean, it's just the truth. She may not have even had an eating disorder, as far as I know she was just doing it for the attention. Once again I'm sorry if this sounds like a harsh judgment and I don't mean to be cruel or unfeeling, that's just the way I saw it. In this particular case, her "eating disorder" seemed to stem from a problem of lack of attention.

I thought Marcy's diaries were interesting. I especially liked the two stories in her first diary in which she showed us how it felt to be a tomboy. I do, however, have to analyze it. In the beginning of her entry she says "I am quite certain, however, that this is for social (not psychological) reasons." Then at the end of her essay she says, "This is a brief explanation of the psychological confusion I feel just from being a woman." This is clearly a contradiction and it makes me feel, as a reader, that this person throws around words like "social," and "psychological" without really knowing there true implications. One of my main problems with people who claim to have eating disorders is that they often blame it on someone besides themselves. It is either societies fault, their peers' fault, or their parent's fault. They bring all society on trial because they feel like they are not skinny enough. If I'm generalizing here it is only because I have not been exposed to many people with eating disorders.

Marcy has a big problem with there being pretty women in the movies and as models. This to me is just absurd. It is ridiculous to tell a culture of people why they should and should not find attractive. Furthermore I believe that it is ridiculous to be so obsessed with an advertising image that you would risk your health to copy it. Marcy says of the media "It tells us we should be thin thin thin." I would just like to ask her, when does the media say that. I have never seen a news broadcast that says, "attention, you must be thin in order to be happy or successful in life." Maybe I just don't watch the news enough. I would suggest a look at real life instead of the movies and the media. I look around me and I see people of all different heights, weights, races, and sexes able to live happy and successful lives. Are they not getting the same messages as Marcy is, or do they simply have the strength of character to live as they would like?

As for the part where she talks about all the "women who are victims" in her second entry, I find it completely biased in that she doesn't mention that men do these things too. I myself often find myself either full to the brim and wanting to eat some desert, or starving and wanting that piece of chocolate cake. The decision to lead a healthy life is a decision that calls for pain and sacrifice in order to gain, but it is still a decision, and one that should be made by only myself.

Marcy then describes her own bouts of anorexia and labels them "the unhealthy and life-threatening reaction of women to the bogus beauty ideals created by men." I can't even begin to describe how this statement makes me feel. Am I at fault because I find a certain type of woman attractive? Is my idea of beauty bogus because I am a man? Should I alter my tastes to ease the suffering of some delusional girl? I think "no" would be the answer to all of these questions.

This issue of eating disorders brings up discussion of many other issues such as: sexism, media influence, should the media influence, what is beauty and so on. I write this paper as merely an argument. If I am wrong in some of the things I have said I truly apologize and I will keep my mind open to new thoughts on this subject with no bias at all.

I knew as soon as I read Charlie's essay that it would ignite a firestorm in the classroom. He acknowledges in the opening paragraph that despite his best efforts he cannot understand or sympathize with those suffering from eating disorders. He views empathy and truth as mutually exclusive, not realizing that he would have greater access to the truth if he were more empathic. How does he know that the young woman taking diet pills "was loving" the attention she received? Why does he assume that others are listening to her now when he is not listening himself? He realizes that his generalizations, based on lack of experience and knowledge, are likely to offend his classmates, but he nevertheless proceeds with his argument.

One of the problems with Charlie's essay is its abrasiveness. By placing quotation marks around the word "disorders," he suggests that they are unreal problems that lead to imaginary suffering. He anticipates that his words will seem harsh and judgmental, but he cannot find the language to avoid wounding his readers. It is easier for him to critique Marcy, one of the diarists in the chapter he has read, than to analyze his own conflicted feelings. I suspect that Marcy would have been able to cite many examples of how culture and the "media" portray unrealistic and unhealthy images of the female body. Angered by Marcy's feminist analysis of anorexia and bulimia, Charlie seems only partly aware of how his own essay will anger his classmates.

How could I allow Charlie to read an essay that I knew would threaten if not destroy the empathic classroom atmosphere that we had worked so hard to create and maintain? Anger may sometimes be productive in the form of release of pent-up emotion, but its salutary effects are generally temporary rather than permanent; moreover, anger inevitably ends thoughtful discussion in the self-disclosing classroom. Rarely does anger lead to heightened understanding of another person. On the one hand, I didn't want to silence Charlie by asking him not to read his essay aloud, but on the other hand, I didn't want him to offend classmates who might be self-conscious about their weight or eating habits. Disaffirming many of his classmates' experiences, Charlie's essay threatened to shatter the strong attachment bond that had developed during the semester. I knew that many of his classmates were already upset because they had read the essay before coming to class. And so I asked him at the beginning of class if I could read aloud an anonymous essay on eating disorders before he read his paper. He agreed, and I hoped that the essay would sensitize him to the shame surrounding anorexia and bulimia. Marcy was a former student of mine, but she was to Charlie only a character in a book; by contrast, his classmate Amber wrote the following essay, and thus its reality was greater to him:

Amber: "What Do You Do When You Get Something That No One Knows about or Won't Admit Exists?"

Reading the chapter "Hunger Artists" from Diaries to an English Professor *was hard for me. From an early age I have had issues with weight. I never considered myself to be at risk for any sort of eating disorder because I was too smart for that. Up until last semester I honestly believed that I had everything under control. Around that time one of my classmates started to discuss her issues with weight and food. Sitting up with her at night, listening to the torment she felt when she ate any type of unhealthy food made me start to think. It started to make me reexamine my own issues with food.*

As she poured out her heart to me, I started to tell her what few people know about me. I have an eating disorder. Mine isn't as blatant as anorexia or bulimia but it's there just the same. It's with me when I wake up, go to bed and at every meal. Everywhere I turn, it's there waiting for me. My eating disorder has characteristics of anorexia and bulimia but has no name that I'm aware of. I never throw up after I eat but I will go on eating binges. The guilt that follows is incredible. It can be so powerful that purging becomes an excellent idea, I can never bring myself to execute. Like an anorexic, I will deprive myself of food but never to the full extent. I have tried every diet I could think of that didn't include any type of pills.

As I look back at what I have written, I can just imagine how this sounds. I guess to understand where my obsession with weight comes from, I should go back to the beginning. Around the age of nine or ten, I realized that I wasn't exactly tiny and I couldn't understand why. I've never been a big eater. I was always dancing, so in my mind I should have been extremely thin. Well, that was definitely not how it was. I became very uncomfortable and insecure. What made this time even worse was that my family noticed my weight gain and they were a constant source of nagging. Despite their heart being in the right place, they went about it the wrong way and continue to do so.

Adding to my insecurities and low self-esteem was a boy named Mac. Mac was my age and lucky me to spend my entire education in the same schools as him. He wasn't very bright and was always getting into trouble. His family life wasn't perfect and neither was he. This boy tormented me up until high school where I learned to defend myself. Because he felt like shit, he went out of his way to make me feel the same. It took me a long time to realize that he was the one with the problem not me. It's hard enough to deal with people like this when you are older but at a young age it can be devastating. I don't even remember how many times he brought me to tears and completely humiliated me.

My doctor even passed comments about my weight. I started to hate him because in my eyes, he was just as bad as Mac even though it was health related. Due to instances like this, I absolutely despised going to the doctor. Just the thought of getting on a scale frightened me. The actual moment was terrifying. Having someone there with me was indescribable. At the age of 20, I still dread stepping on a scale.

Due to all these negative experiences, the pleasure most people experience when eating has been taken away. If I ever enjoy eating a meal, I usually am overcome with guilt. Guilt has become a huge influence over my life. Every time I don't exercise or eat too much I become miserable. When I look back I see how this came to be but how could I let this happen to me? I've always been educated when it came to eating disorders.

I always use to feel relieved when I thought about how I didn't have one. Little did I know that I've spent my whole life fighting one. I think that's the *scariest part. What I have doesn't have a name and just crept up on my mind without warning. It's easy to fight something when you know it exists. What do you do when you get something that no one knows about or won't admit exists? After all the education I received throughout school about eating disorders, they never told me that there were other forms of anorexia and bulimia. After seeing how tormented my roommate is, I realized that I have a problem too and need to deal with it. Maybe one day I'll seek outside help but as for now I want to get through it on my own. No one can give me the self-esteem I need to get through this but myself. It's taken me over 10 years to realize I have a problem. I just hope that it doesn't take another 10 to correct it.*

Amber's essay helps us to understand what Charlie cannot imagine, namely, what it feels like to be ashamed of one's body. Nothing in her essay suggests that her desire not to eat is symptomatic of the need for attention, as Charlie speculates about another woman's eating disorder. Nor does Amber want people to feel sorry for her. Rather, she describes a problem that makes her feel acutely uncomfortable and insecure. She neither blames anyone for her problems nor regards herself as a victim—two criticisms which Charlie makes of Marcy. Amber values self-control as much as Charlie does, and she would agree with his observation that the "decision to lead a healthy life is a decision that calls for pain and sacrifice." But whereas Charlie cannot fathom the degree of pain and humiliation associated with eating disorders, Amber can, and her essay enables the reader to understand the torment of "hunger artists." Hearing an essay written by a classmate who is sitting a few feet away is more powerful than hearing dry facts—even if those facts suggest, as does an article in the *Boston Globe* published on the day I am writing these words (August 5, 2001), that, according to Dr. David Herzog, a Harvard professor of psychiatry and president of the Harvard Eating Disorder Center, "anorexia has the highest death rate of any mental illness; many of these deaths are from suicide."

After reading the anonymous essay, about which there was no discussion, I then prepared the class for Charlie's essay. I anticipated that he would feel uncomfortable reading his essay, and I did not want to make him feel like a pariah. Nor did I want to shame him. "A person too anxious about being shamed cannot learn," the Hebrew sage Hillel observed more than two thousand years ago (cited by Kindlon and Thompson 26). This was not *The Breakfast Club*, where students take turns humiliating each other, but a class devoted to good writing. We were also pursing an education for life, which means acquiring those skills that help us to grow as human beings. And so I told the class that I was unaware of eating disorders until I began receiving diaries from my literature-and-psychoanalysis students in the late 1970s about their obsession with weight and dieting. Indeed, I didn't know what the words "anorexia" and "bulimia" meant when I was in college and graduate school. My former students educated me about a serious illness, and I hoped that my present students would educate each other about the same illness.

I could have also told them that anorexia is one of the most striking examples of a biosocial disease, a disease, David Morris notes in *Illness and Culture in the Postmodern Age,* "of women, white women, especially middle- and upper-class white women in Western industrial countries" (153). My classroom strategy was to identify myself—or a younger version of myself—with Charlie's lack of knowledge to lessen his classmates' anger toward him. I asked the class to realize that Charlie was describing a problem that he had not experienced himself. We had all agreed, at the beginning of the semester, to respect each person's point of view, but now we were in a situation in which one student's view clashed with or disaffirmed a classmate's point of view. I then asked Charlie if he wanted to say anything to the class before he read his essay. "I would like the class to keep an open mind about my essay and I'll try to keep an open mind too." After he finished reading the essay, several of his classmates were visibly upset. We were almost out of time, and no one wanted to speak. Finally Mia said, hesitatingly, "Charlie's essay makes me angry. When he was reading it I felt like . . ." and then she paused. "Strangling him," I said, completing her sentence. Several people laughed, and the tension was broken. Other students spoke briefly, including a woman who unexpectedly supported Charlie's argument. The class then ended.

To what extent did Charlie's essay offend his classmates? I didn't know, but I did not want to raise this question in class since it would probably make Charlie feel more defensive and perhaps worsen the situation. An opportunity arose two weeks later when I had a second conference with each student in my office. I asked each person if he or she felt there were any empathic lapses in the course. About a third said "no," while the rest mentioned Charlie's essay. Amber was the angriest, and I asked her if she would write an essay describing how she felt about his paper:

I want to start off by saying that I had read Charlie's essay before class had started. Everything Charlie wrote drove me crazy. Hearing him read it out loud made me feel worse. As he was reading it, I started to clench my fists. By the time he was done I was seeing red. I had to remind myself that he was entitled to his opinion even if I know he is COMPLETELY wrong. Unfortunately Charlie has no experience with eating disorders. I don't wish that on anyone but this is why he was not empathic. I also want to say it's because he is a guy but I think that is letting him off the hook. Most guys don't understand why girls develop eating disorders but that doesn't mean that they are all like Charlie. When you don't understand something someone is going through you should at least try and understand. I was able to remain slightly calm because I teach Intro to Feminism and encounter ignorance all the time. Yelling at people because of their opinions won't help change them. Since this is not a discussion class, I opted to remain silent. Everything I had to say had nothing to do with his writing and everything to do with what he chose to say. I think professor Berman handled the situation well. He warned the class before Charlie read his paper that some of us might be offended by it and he was right. I think he softened the blow for Charlie. Charlie has every right to have his own opinion and voice it. I have to respect that as much as it is hard and hurt me. After our class ended I was irate. I went home and screamed in my housemate's bedroom for a good twenty minutes. It is hard to see Charlie in class because I do hold resentment towards him. There is a part of me that knows I shouldn't. It is hard for me not to though because what he wrote hurt me. In my eyes Charlie denied that eating disorders really exist and said that girls make them up. I hope no one he is close to goes through what I am.

Although Charlie's essay was more offensive to his female classmates, a male classmate was also disturbed, and he made the following observation in his final essay:

Inevitably, when handling sensitive material, there are times when discomfort, and even anger, finds its way into the classroom. I can recall only once when the balance in the classroom was threatened, and even this situation was handled well by both our professor and the class at large. We were discussing eating disorders, and one of the male students read an essay, conveying his opinions on the subject of eating disorders and the women who suffer from them. Before he read the essay, our professor addressed the class and made us aware of the substance of the student's essay, and offered his own experiences as an outlet to interpreting the essay. He made us aware of his own inexperience with the matter until students began writing about in journals. From what he said, I gathered enough information to vaguely comprehend the substance of the student's essay. The silence that followed the reading was a clear indication of the frustration pitted within many students in the classroom. The student denied the validity of any disease associated with an eating disorder, and suggested that women who do suffer are starved for attention. I'm sure a few rash comments were subdued by the normally empathic class, and the comments that were vocalized were less angry than I anticipated. The careful manipulation of the situation by our professor and the empathic strength of our classroom diverted a seemingly explosive situation, and created an important lesson.

This lesson is another testament to the success of the course. Anthropologists use the term "cultural relativism" as a liberal concept that has changed the way we look at culture. This idea works on many levels, and we have worked on one of those levels in this past semester. We must look carefully at what other people are doing, and try to understand their behavior in a specific context before we judge them. Different behaviors reflect the fact that people have different beliefs, different choices, and different stresses. In an English course where you are discussing issues as sensitive as suicide, divorce, and eating disorders, one must maintain an open mind and be able to understand the differences in perception within each and every one of us.

How did Charlie later feel about his essay? When I asked him during our conference whether he thought there were any empathic lapses in the course, he quickly said "no" but after a brief pause, he reconsidered. "Maybe my paper on 'Hunger Artists.'" He was distressed when I told him that some of his classmates were offended by it, and he agreed to write an essay describing how he felt before, during, and after his reading of the paper:

I was taken back by the honesty and pain in the diary entries. They made me sad and a bit angry. At the same time though, I couldn't shake the picture from my mind of some skinny little drama queen who was popular and beautiful, crying wolf to get some attention. Eating disorders seem like a serious thing to me. I am thankful that I never had one or knew of anyone who did. I don't take the issue lightly and I am not against those who have eating disorders. I am against those who claim they do; and don't.

When I started reading Marcy's diary, at first I was interested in her case. She tells two intriguing stories of her tomboy youth and at first I enjoyed them. Then as I read further, I wondered why she was including these stories in her entry on eating disorders. The points Marcy brought up dealt with her own gender confusion, "sex-role stereotypes," movies, voyeurism, and the all inclusive "society." This is where I begin to have a problem. One can not even begin to respond intelligently to an essay like this because it is so scat-

tered and non fact oriented. She does not bring up one fact or piece of evidence. She does not back up any of her outlandish statements. And she does not even speak of the issue at hand. . . .

At this point she actually diverges into a personal story, which, if it is true, is the most informative and useful part of the entry. This is the type of information we need. But, like the style of many other writers, that was the meat of the sandwich and now we are forced to listen to more accusations, political judgments, and gender bashing. Marcy, in her all knowing way, goes on to label anorexia for those of us who have not had the experience as "the unhealthy and life threatening reaction of women to the bogus beauty ideals created by men." If that is not a sexist stereotype then I don't know what is. So once again we are back to the beginning. Feminist's bashing men who supposedly bash women. Fat people bashing skinny people who allegedly bash fat people. Skinny people hating everyone skinnier then them. This does not seem like an eating disorder problem, it seems like a severe social, yet personal, disorder. Marcy seems to have many issues that she needs to work out, the least of which seems to be anorexia.

It is with all of this in mind that I started preparing my paper. I was mad. I was mad at all the dumb girls that I've known and heard lie about a problem as serious as that just to get attention. I was mad at the people in this world who are not intelligent enough to solve their own problems and instead blame them on the society or the media. And I was mad at Marcy for daring to say that I myself, and my personal tastes, were responsible for her's and other women's anorexic ways.

When I finished writing my paper it was the day before class. I knew it was my turn to read out loud and I had some doubts in my mind as to how my paper would be received. . . . I took the paper downstairs and showed it to two of my female friends. One of them had a good knowledge of anorexia because she had her own trials with eating disorder and had done research on the subject for a paper of her own. The other was just a typical girl. I figured I would run it by them and see what turned up. They both read the paper and neither of them had a problem with what I was saying. I made sure that I included in my paper that my intent was not to harm anyone and only to raise a counter point of view. They were fine with it.

I suppose then that I can say that I was not any more nervous than I normally am upon entering Jeff's class. I don't think I'm a great reader so sometimes when I know I will have to read aloud, I get nervous. I knew my paper was good, and I knew it was what I was feeling. I will never be afraid to say how I feel nor will I ever change how I feel, or how I speak because of the feelings of another. That wouldn't be fair to either of us. If you have a *good heart and a good mind, and you are speaking from the heart or the mind, you can't go wrong.*

At the start of class that day Jeff made an unusual announcement. He asked me if I would mind moving my reading from first to last. I said I didn't mind and we went on with class. When it was my turn to read Jeff broke in with another announcement. I forgot what his exact words were but they were something to the effect of asking the class not to judge me based on my paper or to be empathic etc. This made me nervous because I knew then that Jeff was nervous. I read the paper though and when I was done I looked up. No one was crying. No one was scowling. I thought it was a success. To further affirm my thoughts, the comments made by the class were purely positive. One person, a woman, said she agreed with many of my points and thought that my paper was well written. It wasn't until weeks later, about one week ago, that I found out the actual response of the class. I had a private meeting with Jeff and he told me the other student responses to my paper. Some of them apparently were upset. This came as a surprise and that's why I agreed to write this paper: to clarify, if possible, my position.

What would have happened if Amber had criticized Charlie's essay in class? I suspect there would have been a heated exchange between them and that others would have joined in, inflaming the situation. Charlie probably would have felt too defensive to understand Amber's mortification, and it is not likely that he would have changed his point of view since, as he observes in the above essay, "I will never be afraid to say how I feel nor will I ever change how I feel, or how I speak because of the feelings of another." Had such a debate taken place at the time, Amber and Charlie would have only hardened their positions and perhaps made statements that they would later regret. They and their classmates would be less inclined to be empathic in the future. Not only would writing about sensitive subjects be more difficult, but there would be less inclination to understand other points of view.

What would have happened if I had criticized Charlie's above essay in class? He probably would have felt defensive no matter how sensitively I expressed my criticisms. I disagreed with many of his statements, including: "If you have a good heart and a good mind, and you are speaking from the heart or the mind, you can't go wrong." Countless people go wrong every day by trusting hearts and minds that are not as good as they believe. Nor are people with good minds and hearts always right in their words and actions. Perhaps I could have persuaded Charlie to agree with me about this, but how would he have responded if I observed that he engages in the "accusations, political judgments, and gender bashing" of which he accuses Marcy? I might win the point if I were publicly debating Charlie, but it is doubtful that I would succeed in opening his mind. He would perceive me as another teacher who is "feeling sorry" for a woman searching for attention. Or he would view me as one of the feminists "bashing men who supposedly bash women." From his perspective, my criticisms would perpetuate the cycle of bashing.

Charlie's nervousness over my comments in class suggests that students have difficulty, like everyone else, in accepting criticism, even when that criticism intends to deflect further criticism. They may also have difficulty knowing when they are unempathic toward a classmate. I don't believe that empathy is a panacea, but I do believe that it is an essential pedagogical strategy for courses that promote personal growth and development. To empathize does not mean to condone or approve; it does mean to try to understand other points of view even when they differ from one's own.

Sabreena: "Suddenly Everything I Previously Felt about the Assignment Came Back to Haunt Me."

There was one other classroom situation that could have resulted in the breakdown of empathy. Instead, the event proved to be the defining moment of the semester, involving, ironically, the one student who did not find the "Letter to and from a Parent" assignment valuable. Like many of her classmates, Sabreena imagined how her life would have been different had her parents not divorced, but she did not see the value of raising an unanswerable question:

Whenever I begin wondering what my life would have been like if my father were a part of it, I get angry. The ironic thing is, I do not get angry at my (lack of a) father, but I get angry at myself. I find it pointless to be pondering "what if" and "why" when there is nothing I can do to go back and change the situation. I realized at a very young age that my father did not leave because of me. I went through years of counseling because my mother did not want me to have any "unresolved issues or anger towards my father when I grew up." The counseling, though, was not helpful. I knew the divorce was not my fault. It was other aspects that confused me. I did not see how someone could produce another human being and then decide they were going to remain absent from watching them grow and change. He did not even care to see it from afar. Instead, he chose to (eventually) become virtually non existent in my life.

I was not surprised of the impact that divorce had on the given students. I am, after all, a product of divorce. I can easily understand why the majority of them were feeling the ways they were. I most closely related to the female students, in particular Mara. I also find it difficult to take orders from a male. Growing up, the only caregiver I knew of was my mom. Like Mara, I believe that my dad is selfish for what he did.

My father used to call me every night, like clockwork. Then, the calls became sparse, and I chalked it up to his busy schedule. (I had always imagined him as a busy working man, although in reality I had no idea what his job was.) Eventually the calls stopped. Not that it mattered so much, because all we would ever talk about was nonsense and small talk, but it gave me the sense that he had taken some active interest in my life. When he stopped calling me, I began to forget. I'm still trying to forget.

Looking back in retrospect, the few memories I have of my father are not even happy ones. Once when he was living in Seattle, I went to visit him. We went to a restaurant and I left my jacket there. It had Rainbow Brite on it. We left the restaurant and when we went back it was gone. My favorite jacket. I cried, and he told me not to cry. My mother never told me not to cry. He said that it was not a big deal because I can get another jacket. I knew that he did not understand. It felt awkward for him to be telling me not to cry, because I was only used to my mom teaching me right from wrong. She would never tell me not to cry. She would have known that it was my favorite jacket, and for a 6 year old, losing it was devastating. She would have allowed me to be upset, and then taken me to look for another extra special jacket. My dad bought me an ugly sweatshirt to replace my jacket. I pretended it was good enough, and smiled for the rest of the trip. In reality, I was suffering with a smile because from then on I wanted to go home. I never wanted to go back to Seattle to see my father again.

I resented my father for acting like he cared because I knew that he was doing just that—acting. His insincerity was completely blatant, but I kept wanting to believe that he loved me, so I kept visiting.

He came to New York once for business, and I met him in the city. This was the first time I had seen him in five years. We walked around Times Square and went to a record store where he bought me two or three CD's. That was reminiscent of when he used to take me to Toys R'Us and buy me toys to make me feel happy. It was also similar to the Care Bear he left on my bed for me to wake up to the day that he left. The entire time we spent together in New York, he insulted me. He informed me that I was becoming like my mother, as if that were bad.

The last time I spoke with my father was on my "Birthday" this year. He called me the day before my birthday and said "Happy Birthday Sabreena.

How old are you this year?" It made me wish that he did not call me at all, because it was insulting. In my opinion, if you have to ask your daughter how old she is on her birthday, and you cannot even call her on the correct day, it is better not to call at all. My mother tells me that my father is "passive aggressive." She suggested that this is why he chose to call me not on my birthday, but the day before. He made believe that he was doing a good deed by calling me, but it was more hurtful.

I also see a parallel between Mara and me in how she views her relationships with men now. Like Mara, all of my previous relationships were hindered because of my fear of rejection from another man. My boyfriend and I have been together for three months. His parents are divorced as well, and it is obvious that both of us coming from broken homes has affected our relationship. I never learned how to accept affection from a man. He was never given the opportunity to be a boy, because when his father left he was all of a sudden supposed to be a man. I discovered that both he and I shared the same feelings about our parents' divorce. We both felt inadequate when we saw our peers with both of their parents at school functions, and we had just one parent to watch us in our play or dance recital.

I also feel similar to Mara in that I feel guilty for my mother never remarrying. For quite some time I felt as if she should not be seeing other men, because I knew how hard it was for her to be the sole caretaker of my sister and me, and I thought she would not have enough time for us if she dated. When she did have a boyfriend, every time he came over I would go into my room and slam the door. I refused to speak to him. Looking back, I realize how I must have embarrassed my mother with my bratty behavior. I never meant for that, but the feelings I had at that time were strong, and I believed my intentions to be good.

Reading the chapter did awaken strong emotions in me. Each time I thought about how my life would have been different if my parents were not divorced, I forced myself to stop. I would tell myself that there are plenty of people out there who are in the same situation as I am. I would think that I was not any different than them, and no matter what happens in life you should be able to compensate. After completing this chapter, I realized that it was alright for me to draw parallels between my parents divorce and the way I am today.

I also used to just ignore the fact that my parents were divorced. As far as I was concerned, my mother was the only person who raised me, therefore the only one deserving my love and attention. The modest family of my mother, sister, and I was the only thing I was used to. I stopped missing my father, and eventually ignored the void (of a father) in my life.

More recently, I discovered that my father has a web site. It is called "Avenues of Love." The site consists of his poems, all of which are about love and romance. They all seem contradictory to me, because I do not consider this man to be a loving person. On his web site, he lists the things which are important to him. They are his car, dogs, and computer. I was never expecting him to mention the fact that he has two daughters, because it seems to me as if he does not think about us often. The site depicts that he is materialistic and childish. Viewing his web site almost made me glad that I do not have a relationship with my father. I wondered if I even wanted to have anything to do with this man.

From reading the chapter, I acquired knowledge from people who feel the same way I always have. It made me feel that I am not alone, and in a world where divorce is becoming more common, it gave me a sense of hope. Although each person's situation is different, I related with many of the student's essays. I do hope that one day my father and I can have somewhat of a healthy relationship, because I do not want to look back and regret not knowing him, but at the same time I can only wish for what he is willing to give in return.

Sabreena says that it is pointless to think about a father who has absented himself from her life because the past cannot be changed. She becomes angry at herself for thinking about her father; twice she says she is trying to forget him. She does not deny the possibility that she and her father will have a relationship, but she thinks that it is unlikely to occur in the near future. She returns to this idea in the letter to her father, in which she verbalizes her anger and resentment:

Dear Dad,

It's funny. Just when you think you have things figured out, something comes up, and it sets you right back to the beginning. There is not much that I remember about you. I do remember an email you sent me awhile back, though. At the bottom of the letter you typed "Live and love with an open heart." These are the only words of advice I have ever received from you. I cannot even follow them.

You left when I was three years old. I had little comprehension as to what was occurring then, and I am still confused. I understand if things with you and Mom weren't working out as you had planned. These things happen, and things (as I have learned in my life thus far) do not always work out as you hope.

When you decided to leave, I had no control of the situation. I just wanted to have two parents, like the families I saw on TV. I understood though, why you and Mom split up, and I still do. (I have learned a good deal about relationships in my 20 years). I do not, however, understand the decisions you made after you left. When was it that you decided you were going to ignore the life you made in New York? When exactly did you think it would be alright to leave two children and a wife and go all the way across the country? What happened to the fun times we had playing Atari and going to the toy store to look at the new Cabbage Patch Kids? I tried to put myself in your shoes (not an easy task for me being that I have never and will never want to be in your shoes), and I do not know how you live with yourself. You marry someone you claim to love. You have a child. You decide to have another one. A few years pass, and you start fighting with your wife. Ignore your whole past life. How do you deal with that kind of information? I would love to know if you have ever regretted your choices, or felt guilty that you were not present when my sister and I were growing up.

Now that I am in college, I have greater knowledge of myself as well as the world and life in general. I used to resent you for not being an active force in my life. I do not know how she did it, but mom was there for me and provided me with everything I needed. I feel that if anyone should resent you, it should be her.

Thank you for the advice, though. I will try to live and love with an open heart. I will have spent the majority of my life trying to overcome my fears of rejection because of you. I have always had to push people away from me for fear of getting too close. So this is my advice to you, Dad. I think that you should not "live and love with an open heart" if this means being able to love, move on, and then forget. You should love unconditionally, especially your own children. As for me, I will try to use your advice. I have begun to allow people past the wall I have put around me. I am starting to let myself trust people. I realize that the past is worth remembering, but not worth living in. I do not respect the choices you have made, but I do respect you as a person and my father, and should you ever decide to care about me and my life, you know where to reach me.

Your daughter,
Sabreena

Dear Sabreena,

There is not much I can tell you. You were just a child when your mother and I decided to get a divorce. I knew that you would not understand at the time. I did know that you and your sister would be angry with me. You two were staying with your mother, and I had always just assumed I was made out to be the bad guy. The only thing I did was run away. I went to Seattle because that is where the company I work for sent me. I did not especially choose to move there.

It hurts me to think that you believe I did not want to be there for you as a child. I would have loved to watch you leave for your first day of school every

year. I would have liked to be at your high school graduation. These are memo-
ries I will never have. Do you think you are the only one who is missing out?

My advice to you was written for you to think about. I realized that you might
have difficulty with your own life and the relationships you form. I want you to
be a compassionate and caring person. I want you to trust people. I am sorry if
you feel that I do not care about you. I always have. I do not expect you to
understand, but just know that I do care.

Love,
Dad

The central question in Sabreena's letter is whether she should accept
or reject her father's advice to live and love *him* with an open heart. She
asserts in the first paragraph that she cannot follow the advice, but in the
last paragraph she changes her mind, stating that she will try to take to
heart his words. Anger compels her to offer some advice of her own: words
of love do not mean anything unless they are supported by loving actions.
In the fictional letter, her father expresses love for her, but despite his
efforts to narrow the distance, they seem emotionally as far apart as the
three thousand miles separating them.

In her response essay, Sabreena indicated her difficulty with the assignment. "I sat at my computer staring at the screen and nothing came to
mind." She knew immediately that she was not going to read the essay to
her classmates. She felt "aggravated" while writing the assignment, and
the hardest part was imagining her father's response. "I have no idea how
my father would respond to my thoughts, and I do not care to know. I felt
like I was idealizing him because that is how one would expect a father to
respond to his daughter. After completing the assignment I felt as if I did
not want to hand it in. The only thing I wanted to do was delete it from my
computer as well as my mind." She added that it is difficult to imagine her
father's response because she does not know much about him. The only
way to determine whether she is successful in understanding his perspective is to send the letter to him and wait for a response. "My dad's point of
view is something I cannot begin to imagine." She doubted whether she
would show him the two letters. "I would maybe consider showing the
assignment to my dad, but that feeling would quickly be disposed of when
I remind myself what type of person he was. If I did show him, I feel he
would act hurt or touched, but I would not expect that. (I stopped expecting anything from him a long time ago.)"

The assignment was helpful for Sabreena in only one way, allowing her
to realize that many of her classmates have similar problems with one or
both parents. "There are many who are in even worse situations than I

was, so it helped me to put my life into perspective. When my classmates read their letters aloud I felt relieved to know that I was not the only one who came from a broken home and suffered from it. I was also impressed at how many of them seemed to capture his or her parent's response in a believable way. That was near impossible for me." She concluded her response essay by stating that the assignment was valuable for her classmates but not for herself. "When the assignment was first given, I attempted to write it numerous times. Each time I ripped up my paper. When it came time for the paper to be due, I wrote a very quick letter, trying to avoid putting a lot of emotion into it. I was not satisfied with the result, and I know I can do much better, but it has to come from real feeling, and not because I know it has to be done. I think it is a good assignment to give, but keep in mind how frustrating it can be. For some students, though, it can be a wonderful growing experience. Maybe I am just weird."

Two weeks later Sabreena told me, after her classmates had left the room, that a startling event had just occurred: her father had made an effort to reestablish communication with her. She felt confused and overwhelmed by her new situation, which she had long assumed would not happen in the near future. We were both silent for a moment, and then I told her that, based on the response essays, she was the only student who did not find the letter assignment valuable. I wondered whether this new development in Sabreena's life would change her attitude toward the assignment. More importantly, would the letter assignment cast new light on their relationship? Without giving her advice about whether to see her father, I suggested that she might find it helpful to write an essay about her feelings: perhaps writing about the new situation would aid in problem-solving. She said she would think about it, and following spring recess, she brought multiple copies of the following essay and distributed them to her classmates, prepared to read her essay aloud:

I was the only person in class who was not affected by the "Letter to a Parent and His or Her Letter to You" assignment. Or so I thought. I found it to be difficult. I struggled with my thoughts for days until I wrote a half-hearted letter which came from the surface. I felt blind writing the letters because I never got to know my father. Imagining what he would have to say to me was nearly impossible, and my essay turned out to be fictitious. In my responses to Professor Berman's inquiry about whether the class found the assignment beneficial, I claimed that I would not consider showing the assignment to my father. He hurt me in the past, and I have no reason to share my thoughts or feelings with him. I also stated that, "The assignment did not increase my understanding of my dad. I think the only way I can achieve that is if I speak with him." It is hard to envision a person's reaction if you hardly know him or her. I placed the assignment in the back of my folder without further regard. Then it happened. I was on America Online, conversing with some friends. I received an "Instant Message" from someone with a screen name that was unknown to me. After questioning the person, I discovered that it was my father. He was able to locate my e-mail address. Suddenly everything I previously felt about the assignment came back to haunt me. I found myself wishing I could retrieve my true feelings—the ones I wanted him to know. Instead, I had to work from my mind, because I did not do the assignment with the idea that I would use it one day.

The following is the conversation between my father and I (Who I had not had relations with in over six years). I have edited the greeting section of the conversation for the reader's best interest. The typing and grammar are informal, due to the nature of the Internet.

Dad: I'd really like it if you came to Seattle to visit. Even if you don't like me.
Me: Its not that I don't like you.
Dad: Oh?
Me: I just don't understand why you have decided to take an active interest in me all of a sudden.
Dad: I didn't earlier because I thought you wanted nothing to do with me.
Dad: That's what I felt.
Me: What would have given you that impression? I mean, yes, I grew up fine without you because my mother did an amazing job, but there were still times it would have been cool to have a dad. But whatever, I came to terms with that a long time ago.
Dad: I know, and nothing I say or do will make up for that.
Me: True.
Dad: I also live with that.
Me: As you should. It's not like you should regret not knowing my sister or me, because, well, I'll speak for myself when I say I'm doing just fine. Not to distance myself from you or anything, but my whole life I grew up not having a dad, and that's what's normal to me. Anything else seems weird to me.
Dad: I understand, I really do. And of course I can't make up for the past. If I could, I would. Believe me. There aren't words to express some of the stuff I feel. And yes, I am still in counseling.
Me: I find it hard to believe that you decide to tell me this on AOL. I mean you have been absent my entire life, and now all of a sudden I'm supposed to talk to you like we're related? Like you actually care? OK, I'm not going to

put words in your mouth and say that you don't care, but that's what I get out of it. If you were feeling these things and regretting not knowing me, you could have called a long time ago. And by the way, I saw your website a long time ago, and I found myself embarrassed for you. You actually think that music is good?

Dad: *Every time I called or saw you, I was rejected. I'm not placing blame.*

Me: *Rejected? Do you not recall every time after visiting you how much I cried?*

Me: *Well, that's not important*

Dad: *I accept responsibility for a lot of it. And I tried, I really tried. I didn't know about the crying. And I cried after you left too, by the way.*

Me: *But about your website, "Avenues of love." Could you possibly get anymore cliche?*

Dad: *Forget the website—it's geared towards older people anyway—and yes, maybe I am a cliche.*

Me: *I USED to cry in the airport and come home to my mom crying, and that must have been horrible for her to see. She was the only one who cried about me, and I didn't cry when I left HER.*

Dad: *Sabreena, I cried too. I still do for what has happened. If you can ever see yourself having some relationship with me, I'd like that. But if you really truly can't, I understand.*

Dad: *But I don't think I'd give up trying.*

Dad: *I know I wouldn't.*

Me: *I think it would take me a long time to forgive you, if I ever do. I mean as of now, you are a stranger to me. I think that if I saw you walking down a busy street I wouldn't even recognize you, and I'm just wondering how you decided you were going to have 2 kids and just leave and remain absent from their lives. I know I would never be able to do that. But I don't take that personally, I understand you have issues. Obviously major ones.*

Dad: *Yes, issues that I am dealing with now. And having children when we did was a blessing. You and your sister are that. I feel as bad as you, Sabreena. I too live with it every day.*

Dad: *The issues were between your mother and me. Your sister and you were not any part of the reason for the divorce.*

Me: *OK, well, I have to go now, because I have a 9 am class.*

Dad: *OK, but if you don't want me to contact you, you need to tell me that.*

Dad: *Otherwise I will keep trying.*

Me: *I really don't care what you do.*

Dad: *Then I will continue. Sweet dreams, Sabreena.*

Me: *Bye.*

Since that conversation took place, I have chosen to ignore my father. At this point in my life, I do not see myself having a relationship with him. I told my mother about what occurred and she told me that I am old enough to make my own decisions and to do whatever I feel is right. Maybe one day soon, I will call him and tell him to send me a plane ticket to Seattle. Perhaps when I follow through on my dream to go cross country, I will stop in at his house. For now I am content ignoring his "Instant Messages," hoping that maybe he will feel the neglect that I felt my entire life. Is that immature and arrogant? Probably. I need to live with that. Maybe I should not be so angry at him anymore, and I should get over my childhood to start anew. But as I ended my response assignment, "Maybe I'm just weird."

I did not comment on the differences between the letters Sabreena wrote for the class assignment and the Instant Message conversation, but I was struck by the irony appearing in the first paragraph of the former: "Just when you think you have things figured out, something comes up and it sets you right back to the beginning." The father's unexpected and apparently unwelcome communication confirms the adage that truth is stranger than fiction. Sabreena maintains greater emotional detachment in the fictional letter than in the Instant Message exchange, implying in the former that she has largely come to terms with the void created by her father's absence. She is sarcastic and detached, and while she does not close the door to a reconciliation, she does not expect it to open. "I tried to put myself in your shoes," she tells her father, but she cannot: she never wants to be in his shoes. In the fictional letter, her father attempts to explain the reasons for leaving his children and conveys sadness and regret, but he seems as detached as his daughter. He admits to running away from his family but then states, without any apparent awareness of the contradiction, that the reason he moved away was because of his job. He ends the letter with "Love," a word that his daughter conspicuously avoids.

Both father and daughter appear more vulnerable in the Instant Messages than in Sabreena's two letters. His complexity is more visible; he seems wounded and grief stricken. He mentions feeling "rejected" whenever he called or saw his daughter but then immediately qualifies himself by stating that he is "not placing blame"—a qualification that nevertheless provokes Sabreena's ire, perhaps because she regards it as manipulation. Father and daughter struggle to express their pain while maintaining their composure. Despite his statement that there "aren't words to express some of the stuff I feel," both he and his daughter do convey many of their feelings: regret, sadness, loss, confusion, and hope. Sabreena is skeptical over his feelings for her but promises that she won't put words in his mouth and pretend that he doesn't care. Their Instant Messages end inconclusively with the father reaching out and the daughter uncertain whether to make contact.

I asked Sabreena before she began to read her essay aloud whether she wanted to have a male classmate read her father's words, and she agreed. Nat volunteered, and the reading was uneventful. Nat's reading was more expressive than Sabreena's, for she read her words quickly and un-emotionally, as if she were writing about characters to whom she could not relate. The statement she made in her response essay—"When it came time for the paper to be due, I wrote a very quick letter, trying to avoid putting a lot of emotion into it"—characterized her reading as well. Before I had time to ask her classmates to offer their impressions of the essay, Matilda, distressed by the Instant Message conversation, began to give advice to Sabreena that went beyond the usual discussion of diction, tone, and grammar. "You should take advantage of the opportunity you have, because some people will never be as lucky as you." Sabreena did not have to love or even like her father, Matilda continued, but she should see him again. And then Matilda said that she was jealous of Sabreena's situation and wished that she could see her own father again. With those words, Matilda left the room, engulfed in tears.

Sabreena and her classmates were stunned by Matilda's response, which was a violation of the course's explicit ground rules, established on the first day of the semester, that no one would challenge a writer's point of view or offer unsolicited advice about the content of an essay. Sabreena looked dazed and turned to me in confusion. Nothing like this had ever happened in any of my writing classes. I didn't know whether Sabreena was more angered or hurt by her classmate's words, and for a moment I was unsure what to do. Finally I told the class that they would be able to understand Matilda's reaction after hearing her read an essay about her own conflicted relationship to her father—an essay that, like Sabreena's, focused on paternal loss. Matilda had written two essays on her family, beginning with the assignment on "Sins of the Fathers":

Matilda: "I Can Never Hear My Dad Tell Me He Loves Me"

The voice on my answering machine at nine o'clock that Saturday was so muffled and so low that I could scarcely tell whose it was. We had just returned from an unusually long dinner at the Spaghetti Warehouse and I had barely hung up my coat before the sound of my grandmother's voice on the answering machine overwhelmed me with intense fear. I knew there was only one reason she would be calling. I ran upstairs to my mother's room and asked, "What happened to dad?"

My father was a drunk. This thought plagued my mother's mind as we settled into our new house with hardwood floors and a newly painted interior that signified for her a fresh start. It wasn't until years later, after the fresh white paint had faded, that I realized this house was the beginning of the end of my family. Life continued as normal; dad went to work every morning, and while my brother and I adjusted to a new school, my mother stayed home and baked apple pies.

As summer changed to fall, and fall to winter, my brother and I were exposed to a side of my father that had been hidden from us. Some days, we waited for hours after school for him to pick us up, with the principal who impatiently checked her watch while a list of emergency contact numbers lay ready on her desk. His drinking problem had become so bad that if he wasn't out drinking with his co-workers, he was at home, not just drinking, but getting drunk. My mother's resentment and intolerance had reached boiling point. At night, their fighting was so loud it vibrated my bedroom walls.

"Kids," my mother said to us after dinner at Pizza Hut some time in 1986, "Your father and I are getting a divorce and I want you to come live with me." My parents' divorce did not become real to me until we sold our house and moved into an apartment with my mother where weekend visits with my father became something to look forward to. When the divorce was final, and my mother was awarded custody of my brother and me, my father stopped picking us up on weekends and stopped paying child support. He simply vanished. Life continued this way for seven years, during which time my mother and my aunt poisoned us against my father and almost convinced me that I didn't want to see him. After all, I had a right to be angry. He wasn't helping my mom, wasn't making any attempt to see us, and had ran to Texas to escape paying child support. Sometime during these years we heard that he had a brain tumor, but didn't believe it.

The apartment was making us claustrophobic so my mother moved us into a new house in typical suburbia. I think she was trying to make life normal for us. As much as I felt guilty for missing my dad, I thought about him everyday and wondered how he felt about leaving behind two children. I understood that my parents couldn't be married, but I couldn't understand how my dad could abandon us for so many years. There were so many questions I wanted to ask him and so much I wanted to tell him about myself.

"What happened to dad?" was all I said before breaking down into tears. Just that week I had dreamt about him and had woken up feeling like I

would be seeing him soon. My mom called my brother into the room, took each of us by the hand, and told us that the brain tumor my father was rumored to have was real, that he never fully recovered from it, and that he had died the afternoon before.

It's hard to explain the feelings that cloud your mind when a parent dies. I never expected it to happen, but I guess no one ever seriously considers it. I had thought about his death before; it's amazing what kind of morbid thoughts accompany the disappearance of a parent, but I always felt like my dad was safe, whatever he was doing. My first reaction was to find pictures of him. I dug for hours through drawers and boxes of pictures trying to spark any memories I could. It had been so long that I didn't even remember what he looked like.

For the next few days, my brain flip-flopped over believing that he was dead, and thinking that he was alive in Texas. At the memorial service, when my mom led us up to the casket, I thought we were in the wrong room. I had expected him to look the same as he did when I was six, but instead he looked more like my grandfather. Had he aged that much? The funeral was worse; it meant the end. Now I wouldn't see him again. I walked behind the casket to the altar and if my brother hadn't grabbed my hand, I would have turned around and run out of the church. I was so ashamed for resenting him for almost my whole life and now there was no chance for me to apologize. Before he died, there was always a chance that he would come back, but now, I can never get the answers to the questions I have asked a million times in my head. I can never hear my dad tell me he loves me.

There has not been one day in the six years since my father died that I have not thought about him. Although my mother managed to hold my family together, I often wonder how different my life would have been if my dad were around.

Matilda makes no effort to conceal or rationalize her father's failures. The opening sentence of the second paragraph — "My father was a drunk" — abruptly characterizes him. Nor does she excuse his failure to pay child support. But the question she twice raises — "What happened to dad?" — suggests that the years of anger and resentment she felt toward him for abandoning his family have not put an end to her yearning for him. Her essay compresses into a few eloquent paragraphs the grief she lives with every day. She captures a daughter's confusion over a parent's disappearance from the family and a mother's determination to protect her children. "What happened to dad?" haunts the essay, and no explanation can assuage the writer's grief. Like Sabreena, she cannot understand how her father could have abandoned his children, but her bitterness seems to have been washed away by his death. She cannot stop thinking about him despite the fact that he died six years ago. If his death prevented her from apologizing to him for her resentment, she nevertheless asks for *his* forgiveness—*she* has already forgiven him.

Matilda penned on the top of her essay the words, "Let's make this anonymous and not read to the class." She had mentioned briefly in her autobiographical paragraphs her parents' divorce but did not reveal her father's death; consequently, no one in the class knew about this. In her letters to and from a parent, she imagined conversing with her father:

Dear Dad,

Beginning this letter is difficult for me, because it's like I'm writing to a stranger. How many years has it been since we sat down and talked or watched a movie together? How many years has it been since I last saw you? Over ten? I wish you had stayed around to watch us grow up.

I wasn't ready for you to die dad. I wasn't ready to stop being angry. What were you doing all the years you didn't call on birthdays or Christmas? My brother and I were always waiting. Before Aunt Maureen told us about your plan to come home, I thought you were a coward for running from child support. She's the only one who has told us anything about what your life was like. Everything except what Aunt Maureen has told me about you is a mystery. Running away should not have been an option for you and I can't understand why it became the solution. Was it hard for you too?

Lately I've been thinking about how it would be to have a dad who lives at home. Would we eat dinner together and go out to breakfast on Sunday mornings? I know mom would be happier. Sometimes I wish she had remarried even though it would be hard for me to accept a new father figure in my life. Would we still eat donut holes and Dunkin Donuts everyday after school? I have become so accustomed to living with only mom that the idea of having you at home is foreign and strange to me.

I miss you everyday dad. I miss the smoky smell of your clothes and the brown of your hair. Your skinny body and your big head. Your Mick Jagger impression. Hearing Puff the Magic Dragon on your guitar. Catching crayfish at Stoneybrook. I miss calling someone dad and going to bed after kissing two parents' cheeks.

It always hurts me to think about you. Aside from the loss, I am plagued with constant yearning. That feeling is the worst. I doubt that my questions will ever be answered. When I was little, we talked about my wedding and made a list of songs that we might dance to. Who's going to dance with me now? Who's going to walk me down the aisle? If you hadn't died dad, I would have found you. I am old enough now where we could develop a relationship. I'm not angry anymore; it's futile. Although I could write for days to you, I am ending this letter. I thought that writing to you would make me happy, but there is no end to my grief.

Love,
Matilda

Dear Matilda,
    Since the surgery I've been wandering around here trying to make ends meat. It has finally come to a juncture that I have to return to New York or just give it all up. But, I have no faith in the "justice" system after spending five years in divorce court.
    I don't think casting blame is an effective remedy for anything, so I try to stay away from that these days. I know you never wanted things in our family to turn out the way they have.
    I just wanted you to know that I never wanted to be "bad," that seems to be the way I am characterized. I feel so emotionally drained and live a life of constant pain missing and feeling bad about my children and the rest of our family.
    I do not absolve myself from any wrongdoing—but everything has not and could not be my fault. When I look at my life, it seems insane. Brain tumors, malpractice suits, and all the hate. I can't see it getting better and I have no answers for anything. I can say though, that the only happiness in my adult life I ever felt was when I was married and helping raise you and your brother.

In the fictional letter, Matilda imagines her father as dwelling in a limbo, neither fully alive nor dead. He offers no defense for his actions but asks her not to condemn him. Indeed, to judge from the two letters, Matilda is beyond accusation and recrimination. Nothing can mitigate her suffering except the knowledge that she loves her father and the belief that he reciprocates the love. She does not merely tell her father that she loves him; she shows this love through evocative details of the past and future.

Matilda began her response essay by stating that initially she did not like the assignment. "I try to avoid thinking about my family and my father, and writing about it made me do that. When a parent dies, it's hard to make sense out of your feelings to actually write them down. I put off writing the letter until the last minute." She cried when she finally sat down to write the two letters: She wanted to write something that her father would admire but found it difficult to express her feelings. She didn't know whether she succeeded in re-creating her father's voice, since he had died so many years ago. "There isn't really anything for me to check his voice against. I would like to think that what I wrote is how he felt. I would be glad if my father's voice and point of view were similar to mine. I like to think I am like him." After finishing the letters, which she rewrote several times, she considered reading them to the class but decided against it. "Something like this is too personal for me to share with the class, especially since my classmates are practically strangers."

Matilda would have sent the letters to her father if he were alive and if she had known his address. "I have too many years and too many feelings stored away to not open up if given the chance. Keeping feelings hidden is not a good idea for anyone." She added that although she has often spoken to her mother about the divorce and her father's death, rarely has she been able to do so with her brother. She concluded her response essay with an observation that foreshadowed her response to Sabreena's essay:

I have strong opinions on how people should feel about their parents, even if they have a bad relationship. I realize that everyone's situation is different, but I think others need to realize that we only have two parents and that they can't be replaced. There is no excuse for parents to leave or hit their kids or to blame their children for marital problems. If this happens, it's natural to be upset, but realize, there is always a chance that you will never see that parent again. You never know how hard it will be, regardless of how many times you say you don't want to see him.

In light of her feelings about her father's loss, Matilda's spontaneous reaction to Sabreena's essay is understandable. She projected herself into Sabreena's situation and, recognizing that her classmate had an opportunity forever denied to herself, expressed heartfelt words. But since no one else in the class knew about Matilda's situation, her classmates did not grasp why she reacted so spontaneously to Sabreena's essay. Coincidentally, Matilda turned in an essay that week on how the letter assignment was useful for problem-solving. She wrote the essay only for me, but when I telephoned her the morning of class to ask her if she was willing to read it aloud or allow me to read it anonymously, she readily agreed to the former. I had found the essay moving and thought her classmates would too. I did not realize, however, that Matilda's essay would be so relevant to Sabreena's situation:

It is easy for me to decide which assignment I related to most this semester, the one on divorce. Writing about my parents's divorce helped me sort through some feelings I thought had faded away. As much as I am no longer angry with my father for leaving us, I realized that I am still frustrated that I will never have answers to the questions that replay themselves over and over in my mind. Yesterday my brother called me and he actually mentioned my dad. I don't know if I ever wrote about my brother's reaction to the divorce and to his death, but he has never spoken with me about it. There have been so many times where I have come close to asking him about my father hoping that he might say something that will spark a memory or tell me something I didn't know. I always stop myself from asking him because I feel uncomfortable. I don't want to force him to think about it and cause him pain. Last night, however, he brought it up. In his first comment, he said, "mom and dad." It has been as long as ten years since I used those words together. He stopped himself after those three words and we talked about how strange it was to say those words. Afterwards, I wanted to ask him about my dad, but I didn't. He has too much on his mind right now. In the future though, I think I will be less apprehensive speaking about my father because I think my brother was telling me yesterday that it is all right to talk.

When I heard my classmates read their essays, I was relieved. I am glad to know there are families just as dysfunctional as mine. It was saddening that some students had two terrible parents instead of just one. I am lucky to have my mom. She has always been responsible and grounded. Sometimes I think she goes out of her way to be supportive of us because she knows that we don't find support from any other outlet. Hearing those essays, especially Nat's, made me appreciate my mother so much more. I cannot imagine how my life would be if she had been an alcoholic like my father. She helps me when I'm in trouble, and she helps me avoid trouble. I wish that she could see how much I respect her and realize that she is everything to my brother and me. I could go on and on about all of the things my mother has done for me, but I will move on.

Hearing the essays made me realize that my resolution that all parents deserve second chances does not apply to every family. Ten years ago, I felt the opposite. I didn't want to know my father. I thought that any man who would leave his family and not pay child support was a loser and should be put in jail. My opinion changed when he died and in writing my own paper, I realized that this was not fair for me. When my father died, I dismissed all the bad he had ever done and all the anguish he made me experience. I decided that every parent should see his/her children, no matter what legal repercussions they faced. I thought that every child should want to see his/her parents, regardless of the past. To me, we only have two parents, and to deny them in our lives is to deprive us of a piece of ourselves.

After writing this paper, I realized I was too easy on my dad and that it is justified for me to still be angry. I also realized that not all parents love their children and forcing a relationship could be even worse than just moving on. *I learned that there is no definite rule when it comes to families. Parents don't always stay in love. They don't always love their children, which is the harshest reality of all. It was so relieving to read letters my father had written while away and see that he truly loves us and was sorry for what he had done. It must be the worst feeling to know that one (or both) of your parents doesn't want or love you when we rely so heavily on love and support from our parents. I have changed my opinion. Not all parents deserve second chances. Not all parents deserve to have children. I do believe, however, that both the parents and the children, if they have been separated for any reason, wonder about what the other is doing and how his/her life is going.*

Many essays, especially the letter to our parents, made me depressed. How many times have I wished for a normal family? It's hard for me to see other people interact with their fathers. I honestly don't remember what it is like. I deal with this daily. Many students wrote to their parents to tell them how much they love them and to thank them for always being there and supporting them. Then there's me, who hasn't even said "mom and dad" in ten years. The worst part is that it will never change. I will never call another man dad. Do I feel like I've been cheated? Hell yes. I would give anything in the world to change that. I will continue to see people with their parents and I will continue to wish I was they. I often think about what my life would be like if my dad were here, not necessarily how I would act, but what it would be like to be at home with two parents. Would there be enough spots for everyone to sit down and watch television? Would my mom cook dinner? Would I call my dad "dad" or "daddy?" My brother would be very different if he had had a male influence around. He's so irritated dealing with all women all the time. I hope that my classmates who wrote about a healthy relationship with their parents will take advantage of what they have.

Like I have written and said several times, there is no way to change my situation. Nothing I learned about divorce this semester can directly change my situation. All I can do is reflect. I can think about my mistakes and my parents' mistakes, but I can never change anything. I am lucky to have had the opportunity to write about these issues and came to numerous realizations in the process. I just wish I could do something with them.

I had intended to have Matilda read her essay immediately following Sabreena's, but since she had not yet returned to the room, I didn't know whether to dismiss class or continue. Everyone was still distressed by Matilda's reaction to Sabreena's essay. I decided to read two anonymous essays. By the time I finished, Matilda was back in her seat, composed, and when I asked her if she was ready to read her essay, she nodded. As she started to read, she choked up and once again began to cry. After a few seconds, she asked me if I could read the essay. I nodded, but by this time I was feeling shaky myself, and before I could reach the second paragraph, I found myself welling up with tears, unable to continue. I could feel my face burning, my heart racing, my nose running, my glasses fogging. No longer able to control my body, I burst into tears and sobbed as I hadn't done for years.

Crying in the Classroom

For more than twenty-five years I had read to my students emotionally charged diaries and essays, and though my voice had occasionally faltered and my eyes become watery, I never failed to complete a reading. Matilda's essay was not the most wrenching of the semester, yet I found myself unable to hold back the flood of tears. When I regained my voice, I apologized to Matilda and asked her if another person could read her paper. She nodded silently and then her classmate Mia began reading the essay in a steady voice while the rest of us struggled to regain our composure. The class was as startled by my tears as I was, and I could hear muffled sounds from several people. There was no wailing or convulsive sobbing, as one might hear at a funeral; rather, what I heard were sniffles, as if the members of the class were battling a cold. I thanked Mia for her strong reading, again apologized, and dismissed the class. The students silently filed out of the room, averting their eyes from each other. After everyone left, Sabreena slowly approached my desk and then burst into tears. "I feel like I'm such a bad person," she exclaimed. "I wish I didn't feel so angry at my father. I'm so selfish." I assured her that she had every right to feel angry, and after talking for a few moments, we left the class, both of us wiping away the tears and reflecting on the significance of what had just happened. I wanted to ask Matilda if she was okay, but she was nowhere in sight.

Why had I cried? And why was I so embarrassed by my tears? I have always maintained emotional control in the classroom, and I did not like the experience of being out of control. Ironically, on the first day of the semester I had told my students that some of them might find themselves crying in response to a sad essay; but I never thought I would be joining them. I have never heard of a college teacher crying in front of a group of students except for those who became misty when teaching their final class before retirement. None of my colleagues has ever spoken about crying in the classroom, and I suspect that none would talk about such an event. I have read many articles and books on pedagogy but cannot recall other instances of teachers crying in the classroom. As Jeffrey Kottler points out in *The Language of Tears*, crying is permissible in some professions but not in others. "Therapists cry. A lot. Engineers don't. Stockbrokers don't, although they often feel like it. Truck drivers don't cry (except in country-and-western songs). Soldiers don't generally cry unless they reach a place of prominence in which they are permitted to do so on behalf of all the others who would like to weep. Nurses cry. Nurses *have* to cry in order to deal with the pain they get so close to. Doctors, however, rarely cry. They insulate themselves from pain—their own as well as that of their patients" (119).

Teaching is not a profession that typically sanctions tears, nor does our culture endorse male professors weeping in the classroom. College teachers are supposed to be analytical rather than emotional. The popular stereotype of an English professor is that of a man wearing a tweed sport jacket, looking urbane and sophisticated. If he is middle-aged, he may lament the loss of his hair or virility, and perhaps secretly (or not-so-secretly) lust for his female students, but there aren't many novels or films in which the professor breaks down in class, crying over a student essay. (He may feel like crying when reading a pile of poorly written essays, but that is for a different reason.) Tears well up in Robin Williams's eyes in *Dead Poets Society* in response to his student's suicide, but he cries in an empty classroom. We recall that Mr. Chips cried when reading the list of Brookfield graduates who were killed in the Great War, but he was permitted to do so only because of his age. "Well, why not, the School said; he was an old man; they might have despised anyone else for the weakness" (101). Norman Holland never cries in *Death in a Delphi Seminar*, not even when he discovers to his horror that he is a suspect in the murder of his graduate student.

Another reason contemporary college teachers do not cry is because postmodern sensibility privileges irony, skepticism, and detachment over sincerity, belief, and involvement. We live in an age that is suspicious of both understatement and overstatement, and nowhere is this suspicion more evident than in crying. Tears are not always genuine or sincere, and it is not only actors and actresses but politicians and corporate executives who can cry on demand. Iconic writers like Ernest Hemingway contributed to the cultural suspicion of tears. "I mistrust all frank and simple people, especially when their stories hold together," proclaims Jake Barnes at the beginning of *The Sun Also Rises* (4). He reserves his greatest mistrust for those who are "sentimental," by which he means people who indulge in weepy excess. Apart from the irony that Jake is preoccupied with his own physical and psychic injuries and prone to crying in private—"It is awfully easy to be hard-boiled about everything in the daytime," he admits, "but at night it is another thing" (34)—it is difficult for a male to acknowledge strong emotions without incurring the suspicion that he is "unmanly" or a "crybaby."

I was embarrassed because I had suddenly gone from being a witness to another person's pain to a fellow sufferer. I felt as if Matilda's and Sabreena's words had pierced my heart, and I identified with the sorrow and loss in their essays. I knew how unbearable it would be for my wife or me to be estranged from our grown daughters, with whom we are in daily contact. But I also identified with Sabreena's and Matilda's fathers, for I could imagine their anguish along with their regret and guilt. My own father had died three years earlier, and while my parents were married for more than fifty years and enjoyed what appeared to be a successful marriage, I have always felt that my father was emotionally unavailable to his family. Like so many men of his generation, he could not talk about his feelings, and it was only when he was literally on his death bed, and not fully conscious, that he said "I love you" to me for the first and only time. I grieved my father's death but have not yet resolved my disappointment with him or my guilt for being so judgmental. "The bitterest tears shed over graves," Harriet Beecher Stowe observes, "are for words left unsaid and deeds left undone" (128–29).

I did not weep at my own father's funeral, but I did weep when I tried to read a student's essay mourning the death of her father. How strange the mourning process is, filled with so many unpredictable temporal and spatial discontinuities. Grieving is rarely a simple or direct process; we may grieve months or years after a loved one's loss, and sometimes we may grieve not for the loved one but for a surrogate, a person we have never met. We may cry our hearts out for a fictional father or, in this case, a real father whom we have never met, yet remain dry-eyed during our own father's funeral. Who can predict when a stranger's death will trigger tears for a loved one's death? And who can know when, crying for others, we are also crying for ourselves? In Saul Bellow's masterful novella *Seize the Day*, Tommy Wilhelm has a conflicted relationship with a stern, disapproving father who wishes him dead. The defeated son, who is so terrified of his father that he cannot stop shaking and twitching in his presence, finds himself drawn to a stranger's funeral. As he looks at the body lying in the casket, Tommy begins crying softly at first from sentiment but then from deeper feeling. The tear imagery combines with sealike music that enters his protagonist's tortured consciousness. Bellow ends the story on a haunting, elegiac note: "It poured into him where he had hidden himself in the center of a crowd by the great and happy oblivion of tears. He heard it and sank deeper than sorrow, through torn sobs and cries toward the consummation of his heart's ultimate need" (108–9).

It was only after I had broken down in class that I began to wonder about the cultural and psychological significance of crying. I knew that crying is a universal phenomenon that is shaped by cultural factors, but I was only dimly aware of the complexity of these issues. And so I began to research the subject. I discovered, not surprisingly, that many books have been written on crying. "Tears are the most substantial and yet the most fleeting, the most obvious and yet the most enigmatic proof of our emotional lives," reports Tom Lutz in his book *Crying: The Natural and Cultural History of Tears* (29). He states that the "prohibition against male tears . . . only takes center stage in the middle of the twentieth century, and even then it was not fully observed, as we can see in the weeping of film stars and crooners" (64). With more than a little sardonic irony in his voice, Lutz opines that "[t]ears often resist interpretation, and an explanation that is obvious to the crier may be lost on the person whose shoulder is getting wet" (19). I found myself agreeing with several of Lutz's observations. We tend to cry only to a receptive audience; additionally, crying is simultaneously a performative, expressive, and empathic act. Lutz's fondness for paradox — "[w]e can cry in public as long as we look like we are trying not to: we are less likely to get in trouble for breaking the rules if we pretend that we are not breaking them" (295) — sometimes blinds him to simpler truths, namely, that crying is not always a staged or veiled act. Some of his assertions strike me as questionable, as when he agrees with Arthur Koestler's statement in *The Act of Creation* that the "self-transcending emotions," which include sympathy, empathy, and identification, do not tend toward action but toward quiescence and catharsis (246). In Lutz's words, "[e]mpathy requires identification. To identify with another inhibits the self-asserting tendencies that lead us to action, and therefore empathy is a passive emotion that leads to no action"(246).

Kottler takes a more psychological approach in *The Language of Tears*, offering several theories of crying. "Most obviously, tears are a bodily fluid excreted just like urine, saliva, sweat, or digestive juices. As such, crying may symbolically be viewed as part of the immune system, an aggressive defense against emotional trauma" (93). Psychoanalysts view crying as both a "compensatory defense against other internal drives" and an "act of regression in which we retreat to the earliest preverbal stage of life" (94). In its largest psychological sense, crying is an expression of loss — which perhaps explains why, in every culture with the exception of Bali, crying is a universal response to death. (The Balinese do not shed tears at funerals because of their Hindu belief that one must remain serene in the presence of death.)

Kottler is especially perceptive in pointing out the gendered nature of crying, and his discussion helped me to understand how I fulfilled gender stereotypes when I apologized (twice) to my students for crying. "*Men apologize for their tears.* Not having been rewarded very often for crying, since such behavior represented a humiliating loss of control, men are likely to feel remorse and shame after letting their tears show. Rather than feeling good about their authentic expressions of self, or even relieved at the release of tension, they more often feel some degree of regret and re-solve to show more self-control in the future. The result of this self-re-straint is that the average man cries only once per month, roughly one quarter as often as women" (151; emphasis in original). Kottler's observa-tion that "men work hard to suppress and curtail their tears" (151) also applies to me, as does his explanation why I felt better not *while* I was crying but only when I *stopped*. "It is only in the act of resolution that crying can become therapeutic. In their analysis of this phenomenon, Jay Efran and Tim Spangler found that it is the *recovery* from tears, not the act of crying itself, that is experienced as most therapeutic. The implications of this are, then, that helping people to feel comfortable crying is indeed important, but not without also helping them to dry their tears and make sense of the experience" (195; emphasis in original). Not all of Kottler's observations, however, ring true for me. He argues, for example, that "men are not inclined to explain their tears" (150), a statement that contradicts my need to become, however briefly, a student of tears.

"There is little that can move a man to tears," observe psychologists Dan Kindlon and Michael Thompson in their book *Raising Cain: Protecting the Emotional Life of Boys*. "He can talk about a failed marriage, disturb-ing children, career disappointments, ruinous business decisions, and physi-cal suffering with dry eyes." I was struck by the accuracy of their next sen-tence: "When a grown man cries in therapy, it is almost always about his father" (94). In *The Grief Taboo in American Literature* Pamela Boker ar-gues that "[e]motional honesty, vulnerability, and expression, along with the valuing of personal ties, are customarily associated with a feminine sensibility in patriarchal culture" (2–3), hence, men's repression of grief and the inability to mourn.

Over the years I can recall dozens of women crying or teary eyed in class but no men. Most students who acknowledge crying when writing an es-say or diary are women. Male students sometimes report crying when no one is around, but rarely in front of other people. In the essay about her parents, for example, Sabreena writes about her father's insensitivity to her crying. "I cried, and he told me not to cry. My mother never told me not to cry." In the Instant Messages, however, her father tells her that he also cried but only after her visit.

Some male students have asked me to read their essays aloud, presumably because they did not trust themselves to remain composed, and others have stopped in the middle of an essay to ask me to complete the reading, but no man has cried. Students who occasionally leave the classroom when a classmate or I read aloud an emotionally charged essay are nearly always female. Apparently most men feel, consciously or not, that crying is a symptom of weakness or helplessness rather than a sign of emotional engagement. Recall the student who said that he felt at risk when writing the letter assignment: "I felt as if some type of emotion would overcome me. Since a young child I was taught not to cry in front of others because it shows weakness. I thought that reading my paper aloud would evoke very strong sentiments that I would not be able to control."

How did the students view my crying? I sat with my head bent down while Mia read Matilda's essay, trying to wipe away my tears; I observed everyone with bowed heads the one time I looked up. No one looked at Mia, Matilda, Sabreena, or me. It was as if everyone sensed that privacy had to be respected and that each person needed to be alone. Each seemed to be unaware of his or her classmates' existence, yet at the same time there was a connection, a bonding, suggesting that everyone was emotionally attuned to the sadness and loss about which Matilda and Sabreena were writing in their essays. The silence that arose in response to Mia's reading struck me as profoundly respectful. They knew that Matilda's essay had moved me deeply and that my tears demonstrated the power of her language. My tears gave them permission to feel moved themselves.

Although I wished I had not cried, I felt closer to my students afterward, the way they feel after disclosing a painful or shameful experience and receiving their classmates' support. They sensed that this was a noteworthy moment; their response surely would have been different had I cried every week. They did not know why I cried, but they knew that it had something to do with Matilda's essay. If they were frightened or distressed when they saw me crying, they must have felt reassured when they saw me stop crying. Similarly, if for a few seconds they discovered that words failed me, replaced by expressive but enigmatic tears, they witnessed words gradually returning to me, the teacher once again in control.

Much of this is speculation, however, for although I knew how I felt, I did not know how they felt. Would they look at me differently in the future? How would Sabreena and Matilda be affected by my tears? Empathy requires both identification and detachment, and I wondered whether my temporary loss of self-control would be upsetting, even traumatizing, to Sabreena, Matilda, or their classmates. Recall Danielle's observation about "trembling at certain descriptions" of her classmates' childhoods: "There have been a number of times when it took everything in my power not to openly weep. I don't define myself as at 'risk' but I could see the potential for it when I hear these accounts."

By chance, I had scheduled a conference with Sabreena after class, but we decided to postpone it until the following Tuesday. Over the weekend I brooded over the class, still shaken from the event. I had called Matilda several times on Saturday, Sunday, and Monday, but no one answered the phone. Sabreena and I met on Tuesday, and she assured me that she was grateful for Matilda's comments. We spoke for about half an hour, and she gave me an essay that she had written over the weekend explaining what she had learned from the experience. We walked to class together, and I noticed that Matilda was absent. Nearly all the other students were present, however, and I told them that before I explained how I felt about the preceding class, I wanted to know how they felt. I asked them to respond anonymously to the following question:

> Last Thursday, while reading Matilda's essay to the class, I lost my composure and was unable to finish the reading. Mia helped me out, completed reading the essay, and then the class ended. Would you please describe in a paragraph or two how you felt during that class. I'm also interested in your reactions after class, when you had time to reflect upon Sabreena's and Matilda's essays. If you didn't attend that class, speculate on how you might have felt.

As I explained when we met before class, I felt confused when Matilda began voicing that I should try and make amends with my dad. After her essay was read I understood why she said what she did. I felt embarrassed at first because my essay seemed invalid to me after hearing Matilda's. I think that having Mia read it was a great idea because she provided a mediator's voice and did not know what to expect. I was upset after class for quite some time, but I think last Thursday's class definitely helped me to understand myself and others.

I was so surprised to see such an outflow of emotion this late in the semester. While students have been affected by the writings, it was unusual to see this so suddenly. I am not afraid that anyone in the class was affected negatively by Prof. Berman's self-described loss of composure. While most professors and faculty as well as others would frown on this, I found it particularly refreshing. In essence, this is one of the things academia fears from classes that deal with personal subject matter; a weakening or disabling of the relationship between student and teacher. Since that relationship is usually defined by power and the issue is learning and education, I have mixed feelings. But while some see this as dangerous, I believe it leads to greater communication.

I cried. I felt Sabreena's essay illustrated how there is a man who wants to be her father. But she can not connect to a father figure because she never knew him and now after all these years, he wants a daughter. And she does not want to have contact with him. Matilda's paper told her story of the chance to get to know her father but couldn't because of his death. I cried because Matilda described situations at the dinner table, and in the living room watching tv with the family that has happened to me. Remembering that my dad still calls me his princess or baby girl or that we still hold hands to cross the street like when I was four. I felt saddened because both girls don't have the chance that I do and it made me feel guilty and selfish.

I felt as if nothing was moving in the class while Matilda's and Sabreena's essays were read. As Matilda started to cry, I started to see the rest of my classmates sink into their chairs. The room was very tense. I noticed Nat putting on his sunglasses. About half way through Matilda's essay, I felt an enormous craving for a cigarette. I needed to get out of that classroom. All of the feelings were too much for me. I felt relieved when I was finally outside getting fresh air.

I'm glad you asked this question. Driving home that evening I cried. I wasn't hysterical, but I cried. I felt for both Matilda and Sabreena in a way that I didn't think was possible, up to this point. I wasn't just hurting for one of them, it was the combination of both. When Matilda told Sabreena to talk to her dad, and she started to get upset, I think that affected Sabreena a lot. I wonder if she thought about what Matilda said? During the class I was stunned. The tone was so heavy and one could just feel the weight in the room. I saw Matilda on the road that evening. I was expecting to see her breaking down at the wheel, but she wasn't. I give her a lot of credit for coping so well and sharing such a depressing area of her life.

I felt awful for Sabreena, Matilda, and the professor. Primarily, I was concerned for Sabreena. Sabreena was addressing her strained (and nonexist-

ent) relationship with her father. Given the history of their relationship, it is extremely understandable why Sabreena had such animosity towards her father. Not many people have learned the life lesson that Matilda was forced to. Sabreena's anger, in my opinion, was completely natural. For her to feel awful about the feelings she has for her father would be to deny her role as a human being. My heart went out to all of those people involved, but I really could not help but to reflect, primarily, on Sabreena. She reacted to her situation with her father as most people would. As for the professor's reaction, initially I was scared. The type of scared you get at a small child witnessing his/ her parent crying. That fear was quickly replaced by comfort. In a way, the professor's tears had allowed the students to feel comfortable in their sorrow. It made all the words from Mia's mouth consume each of the listeners and to actually allow the students feel acceptance in their sorrow. The paper and the professor's reaction made the expression of sorrow acceptable.

I was not present for last Thursday's class, but I know that if I was here, I probably would have become emotional as well. There is a strange, unspoken rule that states that teachers are supposed to be formal and unemotional during class. I know that I would have been very shocked to see my professor lose his/her composure during class time. I probably would have felt like I wrote a great, yet poignant essay if it was my essay you were reading.

To judge from their words, the students found the class wrenching, but they were not judgmental or disapproving. Several reported crying during the class or afterward, and nearly all experienced empathic distress while hearing Sabreena's and Matilda's essays. They admired the two students' courage and gave them credit for coping with difficult family situations. They believed that my loss of composure had positive consequences. One person believed that it led to "greater communication" between teacher and students; a second felt that my response indicated "care" and brought me "a little more down to earth"; a third believed that my tears "allowed the students to feel comfortable in their sorrow." Those who felt momentarily overwhelmed believed that their response befitted the intense emotions elicited from Matilda's and Sabreena's essays. Audrey, who had noted in earlier essays that she was adopted, felt a longing to discover her biological parents. Two students expressed gratitude for having loving relationships with their fathers. Those who missed class predicted that they would have felt upset, sad, or choked up. There was only one student whose response was unambiguously negative:

Class was conducted different than any other previous class. Sabreena's paper was read, and then it was openly discussed. The discussion went too far as to discussing the topic. The environment became too emotional and tense when Matilda started to tell Sabreena that she should be grateful that her father wants to be part of her life. I thought it was an inappropriate time for a discussion on that level. This class is about grammar and style, it should not stray into an emotional fiasco. The reading of Matilda's essay was also inappropriate at that time. The reason being that it was an anonymous essay and the name of the author was revealed, not only to Mia but to the class. I feel that if an essay is too disturbing for the professor to get through that it is not appropriate for the class. It raises too many emotions that could not be present in a classroom setting.

I don't wish to dismiss this criticism—the atmosphere in the classroom *was* emotionally tense—but there is a factual error here that may have influenced the negative judgment. As I indicated to the class at the time, Matilda had agreed in advance to read her essay to her classmates: there was no breach of confidentiality. Matilda *wanted* to share the essay with her classmates, though neither she nor I realized that it would be so difficult to read.

Apart from the preceding negative judgment, it is possible that other students were less positive toward my crying than they indicated in the anonymous written responses. Perhaps they were being kind to avoid hurting my feelings, or perhaps they were telling me what they thought I wanted to hear. Yet even if these possibilities are true, their comments reveal strong empathy and sympathy for me, both of which they knew I would understand and appreciate. They were mirroring the empathic responses I offer to them, allowing everyone in the classroom to see how an event that might otherwise have been interpreted as a weakness or failure might be viewed as an appropriate response to another person's sorrow.

It would be absurd to claim that the empathic distress my students and I experienced resembled what Shoshana Felman's students felt while witnessing Holocaust videotapes. The Holocaust is an incomparable event in history, and the shock it must have produced in her students is of a different magnitude from the emotions generated over parental loss in my classroom. Nevertheless, all people find themselves unexpectedly witnessing others' pain, and there is the possibility that one or more people may experience empathic distress when traumatic subjects are discussed in the classroom. These moments occur whenever we confront topics of overwhelming importance. Emotions need to be understood, in Martha Nussbaum's words, as "geological upheavals of thought": that is, "as judgments in which people acknowledge the great importance, for their own flourishing, of things that they do not fully control—and acknowledge thereby their neediness before the world and its events" (*Upheavals of Thought* 90). These upheavals of thought may occur anywhere—in the analyst's office, the confessional, or the classroom. In Nussbaum's terms, the crying in our classroom represented a "eudaimonistic judgment, namely, a judgment that places the suffering person or persons among the most important parts of the life of the person who feels the emotion. . . . Thus we feel fear about damages that we see as significant for our own well-being and our other goals; we feel grief at the loss of someone who is already invested with a certain importance in our scheme of things" ("Compassion and Terror" 15–16). However painful these moments may be at the time they occur, they may be viewed in retrospect as momentous, even epiphanic, and they may represent breakthroughs in our understanding of ourselves and others.

These breakthroughs of understanding demonstrate the intersubjective nature of teaching, in which teachers and students influence each other intellectually and emotionally. This influence is itself shaped by conscious and unconscious forces. As hard as I tried to remain detached and objective while reading aloud Matilda's essay, I could not: my observation and participation were inseparable. Nor could Matilda's classmates remain detached, for they, too, were involved with her and my tears. Teacher and students participated in a mutual and reciprocal relationship that involved not only the present moment, the reading of an essay, but also past moments, or histories, of each person in the classroom. No one can predict when these past experiences, conflicts, or issues will erupt suddenly in the classroom and influence everyone else.

Unlike Shoshana Felman, who was advised by psychoanalyst Dori Laub to "reassume authority as the teacher of the class" and "bring the students back into experience," I did not worry about losing my authority in the class. My main concern was to make sure that no one was harmed by the outpouring of emotion in the preceding class, and I felt reassured when I read the students' anonymous responses. I typed up the responses, photocopied them, and then distributed them during the next class. Each student could then see how his or her classmates reacted to Matilda's essay. The result was not only increased awareness of each person's subjectivity but also a recognition of the humanness—and humanity—of every person in the classroom.

We often use metaphors such as "flood" of tears and "overflowing" tears to describe crying, suggesting our cultural fear of being "swept away" by dangerous emotion, "drowning" in tears, but the reality is that we stop crying after a few seconds. Rarely if ever do people perish from tears. Indeed, clinicians believe that the opposite situation is far more deadly: being unable to cry and thus unable to find an outlet for potentially explosive emotions. My father never cried, not even on his deathbed, and I often wonder whether his refusal to express any emotion about his illness hastened his death. I no longer feel ashamed that I wept in class, nor do I feel proud that I have now written about the experience. If I cry again in class, it will no longer be an experience to cover up—or cry about.

Sabreena: "I Began Seeing a Different Side to the Story"

We did not read aloud or discuss the students' anonymous responses to my question, but I did speak briefly about my reactions to the preceding class, including my conflicted relationship with my father. I then told the class about an essay Sabreena wrote over the weekend that she was willing to share with her classmates. With Sabreena's permission, I asked Mia to read it aloud:

"I Drew You Pictures of My Pain. They Were Pretty . . . So Vain"—Jawbreaker

Having to sit through last week's class was one of the most emotionally draining experiences I've had to endure this semester. After class I broke down. I walked out of the classroom feeling more unsure about my life than I think I have been. I began questioning my intentions. When Matilda began crying, I wanted to hug her. I wanted to tell her that I felt her pain. Instead, I felt like the worst possible human alive. As she voiced to me that I should take advantage of my father's attempts, I began seeing a different side to the story I have known only one side of my entire life. In my essay I explained that I did not want to accept my father's pleas to reconcile. I left it that I was not ready to make amends with him, and maybe when I got around to it I would give him a chance.

At first, I was confused that Matilda was jealous of my chance to see my father. Everything she talked about was reinforced when her essay was read aloud. I am faced with an opportunity that Matilda would love. Suddenly I feel selfish. How could I take advantage of the fact that my father is actually trying? (No matter how false I believe his words to be.)

I talked to my father after class that night. Ironically, I got an email after class from him. He offered for me to stay with him this summer. Because of this class, I came to a decision. I am going to visit my father this summer. I do not think I am going to stay for the duration of the summer, because I feel that I should take things one step at a time.

People have always told me that I should reconcile with my father before it is too late. I was always too immersed in self-pity to care. Matilda's essay put into perspective how important NOW really is, because "Too late" can be a month or a minute from now. It made me realize that I should "Seize the day" because "Too late" can be all too soon.

I believe that each of us has grown as a writer and humanitarian throughout the semester. We have been exposed to each other's personal lives. We learned about each other, and gained knowledge that the author's closest friends might not even know. I will remember each of you as individuals. Many of your essays forced me to rethink my past. Many of them had profound impacts on me. I have made decisions about my future that I would not have made without hearing all your essays. I would like you all to remember me the same way I will remember you; as a flawed but honest person. I consider myself lucky to have been trusted with your personal writings. We are all the Dead Poets Society, and Jeff is our Robin Williams. He provides us with the inspiration we need to improve as writers, and teaches us to grow and reflect while doing so.

I feel as if I had an epiphany this semester. I made a decision that might alter my life. Because of your essays, I might have a relationship with my father. I am grateful for being able to share my Tuesday and Thursday evenings with you, where "through our suffering, we are one" (Unknown).

> *Sincerely,*
> *Sabreena*

After the semester ended, Sabreena left me a short note in which she brought me up to date about her summer plans, including a visit to her father:

Professor Berman,

I stopped by to say goodbye and thank you for a wonderful semester. I hope you have a great summer and an inspiring semester off. I will see you when I get back from Seattle (after I get reunited with my dad). I am scared and excited but I feel a stronger person because of your class. (And I am equipped with the power of words if they have to be used against him.) You will be missed!☺

> *Yours truly,*
> *Sabreena*

Sabreena does not allow herself to become unrealistically optimistic about the outcome of her visit, but she is now armed with the "power of words." Contrary to Arthur Koestler's and Tom Lutz's claim that empathy inhibits the self-asserting tendencies that lead to action, empathy enabled

Sabreena to undertake a new and potentially transformative action, reconciliation with her father. And contrary to the reference to *Dead Poets Society*, none of the students in the class was hurt, nor did the teacher incur the disapproval of a school administrator.

Part of the challenge of teaching is that one can never predict the direction of an open-ended class discussion. Nor can one foretell, regardless of years of teaching, how a student will react to a topic. Suppose Matilda was not a member of the class or that no one had responded to the content of Sabreena's essay. Or suppose Matilda responded in the way she did without telling anyone about her father's death. Or suppose Sabreena did not read her essay aloud. Would she have then reached a different decision about her father? I have no answers to these questions. As happens so often in life, there was an element of luck here: a fortuitous constellation of events led Sabreena to a conclusion that she might not have otherwise reached. For example, she told me during our conference that she would have felt too embarrassed to read her paper if Matilda had first read hers. However serendipitous the events were leading up to Matilda's comment, and however heartfelt her advice was—and it's too soon to judge its long-term impact on Sabreena—I still believe that it is better for teachers and students to avoid telling each other what to do or not do with their lives. Such advice is fraught with dangers. There are exceptions, of course. Advising students who are struggling with psychological problems to visit the university counseling center is an obligation; notifying campus security that a student might commit a violent act is also a duty. But in general I don't believe it is appropriate for teachers to advise students on personal issues. Rarely do students ask for such advice—Sabreena did not, for example—and if they did, I would be loath to do so.

"What's the Catch?"

Sometimes my reluctance to give advice leads to a student's frustration. For example, the student who stated enigmatically in an anonymous in-class exercise that there "has to be a catch" to personal writing identified himself during a conference, and he wrote the following explanation when I asked him to elaborate on what he meant:

I wrote about my life. I wrote about my pain, struggle, discourage, and love. I wrote from the heart and dug deep into my soul to express my true feelings. My job was to be honest, empathic, and sometimes sentimental. I did this perfectly. But I got no response. Jeff was too busy looking for gram-

matical errors and colloquialisms to even inquire further into my thoughts. So I ask you Jeff: What's the catch? When I say catch, you might think of a deceiving act, like someone trying to lure you into some kind of a trap. I do not mean it in this context. I am talking about the reason he does not inquire about the content of our work, but rather the style and mechanics. Why do we have to open ourselves up, with no advice received from the professor? Some of us want to be helped: some of us need you to be our shrink. Yet you do not play that role. Do we have to pay you, you know, slip you a bill or two? I wish I knew the damn catch. If I were to get a call saying that I won a free trip to anywhere, I would say what's the catch, and they would say, "Well, you have to buy $10,000 worth of appliances during the next six months." Hell, I spend 10 grand and all I get are some toaster ovens and some plane tickets? Sorry, maybe next time. The point I am trying to make is a simple one. Are we writing so that we can analyze ourselves and come to a self-realization, or are you reading our lives to use the content in some thesis? The question lies, possibly with no answer.

I think the question *has* an answer, one which the writer has himself articulated: teachers encourage students to analyze themselves and come to their own self-realizations. Indeed, this is far preferable to teachers telling students what they must do or not do. It was not that I was too busy looking for grammatical errors and colloquialisms to inquire further into my students' lives, but rather that I was trying to help them find the right words to reach their own conclusions. This is the role of the teacher; anything beyond this role has the potential for harm.

Matilda: "After I Wrote It, I Felt Better"

How did Matilda feel about breaking down in tears while disclosing her father's absence from her life? How did she react to my own tears? She told me, when I finally reached her by telephone, that my response did not upset her further. Nor did she remain distressed after class ended. She turned in an essay at the end of the semester describing the class's impact on her:

If I had to explain this class to another person I would tell him/her that it is like no other class he/she will ever take. On the first day of class, when I walked into what was then a room full of strangers, I wasn't sure what to expect. I couldn't imagine, after you told us that many of the students cry in the class at some point during the semester, that it would actually happen, and especially that it would be me.

I am going to be honest. I chose this class out of the other expository and critical writing classes that are required for my major because when I read the description, I figured it would be the easiest one. Why would I write travelogues when I could write essays about real events in my life. So I made my decision, joined the class, and thought it would be just another class. Naturally, I was wrong.

After the first few assignments, I still felt detached from the class. I wasn't feeling any emotional drain from what we were writing about and I was not expecting to hear the stories from the other students that would change my opin-ion of them, and make me realize that I am not the only person with problems, and that my family is not the only one to experience suffering. At this point, I was enjoying the class for your emphasis on grammar and writing skills. I still didn't think that I would be revealing anything too personal to the class.

Then we were given two assignments on divorce. I wrote the first paper with the intention of reading it in class, but realized when I was finished that I wasn't ready to share with the class after all the tears that went into writing it. The letter to a parent was even worse for me. I was no longer just telling a story, but actually bringing another person into it, my father. My feelings and frustrations came out in this paper and it was hard for me to deal with. After I wrote it, I felt better. It is hard to describe what I mean by "better" because the feelings and emotions that come with the loss of a parent are difficult to decipher and describe to a person who has never expe-rienced it. I guess I could call it a feeling of release, especially since we had to imagine what our parent would write back to us.

Colin: "There Is Nothing Worse Than Hating Yourself and Not Knowing Why"

There were many other students who wrote memorable essays, but I want to close with Colin's, which was the last one read on the final day of the semester. Colin believed that his essay could not be understood without an awareness of the letter to his father:

Hey Dad,

It's Colin here. How are things going? It's been awhile since I talked to you last and I'm not sure why that is. I have some unresolved issues that I need to address to you but I'm not sure how to do it. I've been sitting at my desk for over an hour now thinking about whether or not I should write this letter. This is probably my tenth draft and I haven't written more than a paragraph. I'm not sure why I'm writing it now or at all and maybe that's why I'm at a lose for words but something tells me it's long overdo. I'm trying to make sense of all the anxieties I've been having lately and perhaps I can articulate them here in a clear and honest way. If I can't, you won't be receiving this letter and don't have to worry about it.

I've been reading journal entries submitted by students in the past about their experiences with divorce in one of my English classes. At this point I'm sure you know where this is going and I understand that this is a bad time for me to complain to you about your horrible parenting but I need to settle my mind, if only for a minute. Listen, that's all I ask of you. Many of the students, in their essays, expressed hatred for their fathers and admiration for their nurturing mothers while others were confused about how to feel at all as a result of their parents divorcing. The essays were honest and personal and the varying emotions expressed by the different writers dripped from the pages as they have from my mind for so many years. I just felt so god damn confused after reading them, Dad. It was like all the memories of my youth came crashing down upon my head. As I was reading some of them I found myself despising these terrible parents and feeling sorry for all those confused kids. I left it alone for a while and went out that night. When I got home I lay in bed and listened to some music and gave it all one long drunken thought. I came to the realization that I didn't really feel sorry for these kids at all, I was feeling sorry for myself and that pissed me off. I understood their pain and confusion but in the end I found myself comparing them to my own. I blame you dad. I blame you for how I feel right now and for making me feel sorry for myself. Its been twelve years now since you left and, even though things have been better between us in the past few years, I have so much unresolved anger laying heavy on my chest that I need to let go.

Maybe I need to beat the shit out of you, who knows? Or maybe we need to talk as adults about how bad a father you were to us growing up. In the past, I've noticed that every time that question is alluded to in any way, you change the subject or bring up the good old Cub Scout days. First of all, you and my brother were the ones that went camping and did the Cub Scout thing. I was the eight year old that learned from my brother what you probably think you taught me. It doesn't really bother me that you weren't there when I wanted to play ball or go fishing as a kid. I mean there are people out there that have it much worse than I'll ever have it. It's the fact that you walk around not blaming yourself for it all. Maybe I want an apology from you or maybe I need to let it go?

I really think you are a decent man, dad, and probably regret what you have done in the past. It just seems like every time I need your guidance you screw up somehow. I'm sure you won't understand what I'm saying until I give you some examples. I'm thinking.

Do you remember how long it took you to contact us after you left home. Well, it was one year, one month, and three days I think. I lost count after a year. That day I heard mom say that you were on the phone, my eyes lit up brighter than they ever had before. I was so excited to see you, your new house, and new dog. I thought I would be ecstatic when I saw you that morning but when I looked into your blood shot eyes I knew why you were gone in the first place. I don't remember if you hugged me or kissed me but I do know I was close enough to smell the cigarettes and beer. Why did you come get us that day? You couldn't possibly think that was the best thing for us. We did have fun throwing empty Bud cans at you while you were passed out on the couch but from your side that was terrible reentry into our lives.

We didn't see much of you for the next three years. I guess you had pulled out all the stops on that first reunion. Ahhh, then we took that trip to Vermont to go skiing. That's the trip I talked about for over a month in class. The one where the irresponsible father takes his kids away for the weekend and smothers them with attention and presents in an attempt to reclaim their love. You decided that introducing us to your new girlfriend was the better path, though. I do applaud you on your effort. And who can forget our wonderful trip to Florida a year later that wasn't about a family reunion at all. It may have been a reunion for you but it was a nightmare for us. Thanks for letting us know that you were getting married while we were in Ohio. That was just short of 600 miles from where I wanted to be then and forever.

I tried not to be sarcastic here but your stupidity demanded it. Dad, you've had so many chances to make things better and you've let them slip through your fingers every time. Now, I'm an adult now and have my own problems but I'm never going to be completely at peace with you until I have some closure. I have gotten by without your help but I've been lucky. I might need you in the future and need to know if I can depend on you. I don't have much left to say, it's been hard enough expressing this much emotion to you. I've written more here on these lines than I've ever revealed in real life. I guess I have a long way to go. Don't hurry a response. Sit on it for a while and let me know how you feel some other time. Take care.

Colin

Dear Colin,
How are you doing? First of all, I think I know what's wrong with your car. Call me after you receive this letter and I'll let you know what I think. We won't discuss what I've said in this letter at that time in less you want to. Well I'll tell you what, son . . . you really shook me up with that stuff. I don't remember how many times I've read it and just plain stared at it. I want you to know that I love

you and your brother and sister. With your sister getting pregnant and all and the term, grandpa, bouncing around in my head, I've had a lot of revelations. I've told you before that how ever bad my marriage was to your mother I don't regret any minute of it because if I had left after having your sister, which I wanted to do, you and your brother would not be here. I'm proud of all of you and I guess I'm proud of myself for bringing you guys into the world.

There are so many issues that I could never express to you when you were a kid and will probably have trouble expressing now but those I will leave to another time. Most of what I want to say can't be expressed in words so I'm not going to waste your time trying to write how I feel. What I can write is my sorrow and guilt for leaving you kids so long ago. That time in my life didn't make a whole lot of sense to me and your mother and I got to the point where we couldn't stand to be around one another. That meant I couldn't see you guys the way I wanted to see you and finally I gave up. I gave in to drinking and feeling sorry for myself. It took me a long time to realize that it was myself who I had to blame. That didn't happen after I left you guys. It didn't even happen after I divorced your mother. It happened just a few years ago when I saw in you kids the adults that I never saw in myself.

To answer your question Colin, I blame myself for treating you kids the way I did. I know this isn't enough for you and it shouldn't be. It feels like shit when your kid can't say "I love you" back but I deal with that and I probably deserve that. I would like to solve all those problems for you, Colin, and I think by sending that letter, you are old enough to know the truth however painful it may be. If we can begin to work this out I think we will be much better off in the future. I'm sorry that I can't say more here, son. I need to speak with you in person and see your face when dealing with this. I am very proud of you and will be there for you as much as I can. We should arrange a couple of days where you can come out and we'll go from there. Until then, take care son.

Love,
Dad

The letter assignment was so important to Colin that he wrote two different response essays, one immediately following the assignment and the other a few weeks later. He stated in his first response essay that he was "thrilled" when he first received the assignment. "The idea of expressing my emotions toward my father in a controlled atmosphere made me feel comfortable. The anger and frustration I have for him runs much deeper than any words could describe but I felt the experience would be rewarding to me nonetheless." He was also intrigued by the challenge of imagining his father's letter to him. "I feel I know his personality and I presumed that hearing his voice through my own would help me come to terms with my own insecurities and pains." The assignment turned out to be much more difficult than he expected. "I must have had at least ten sessions where I stood at a blank computer screen struggling with my emotions, hoping to pull them from the remotest parts of my subconscious. I thought I knew the words to express my feelings of abandonment and sorrow but I only got broken fragments of a once angry child. I realized, as I fought to extract hidden memories, that I had lost so much time trying to forget the circumstances of my childhood and blanket the consequences with less painful ones."

Colin felt a "sigh of relief" after completing the assignment. He believed that the emotions he expressed to his father were "heartfelt and honest" but acknowledged that he still had a "long way to go" before their relationship would improve. Reading the entries in *Diaries to an English Professor* helped him to recall distressing memories of his past that had been "lost in an abyss of denial for many years." The letter assignment was valuable, but he did not expect to show it to his father in the near future. "I wonder if I could put these letters in an envelope and send them to my father? I imagine myself at some corner mailbox, my hands sweating as the envelope gets closer to the mail slot. I see myself retracting the letter and cursing myself with head hung low as I shamefully walk back to my apartment. No, I couldn't send it. I would love to but I can not send it. I know I'm not ready to confront him with my anger. There will come a day when I can confront him with a strong voice and a steady eye."

Colin continued to brood about his father, and in the second response essay he tried to find a way to convert the letter assignment into a life-changing event. "When I began the letter to my father, I was unsure how I would deal with my anger toward him. We had been getting along for the past couple of years, and I thought the letter would bring to mind memories I had previously chosen to forget. When I finished the essay for class, I saw in it an opportunity to approach my father with my anger, and put to rest the anxieties I had been struggling with for so long. I needed to release all that was bothering me. The pain in my chest and the emptiness in my heart were festering, and I felt he was the center of it all. The more I thought about the letter, the longer it became in my mind. I knew the assignment only scratched the surface of what was truly bothering me, and I made an attempt to draw from my anger a solution and a peace."

Colin wrote in his second response essay that he was struck by one of my comments to his letter assignment. "I came to a section that Jeff had commented on, and I paused. I read over my sentence and his response. The more I thought about them, the more frustrated I became. I wasn't frustrated with what Jeff had written. I was frustrated with what I hadn't written. I stated, 'I've written more here in these lines than I've ever revealed in real life.' Jeff's response was, 'Is this true?' I thought I had written in two pages all the anger that I had ever felt for my father, but there was so much more within me that needed to come out. I knew the only way to ease my frustration was to confront my anxieties, and direct them right at my father. The letter had been therapeutic as far as I was allowing it to be. My problem was that I was viewing it only as an assignment." After reading over what he had written and what he thought his father's response would be, Colin concluded that he had to sit down and talk with him. But it was not easy to do this, for each time he visited his father after writing the letter, he became anxious. "I have talked about him to counselors and friends, and have unraveled almost all my hatred and disgust for him. I feel I must bring this all to his attention, but instead, I become more frustrated. I am not angry because I can't tell him. I am angry because I won't." Colin then described what he learned most from the letter assignment: the need to accept his father. "I can't judge him for being the man he once was, because I can not confront him with that. I have learned how people can change, and how holding onto fragments of the past can leave you in anguish for the rest of your life. I look at my mother, and I see a broken woman who never came to terms with the fact that my father left her. She is scarred from the physical and mental abuse he laid upon her when they were together, but she has not released that hate to anyone in a meaningful way. Unfortunately, the only way she could express her pain was by screaming at her innocent children when they were growing up without a father. I know she is sorry for this, and I forgive her. But she will never be happy because the pain is tied way too deep within her. I don't want that to be me in the future. If I can not confront my father with my anger, at least I will give him a chance to become a better man in the future. At this point in my life, that will suffice."

It is against the backdrop of the letter assignment and the two response essays that we can appreciate the significance of the essay Colin submitted near the end of the semester. It is the time when students often turn in their most self-disclosing essays because they realize that it is their last opportunity to share a life transforming event with classmates, one that they have generally concealed from all but their closest friends. I had wanted Colin to read his essay during the next-to-last class, but because of a backlog of papers, we did not get to it until the last class, which was reserved for an in-class party. Colin wondered whether it was an appropriate time to read his essay, not because he feared it would be anticlimactic, but because its tone was hardly festive. I assured him, however, that the paper was too important to ignore. He had described in his earlier writings the feeling of abandonment he and his siblings experienced when their father divorced their mother and moved away, and he links that period in his life to a later experience that he recalls in vivid detail:

I had been sitting on my rooftop equipped only with my thoughts, and even they were escaping me. I was feeling so alone and empty. I kept asking myself the same question. How the hell did I get like this? These words echoed loudly throughout my head every day and every night. I felt they would never go away because I didn't know how to answer them. My mind was only hearing the sorrows and cries of my own self-pity. I couldn't seem to get a handle on my life, and wondered how I had become so worthless to myself and the world around me?

There is nothing worse than hating yourself and not knowing why. Even as I sat there in the dark, staring blindly at the night sky, I couldn't figure out why I was here and what I was saying. I did know that my life was taking a bitter turn, but I didn't know where to go. I had withdrawn so much of myself from the environment around me and I was filling that void with nothing but self-hatred. I woke up some mornings not knowing where I was, and it scared me back to sleep. So I would close my eyes and dream a while longer. At least there I could pretend. In life, I had nothing to pretend about. I was staring out across the skyline of Manhattan, and began feeling more alone. I gazed at the people on the street below me, knowing they didn't care. I stood up and walked forward, dragging my feet along the gravel floor of my roof, and grasped the brick ledge with my hands. I lifted my body over the wall and sat with legs dangling below. I peered down five stories and began asking myself, had my life come to this. My body was shaking and my fingers were digging into the ledge at my side, but my mind was screaming . . . Let Go. Just let go.

And so I did. I took a deep breath, closed my eyes, and leaned forward. I felt my fingers scrape the bricks on the ledge, and then, let go. My heart was pounding, and for that brief second, I thought I was dead. I panicked and opened my eyes soon enough to grab hold of the ledge before it was out of reach. I pulled myself over the wall with the little energy I had left, and collapsed on the roof. I cried for over an hour, curled up in a tight ball, clutching the loose gravel with my bleeding fingers. My body was numb and shaking, but I lay there throughout the night, and managed to drag my feeble body down four flights of stairs early that morning.

I think of that moment when I let go. I remember how it felt with my eyes closed. I remember how the cold October wind felt on my wet face and how I was not scared at all. For a brief second I was not afraid of dying. I won-

dered why it was so easy to remember all the pain and traumatic events leading up to that night on the roof, and forget all that was wonderful in life. I began thinking, what if I wasn't scared for just one more second. Would my life be over? I remained in bed for three days following the experience, staring at shapeless images on the television and smoking one cigarette after another. I couldn't eat and I couldn't sleep. The knowledge of my failed attempt, and the fear of doing it again left me more vulnerable than I had ever been in my life. I remained buried underneath my warm blankets, and cried most of the night.

I began having flashbacks of my youth. The darkness in my room reminded me of a time when I was twelve years old. It was weeks after my father left us and I was alone, facing all the fears of an abandoned young boy in the darkest hour of the night. My eyes were swimming through the blackness of my room, seeking solace from someone or something. Minutes before, I was clutching my mother's warm arm and I was laughing with my siblings. We were all abandoned, but we were braving the storm together, holding on to one another night after night in her bed. I can't remember why I was thrown out of the room, but I know it was final. I never felt more alone in my entire life. I held my breath so I could hear into the other room, but there was silence. Maybe the fear of being exiled scared my siblings quiet, or maybe they all fell asleep in a peaceful embrace. Either way, I was left to bear the silence alone. I began feeling insignificant and scared, and as the tears began to choke me, I thought about suicide for the first time in my life.

I was going to a counselor at this time, and I remember being confused about how to deal with my new darker emotions. She was a nice woman, but inexperienced. She had come from a broken home as well. Her father left when she was in high school and she hadn't seen him for years. I always felt uncomfortable around her because I was only twelve, and I felt I was less equipped to handle a divorce than a young woman. She was much older, and I was embarrassed about my feeling of neglect and these strange self-destructive thoughts that beamed in my head. After a few months and more thoughts of suicide, I approached her with it. She remained calm, but I could see her shaking behind her plastic face. She asked me how I felt when these thoughts came to me, and how I got over the numerous urges. I don't remember the language she used, but it was sweet and heart felt, so I let her inside. She put me on medication that I adamantly refused but my mom shoved down my throat every night. As the weeks went on, our meetings became more comfortable. I began seeing Esther, not as a counselor, but as a friend and guide. It was about this time that my father came back into my life, and the momentary service she was providing me became an essential part of my life. His unfulfilled promises and lack of interest became Esther's problems, and she handled my feelings of abandonment with the care only a grandmother could offer. My mother was lost in her own world of agony and abandonment, and her pain was not the type three children could remedy. We would stand in front of the bathroom door some nights, and cry back the tears my mother was expelling on the other side. We were an army of lonely children that strengthened one another, but couldn't bring a smile to our mother's weathered face. My siblings and I formed a strong union that built up its defenses against the material world around us, while Esther and I battled the demons in my head. My suicidal feelings began to diminish, and the neglect of my father didn't bother me anymore. I had the union with my siblings and the strength of Esther.

Around this time, my brother had discovered a hidden section in our yard that was covered densely by trees. He brought my sister and I into it one day and we knew immediately he had found something special. The pine trees hung heavy over us, creating a thick wall and ceiling that was hidden from the outside. We raked the floor and placed planks of wood on the earth to serve as our carpet. We brought in a ladder that had fallen off our swing set and placed it against the center of one of the pine trees. It was our tower. We swore we would never tell anyone about "The Secret Passage," as we called it. We never did. When my mother would slam the phone down, presumably on my father, and begin throwing silverware and dishes across the kitchen, we would run to "The Secret Passage" and hold one another until silence and peace was restored. She couldn't be there for us, so we were there for one another. Esther played a similar role for the next year or so until she was finally transferred. She had helped me deal with those times I was in bed, alone in the dark. She reminded me of all that was important in my life, and gave me the confidence to keep fighting.

I know now why I didn't jump that night. I had been tired of being alone, and not having an outlet for my pain. I lost trust in everyone that was close to me, and I allowed no one new into my life. I didn't have an Esther to talk to, and didn't have a "secret passage" to escape to anymore. I felt I had lost everything that ever meant anything to me, and I thought, for that one long second, that dying would release all the pain I had ever endured. I didn't jump because I didn't want to die. I had been walking around for months, feeling sorry for myself, and the sorrow just kept building. My life wasn't easy, but I was making it worse every single day by not acknowledging it. I would look at myself in the mirror, and see through my hollow eyes. Inside there was nothing. My strength and my faith were absent, buried deep beneath months of self-torture. That brief second on the roof did not only make me realize how confused I was. It let me know that there was still life left in me. I just had to find it.

I got out of bed after reflecting upon my youth and the circumstances leading up to that. For three months, I had been walking around in no particular direction. I didn't know how I ended up on that roof and, ultimately, on that ledge. I was scared and I didn't want to hurt anymore. That one second of obscurity opened my eyes to a world I had not seen in a long time. After recovering from the stress of the moment, I stared at a mirror, and for the first time, I saw the pale hollow mask I had been wearing for six months. I ran to my phone and called my best friend. I laid bare all the pain I had inflicted upon myself, and exposed the scars that were killing me. He opened himself to me, and absorbed my tears with understanding and comfort. It was the first time in six months that I had allowed anyone into my life. That small window of hope became a pathway for all the grief that I had displaced, and I began a long and wonderful journey back to the world I had once loved.

It is not a stretch of the imagination to see how Colin's writing class itself became a "secret passage" to explore life-threatening issues that are seldom discussed in the classroom. The mirror into which he peers, seeing his own hollow eyes, is a metaphor of the writings he and his classmates turned in every week. Some were joyful, many others were not, but all contributed to increased clarity, self-understanding, and connection. Like the friend to whom Colin poured out his feelings, and who "opened himself to me, and absorbed my tears with understanding and comfort," so did Colin's classmates perform this role for him and each other.

We can also see in Colin's essay, along with those of several of his classmates, a process of self-forgiveness. Self-hate brought him to the edge of the abyss—in this case, a five-story Manhattan rooftop—and although he felt relieved that he did not jump, he also felt increased shame over the failed suicide attempt. "I remained buried underneath my warm blankets, and cried most of the night." Once again we see male tears concealed from the world. He links the flashbacks he began experiencing to the period in his childhood following his father's departure from the family. Like so many of his classmates, he describes the traumatic nature of a parent's abandonment. With the help of his siblings, therapist, and close friend, he slowly regained self-confidence and trust in others. He ends the essay with the image of a "small window of hope" that gives him a larger perspective of the world than the frightening rooftop on which he began the essay.

During the semester we never discussed the genre of illness-and-recovery narratives. Only after the semester ended, in reflecting upon his writings, did I realize that Colin's story ends with the glimmer of hope that can be seen in novels like *I Never Promised You a Rose Garden*, *The Bell Jar*, and *Girl, Interrupted*. What makes Colin's essay unusual is that unlike the protagonists in these autobiographical novels, he attributes his recovery, in part, to his participation in an empathic classroom. He makes this clear in an essay submitted after the semester ended:

I enjoyed being part of this class, and hope that I take from it everything I think I have. When I walked into the room on that first day in January, I scanned the faces of my peers as I normally do the first day of school. I didn't know a single person in the class. I had seen some of them in previous classes, but never had talked to any of them. So the semester began as it normally does for me; a semester of a few expressions and even lesser words.

You see, a couple of years ago I suffered from an anxiety disorder that disrupted my life significantly. For the first few months I denied I had any problems, and tried to make it through each day without having an anxiety attack. Life became progressively worse, culminating in my withdrawal from college. I went home for a year and worked, and became more and more miserable. I came to Albany the next year, hoping to find solace from my self-pity and loneliness. I did not find it. I began having attacks in class, and missed most of my first year. I spent most of my days in bed or staring at the television. If I went to class, I would put my head down and withdrew myself from all classroom activity. I feared I would embarrass myself by passing out, or worse off, have a heart attack. I went on medication for some time, but took myself off it because it interfered with my drinking habits. I don't want to go any further into my personal decline, because it has little to do with this assignment. What I wanted to do is acknowledge my weaknesses, and attribute my recovery, in part, to the success of this class. I had been feeling better prior to this semester, but I still lacked an adequate outlet for my emotions. Two years ago, I was reading a book and writing almost every night. I found refuge in a character's world, and therapy in my own words. But the more I broke down over the next couple of years, the less I would read and write; the less I would read and write, the more I would cry and feel sorry for my pathetic self. What I found in this course was an outlet for many emotions that have remained dormant within me for so long, and an opportunity to dissect them in a cooperative atmosphere.

You may ask how this class has aided in my recovery? The cooperative atmosphere was essential to the success of the class. Early on in the semester, we were given a handout that broadly defined the term, empathy. Over the next several months, the term became more and more dynamic. It filled the room every class period, and created the essential atmosphere that was needed for all students. We conveyed many personal experiences that, for some of us, were hard to deal with. Imagine a room full of strangers, listening to your crackling voice as you express your hatred toward your father, and tell me you wouldn't feel vulnerable, if not for a second. The atmosphere we created softened the direst of emotions so that our own vulnerability was swallowed up by the comfort and compassion offered by others. Looking back on the experience, I wish I had shared more with my classmates and professor, because they have given me so much themselves.

Try to imagine our classroom. There are twenty people in a small class, circling around three of the four walls in the room. You can see everyone's faces without having to move your head. Everyday, four to five students read aloud from their personal writings, and the class comments on them afterward. It seems to be a relatively basic concept, but the way in which it was performed was far more powerful. I can recall one day when we were discussing an essay about our parents. The point of the assignment was to write a letter to one or both of our parents, and convey how we feel about them. In turn, we would write a letter back from our parent, using his or her voice. The day I am referring to involves me reading my assignment to the class. Mine was the second of four essays read aloud and I was nervous about reading my assignment to the class. The student before me spoke of her parents with an animated voice, and expressed her feelings for them with love and respect. I was weary to read my essay after hers, since mine was much darker. I spoke with an unsteady voice, and I could feel the eyes of my classmates peering through the words I had written. It wasn't a happy essay, but it was an honest one. I thought to myself, maybe they will see through all the gloom and recognize the sincerity in my words. Maybe my essay was a fitting transition in the mood of the classroom. The only difference between my essay and the one before mine was the voice. They were both honest and powerful, and as I read mine aloud, I just hoped that everyone would see it that way. And they did. That is the strength of empathy. The strength of seeing people individually, and understanding the differences in each and every one of us. The following two essays were meaningful in their own individual way, and my classmates handled them in the same fashion. That was a good day. I began to respect the consideration each student put into one another's efforts, and it helped make my own compassion more accessible to the classroom.

The Self-Disclosing Classroom: "Come Off the Page, Come to Life"

How did the students finally judge the impact of self-disclosing writing? I asked them near the end of the semester to write a brief, anonymous response to the following questions:

> Nearly all of you have disclosed painful and/or shameful experiences that you have never written or spoken about before. Some of these self-disclosures have been in the form of signed essays that the writers read aloud, and others have been in the form of anonymous essays that I have read aloud. I suspect that most of you have been surprised if not shocked by these self-disclosures.
>
> Would you please write one or two paragraphs about the impact of these self-disclosures on you. How did you feel about your classmates on the first day of the semester, and how do you feel about them now that the semester is almost over? To what extent has this course affected your understanding of people in general? Has the course affected your empathy? If so, how?

Hearing other people share personal experiences makes me feel closer to them. My usual reaction is not to dwell on their experience but to think about how it relates to me. If someone's parents hit them it makes me think about my parent, or about how I will one day be a parent. If someone writes about how they felt sexually pressured, it makes me think about my sexual behavior; have I done that? Has someone ever done that to me? This is good! This is what English/literature is supposed to do: come off the page, come to life, say something about not only the characters involved, but also about the person reading it.

Just like any other class the first day is filled with uncertainty of who is sitting next to you and surrounding you. You don't know what to expect. After seeing these people for weeks now I have befriended some. I have learned enough about the rest of my classmates that I feel I know them. Throughout this course I have learned that people in general have lived through many challenging situations. I learned that people are made stronger by the situations they have survived. I have learned a great deal of empathy. I will think again before judging someone and their actions. Hearing about various circumstances I have learned that there are real reasons people act and behave in a certain manner.

I have had so many classes with many different individuals, and so often an entire semester goes by and I don't even know any of their names. I feel that I've learned so much about my classmates and I feel honored that I was allowed to hear some of their most painful and embarrassing experiences. What I learned and feel to be most important after taking this course is that every individual has experiences that are just as heart-wrenching, if not more so, than my own. I do feel I have a greater sense of empathy and a greater understanding of life in general. This class has helped me put my life into perspective.

The student responses reveal remarkably similar attitudes toward self-disclosure. They were anxious in the beginning of the course, unsure whether they wanted to self-disclose to a group of strangers. As the course progressed, they overcame resistance to self-disclosure and experienced a growing attachment to their classmates and teacher. Given the reciprocal nature of self-disclosure, the more they revealed about themselves, the more their classmates revealed to them. Nearly all commented on the relationship between the growth of their self-understanding and their understanding of others. Several wrote essays focusing on parental loss, mourning, and posttraumatic growth, and nearly all were sensitized to suffering. The empathic classroom allowed students' stories to "come off the page, come to life," and the stories were thus able to "say something about not only the characters involved, but also about the person reading it."

Being a Character in a Book

How did my students feel about being characters in their professor's book? This is one of many questions I asked during interviews conducted six to twenty-four months after the course ended. This was the first time I have interviewed students after the completion of a course. Before the interviews, I showed the students an early draft of the book so they could see how I was representing them and to make sure that no further disguises were necessary. Included in this two-hundred-page draft was a brief discussion of forgiveness, which I discovered in retrospect was a common theme running throughout many of the essays and letters on divorce. I was interested in how students felt rereading their own writings as well as their classmates', the course's impact on their lives, and whether they had shown their essays to relatives or friends. I tape-recorded each interview and, in what follows, offer updates about most "named" students.

To begin with, all the students felt comfortable with the way I represented them, and none asked for additional disguises. All but one wanted me to include their real names in the acknowledgments page, though they realized that their anonymity might be compromised. They believed that I had represented their point of view accurately and that I hadn't omitted anything important that occurred during the semester. They were excited about appearing in the book, and most said that they had already shown, or intended to show, their writings to relatives or friends.

Cory: "I Think about Empathy All the Time"

"It's a bit awkward [rereading my writings]," Cory stated at the beginning of our interview, "like seeing yourself on videotape or hearing your voice on an answer machine." He said he didn't anticipate becoming a "character" in the book, but that's how he felt while reading the manuscript. "It seemed like I was back in that class, and the book triggered a lot of memories, not just of that class, but of the entire time. Reading it was almost like going to a reunion. I really miss the class. I started thinking about the commute to campus, either being flustered because I had just finished my writing assignment or nervous because I wasn't prepared for class or excited because I thought I wrote a killer paper."

Since graduation from college, Cory has been pursuing a master's degree in English education so that he can become a high school English teacher. Much of the writing he did in English 300 now seems "melodramatic" to him. "During your teenage years you are the most melodramatic person in the world, and that begins to fade when you get older." He was surprised by how personal his writing was; he would not have predicted many of his self-disclosures. Cory said the main strength of English 300 was its ability to improve his writing. "I really learned how to write, how to choose my words carefully." He attributed this improvement partly to the sentence revisions we did at the beginning of every class—"It was one of the most effective grammar lessons I've ever had. The sentences weren't from a textbook but from our own essays"—and partly to the self-disclosing nature of his essays. "The writing became better because it was so emotionally charged." A weakness of the course was that the structure became repetitive. "Perhaps we should have read a short story or two."

Apart from improving his writing skills, the course's greatest impact on Cory was its emphasis upon creating a safe classroom in which students could write about risky topics. "What amazes me about the class was its empathy. . . . I think about empathy all the time. It's something that is very dear to me, and I'm always going to be an empathic teacher to my students and an empathic father to my children. It's the cornerstone of my outlook to life." He felt that the "proof" of the course's empathy occurred when several of us cried during Matilda's essay: our tears affirmed the existence of emotions that are often too powerful for words. "I've often thought about how the feeling of love completely rules our society. There's really no proof that love exists. Crying is one of the closest things we have to prove that something exists that is indescribable. There was a period in my life that I actually doubted love's existence—love is a maddening thing that causes so much inner conflict. Crying is a curve ball because our eyes explode with water." Cory said that although he is a firm believer that the opportunity for growth arises from mistakes, sometimes it is too late to express forgiveness, as Matilda's essay revealed. He felt that crying in the classroom was the defining moment of the semester, one that he will never forget.

Danielle: "I've Lifted That Weight, Which Was My Father"

"It's very strange being in your book," Danielle exclaimed. "I wasn't in class when you read the piece on my father—it was a last-minute decision not to attend that class." She said that although she wanted me to read the essay aloud, she did not want to be in the room to hear it: she was afraid that it might be too painful to hear and that she might give herself away. But having read the book, she now regrets having missed that class. She was both surprised and pleased by her writings: surprised that she was so self-disclosing and pleased that her writings conveyed what she intended. She said that everything she wrote about her father was truthful, but that in retrospect she did not want to convey the impression that he is a terrible person. "He has many wonderful qualities, including his love and protectiveness of his wife and children." She felt disloyal in writing about him, but she was glad that she did not embellish or gloss over the truth.

"This is the one course I've taken that sticks out," Danielle said, "the course that has been the most beneficial." Writing about her father was a turning point in her life, and as a result of the course, she felt increased understanding and forgiveness. "Being able to re-create what my mother would say to me gave me a little more ammunition to forgive my father. It gave me his point of view from my mother's point of view. It made me understand a little more. With my father, I used to worry constantly. Even when I was in college, I felt guilty about leaving my family and what he would do next. Since I have written that, I guess my form of forgiveness has been indifference. I can't control his actions and spend my life worrying about what he was going to do. Not that I don't care, because I do. I still do. But it doesn't control my life as much." When I asked her if "indifference" was the right word, she paused and then said that "no, acceptance would be a better word. I guess acceptance is a form of forgiveness."

Colin's last essay made the strongest impression on Danielle. "That was the most powerful essay of the semester. After class I approached him—I don't typically do that, and I never would have done that with someone from another class. I told him that it was one of the most powerful essays that I read. He responded positively." She was also impressed with Nat's letters. Danielle said that she thought her classmates demonstrated "courage and strength" by reading their essays aloud and wished she could have done so too. "I chickened out," she said, to which I responded: "But every person has a different comfort level. I don't think that the decision to remain anonymous has anything to do with a lack of courage or strength."

About a month after the course ended, Danielle decided to show her writings to her brother. She was startled when he started to cry as he read the letters. His crying made her nervous, since he is not an emotional person. She then showed the writings to her mother. "She wanted to read the letter aloud, but I said 'no, I don't want to hear it.' She read it, and her reaction was similar to my brother's. She just kept nodding her head, especially during her letter. She kept saying how honest everything was. She was surprised that I was able to capture exactly what she would say and think." Danielle believed that she succeeded in conveying her mother's protectiveness of her husband as well as her helplessness and sadness. They discussed whether Danielle should show the letter to her father but concluded that although it would be valuable for him to read, he was not ready to do so.

Showing the letters to her mother has changed their relationship. "I think I have a better understanding of her; she thought that maybe my brother and I were blind to everything—I think she thought she was in this alone." Now Danielle's mother sees how her children are involved in the situation. Danielle thought that her mother might "cringe" when reading the letters, but she didn't: "she actually liked the way I handled the whole thing." Danielle believed strongly that writing about her family has been a transformative experience; her writings might not change her father's life, but they have changed her own. "I don't know how to articulate what my writings have given me, but I was constantly anxiety-ridden about my father. When I got all of that on paper—and I only noticed this after reading your chapter on forgiveness—I honestly haven't let [my father] in the last six or seven months be the main focus of my life. I've lifted that weight, which was my father." Although she is still concerned about him—and although he still drinks—she has accepted the situation. Our interview was right before Christmas, and she said that unlike previous years, she was now looking forward to going home for the holidays. "I used to get really anxious before going home—Christmas always used to be awful because that's when it was worse for him. Now I'm really looking forward to going home and spending time with both my parents, but I'm not so nervous now. I don't have all the fears and the anger that I guess I did last year, when I went home."

Lydia: "I Learned That It's a Lot More Difficult to Forgive Than to Hold onto Anger"

"Rereading my writings in your book reminded me how intensely I felt being at home with my mother," Lydia declared; "I realized that I was not over my feelings." When I asked her what she meant by "feelings," she responded without hesitation: "anger, pain, and vulnerability"—emotions she did not want to have. "I'm glad I wrote those essays, but I'm also sad that they contain so much anger."

Lydia said that she never realized the extent of her anger toward her mother until she reread her writings. Hearing her classmates' essays helped her to realize that they too had parental conflicts. She identified with many of her classmates, especially Cory. "I see now that parents aren't perfect. It's very possible that my parents set out to do the right thing. I wouldn't have thought of that six months ago. I'm learning that my parents are people." She believed that she portrayed her mother as accurately as her perceptions allowed her to. "It's how *I* see her." Rereading her own writings and her classmates' writings enabled her to change her self-perception; whereas she used to blame all her problems on others, now she felt she must accept responsibility for her actions. "I used to be angry at people, especially my mother, but now I'm picking my battles. The course has helped me figure out how I felt toward her. The course helped me put these feelings on paper and organize them in a way I wouldn't have done ever. I was much more conscious of what I was trying to say, and by doing that, it made me think about what I was truly thinking. I could then go back and look at my writing and say, 'no, that's not right, that's not what I meant.' I can't say that my relationship with my mother has changed, but I think that my understanding of her has."

Lydia corrected a factual mistake I had made in my discussion of *The Breakfast Club*. "The film takes place not in the school gym, as you wrote, but in the library." She said that film was a rite of passage for anyone who grew up in the late 1980s and 1990s and that she saw it about twenty-five times. "*The Breakfast Club* has such an attitude of hostility that I can't imagine sharing the type of things we shared in our class."

Lydia couldn't wait to share her letter to her mother with her classmates.

"Even though when I read it aloud it felt like I wanted to cry, and I was shaking, I felt it was the next best thing to telling my mother what I thought about her." She was pleased with her classmates' responses, and although at times she wanted the class to be like group therapy, she was glad that it didn't happen. "The class remained really focused on the writing. The reason everyone felt so comfortable was that they knew they didn't have to hear other people's opinions about their opinions. They're only going to critique my writing and, in the process, make me a better writer. When you feel passionately about a subject, you write most clearly, and using personal topics to write about made it so that we cared more about how we expressed ourselves. . . . It's so important to you that others get what you are saying. Everyone was very respectful." The only aspect of the course that she did not like was the emphasis on grammar. "I hated all the grammar but it was necessary, so I can't say it's a negative. It's a positive disguised as a negative."

When asked what readers should know about her that she has not yet revealed, Lydia replied, "it's quite possible that I have manic depression." She couldn't remember whether she had disclosed that her mother was also suffering from this mood disorder. (She hadn't.) Lydia added that for years she has been struggling with an anxiety disorder and depression. She had no objection to my including this information in the chapter because she thought it would help readers to understand her. One of her fears, she said, is that she might become like her mother—a fear that she consciously realized only during our interview.

How did Lydia feel about being a character in a book? "It's weird because I feel like I got approval from you." She felt that she was now in some ways "more like a colleague than a student. It means a lot to me to receive approval as a writer." She hoped that I would include her writings and for that reason paid more attention to word choices than she would have otherwise. "It made me self-conscious in a good way." She realized the necessity to use a pseudonym but at the same time wished that she could use her own name so that she could "own" her writings. Like Danielle, Lydia said that she hopes to be a writer one day and use her own name but, until then, would "settle for an acknowledgment."

One of Lydia's most important realizations from the course is that words can be both wounding and healing. She felt that the course enabled students to look into themselves and heal from each other's writings. "I learned that it's a lot more difficult to forgive than to hold onto anger for the rest of your life. I felt sad when I read Sabreena's Instant Messages with her father. As an outsider, it made me realize, "well, no, she should just forgive him and give him another chance. And then I applied the same logic to myself." Lydia then observed that if she were writing a letter to her mother now, it would probably be very different from the one she had written in class. "I no longer feel so angry. I don't want to be an angry person. That's what I talk about in therapy. You can write that in your book too."

Nat: "I Always Knew My Mother Would Be the Most Fascinating Character I Could Read or Write"

"It was interesting to read my writings in your book," Nat remarked at the beginning of our interview. "It seemed to give it some importance that I wouldn't have normally thought it had." Writing about his mother was not a transforming experience for Nat; his attitude toward her has not changed. Nevertheless, writing was a "way of abbreviating, a way of clearing up, almost a finalizing. Each time I reread my writing, it reminds me that these issues in my life have now come full circle. This isn't to say that I won't continue to have observations about my past from future experiences, but the majority of what I have learned has, I think, already been done, and the psychological comfort has been attained." Nat believed that he completed a chapter in his life, but he was not sure if he knew what closure is. "When you have something traumatic happen to you, I'm not sure that the word 'closure' makes any sense. But in terms of getting to the point where your life is enriching instead of negating, then I have reached closure."

What most surprised Nat about his writings was his ability to re-create his mother's voice. "I always had problems trying to explain what my mother was like when I talked to other people. I was frustrated because people didn't understand how I could have these sorts of feelings about my mother. [They would say] 'She's your only mother and you have to love her.' Yeah, it was really frustrating. People would meet her and say she was the most wonderful person in the world and believed she had a very impressive personality. It was only after years of knowing her or living with her that people would finally understand, as some people did. I was surprised that for one of the first times I was actually able to make sense and convey her personality. I always knew my mother would be the most fascinating character I could read or write, and knowing that I was able to do that surprises me."

Nat singled out Sabreena's letter to her father as among the most moving of the semester. "Reading her essay greatly increased my respect for her. I hate to say that I don't have respect for someone until I realize that they have undergone pain just like me, but as humans we tend to think that we feel pain more than other people and less pleasure. By feeling her pain, I gained more respect for her experience, for her emotional intelligence. Sometimes I think I'm more emotionally intelligent because of the experiences I've had, but that's not true. I noticed that Sabreena was handling the situation very maturely."

The course sharpened Nat's writing skills—that's what he liked most about it. "My biggest improvement came in my compression of language. Also, I now have more pride in my writing." The catalyst for this improvement was that he was writing on important subjects. "For the first time in my academic career, I found myself rechecking my language more than once." He also commented on the "aesthetic pleasure" he experienced while writing the letters to and from his mother.

Writing about his mother has resulted, paradoxically, in thinking about her less. "It was not so much the act of writing but reading about what I wrote that was more beneficial and therapeutic." I was surprised when Nat said that rereading the letter a day after he wrote it gave him the same degree of objectivity as rereading it six months later. "While I was writing the letter I was caught up in the detail, caught up in the idea of the particular sentence I was working on, but reading it gave me the big picture." He had no intention of contacting his mother in the future, but the idea of showing her his writings was nevertheless enticing. "But whenever I think about that, the only motive seems to be vengeance, so in the end it doesn't interest me." He believed that he achieved self-forgiveness when he was fourteen or fifteen and realized that he was not to blame for his parents' divorce. He didn't know whether he would forgive them, but he no longer blamed them for problems in his life.

What should readers know about Nat that they don't yet know? "I guess I could update you on my continuing lack of a relationship with my mother. This summer I went to Europe and met my dad in the airport for lunch, right before the flight. We sat down and were eating, and just as I had the first chicken McNugget in my mouth, he hands me a letter and says, 'Oh, by the way, this is for you.' I knew as soon as I touched the letter, like some type of magnetism, that it was from my mom. I opened it, and since it was getting very close to my birthday, she had sent me a birthday card that said, 'Happy Birthday.' She gave me her new phone number—apparently she had moved—and then a check, a gift certificate to Barnes and Noble. I didn't know which part was more disturbing, that she had contacted me or that she had given me money. In some ways I felt like I was being bribed to contact her. I tried to understand if this was a continuation of her old methods—bribing was one of the things she used to do at times. It was really disturbing. At first I thought, is this going to be on my mind during the whole trip? It wasn't, but I did have to spend several hours thinking what this meant to me and if I was going to react or not. I didn't actually come to a conclusion really quickly, but by the time I got back I had decided that I would not write her back. What required a decision was that I would not write down her phone number on the card. My first thought was to send the gift certificate back, and then I thought, 'well, that could be one of her tricks so that she could get my return of address.' I decided not to contact her and I went and spent the gift certificate on a book. I didn't feel guilty about it at all."

Amber: "I Had Never Put It Down in Words Before"

Amber said that she "almost started crying" when she reread her essay on eating disorders, largely because she first acknowledged the problem to herself while writing the essay. "I can't believe I wrote that. I had never put it down in words before. I had never admitted it to anyone. I felt scared and shocked when I realized, while writing the essay, that I have an eating disorder. But afterward, it was kind of nice to be able to talk about it and to know that I can get through this. Last semester was when I really started to talk about it. When I wrote it for you in class, I could pretend that no one else was going to see it."

It was painful for Amber to write the essay, but in retrospect she was glad she wrote it, for it proved to be a defining moment in her life. Without the anonymity option, she never would have written about her eating disorder. As a result of the course, she has acquired a new openness about eating disorders: her classmates' self-disclosures emboldened her own. The two most memorable essays for her were written by Sabreena and Colin. "It was powerful and scary that Colin felt that way. I could just see him sitting on that ledge and wanting to jump and then pulling himself back up. I could visualize him doing those things. I was shocked when he was reading it. It was nice that he could really open up." She has herself opened up about her eating disorder, and not long after writing the essay, she showed it to her aunt, who was sympathetic. Amber was not ready to show the essay to her parents because she knew they would be upset. "I told my mom that I'm going to be in your book, but she has no clue what I wrote about. I just couldn't tell her. I know it would hurt my parents to read the essay, and I don't want that to happen. They are very protective of me." Amber felt that the course was supportive without being a support group. "For me group therapy would be talking about your feelings, giving each other advice. We didn't do that. We were open to each other, but we focused on the grammar, and then we left it at that."

Amber wanted her readers to know that she has always shied away from attention and pity, contrary to Charlie's assertions. His essay on eating disorders infuriated her, and it was difficult for her to remain silent in class. "I wanted to cross the line hugely; I wanted to jump over it, and I couldn't because it wasn't the right time. But I think the way I would have yelled at him would have been too confrontational to have him understand what I was saying." I asked her to speculate on what might have happened if she had verbalized her feelings about the essay. "I think the class would have ended in an abrupt fight. It would have been very tense, and I think that when we came back the following class, it would have continued to be tense because we had just had a confrontation. It might have disrupted the way our class interacted with each other. The class might not have wanted to deal with Charlie, or he might have been polarizing because he felt so alienated." Nor did she feel less angry after she read his two eating disorder essays in the book. "When I reread his first essay, I got upset all over again. 'Oh my God, why are you saying this? You don't get it.' And then I read what he wrote in the second essay and understood where he was coming from. The way that he read the [first] essay in class was so harsh and matter-of-fact. I think he completely trivialized everything that society can do to someone."

Charlie: "I Try to Be Empathic, but I Have a Lot to Learn"

"It's cool that I will be in your book," Charlie said with obvious pleasure at the beginning of our interview. "A certain pride comes with that. A lot of times people ask me about the class, and I can show them the book. It's something that I will have and remember for ever." I was gratified that Charlie felt so positively about being in the book; I wasn't sure how he would respond to Amber's criticisms, which he encountered for the first time while reading the chapter. Much had changed in his life since completing the course: he had injured himself in a skateboarding accident and then had to miss the next semester because of a serious illness, from which he has only partly recovered.

Charlie said that he would make a few changes if he were rewriting the eating disorders essay. "I wouldn't have changed it completely, because it was an essay I felt strongly about. I knew it would bring up a strong reaction. But there were some things I might have changed, certain words." When asked what these words were, he replied, "I would have omitted the sentence in which I said that I'm 'skeptical of people who claim to have eating disorders.' That's a trouble-making line." Charlie wanted his readers to view him not simply on the basis of the first eating disorders essay but on the second essay as well. "If they were just to read my first essay, they might think of me as a mean person, someone who doesn't understand, someone who is unsympathetic, but the fact that I wrote the second essay, and that you included it in the book, will, I think, help people understand that I'm not really a mean person. It's just that, unfortunately for me, I've been exposed to some bad experiences with eating disorders. Not that my friends have had them, but I've seen them used for personal gain rather than for the very sad thing it is."

As a result of the course, Charlie believed that he has become more open-minded and empathic. "It opens your eyes to the fact that not everyone is the same as you. We all come from a million different places. You really do have to be empathic about other people's situations." He admitted that it was not easy for him to be empathic because of his family upbringing. "Both my father and his father are police officers, and I have other relatives who are police officers and lawyers. My family is very skeptical. Dinner at my family is more like an interrogation than a conversation. My parents were very good at picking out when I lied, and I think I'm also very good at finding when other people lied. I can't help it, and I don't think it's a good characteristic, it's just the way I am. I'm always thinking of the possibility that people might not be telling the truth. It's not my favorite part of myself, but it's just the way I am. I try to be empathic, but I have a lot to learn."

Apart from developing his writing skills, the course helped Charlie realize that there are always multiple points of view, not just his own, as he had previously believed. This was an important revelation to him, for he came to believe that increased understanding leads to both healing and forgiveness. We can also see a shift in his thinking away from an interrogatory, accusatory position to a more empathic mode. If he had trouble identifying with the eating disorder assignment, he had no trouble identifying with the letter to and from a parent, which was his favorite assignment. "While I was writing it, I realized that my relationship with my parents is not so great." Sabreena's essay taught him the value of multiple perspectives. "The letter to her father makes me look at my own situation and made me more open to the idea of forgiveness and the healing that goes along with it. Not to be able to forgive your parents or friends is sad. Her essay showed me that forgiveness is a two-way street."

Charlie knew that the eating disorders essay would be "tough" for his classmates to hear, just as it was difficult for him to write, but he could not foresee that it would provoke so much anger, indignation, and distress. He said that, contrary to my speculation that he might become defensive if Amber had criticized his essay in class, he would have welcomed her point of view. But he agreed with my statement that he would have become defensive if I had criticized his point of view in class. "When a teacher says something, it's the final word on the subject. I guess I'm glad you didn't do that!" He concluded by saying that "it would take an interview like this for people to understand that I didn't mean to invalidate those with eating disorders."

Sabreena: "I Learned the Things My Mother Told Me about Him Weren't Lies"

"It's bizarre to be reading yourself as a character," Sabreena observed at the beginning of our interview; "it's interesting because you have a different perspective on yourself. It's like taking a step back and looking at it from another point of view. I never expected I would be like one of the characters in *Diaries to an English Professor*." She was surprised by her self-disclosures. "Normally I don't expose myself very much, and when I was writing, I was writing only for the class." She said that although she might not have been so personal if she knew she was writing for book publication, she did not want me to omit any of the details of her writings. "I know that these details expose me to readers, but they add to the authenticity of my writings."

Sabreena said that class never turned into a "pity session" because everyone knew that it was a writing class rather than a therapy session. She tried to make every essay into a "work of art," and she felt that her classmates also focused primarily on crafting their writing. Yet at the same time, the course was a growing experience, and she discovered that writing is a "method to release emotions." She learned a great deal from her classmates' essays. "From their writings, you can see the person and understand what they went through. It's much more personal reading a classmate's essay than reading about past students in a book." She felt a greater connection with her expository writing classmates than with those from other courses. "The knowledge I have of them is like a gift. It's interesting to know that every person has his own story. Whenever I see a former classmate, I always stop and talk with them for awhile. You know a little piece of that person." She identified with many of her classmates' essays and now sees herself as more similar to them than different. "I no longer think that I'm the only person whose parents have divorced." Reading a draft of this book allowed her to see that forgiveness was a "common thread" running through her classmates' writing and an "ongoing question" in her own life.

In one of her early essays Sabreena remarked that it was "pointless" to think about her absent father, for there was nothing she could do to change the situation, but she was glad that she wrote about him. When asked to compare her fictional letter to her father and the Instant Messages, she said, "I wasn't expecting him to get emotional in the Internet letter, but at the same time it was hard for me to think that he truly meant it." She agreed with my characterization of her reading in class as detached and said that she tried to "dissociate" herself from her words. She felt that her father was a "sappy person, over-emotional." "He writes poetry," she added. We both laughed when I reminded her that she is an English major, hence, a student who reads poetry. "He doesn't write like e. e. cummings," she rejoined, "but like someone who writes 'love cards.'" As a result of the course, she accepted her father's invitation to visit him in Seattle shortly after the end of the semester. She didn't regret the visit even though it did not go as well as she had hoped. "I now know that I don't really want him in my life." After the visit he has called her only once, from which she concluded that he isn't serious about resuming a relationship with her.

Sabreena was "shocked" when Matilda left the room crying, and at first she became defensive, thinking, "who are you to comment on my life?" She didn't know why Matilda was so upset. When I started crying, Sabreena tried to restrain her emotions: she didn't want to turn the class into a "major tear session." She started to feel "really bad," like she was a "really bad person," while Mia was reading Matilda's essay. "I felt awful, horrible, disgusted with myself when I realized that I was given an opportunity that Matilda would never have." A long pause followed when I asked Sabreena how she felt while I was crying. Without directly answering the question, she responded, "I was surprised and pleased that you offered me a ride home after class, since that is something that professors do not usually do. It felt like you were still speaking to me as a professor, but also speaking to me as a person. The boundary between teacher and student was broken down, but not in a bad way. It helped me to realize that teachers aren't weird. Teachers are just people who want to help you." She felt that my tears brought the class closer, demonstrating that "it's okay to have a breakdown. If anything, it's a learning experience."

What would have happened if Matilda was not in that class or did not make her comment? "I would have put the assignment away and not have thought about it again. I would not have visited my father that summer and would not have realized that I am better off with him not in my life. Now I know for sure, and I'm glad that I did this. It's something I had to do to make that judgment." She felt that the realization that she did not want her father in her life was very important. "I learned the things my mother told me about him weren't lies. I'm doing fine without him. I don't forgive his actions for what he did. I think it was cowardly of him to leave his wife and kids. But now I have a better understanding of the person he is, and I know why mom fell in love with him. As a result of seeing him, I don't see myself as a bad person anymore. I learned that having him back in my life isn't an option."

After the semester ended, Sabreena showed her writings to her mother. "She was shocked because I had never really talked to her about my father. She was shocked that I wrote about my father and shocked that I read it to the class." Nor had Sabreena discussed her feelings about her father with her therapist years earlier. Thus, no one knew the importance of this subject—not even Sabreena herself. "This is the only class in college that I have taken, other than an art class, that I am going to use for my life as opposed to my career. It helped me grow as a person. It was unique, and I will never forget it."

Matilda: "Writing Put Some Permanence into His Presence"

"It feels very strange being a character in your book," Matilda said. "The idea that someday there's going to be a book on a shelf and that I might be there is weird for me. Everyone in my family is very excited." Rereading her writings helped Matilda realize that her feelings toward her father are more complicated than she thought. "That I couldn't keep my composure in class was a big thing for me. Because my father was gone for so long, I felt sometimes that I wasn't feeling the same things that another person might feel if he had been around all the time. I felt guilty sometimes for feeling that I was not feeling enough."

Matilda was surprised that she wrote about her father. "I really attempted to avoid the whole thing from the beginning, but the assignments were so directed that I said, 'OK, I'll do this.' I've written about this subject before, for myself, but I'm surprised that I put it into a paper that I would be handing in and sharing with other people." When I asked her why she decided to write about her father, she said, "Maybe it was just a need for the situation to be acknowledged. I felt like it would be a good thing for me to do, and to organize my feelings into a real essay would help me see what I was dealing with."

Matilda wanted readers to know that her understanding of parent-child relationships has changed as a result of the course. "One of my friends has problems with his parents—his mom has mental health problems and so she's been in and out of the hospital. His dad tried to have him arrested. Before the class I was less understanding of parent-child conflicts than I am now. I have a deeper knowledge of and sympathy for people who have conflicts with their parents." She wanted readers to see her as a strong person who is in control of her life. "I hope they don't view me with pity. I got over wanting to feel sorry for myself about two weeks after my dad died. I don't feel sorry for myself. Things happen, and you learn how to deal with them. I hope readers will see that I'm learning to deal with it and that I can deal with it."

As a result of the course, Matilda's attitude toward forgiveness changed, but not in a way that one might have expected. "I don't think that everyone deserves forgiveness anymore. In the beginning of the course, I felt that my father deserved and received all my forgiveness despite all the bad things he did to us. After reading other people's papers, I realized that parents do some really bad things and that they don't always deserve second and third and fourth chances." Sabreena's feelings toward her absent father compelled Matilda to take a harder look at her deceased father. "It was just so easy for me to throw everything out the window [when he died], but writing about it and actually having to look at his faults made me put a little more blame on his side now. I've definitely started thinking more about the reasons why I was mad at him, thinking them through more. After taking the course, I realize I was too easy on him. I saw how other people were still angry at their parents for doing things that were very similar to what my dad did, and I didn't feel that I was unjustified for being angry at him. The whole idea surrounding death and his dying made me feel until recently that I was totally unjustified for being angry at him, for holding any negative feelings toward him. Now I feel more justified." Matilda didn't believe that her negative feelings are unhealthy. "It's not really anger but frustration that I feel. I'm frustrated that he would do those things and not give me a chance to yell at him. I could definitely see how it would be unhealthy to hold onto these feelings, but trying to think about them and work through them make me able to come to terms with them."

I asked Matilda to elaborate on one of the sentences she had written to her father—"I thought that writing to you would make me happy, but there is no end to my grief"—one of the saddest sentences anyone had written during the semester. "I knew that I wouldn't accomplish anything by writing the letter. I knew it would stir up all of these feelings. It was a nice outlet for me, but these are feelings I've had and will have for ever, and I will never be able to talk to him about it. Nor will I be able to get his feedback, so it leads to more frustration. I had never written a letter from him to me before, to try to imagine what he might have said, and it made things more difficult because I never really looked at it in a way that might see what he would say. Trying to make up his response was—I didn't really know what I was doing." Nevertheless, Matilda was glad that she wrote the letters to and from her father, for they helped her to feel closer to him, almost as if he were returning to life. "I like to think that he's looking over my shoulder and that maybe he knew what I was writing about. Writing put some permanence into his presence, and that my writings are going into your book brings even more permanence into him because if I ever need to, I can open your book and read what I wrote."

Matilda felt fortunate that she had the opportunity to write about these issues and came to several realizations as a result of the course. "Definitely number one was about forgiveness and about second chances, and how not everyone deserves them. Another thing I realized is how I've lived without two parents for so long that I can't even imagine what it would be like to have two parents living in the house. I think about it a lot now, and I have no clue about how my parents would interact and if I would have as many freedoms as I do. Another realization was not to feel so uncomfortable about bringing the situation up with my brother. The class definitely made me talk to him about this more. Now I feel that since we've talked about it, we can continue to talk about it. This is an important development because before the class, we really didn't talk about our father at all. A week or two after dad's funeral, I went into my brother's room; he was sleeping and I woke him up, and he kicked me out of his room. He was angry and didn't want to talk about our father."

Matilda was surprised by her comments to Sabreena and even more surprised that she became so emotional. "I didn't want my comments to come out like that. I realize that my comments contradicted what I had written in my own essay, when I said that parents don't always deserve second chances. My comments were so different from what I meant them to be. I wanted just to tell Sabreena that if she was uncertain about the decision to see her father, she had to do it—no, that she should do it, or that she should think about doing it, because you don't know what is going to happen. I never expected this to happen to my father. I figured that someday he would pop back into my life, although we wouldn't necessarily have a really strong relationship. I know that if I was given the opportunity now, I would jump all over it. I know that, even if I was angry. I wanted to open Sabreena's eyes to the possibility that something could happen that could ruin the possibility that she could have a relationship with him in the future."

Matilda speculated that her remarks must have made Sabreena feel guilty, though that is not what she intended. "I think if I were in Sabreena's position, I would have felt uncomfortable hearing these words from a stranger." Matilda said that she did not realize that her comments violated the class's agreement not to offer advice to a classmate. "I became overwhelmed and couldn't control myself." Nor did Matilda realize when she returned to the classroom and began reading her essay that she was still feeling distraught. "I don't think I was done crying when I came back to the room. I felt stupid that I had gotten so overwhelmed. I felt that I had overstepped the line, and I wished that I had not said anything and just read my paper instead. And that was what I had planned on doing when I walked into the room." She was startled when I started crying. "I was more shocked than anything else. I didn't realize that my and Sabreena's stories could be so touching to other people. I always think of people as being so detached from everyone else's experiences. I believe that people sometimes fake feelings. You definitely weren't faking, so it was refreshing to see that someone could actually be that empathic toward another person." It was the first time she had seen a professor cry.

After the semester ended, Matilda told several of her friends about the chapter and showed it to her mother. "I was very nervous to let my mom read it. A lot of times she feels like she's a terrible mom and that she has done these horrible things, but this is so far from the truth. Showing her my writings in your book shows her how grateful I am to her for being so supportive of us and to have helped us get through. She was sobbing when she read it. I was in another room, and I could hear her crying. When she finished, I walked in. She said that she started crying with the first line—'I can never hear my dad tell me he loves me'—and that she cried the whole way through. She told me that I captured everything very realistically and that she wasn't surprised that I was having these feelings because she herself was feeling this way too. And then I came back to Albany and she called me a few days later and told me that she had spoken to my aunt about it—my father's sister—and that my aunt had started crying. My aunt is so emotionless—the only time I heard about her crying, except for this, was the night we found out my father died. Based on her reading my writing, my aunt has a new respect for me. My mom likes the chapter because we can all read it, and they can understand my feelings about my father. The majority of what I feel is on those pages."

Colin: "I Brought the Reader to the Edge of the Roof"

"I used to write tidbits about the way I was for those few months when I was really depressed," Colin began. "They were diary entries and were always very morbid. I never showed them to anyone. This semester, when the topic came up, I decided this was a writing class about self-expression, so I decided to try this out. I brought the reader to the edge of the roof and then brought the reader away from the edge."

Colin was anxious about reading aloud his final essay because it was the last class of the semester, and he didn't know whether it was appropriate to read it during a party. His anxiety disappeared because of his classmates' empathy. He had completed the essay three weeks before the end of the semester but didn't hand it in; "perhaps there was an unconscious reason why I left it for the end." He said that he might have felt disappointed if I did not ask him to share it with the class, though he was interested mainly in my response. "I wanted your reaction to the way I wrote the essay. Your comment that it was a 'powerful essay' was important to me, since that validated my writing skills."

Originally I had not included Colin's essay on divorce in the book, but he felt that I should because divorce is "such a huge part" of his life. In his view, the underlying motives behind the suicide attempt can be traced to the feelings of abandonment arising from his parents' divorce. Only a few friends know about this dark period in his life, and he has not disclosed the suicide attempt to his parents. "My mother would be in complete shock if she read the essay, and she would probably blame my father for the suicide attempt. She wouldn't be able to understand why I did it. My father would be a little shocked if he read it. I was almost 20 when I was on the ledge, and I cut myself off from everyone around me and fell into a deep funk for several months. I still have serious bouts of anxiety here and there, but the depression has subsided a lot, and I've learned to deal with that. I have great friends, and I'm creating new bonds with my family that I never really had."

Colin believed that the major strength of the course was its focus on empathy. "I've always been a very empathic person, and the class has strengthened this side of my personality." He said that he initially felt like a "guinea pig" when I asked him for permission to use his writings, but he no longer felt that way after reading the chapter. The most memorable essay for him was Danielle's anonymous letters about her alcoholic father: "The essay was really expressive and emotional, and it became even more emotional when you read it aloud." He felt increased closeness to his classmates after reading their writings. "You can see a progression in the emotion of their writings from the letter to a parent assignment. You can definitely see how the students grew and understand their emotions more as a result of being in the class and sharing that information and writing it down. That's how people really develop." He also saw a progression in his own writing. Like Nat, he felt that the writing techniques he learned — especially compression — are more important than the life lessons he acquired. Above all, the course gave him the incentive to continue writing. Colin observed at the end of our interview that he began thinking about forgiveness only when he read my discussion in the book, where I state that the subject runs throughout the divorce essays. Now he believes that forgiveness is a long process that must come from within. "Personal writing is a way of developing the process of forgiveness."

Summing Up: "The Shock of Creative Discovery"

For Colin and his classmates, personal writing proved to be not confessional but transformational, resulting in heightened (self-)empathy and (self-)forgiveness. In many cases, they felt heightened empathic understanding of the most formative influences in their lives: their parents. Their writings represented significant learning experiences, acts of creativity that evoke Michael Parsons's description of psychoanalytic breakthrough. "If creativity is the discovery of what we had not known we were looking for, or the making of something, up until now, unimagined, it calls for a special sort of vulnerability. To be open to the shock of creative discovery means putting ourselves at risk and being ready to give up, with no certainty about the future, ways of seeing which up until now have served us well" (150). Each of the "named" students discovered something important about his or her life, and while these insights cannot be reduced to a few words, they can be summarized by a single sentence expressed in their interviews with me after the semester ended. Thus Cory learned that empathy is the "cornerstone" of his life"; Danielle "lifted" the "weight" of her father; Lydia learned that "it's a lot more difficult to forgive than to hold onto anger"; Nat wrote about the "most fascinating"—albeit problematic—character in his life; Amber acknowledged to herself for the first time a serious conflict; Charlie discovered that he has "a lot to learn" about being empathic; Sabreena understood for the first time that the "things" her mother told her about her father "weren't lies"; Matilda succeeded in putting "some permanence" into her father's "presence"; and Colin "brought the reader to the edge of the roof" by sharing an experience about which he had never previously written. They reached these insights on their own, but they were aided by my questions and their classmates' disclosures. In writing about painful and, in some cases, traumatic childhoods, they reexperienced feelings that they could not put behind them, but along with this pain came welcome relief and, perhaps, a degree of resolution and posttraumatic growth. Nat's paradoxical observation that writing about his mother has helped him think about her less often is relevant here; for although he cannot forgive her, she no longer seems to haunt his life.

Class/Family; Teacher/Parent

As they stated both during and after the semester, the students felt a strong bond to each other, far stronger than they feel to students in other classes. The connection lasts long after the semester ends. They feel this closeness for many reasons. They know each other on a first name basis, and since they have written each other's biographies and learned details of each other's lives, they have a knowledge of each other that is rare inside or outside the classroom. Listening to their classmates' essays, they have, in George Eliot's words, a "keen vision and feeling of all ordinary human life," but rather than dying of that "roar which lies on the other side of silence" (189), they come away from their experience with a heightened appreciation of each other's struggles and their capacity to persevere.

It may seem naive or sentimental to describe a class as a family, but for fourteen weeks students took turns writing the stories of their lives and hearing their classmates' stories. They forged close bonds with each other in the process. Their stories were painful to write and sometimes wrenching to hear; few would have predicted at the beginning of the semester how many family conflicts would emerge. In writing about these conflicts, students exposed their darkest secrets to each other, much as in *The Breakfast Club*; but instead of hurting each other through cruel and judgmental remarks, they supported each other. Recall Colin's words: "The atmosphere we created softened the direst of emotions so that our own vulnerability was swallowed up by the comfort and compassion offered by others." Though tensions surfaced on two separate occasions, the empathic atmosphere prevailed; to this extent, the "family" of students remained intact— more intact, paradoxically, than many of their families.

If the class is a family, is the teacher, then, a parent? Audrey's mother, who has been teaching for twenty-five years, thinks so: "I know what you mean when you say teachers have to act like parents." There are, of course, many differences between teachers and parents. Teachers, regardless of the level on which they teach, say goodbye to their students at the end of the semester, and they are responsible "only" for their students' academic development. They generally see their students only for a semester or two, and they usually lose contact with them afterward. Teachers must grade their students, which parents fortunately do not have to do with their children. They may teach thousands of students over a lifetime, so many, in fact, that sooner or later the students may become a blur. Teachers' children age along with their parents, but teachers' students never grow older, though the age gap between student and teacher widens each year. When I first started teaching in graduate school in the late 1960s, I was only five years older than my freshmen; now I am forty years older than they. If I am fortunate enough to be teaching in my seventies, as I hope to do, my students will be the age of my grandchildren. Even now I have difficulty recognizing some of the students I taught only a few years ago. Recall Mr. Chips's final speech to his students: "If you come and see me again in years to come—as I hope you all will—I shall try to remember those older faces of yours, but it's just possible I shan't be able to—and then someday you'll see me somewhere and I shan't recognize you and you'll say to yourself, 'The old boy doesn't remember me. [Laughter] But I *do* remember you—as you are *now*. That's the point. In my mind you never grow up at all. Never'" (89).

The similarities between teachers and parents are no less striking than the differences. Good teachers, like good parents, must be fair, consistent, attentive, supportive, and respectful. They must earn their students' trust, observe appropriate boundaries, acknowledge limitations and mistakes, and remain hopeful about the value of education. The British psychoanalyst D. W. Winnicott's theory of the "good enough mother" comes to mind here: "The good enough 'mother' (not necessarily the infant's own mother) is one who makes active adaptation to the infant's needs, an active adaptation that gradually lessens, according to the infant's growing ability to account for failure of adaptation and to tolerate the results of frustration" ("Transitional Objects" 94). As I suggest in *Diaries to an English Professor,* teachers, like parents, can be either good enough or not good enough, "depending on whether they are attentive or inattentive to their students' needs" (234).

Was I a father figure to my students? I'm not sure. I was not aware of any Oedipal tensions in the classroom: none of my female students called me "Dad," and none of my male students overtly challenged my authority or sought to steal my phallic pen. No one exploited my vulnerability when I cried in class. From my point of view and, I hope, from theirs, there was no transgression of teacher-student boundaries. I did not regard my students as my children, but I remained attached to them, and they to me, and so from that point of view, I was an attachment figure, the recipient and guardian of the secrets they entrusted to me. Several students have asked me to write recommendations for them for graduate school, which I have done gladly, but I do this for all my students, including those in my nonself-disclosing classes.

I never psychoanalyzed my students' writings, nor did they wish me to do so. In my psychoanalytic literature courses I describe myself as both a "Freudian" and a "Fraudian"—one who is sympathetic to many of Freud's theories but who is not a trained psychoanalyst. My expository writing students read *Diaries to an English Professor,* which has a psychoanalytic focus, but I did not import Freudian theory into the writing classroom. (Nat's mother makes a disparaging reference to Freud, which may or may not reflect her son's viewpoint.) Perhaps some of my classroom authority derived from my publications and my age, but I suspect that what most impressed my students was my commitment to creating an empathic classroom where they were free to write honestly and openly about their lives without the fear of criticism or attack.

Those who are interested in my approach to teaching often ask me whether I feel burdened or depressed by my students' self-disclosures. I don't. The reason is that students want teachers to be caring rather than caretakers. Several of us cried in class during the semester, but I would not characterize any of us as "weepers," the pejorative word that appears in *The Small Room.* Like Lucy Winter, I believe that teaching is the "most difficult kind of art in which the final expression depends upon a delicate and dangerous balance between two people and a subject," but unlike Lucy, I believe that the subject may be students' lives. There was no contradiction between my students' desire to improve their writing skills and to pursue an education for life. Like Pippa Brentwood, some of my students were mourning parental loss, but no one appeared needy or clinging, as in May Sarton's novel. The students in my own small room were as respectful of my privacy as I was of theirs. As much as I gave to my students, I received from them: their appreciation, trust, and validation. For fourteen weeks we shared a unique experience, and when the semester ended, we moved on with our lives. There was both sadness and pleasure at the end. I am indeed fortunate that teaching is such a joyful part of my life, one from which I cannot imagine voluntarily retiring. I am not an Aristotelian, but I value beginnings, middles, and endings; the knowledge that the ending of one semester will soon be followed by the beginning of another semester is deeply sustaining to me, for I know that soon I will have the opportunity to meet new students and learn more about their extraordinary lives.

CHAPTER 5

"The Age of Melancholy"
BEARING WITNESS TO DEPRESSION

"Depression is a disorder of mood, so mysteriously painful and elusive in the way it becomes known to the self—to the mediating intellect—as to verge close to being beyond description" (7). So notes William Styron in his haunting 1990 book *Darkness Visible*, aptly subtitled *A Memoir of Madness*. I have taught *Darkness Visible* twice in a graduate course on literary suicide, first in 1992 and then in 1994, and both times students were profoundly moved by the story of his triumph over suicidal depression. One student, Julie, was so affected by the book, which she read while experiencing a severe psychological crisis, that she sent Styron a letter based on the class presentation she gave on the final day of the semester. He responded with a warmly appreciative note, which she received while being treated in a psychiatric hospital. She later told me that she credited her recovery in large part to his heartfelt response. Of all Styron's works, including his masterpiece *Sophie's Choice*, none has had the astonishing popular success of *Darkness Visible*, perhaps because it speaks so eloquently about an illness that affects millions of people. I have never taught *Darkness Visible* to undergraduates, but when I was asked to teach a large course with a guest lecturer component in the spring of 2002, I immediately thought of his memoir and the extent to which literature bears witness to suffering.

In planning Literature and the Healing Arts during the summer of 2001, I knew that a course with more than fifty students would be too large to require each person to write several formal essays, as I do in smaller literature classes. But I did want students to write, not only to demonstrate what they were learning but also to engage with the readings. I could have required one long formal essay, but I wanted more informal and frequent writing. And so I decided on a midterm, a final exam, and reader-response diaries, each constituting one-third of the final grade.

"It is probably no exaggeration to say that the single most common subject of art," Walter Slatoff states in *The Look of Distance*, "is some form of human suffering" (233). The number of poems, stories, plays, and memoirs on the subject of suffering and healing is inexhaustible, and the challenge in constructing a syllabus was not what to include but exclude. Probably no affliction is more ubiquitous in literature than depression or, to use the more poetic word that creative writers have used for centuries, melancholia. As Styron observes, "Through the course of literature and art the theme of depression has run like a durable thread of woe—from Hamlet's soliloquy to the verses of Emily Dickinson and Gerard Manley Hopkins, from John Donne to Hawthorne and Dostoevski and Poe, Camus and Conrad and Virginia Woolf" (82).

Reader-Response Diaries

Students were required to write reader-response diaries on each of the six books in the course: Lucy Grealy's *Autobiography of a Face,* Camus's *The Plague,* Primo Levi's *Survival in Auschwitz,* Leo Tolstoy's *The Death of Ivan Ilych,* Styron's *Darkness Visible,* and my own *Risky Writing,* which had just been published. As I wrote on the syllabus,

> Each diary should be between 2–3 pages long, typed and double-spaced. I have indicated on the schedule when the diaries are due; late diaries will be penalized. The diary should give evidence that you have read and engaged with the book. You can be as personal as you wish in each diary: you determine the degree of self-disclosure. At least half of the diary should focus on the book, including the beginning, middle, and ending. I will not grade each diary, but I will comment on each one before returning them to you the next class. On the last day of the semester, May 7, I will ask you to submit all six diaries to me in a folder (remember that I will have already read and commented on them); I will then grade the diaries and turn them back to you on the day of the final exam, May 14. You will be graded not on the degree of self-disclosure but on your ability to discuss insightfully the book you have read.
>
> What am I looking for in the diaries? I'm mainly interested in your ability to illuminate the story under discussion and to show how the story affects you—both intellectually and emotionally. These are diaries, not formal essays, and therefore I will not have the time to discuss the strengths and weaknesses of your writing (the class is too large for me to do that). Nevertheless, I value good writing, and a well written diary is bound to receive a higher grade than a poorly written one.
>
> I would like to read about five diaries aloud before I hand them back to you the next class. If you do *not* want me to read your diary aloud, please indicate so; otherwise, I will assume that you are giving me permission to read your diary aloud. I will always read the diaries anonymously—no one

will know the diarist's identity. Nor will there be a discussion of the diaries afterward. Each of you will reach your own conclusions about the diaries read aloud. Your grade will not be influenced by the number of your diaries I've read aloud.

I had used this diary approach for a quarter of a century in my literature-and-psychoanalysis classes, with excellent results; the only difference was that now I would be grading the diaries. I didn't want my students to feel that, contrary to my stated intentions, they were being coerced into self-disclosure, but I wouldn't know how they felt about the diary component until the end of the semester, when they anonymously evaluated the course.

I decided to begin with Coleridge's great poem of sin and redemption *The Rime of the Ancient Mariner*. We would then read Hawthorne's "The Birthmark" and Richard Selzer's "Minor Surgery," two stories about the disastrous consequences of "improving" nature through cosmetic surgery. Next would be *Autobiography of a Face*, Lucy Grealy's harrowing account of the dozens of surgeries she endured to reconstruct her jaw following treatment for a rare and usually deadly form of bone cancer. Then we would read *The Plague* and *Survival in Auschwitz*, both of which, it turned out, had uncanny relevance to the September 11 attack. *The Death of Ivan Ilych* was the next story, followed by *Darkness Visible*. We would then conclude with *Risky Writing*.

Thanks to the generosity of Francis Dibner, an alumna of the university and patron of the arts, I was able to invite five guest lecturers. Our first speaker, Iliana Semmler, a professor emerita and the editor of Selzer's forthcoming journals, spoke on "fashioning nature: literature's judgment on aesthetic surgery." With the help of the New York State Writers Institute, I invited Lucy Grealy for a reading. Michael Kaufman, a former colleague and dear friend, gave an insightful lecture on Tolstoy's cautionary tale. The final two guest speakers were Sophie Freud, professor emerita of Simmons College and the granddaughter of the creator of psychoanalysis, who spoke on "the reading cure," and Rita Charon, a professor of medicine at Columbia University and editor of the journal *Literature and Medicine*, who spoke about narrative medicine.

The first reader-response diary, on *Autobiography of a Face*, was not due until the fourth week of the semester, but it soon became apparent that, without these diaries, students were unwilling to reveal their feelings about the sensitive issues that emerged from the readings and class discussions. For example, Iliana Semmler noted in her lecture the curious paradox that although fictional stories like "The Birthmark" and "Minor Surgery" portray the catastrophic consequences of efforts to enhance nature, those who have cosmetic surgery in real life are generally highly satisfied with the results. Cultural historians reveal sharply contrasting attitudes toward cosmetic surgery. Sander Gilman argues that despite the widely held perception that "reconstructive surgery, in restoring function, seems to lie at one end of a spectrum and aesthetic surgery, in improving appearance, at the other" (3), no such distinction exists: "Curing the physically anomalous is curing the psychologically unhappy—this view provides the key to any understanding of the power of all surgery to alter the psyche" (7). For Gilman, the aesthetic has a place in all general surgery. Virginia Blum takes a darker, more judgmental view, maintaining that once you have cosmetic surgery, "you will either have it again or want it again" (280). During the question period following Professor Semmler's talk, a few students spoke out against cosmetic procedures such as rhinoplasty and breast augmentation or reduction, but no one spoke in favor of them. Why? I suspect the reason is that many people stigmatize cosmetic surgery (as opposed to the reconstructive surgery described by Lucy Grealy): it is not something that one easily talks about, even (or especially) in the classroom. If students wrote reader-response diaries on "The Birthmark" and "Minor Surgery," would they be willing to disclose their own experiences with cosmetic surgery? Would they be willing to write about other sensitive subjects that are generally too personal for the classroom? These were questions I was eager to have answered.

The Stigma of Mental Illness

Depression is a far more sensitive issue than cosmetic surgery, and despite the progress that has been made in treatment, it still evokes stigma in most people. In fact, Otto Wahl argues in his book *Telling Is Risky Business* that the stigma of mental illness is sometimes worse than mental illness itself. Wahl uses the word "consumers" to describe "individuals who have had mental illness, psychiatric treatment, or diagnoses of mental disorder" (xvii), a word that, while still controversial, is endorsed by leading organizations of people with mental illness, such as the National Mental Health Consumers Self-Help Clearinghouse and the Consumer Council of NAMI, formerly called the National Alliance for the Mentally Ill. Wahl's research, based on fourteen hundred mental health consumers who filled out a detailed questionnaire and one hundred who were interviewed over the telephone, indicates that having a mental illness label, "even if it comes indirectly from having received treatment, is stigmatizing and leads to reduced social acceptance" (21). Sixty-one percent of his respondents indicated that "they had at least sometimes been shunned or avoided by others when it was revealed that they were mental health consumers"; 26 percent said that this happened to them "often or very often" (43–44). Wahl quotes a 1991 Harris Poll indicating the extent of the public's discomfort with mental illness: "only 19 percent of survey respondents indicated that they were very comfortable with a person with mental illness, as opposed to 39 percent who reported being very comfortable with people who are deaf and 59 percent with people who are in wheelchairs. More poll respondents were comfortable with people who are facially disfigured (28 percent) than with people who have mental illness. 'From the public's perspective,' the Harris poll concluded, 'mental illness is the most disturbing form of disability'" (45).

Given the widespread stigma associated with mental illness, it is not surprising that a large majority of mental health consumers—71 percent, according to Wahl's research—avoid acknowledging their psychiatric history, even if this means being dishonest when filling out written applications. He quotes one respondent saying, "I *never* reveal my illness (chronic depression) . . . and have always lied about it for all applications, including insurance, military applications, and Peace Corps applications" (132). The vast majority of Wahl's survey respondents—79 percent—feared that others would "view them unfavorably because of their consumer status if they found out" (135). The most common long-term consequences of stigma are "lowered self-esteem and self-confidence" (138). Other long-term consequences of stigma include "social isolation, anxiety about disclosure, stressful efforts to conceal, and prolongation of symptoms like depression and distrust" (142). The fear of social stigmatization is so intense that two of the major coping strategies are secrecy and withdrawal, both of which lead to further distress.

How can we overcome the crushing stigmatization of mental illness? One important strategy identified by Wahl is "listening to mental health consumers and providing opportunities for them to tell their unique stories" (25). Telling these stories not only allows consumers to unburden themselves—Wahl describes their enthusiastic willingness to participate in his research project—but also to educate the public about the nature of mental illness and to dispel the harmful stereotypes surrounding the subject, such as the common perception that most mentally ill people are violent. (Wahl quotes a study indicating that more than 70 percent of the major characters with mental illness in prime-time television drama are violent [124].) The overwhelming majority of Wahl's interviewees felt that the best way to destigmatize mental illness is through education. "Consumers believed that, if people understood more about mental disorders and about what it was like to have a psychiatric illness, then they would not be so quick to make disparaging remarks or show such reluctance to employ or befriend them" (153). Wahl emphasizes the importance of consumers' telling their stories from their own perspective—a perspective that he provides in his book and that I try to provide in this chapter.

One of the cruel ironies of the social stigmatization of mental illness is that psychiatric disorders are so common. Wahl states that overall, "estimates from available studies are that from 20 to almost 50 percent of the adult population of the United States will suffer a diagnosable psychiatric disorder at some time in their lives" (xvi). Illnesses such as depression and schizophrenia generally first appear in adolescence and young adulthood—the modal age in which Wahl's respondents reported receiving their first diagnosis was eighteen, the age when most students enter college. This is also the time when students are vulnerable to suicide, which provokes even more stigma than does depression. Not all depressed people are suicidal, but most suicidal people are severely depressed, and suicide remains a leading cause of death among the young. As Tipper Gore, honorary chair of the National Mental Health Awareness Campaign, observes, "In 1998, more teenagers and young adults died from suicide than from cancer, heart disease, AIDS, birth defects, stroke, pneumonia, influenza and chronic lung disease combined" (*Albany Times-Union*, June 26, 2002). Most people are not willing to talk publicly about their experiences with depression or suicide, and these subjects are no less risky in a college classroom. Is it possible to write about depression or suicide in reader-response diaries and share these experiences anonymously in a safe, empathic classroom? This would be part of the challenge of Literature and the Healing Arts.

Depression Narratives

Those who write about depression must make readers *feel* this mysterious disease, and to do so they must depress readers, if only briefly. Most "depression narratives," to use an inelegant term, dramatize the journey from illness to health, darkness to light. Since showing in writing is better than telling, the reader no less than the benumbed protagonist must suffer. The challenge for those who teach the literature of depression is to make these stories and poems about suffering come alive for students without traumatizing them permanently. This does not mean that stories must be depressing from beginning to end. Serious illnesses like depression often seem interminably long and purposeless, unlike literature, which is compressed and purposeful. A story about boredom cannot be boring, at least not for very long; in the same way, a story about depression must remain interesting, unlike depression itself. Teachers who wish their students to engage in a healing narration like *Darkness Visible* must be sensitive to the difficulties some of them may experience as they voyage through the depths of despair before returning to the world of hope. For many students, this journey will not be unduly hazardous; but for those who have struggled with depression in the past or who are currently depressed, reading may confront them with old or new demons they are doing their best to avoid.

"The Age of Melancholy"

At no time did I ask my students to "diagnose" themselves or their classmates. I did not require them to write about clinical depression or other psychiatric disorders. Nor did I during a class discussion or in a response to a diary offer a comment that could be construed as an attempt to diagnose a student. They knew I am not a clinical psychologist. Nevertheless, I wanted to offer as precise a definition of clinical depression as possible, and so I handed out copies of "Major Depression Disorder" from the *Diagnostic and Statistical Manual of Mental Disorders (DSM-IV)* before beginning our discussion of *Darkness Visible*. There one learns in the dry language of the American Psychiatric Association that the "essential feature of Major Depressive Disorder is a clinical course that is characterized by one or more Major Depressive Episodes . . . without a history of Manic, Mixed, or Hypomanic Episodes" (339). The criteria for "Major Depressive Episodes" include five or more of the following symptoms during a two-week period: depressed mood, diminished interest or pleasure, significant weight loss or gain, insomnia or hypersomnia, psychomotor agitation or retardation, fatigue, feelings of worthlessness or guilt, diminished ability to think, and recurrent thoughts of death.

Since most people have experienced many of these symptoms at one time or another, it is not easy to make a self-diagnosis of clinical depression. Even Styron, who throughout much of his life felt compelled to become an "autodidact in medicine," acknowledged that despite reading many books on the subject, including the *DSM*, he was "close to a total ignoramus about depression" (9). The language of the *DSM* is often technical and jargon ridden, making it user-unfriendly, but it does indicate clearly that depression is far more common than most people realize.

Nearly all the available epidemiological data suggest a startling increase in the incidence of depression. David Karp makes three observations in his book *Speaking of Sadness* about how widespread this mood disorder is:

(1) The incidence of depression among those born after World War II is much higher and the age of onset much earlier than in earlier population cohorts. (2) In recent decades, there has been a continuing rise in depression among young women, but a disproportionate increase of depression among men has been closing the depression gender gap. (3) There has been an absolute explosion of depression among "baby boomers." These and similar findings warrant the conclusion that America is in the grip of a depression epidemic; that we have entered an "age of melancholy." (167)

Karp notes that as many as 15 percent of Americans will need to be treated for anxiety or depression, and that only about one in four people suffering from clinical depression is likely to be diagnosed (10–11, 48). A sociologist, Karp discusses the biological, psychological, and cultural factors that contribute to depression, and in extensive interviews with fifty people, he explores the phenomenological aspects of depression. He also writes about his own long personal struggle with this mood disorder. *Speaking of Sadness* thus resembles *Darkness Visible*, Kay Redfield Jamison's *An Unquiet Mind*, and Andrew Solomon's *The Noonday Demon*, books that focus on the authors' own accounts of depression or manic depression while at the same time probing a larger cultural and historical phenomenon.

In the spirit of Styron, Karp, Jamison, and Solomon, I should mention my own involvement with depression. My mother has suffered from anxiety attacks for most of her adult life, although when I was a child no one in my family used that term; instead, she complained of severe heart palpitations and gastrointestinal problems. Sometimes she was unable to leave her bed for days. I never understood the meaning of my mother's anxiety attacks, but I knew that they were somehow related to her terror over cancer: her mother, father, and older brother all died of cancer, her brother in his forties. She remains convinced that she too will succumb to this disease. When she was diagnosed with ovarian cancer in 1988 and scheduled for surgery at Mount Sinai Hospital in Manhattan, she told me that her mother died of the same type of cancer in the same hospital. Immediately before undergoing surgery for what turned out to be a tumor the size of a grapefruit, she confided to me, "I'm glad I finally got it." The comment perplexed me, and after the surgery I asked her to elaborate. Did she mean that the reality of cancer is less terrifying than the lifelong fear of it? No, that's not what she meant; rather, she said she was glad that cancer had finally struck her because it proved that she was not "crazy" for worrying about it her entire life.

My mother is now over eighty and remains, in the words of her oncologist, one of his "best survivors" of this usually deadly form of cancer. Her only surviving relative, a younger brother, has the same morbid fear of cancer. A few years ago he collapsed on a tennis court from what turned out to be a heart attack and was clinically dead for more than a minute before he was revived through CPR. He now says jokingly that there is "no way" he's going to die from a heart attack: like my mother, he believes that he is fated to die of cancer.

I am my mother's son in many ways, and I have inherited—or acquired through learning—her fear of cancer. I've never been clinically depressed or suffered from panic attacks, but I am an anxious person in general— though, curiously, not in the classroom, where I feel relaxed and in control. I have been a student of psychoanalysis for the better part of my adult life, studying for three years as a research scholar at a psychoanalytic institute in New York City, but I have never been in psychoanalysis. My explanation— or is it rationalization?—is that the price of analysis would have made me more neurotic. I suppose that if I felt a burning need to be in analysis, I would have found the money to pay for it. Instead, I have muddled through life on my own, reasonably healthy, though I have long known that I have obsessive-compulsive tendencies: anything out of place on my desk or in my office agitates me. I'm a "neatnick," like Felix in *The Odd Couple*—I vacuum the house when I want to take a break from writing, or do the laundry, and I actually *enjoy* washing the dishes after dinner (though truth be told, I am more concerned with neatness than cleanliness). My children's favorite word to describe me is "anal," which I take as a compliment.

I have always been blessed (a strange word for an agnostic/atheist to use) by the ability to love and work, but when a member of my family began experiencing anxiety attacks several years ago, I too started to become more anxious than usual, and I entered brief psychotherapy—the only kind of therapy my HMO provided. It was cognitive rather than psychodynamic therapy, but it was enormously helpful, and I learned a new word, one that strongly resonated in me: I am a "catastrophizer,"a person who tends to see in every mole a potential melanoma—again, my maternal legacy.

For the past thirty years I have been an early morning person, but a few years ago I found myself waking up earlier and earlier—sometimes 4:30 or earlier, unable to return to sleep. Every couple of weeks I would wake up at 2:30. My mind was instantly alert despite my body's fatigue. I can't explain why I would wake up so early: it was not the dark night of the soul because I did not feel depressed. But I would think about all the things I had to do that day and worry about whether I would be able to do them. I tried many remedies for chronic sleep deprivation, including melatonin, antihistamines, and sleeping pills, but to no avail. About two years ago I was giving my medical history to a new physician, and when she asked me if I had any medical problems, I said, "only chronic sleep deprivation." She asked me a number of questions and then suggested that I try an anti-depressant. I agreed without hesitation. She prescribed an older type anti-depressant, amitriptyline (Elavil), and told me to take one pill, or ten milligrams, nightly for the first week, two pills for the second week, and three pills thereafter. She also said that it would take a few weeks before the medication began to work. When I asked her what would happen if I took only one pill, she said it wouldn't work at that level. Fine, I replied, and proceeded to fill the prescription. The first night I had the kind of deep eight-hour sleep I hadn't had in years. When I later told my daughter, who was in a Ph.D. program in clinical psychology and knowledgeable about psychopharmacology, she said that the antidepressant couldn't possibly work in that small dosage, nor could it work so quickly; "it's probably the placebo effect," she explained. Perhaps, but I remained on one pill, with excellent results. Both my daughter and my physician later admitted that each person reacts differently to medication.

I increased the dosage of antidepressant on August 12, 2002, the day on which my beloved wife of thirty-four years was diagnosed with pancreatic cancer. The catastrophe I had long feared came true but not in the way I anticipated. I never imagined that Barbara, who had no history of cancer on either side of her long-lived family and who could have been a poster child for living a healthy life, would fall ill from this dreaded disease. Nothing can describe our shock and horror upon learning the grim prognosis, which shattered all of our assumptions about the future. Life has become for both of us an emotional roller coaster, especially when we await the results of the latest series of CT and PET scans, but we are managing. The future is highly uncertain, but psychotherapy and psychopharmacology have allowed both of us to cope with anxiety and depression, and we are fortunate to have a strong support system of loving relatives and friends.

I mention the preceding for three reasons. First, since every interpretation implies something about the interpreter, my discussion of how my students bear witness to depression implies something about me: in particular, a belief in the value of talking and writing about stigmatized subjects. My commitment to both the "talking cure" and the "writing cure" extends to the classroom. It is because of this belief that I decided to teach

Literature and the Healing Arts. Second, whereas I used to believe that some solutions to problems are better than others, I now believe that whatever works, works. If a small — or even large — dose of medication gives me an extra hour or two of life-restoring sleep, and if the medication has no serious side effects or harmful long-term consequences, then I have no problem taking it for the rest of my life. This is a minor example, but perhaps it illustrates how little we know about the mysterious relationship between the mind and body, and how what helps one person may not help another. There are a variety of treatments for mood disorders, including psychotherapy, psychopharmacology, and self-help groups. Each form of treatment has its supporters and detractors, and it is not my place as a literature teacher to comment on any of these treatments other than to say that they exist. But it is my place to be as knowledgeable about the subjects I teach as possible, which, in this case, means to suggest to students that mood disorders such as depression and manic-depression are far more treatable than in the past. Finally, I have learned from personal experience that both hope and hopelessness are contagious; unless one is a contrarian, hopeful people generate hopefulness in others. Much of the power of a story like *Darkness Visible* derives from its ability to create hopefulness in readers, especially those who doubt whether they will survive the ordeal described by Styron.

Treating Troubled College Students

"Counseling centers at many colleges are reporting significant increases in the percentage of students seeking treatment for psychological problems, and in the percentage of new students who arrive on campus with prescriptions for antidepressants or other psychological problems." That's the conclusion of Robert Gallagher, a past president of the International Association of Counseling Services. Gallagher conducts an annual survey of counseling directors, and on February 12, 2003, he led an online discussion of mental-health issues on college campuses sponsored by the *Chronicle of Higher Education*. Gallagher first noticed the increase of psychologically troubled students in the mid 1980s, and in 1988 he began asking colleagues in the National Survey of Counseling Center Directors if they noticed the same increases on their campuses. "56% of the respondents said yes. I have asked this question in succeeding years and each year the percentage of directors reporting this trend has gone up until the last few years where it has leveled off at about 85%" (Gallagher). The counseling directors offered three explanations for the rise in serious psychological problems among college students. "Some believe that it is because of the increasing family dysfunction we have been noting for a number of years. Others believe that many in recent years have been overly pampered and haven't had the opportunity to develop good defense skills, such as tolerance for frustration. Another factor is that many students, who in the past might not have been able to get to college because of their psychological problems, now can, because of psychiatric medication." In a related article appearing the same week in the *Chronicle of Higher Education,* a national survey of counseling directors found that "95 percent reported seeing more students on psychiatric medication than in previous years," with elite colleges reporting a greater share of students on psychiatric drugs than other institutions (J. Young).

Gallagher urged colleges to do a better job in identifying at risk students: only 26 of the 125 student suicides reported in the 2002 National Survey of Counseling Center Directors Survey had sought help from a college counseling center. "Faculty members, coaches and residence staffs, for instance, need to focus not only on disruptive students, but also on those who are quietly withdrawn or whose residence hall discussions or classroom essays may disclose student hopelessness or suicidal intent. Sometimes those individuals that notice such behavior are reluctant to express their concerns to students for fear of further upsetting them." But, adds Gallagher, "in my experience, students are almost always appreciative when someone expresses their concern and extends a helping hand. Counseling centers, I believe, need to do a better job of educating faculty and other front line people on campus how to identify student problems and how to make a good referral."

The Gendered Nature of Depression

As the *DSM-IV* notes, "Major Depressive Disorder (Single or Recurrent) is twice as common in adolescent and adult females as in adolescent and adult males"; moreover, the "lifetime risk for Major Depressive Disorder in community samples has varied from 10% to 25% for women and from 5% to 12% for men" (341). The average age at onset for major depressive disorder is in the mid-twenties (less serious forms of depression occur earlier). In about two-thirds of cases, major depressive episodes end completely; there may be partial or no remission in the remaining one-third of cases. As Irene Stiver points out, marriage also affects the incidence of depression, lowering the incidence of depression in men but raising it in women. Stiver adds that single and widowed men are more likely than women to become depressed; men are also more likely than women to become depressed during marital separation (Stiver 154).

Many of these gender differences may be seen in my students' diaries. There were, in fact, two gender differences, which may be related. First, there were many more women taking the course than men: of the fifty-three students, thirty-nine were women, or 73.5 percent. This difference cannot be explained entirely from the fact that there are more female English majors than male English majors at my university. Perhaps the female students were more attracted to the course title, Literature and the Healing Arts, or the course description:

> Many writers would agree with D. H. Lawrence's observation that "one sheds one's sicknesses in books—repeats and presents again one's emotions, to be master of them." In this course we will explore the therapeutic implications of reading and writing, including the relationship between creativity and illness. We will read poems, novels, memoirs, and autobiographical essays that explore injury, illness, and death. Lest this seem unduly gloomy or depressing, our focus will be on the ways in which literature enables the writer and reader to confront and master painful events. We will emphasize trauma theory, bearing witness, and empathic reading.

The greater number of women taking the course pales in comparison with the second gender difference: the percentage of women who wrote about being depressed was much higher than that of men. Although I did not ask students to fill out anonymous questionnaires about their psychological health, which would have provided more objective information, the diaries imply that twenty-three women, or 59 percent, have suffered from some degree of depression: eight of these women experienced mild depression and the remaining fifteen experienced moderate to severe depression. By contrast, only four men, or 28.5 percent, have suffered from mild depression and none from moderate to severe depression. These figures, I should add, are based on how students wrote about their experience with depression. A clinical psychologist who interviewed every student might reach a different conclusion. Yet no matter how imprecise these figures are, it is inescapable that a far higher percentage of women wrote about a personal experience of depression than did men.

Did a literature course with the word "healing" in the title attract not only more female students than male students but also more depressed women who were looking for psychological relief? Were more depressed females drawn to the course because of my reputation as an empathic teacher? These possibilities cannot be ruled out. Nor can I state with any degree of certainty whether the students enrolled in the course were representative of others who study at the university. I suspect that if teachers gave their students an opportunity to write about depression, they too would be surprised by the large number who reveal familiarity with this mood disorder. Given the "age of melancholy," the value of reading and writing about depression takes on great importance, for literature can sensitize us not only to illness but also to the possibilities of recovery.

Bearing Witness to Another's Depression

"The pain of severe depression is quite unimaginable to those who have not suffered it" (33), Styron writes, and even those who live with a depressed relative may have trouble understanding and empathizing. In *Darkness Visible* Styron only hints at the extent to which his suicidal depression affected his family, but a fuller story emerges from his wife's account, "Strands," appearing in *Unholy Ghosts: Writers on Depression*. I read to my students the most moving moment in the essay, when Rose Styron records her daughter Polly's jottings of the night when her father was hospitalized:

> So, I guess I should write this down, or I won't believe it. I came to the house Friday evening because I'd heard Dad had had a terrible night on Thursday and that he and Mum were fairly shaken. I was prepared for a morbid gloom, but not for what the night actually turned out to be. When I went upstairs to his room he was lying there, with his long gray hair all tangled and wild. I took his hand, which was trembling. "I'm a goner, darling," he said, first thing. His eyes had a startled look, and he seemed to be not quite there. His cool, trembling hands kept fumbling over mine. "The agony's too great now, darling. I'm sorry. I'm a goner."
>
> For the next hour, he raved about his miserable past and his sins and the waste of his life and how, when they published the scandal of his life, we should try not to hate him. "You'll hate me. You'll hate me," he said in a whisper. Everything was repeated over and over. "I love you so much. And the other children. And your mother. You'll hate me for what I am going to do to myself. My head is exploding. I can't stand the agony anymore. It's over now. I can't stand the agony. Tell the others how much I love them. I've betrayed my life. All my books have been about suicide. What a miserable waste of a life. I'm dying! I'm dying! I am dying!" And on and on, and over and over, while grabbing me to come closer, taking my head to his breast, holding me closer. My father.
>
> When Mum finally came upstairs, as he held me next to him with his eyes closed, I mouthed the word "HOS-PI-TAL" to her. (133–34)

Rose Styron concludes her essay by affirming her husband's contact "with fellow depression sufferers by mail or by phone" (136). She points out that the novelist who had jealously guarded his privacy and solitude in order to write now gives of himself generously to those who seek counsel. She stresses the importance of bearing witness not only for the sake of others but for one's own well-being—and, in the case of her husband, for renewed creativity.

In what follows, I focus on how several of my students wrote about depression. Not surprisingly, most of these depression diaries were written in response to *Darkness Visible*, but some were reactions to the other books on the syllabus. I did not know in the beginning of the semester that I was going to write about this class; it was only toward the end of the semester, after I received so many diaries on this subject, that I decided to write about how students bore witness to depression. During the last week of the semester I suggested to the students the possibility that I might contact them in the future, after they received their final grade (and after I received approval from the university Institutional Review Board, which must approve all human research), to see whether they would allow me to use one or more of their reader-response diaries, their final exam, or both for the present chapter. What emerged from the more than three hundred diary entries, totaling nearly nine hundred double-spaced pages, was that more than half of the students had some familiarity with depression. Many bore witness to a relative or friend's clinical depression; others wrote about their own experience with depression in the past; and a few were either currently in treatment for depression or feared that they were becoming depressed.

Reading *Darkness Visible* allowed three students—Gabriella, Rita, and Mac—to understand troubling periods in their family history when a twin sister, brother, or mother, respectively, was in a crisis. Styron's story touched them deeply, and their diaries share several characteristics both with *Darkness Visible* and with each other. All three acknowledged a real or perceived failure to respond empathically to a loved one's depression, and in varying degrees they felt guilt, sadness, and shame, feelings they explored in their diaries.

Gabriella: "Reading Styron's Memoir of His Own Struggles with the Disease Hit Very Close to Home"

Although I have never experienced the painful depths of clinical depression myself, my twin sister has battled with it all through her adolescence. Reading Styron's memoir of his own struggles with the disease hit very close to home, and brought back a lot of the memories I have of my sister's inner torment at the time. Right before our thirteenth birthday she scratched up her wrists with a daisy razor as a way of purging her feelings of depression and despair. She was deemed a danger to herself and was admitted into a hospital for mentally ill teenagers. When Styron retold his close brush with suicide and how thoughts of his family and the wonderful memories he'd had throughout his life saved him from committing such an awful deed, I wondered why my sister wasn't stirred by the same thoughts. Could she have thought her life so hopeless and insignificant?

It was also difficult for me when Styron spoke of his wife, who patiently stood by her husband during his illness, even when he was completely oblivious to the outside world. Unfortunately, I was not so attentive and sympathetic to my sister's plight. I couldn't understand why she was acting the way that she was. She didn't want to hang out with any of our friends anymore, claiming, "Everyone is going to die eventually anyway, so why bother getting close to anyone?" She scratched her ankles and face with thumbtacks, and slept all day long. My mother sent her to a therapist, which was supposed to remedy her situation, much like Styron's appointment with the reputed doctor was expected to make all the pain go away. Needless to say, this wasn't exactly the case for either of them. My sister inflicted pain upon herself several times, as well as exhibiting other forms of self-destruction. She stole vodka from a friend's house and downed it with small amounts of orange juice. She began cutting up her wrists, arms and ankles on a regular basis, always being sure to hide the cuts under long sleeves and pant legs. Although her actions weren't deemed true "suicide attempts," she had expressed suicidal thoughts in therapy, which was enough to put her into a psychiatric hospital.

Up until she was sent to the hospital, I was angry and frustrated with her temperament, and believed she was doing it all for the attention it brought her. I had always been the more outgoing between the two of us, so I felt like her actions were a way to take back the spotlight. Looking back, I wish I had known then what I know now about depression, so that I might have been more compassionate and understanding. When she was sent away, it was the first time since we were born that we had been separated. She was institutionalized for three months. They let her out on a day pass on our thirteenth birthday, and a few friends came with us to the mall to celebrate. It was difficult for everybody. When I spoke to her over the phone she sounded listless and disinterested in anything and everything, which made me wonder if being there was actually helping her or making it worse. My mother battled with guilt on a daily basis, wondering if she had really done the right thing by admitting my sister. My sister was angry with everyone, and felt betrayed and isolated by those closest to her.

On the day she was released, I was so excited. My sister was going to finally be free and happy again, like when we were kids. Everything was going to be better. When we walked out into the warm spring afternoon, I kept saying how great she must feel to be out of there, although she remained stoic and expressionless, knowing that she still had a long battle ahead of her.

Just the other night, I was on the phone with my sister, who is still on antidepressants, but a whole world away from where she was at the lowest points of her depression. I told her about Styron's book, and how I really thought she would benefit from reading it, since some other people in the class who had also battled with the illness felt generally moved and inspired by his recovery, as well as comforted by the shared experience. I also mentioned that many other students in the class had said that the hardest part of depression is the lack of understanding and sympathy expressed by the people around them. And for the first time, I apologized for not being able to understand, and not trying to understand. I confessed that I felt angry and resentful, and that it was difficult to be so detached from the one person closest to me in the world, with which I had shared everything. She did not offer forgiveness or reply with bitterness. She just uttered a wise and heartfelt, "I know." And it felt as if the bond with my twin sister was being slowly rebuilt.

Rita: "I Did Not Know How to Deal with the Depression That My Brother Endured"

William Styron's account of his bout with depression in Darkness Visible *is a frightening description of the despair that one inflicted with the disease undergoes. It was saddening to read about the hopelessness that Styron felt when he was at his lowest point in the progression of his depression. It did allow me, however, to reach a better understanding of the emotions that my brother must have felt during his struggle with the disease, and his subsequent hospitalization.*

My brother is eighteen now, and doing well overall. From the time he was fourteen, however, until about a year ago, he was in the throws of a serious case of depression. His psychologists and psychiatrists tentatively diagnosed him with manic depression. There was debate, however, over whether that diagnosis was correct. One woman believed he was simply oppositionally defiant. She was tragically ignoring the source of his acting out, however, in this diagnosis. He was prescribed a number of different anti-depressants during this time, none of which seemed to make much of a difference in his mood. The height of his illness occurred when he became suicidal. He was abusing alcohol and marijuana regularly at this time.

I remember being called to the hospital one evening by my mother who was hysterical at the time. My brother had been found by a police officer lying unconscious on a curb in a pool of his own vomit. When I arrived at the hospital I found my brother strapped to a hospital bed, speaking incoherently about his intentions to kick the doctor's ass. My mother explained to me that they had to pump his stomach, and he had been so violent when they tried to insert the catheter that they were forced to strap him to the bed. This was the most agonizing place, both physically and emotionally, that I had ever seen my brother during his depression.

Things got worse with my brother after this incident. His school filed a petition to the city as a result of his excessive absenteeism. Once there, the supervisors of that facility decided that they were not equipped to deal with his emotional problems, and he was transferred to the mental ward of another hospital. At this time, my brother's description of his stay in the hospital differs greatly from that of Styron's. He told my family and I that he could not sleep because there was another patient there who would bang his head on the wall all night screaming for someone to help him. Also, my brother was traumatized when he witnessed another patient try to slit his wrists with a Popsicle stick. On top of the experience of having to reside with other patients whose illnesses were certainly not in check, my brother became further depressed at the thought of his being associated with them. He began to feel that he must be crazy, and the stigma that mental illness has on its victims began to seep into my brother's psyche further supporting his feelings of hopelessness. In addition to these repercussions, the hospital's psychiatrist ignored the current medication and dosage that my brother had been taking before his admission into the hospital, and prescribed for him instead a medication that caused my brother to be basically catatonic. This doctor did not even follow the correct process of switching medications that Styron describes which consists of a period of weening off one medication in order to begin another, and the gradual increase of dosage in the new medication to allow for the body's adjustment to this new chemical.

The depression did not cease in my brother through all of the placements and medications that he endured. My mother finally convinced the court to allow her to send him to a school in New England at her own expense. The school is an outdoors based program with a very restricted number of "students" (not "patients," notice the difference in stigma) so that personal attention and help can be provided. Activities, trips, education, and therapy are some of the methods that they utilized in creating a healing environment for the troubled youth that resided there. The changes in my brother as a result of his stay there were a miracle.

I did not know how to deal with the depression that my brother endured. Often I was just angry with him. Styron's account of his depression, however, has allowed me in retrospect to attempt to understand how my brother *must have felt when he was struggling with that same disease. Like Styron says, the disease manifests itself differently in every person that it reaches. I do feel, however, that much of Styron's descriptions of his severe melancholy reflect the feelings of my brother. When Styron describes his attendance at the dinner party that his wife had thrown, I can see my brother's face at a family function, completely devoid of any trace of happiness. The support from friends and family that Styron attributes as having contributed largely to his recovery was also a large part of my brother's own ascent from his depths. My mother especially would not give up on my brother no matter how poorly he treated her.*

Mental illness is the most debilitating class of ailments that exists in the realm of physical or mental health. To lose one's ability to think as one should, to lose control over the mind, is a horribly excruciating experience. Styron captures the tragedy of depression in Darkness Visible, *and offers hope to others who suffer from the disease, as well as education to those who do not.*

Mac: "I Thought of My Mother Every Second That I Was Reading This Book"

"Confusion, failure of mental focus and lapse of memory" (Darkness Visible) *are among the scariest things that one can ever go through. These "hallmarks" come with being depressed and for these things there is no real medicinal treatment. Depression is a disease that has to be therapeutically maneuvered; it cannot be prescribed away. That is the worst part of this mind-eating disease; one has to deal with the pain and confusion. The person suffering from depression begins to make irrational decisions, their memory bank begins to skip, and they start distancing themselves from the world that does not understand a thing that they are saying. That is what she did. She used to forget everything I told her and everything that she herself said. I never knew how to deal with my mother's depression, but after reading this book, I see how horrible of a job I did. I had no patience and I see now, I offered no type of therapy. Had I known, what was going on in her head, had I known that she had, like Styron, a "sense that . . . [her] thought processes were being engulfed by a toxic and unnameable tide that obliterated any enjoyable response to the living world," I would have been more helpful.*

I do not know what I would be doing right now if my mother never had sought therapy. I feel guilty as it is for not being able to help her get better and making her do it on her own; I would not want to experience the guilt that comes with the suicide of a loved one. As Styron says about his acquaintance, Abbie Hoffman after his suicide, "the people closest to suicide victims so frequently and feverishly hasten to disclaim the truth; the sense of impli-

cation, of personal guilt—the idea that one might have prevented the act if one had taken certain precautions." This I know I would not be able to handle. My mother made it and I still feel guilty, having her not survive probably would have put me in the same state that she was in; Melancholia.

A great distance is set between a person suffering from depression and all of the things familiar to them. I think that is what did it for my mom. I think that living in the same apartment where she always has really made my mother suffer. This house belonged to our family, and after my dad left, we were everything but that. I know now, through this book, some of the things that my mother must have been facing. Styron tells us how when he moved back to his home in Connecticut, he felt as though his place that was once therapy for him was now making him suffer more. Styron, like my mother, surrounded himself with things that were familiar to him in hopes of remedying his illness. That proved to be detrimental to the process. I remember watching my mother blank out, as I'd catch her staring at the pictures in the house. She would stare at me sometimes without noticing, and I'm sure would think of my father whom I so closely resembled. The more that I think of it, although my mother was not in as deep a depression as she once was, once we moved out of the apartment, her health improved.

Not having the conventions of healthcare, my mother could not go to doctors. She was left to deal with her illness without the help of modern-day science. My mother needed an outlet. As William Styron took to reading and writing (especially in his diary), he felt a little better at times. For my mother, her outlet finally came in the form of my niece; someone new to take care of and to love. My mother never received therapy, she was never hospitalized meaning that she's never seen that "purgatory" that Styron tells us about. Halcion, nor any other anti-depressant for that matter, was not a part of her daily regimen. Her recovery was nothing short of miraculous. I say this now, and not only, because I never knew the extent of which my mother was suffering. I thought of my mother every second that I was reading this book. It made me feel guilty for not being able to help her while she was going through all of this. At the same time, this book makes me better understand that part of my life. I have stopped blaming my mother for the things that I saw growing up; I understand that she herself could not see.

Although the details of their stories differ, Gabriella, Rita, and Mac all acknowledge feeling anger, resentment, and bewilderment during this bleak time. They now believe, after reading *Darkness Visible*, that they would have acted differently, with more compassion and understanding. Styron's story illuminates aspects of their own family stories. While none of them is a published author, they all provide the concrete details to make their stories understandable to the reader, as Styron masterfully does; they capture, as Rita suggests, much of the "tragedy of depression."

The three students' diaries are, like many of their classmates', not confessional but transformational. That is, the diarists acknowledge their failure to understand depressed relatives, and they resolve to act differently in the future. One senses that reading *Darkness Visible* has affected their lives. Gabriella tells her sister about Styron's book and mentions her classmates' experiences with depression. Apologizing to her sister for not being able to understand her depression, Gabriella now believes that their relationship is slowly improving as a result of her new insight. Rita also comments on how *Darkness Visible* has allowed her to grasp how her brother struggled with depression, and she ends the story on a note of realistic hope. Mac feels, along with Gabriella, guilt for his failure to understand depression, but rather than dwelling on blame, he affirms his new awareness of his mother's past illness.

The three diaries are reflective and filled with "insight" verbs. Thus Gabriella refers to "looking back" at her sister's experience. The most noteworthy sentence occurs in the last paragraph of her diary, when she remarks that she "apologized" to her sister for the first time last week "for not being able to understand, and not trying to understand." Rita writes about "reach[ing] a better understanding" of her brother's emotions during his hospitalization; and Mac ends by stating that *Darkness Visible* helps him "better understand" his mother's battle with depression. These insight verbs suggest that the three students see the past in a new way that is associated with emotional and cognitive processing. Each of the three diaries charts a similar movement from confusion to understanding, darkness to light, and each begins with negative emotions that give way to positive ones. These linguistic observations are consistent with the Linguistic Analysis and Word Count, developed by James Pennebaker and M. Francis to predict how the content of an essay is related to health improvement. In a 1997 study of adaptive bereavement, Pennebaker and his associates found that the category of words most predictive of improved health is cognitive word use: words denoting cause and insight. Writers who increased their use of positive emotion words and who used a moderate number of negative emotion words also were likely to derive health benefits from writing.

Bearing Witness to Past Depression

Darkness Visible hit closer to home for those students who had experienced depression in their own past. Most had never before written about these experiences, except perhaps in a private diary, nor had they shared these experiences with anyone other than their parents and closest friends. Although most were women in their twenties, they closely identified with the experience of Styron, a man in his sixties. They felt validated because *Darkness Visible* captured the loneliness, torment, shame, and confusion they experienced during this bleak period in their lives. Angie, Casey, Blythe, Adrian, and Griffen wrote about their own mood disorders. Angie wrote two diaries on depression, the first on *Autobiography of a Face*, the second on *Darkness Visible*. Casey, Blythe, Adrian, and Griffen wrote their diaries on *Darkness Visible*. The five students are no longer depressed, at least not to the same extent as in the past, but it is still difficult for most of them to write about this aspect of their lives. They allowed me to read their diaries aloud, which I did, beginning with Angie's. (I read only her first diary aloud.) The five students cast much light on an obscure time in their lives, and they find many appropriate passages in *Darkness Visible* that relate to their own experiences. They identify with aspects of Styron's life without ignoring the differences between his story and their own. They don't claim that their depression was as severe as Styron's, but they imply that it was serious enough to cause great distress. Writing about a troubling period in their lives, they reveal different subjectivities: a past self that seems significantly different from their present self.

To preserve confidentiality, I have omitted some of the opening sentences of Angie's first diary, which describes her many similarities with Lucy Grealy:

Angie: "I Now Know How Lucy Must Have Felt after Finishing Her Book"

I could relate much of my life to Lucy Grealy's. . . . Although loving and supportive, my family [like Grealy's] also experienced their fair share of financial difficulties. . . . In Lucy's life, it had been her mother that struggled with depression. In my life, it was I who fought against Manic Depression. Our class discussed the effects on a child by being raised by a depressed parent. But with each passing year, I see how raising a depressed child affected and still affects my parents.

I suppose if this were a movie, you could see the blurry, dreamlike images accompanied by the lovely strumming of a harp. Then we would have a lovely flashback sequence to 1999, my senior year of high school. But this is a low-budget diary and there are no such special affects.

Anyway, looking back to February of 1999, I began loathing school, studying, socializing, and everything I normally loved. To everyone, this was so very odd since I was a Straight-A, cheerful, social butterfly. I was beyond exhausted constantly and every action, motion, and thought took great effort. I lost my appetite and I was to the point where I didn't care about anything, even living.

Two months later and sixty pounds lighter, everyone began panicking. I was placed in a Mental Hospital for depression for about two weeks. Unlike Lucy's parents, my wonderful parents handled everything so well. Never fighting, they gave nothing but love, hugs, kisses and prayers.

I remember the night before I was leaving for the hospital, my mother came to my room. I remember crying and telling her that I just wanted it all to be over. Maybe I could be with God and be blissfully at peace. Maybe not, but it would be over. I kept apologizing because I loved her so much and she was the last person I wanted to hurt. Just as Lucy's mother had never done, my mother told me to let it all out and just held me. I cannot remember if she cried then but I do know how much that scene must have crushed her. Her oldest daughter wanted nothing more than to end it all. I can only recall that night with tears.

The next day we left for the hospital. My parents seemed so calm. They stayed as long as possible and visited as much as possible, despite the two-hour trip. While unpacking, I found a long letter from my dad. He wrote how much he loved me and how proud he was of me. Here, my dad acted very similar to Lucy's father. Face to face with me, my dad struggled with expressing himself. Both fathers choose to reveal their feelings on paper with the simple message of love. I cherish my dad's letters and hope that Lucy still might have her father's letter.

Unlike Lucy, I hated the hospital. Of course, I was there an incredibly shorter amount of time and under extremely different conditions. The nurses forced me to eat and gave me strange and intoxicating medicines. I never felt safe. The patients there seemed a million times crazier than I was! I vividly remember seeing a woman down the hall desperately trying to hang herself with a shoelace. She wasn't successful and was punished by having to wear her pajamas all day and night. What a way to cheer up a depressed person!

In her stays, Lucy so fondly recalled the smells of the fresh, clean hospital. The smell I can't forget is the "Hospital Towel Smell." The hospital towels had been washed over and over and over again with unscented laundry detergent. The smell they had was faint but very distinct. I grew to hate that smell. It is always on the towels of any hotel. I mean, what a way to ruin a nice vacation. I take my flower-scented towels now on trips.

My mom later told me that the day I left for the hospital was the worst day of her life. She cried the whole way home and throughout the following days. This hurts me so much knowing that I caused that pain in her life. Later my mom said that leaving me at the hospital was the worst thing she could have done. I remember my parents arguing with the doctors to release me. *My parents felt the hospital was not beneficial for me in any way. The doctors wouldn't release me no matter what, or at least until my insurance ran out a week later. I realize how helpless and infuriated my parents must have been, knowing they had temporarily lost all control over me during the moment I needed them most. I know my parents felt extreme guilt but they did their best and I love them for that and who they are.*

It will be three years in April since my worst episodes of depression and the hospital bills continue to come. Seeing this, I feel guilty within our limited budget. The constant reminder of my stay at the hospital revisits me every night when I take the same antidepressants that I started the first night I stayed at the hospital. These pretty, pink pills also cost money.

Within seconds of talking to me, my mom can now always tell when I become depressed. She knows exactly how and what to do to make me feel better. She does everything she can for me, as does my father. This love and support mean everything to me and without it, who knows where I would be now?

Although I still struggle with depression, life is good. Had Lucy been brought up in a more loving and understanding environment, I feel her outlook on life would have been drastically different. She would probably view herself in a much more positive manner. Thus, her life would have been more enjoyable with more stable relationships.

After writing about such a painful topic, I assumed I would have felt sad or stressed. But after saying everything I wanted, I felt a welcomed relief. I now know how Lucy must have felt after finishing her book.

How to Decorate a Hospital Room When Life Is Not Worth Living

This helpful guide, entitled "How to Decorate a Hospital Room When Life Is Not Worth Living," will address those pesky problems when dealing with the fashioning of a hospital room. It will include insightful tips on how to make your room more suitable towards your tastes. It will also give an autobiographical experience that the reader may draw upon and apply to their comfortable stay at the hospital.

To begin decorating your newly acquired hospital room, there are a few things that must be taken into consideration. For instance, why are you staying at the hospital? This is crucial to the theme of decor. This guide focuses on patients who are severely depressed and suicidal. Let us not confuse these patients with those of pregnant mothers or appendicitis victims. For the course of decoration is entirely different, seeing as the latter generally embrace life.

Secondly, the length of your hospital stay should be considered. This is very important. This factor will determine how much time you will spend in

your room. It will also determine how many guests, if any, may come to see and support you.

Thirdly, how did you get to the hospital? Did you go there voluntarily? Were you forced? By family or friends? Or did you arrive accompanied with the soothing screams of a red and white ambulance?

Lastly, you should consider your state of mind and physical well-being. These factors directly influence how the room will be decorated. For instance, if you would rather force a 12-inch knife through your heart than to be woken up the next morning by the sun's gentle rays, decorating may not be your first priority! Or perhaps, you are too damn weak to pull that heavy scotch tape from its holder and stick that lovely photograph of Scruffy the Dog on the wall. Also, are you out to impress anyone? Do you care how your doctors and psychiatrists evaluate you? This is important because maintaining a cheerful and clean room could determine whether you are released in ten days or ten weeks.

I was admitted to a lovely hospital in April of 1999. My room bore plain white walls. My metal bed was of average height and came equipped with freshly washed white linens. The windows had large metal bars blocking the outside world from me. My older roommate found these bars exceptionally useful for venting frustrations, as she would repeatedly bang her bloody head against them. I was never threatened by her destructive behavior since she was only violent towards herself. William Styron illustrates this notion as he writes, "people with depression are usually dangerous only to themselves." She was simply just trying to knock the pain of depression out of her.

Once my parents had left, I was left to decorate as I pleased. I had the luxury of having a good thirty minutes to pack a suitcase. This luxury was awarded to me since I was not in any immediate danger, since my destructive weapon of choice was through starvation. Thus, I had time to bring a few pictures of family and friends. I advise you to place them near your bed so that you may stare at them through the long hours of waiting to be cured. These pictures can serve as a reminder as to why you are there in the first place. For instance, I was put in this wonderful get-away by people who loved me, in hopes of [being] happily reunited with them later.

Other people may choose not to decorate in this fashion. You may find that just the white wall will suffice. It can be most titillating to watch the white paint slowly peel. It should also be noted that many depressed patients choose this route. Many patients would much rather focus on the task at hand, that of ending one's life, then deciding whether a stuffed teddy-bear better compliments the right or left side of the bed.

I believe that the rate at which you decorate your room is directly propor-

tional to the rate of your recovery. For instance, when you initially arrive at your room, your creative efforts will be minimal. This is due greatly to the fact that slitting your wrists seems like a much more valuable pastime than arranging flowers. As time progresses though you may begin to feel more alive and your interests in life, friends, hobbies, or other various things may increase. It is then that situating a nicer environment for yourself may become much more important.

A variation of this theory is illustrated through the actions of Styron. When Styron first participated in his art class, he was intensely angered at the thought of creating or decorating. He rushed through his class, carelessly scribbling with his crayons. As the weeks advanced, he found his health improving along with his "sense of comedy." He started to take time and enjoy this period of creativity. His creative projects also reflected each "intermediate stage of recuperation." His last project was a "rosy and cherubic head with a 'Have-a-Nice-Day' smile." Clearly Styron had risen to better spirits and now had a cheerful decoration to brighten his days.

As mentioned previously, you may want to keep your newly acquired room nice and tidy. One reason for this is that you may be fortunate enough to entertain guests. This is a rather touchy subject since suicide is tainted with a certain negativity and shame. Styron illustrates this as he reflects on the suicide of Primo Levi. He wrote that people viewed Levi's suicide as a "frailty, a crumbling of character they were loath to accept" and "with helplessness and a touch of shame." These attitudes enraged Styron. He publicized that "the pain of severe depression is quite unimaginable to those who have not suffered it, and it kills in many instances because its anguish can no longer be borne."

I agree immensely with all of Styron's attitudes and statements. This attitude also shows why entertaining a guest can be stressful towards the depressed patient. For example, I greatly appreciated when my best friend came to the hospital to offer her love and support. I worried relentlessly over her thoughts and if she was disappointed in me. I was also embarrassed and shamed that I had brought her to such a place. This also shows that the depressed person may suffer from guilt and shame following a suicide attempt.

Hopefully you have found this guide of some use. You now have a few steps to brightening your very own hospital room. My one and only hope is that it will not be the last room you will ever decorate.

In her first diary, Angie evokes the frightening and antiseptic details of the psychiatric hospital, recalling a patient who tried to hang herself with a shoelace and the harsh hospital towel smell; the diary is reminiscent of the nightmarish psychiatric hospital in Ken Kesey's *One Flew over the*

Cuckoo's Nest. In the second diary, she offers a satirical guide for the depressed and suicidal on how to decorate a hospital room. The sardonic tone of the second diary allows her to detach herself from the pain of her hospitalization, but she never lets the reader forget the anguish she felt at the time, and she ends with a jarring sentence that underscores the seriousness of her theme.

Casey: "This Book Helped Me Realize How Serious My Condition Was"

In my last diary I wrote about The Death of Ivan Ilych *and how it reminded me of my battle with depression. I think it will be more appropriate for me to discuss what I went through in comparison to William Styron's "memoir of madness,"* Darkness Visible. *Much of the feelings described are very familiar to me and this book helped me realize how serious my condition was. Although William Styron was in a deeper, more life-threatening depression, we have shared the same feelings of extreme sadness, anxiety, and "unfocused dread" that characterize this disorder.*

One of the most important points Styron makes in this book is that people who have not experienced serious depression will probably never understand the agony one goes through. After I read the book, I also read the journal that I kept during my therapy in order to recall what I was feeling in this lowly state. I wrote about how when I came home from school for vacation it was "rough because my parents were trying to figure out what my problem was. They thought it could be pinned on one reason, but it was many things that had built up." My parents thought that it would be easy for me to tell them what was wrong with me, when in reality I had no idea; I just knew something was not right. I wrote that my mother had told me that "before I go back [to school] or before she sent the tuition money in, I had to tell my parents why I wasn't doing well in classes and how I plan on changing. She thinks it will be easy for me to share my feelings, but for some reason I don't feel comfortable sharing this with my parents and I don't know how to explain things to them. There are some things they just can't fix." It is not as though my parents didn't care about my condition—they were more than worried about my well being. But, as Styron tells us, "such incomprehension has usually been due not to a failure of sympathy but to the basic inability of healthy people to imagine a form of torment so alien to everyday experience."

Styron's battle with depression was very similar to mine, with only some minor differences. He began his days feeling fine, but gradually got worse as the day wore on. He does make a point to say that most people, including myself, are in the opposite situation. In my case, I was unable to get out of bed in the morning, even though I had to be in class and functioning like a normal person. As the day progressed I would usually stay in bed, either sleeping or just staring at the walls and ceiling of my dorm room. Styron describes how this feels to "lie for as long as six hours, stuporous and virtually paralyzed, gazing at the ceiling and waiting for that moment of evening when, mysteriously, the crucifixion would ease up just enough to allow me to force down some food and then, like an automaton, seek an hour or two of sleep again." I would usually get up only for meals, which were not enjoyable but merely a way to keep contact with my friends. If, for some reason, they didn't call me or come to get me for dinner I would be panic stricken and filled with worry about why they hadn't contacted me. What had I done wrong? Some of these thoughts that ran through my head had been put there by my mother. If I told her that my friends hadn't called she always put the blame on me, thinking there was something that I had done to make them ignore me. For her, and eventually me, there was no way that they could have just forgotten; there must have been something that I had done to upset them. And the anxiety continued with thoughts racing through my head until I finally got up and did something about it.

In the evening, usually after dinner, is when my day really started. When I would hang out with my friends or go out to parties I felt almost normal. It did, of course, take a lot of effort for me to be "social," but nighttime was the best part of my day. Everything seemed fine until I was alone in my room again, and the process started over. I had a great fear of being alone. I even had horrible nightmares in which everyone had disappeared and I was running around in a frenzied search for someone—anyone. Styron writes, "There is an acute fear of abandonment. Being alone in the house, even for a moment, caused me exquisite panic and trepidation." I was afraid there was something going on somewhere that I was missing, or that people were talking about me, or that I just had nobody to turn to. Who could I turn to? I was certainly very uncomfortable talking to my parents about things, and although my friends tried to help, they couldn't understand what I was feeling or give me the advice I needed.

One day, when I couldn't take the agony any longer, I called my mother in hysterical tears and in between sobs told her I wanted to talk to a counselor or therapist. Although she did not know exactly why, she agreed. I also saw my doctor, who prescribed Celexa, a new antidepressant with very few side effects. Like Styron's medication, mine could take up to six weeks to start working. This seemed like forever; I didn't think it was ever going to work, and I eventually stopped taking it. People often think that with medication and therapy one will have a speedy recovery, however, this is not the case. Although I had a few weeks of therapy and had been on medication, I *did not feel my situation alleviate until I took matters into my own hands. I finally realized that I had fallen on my face; my grades were terrible, my emotions were a mess, and my family life was strained. Much of my healing process was self-motivated. I found relief in my journal entries, artwork, music and the company of good friends. I am lucky to have pulled out of such a deep state. While this book was the easiest for me to understand and relate to, it was the most difficult for me to read. I think everyone who has had a family member or loved one suffer through a deep depression should read this because it truly does give a sense of what the disorder feels like.*

Casey quotes from the diary she had kept during her depression in which she revealed her inability to explain to her parents or to herself what she was feeling at the time. Reading *Darkness Visible* has heightened her empathy toward her parents, for she now realizes that their incomprehension of her depression arises not from a failure of sympathy but from, in Styron's words, the "inability of healthy people to imagine a form of torment so alien to everyday experience." Styron's insight seems to lessen her feelings of self-blame, since depression is inherently incomprehensible to those not depressed. Throughout the diary she quotes passages from *Darkness Visible* that resonate with her own life, and she seems both surprised and reassured that Styron's story so closely parallels her own.

Blythe: "I Was Literally Lost as a Human Being for Many Years"

The green pants that I wore faithfully through the year and a half of my severe depression ripped just as I sat down to record this diary. Although I lived in those pants and still wore them quite regularly as if they were my own private Scarlet Letter, I am only satisfied that their moment of ruin was apropos to my diary response. William Styron's eloquent memoir Darkness Visible *captured so many of the aspects of a debilitating numbness that is indescribable to anyone who has not suffered completely the ravages of true depression.*

Four weeks before my twenty-first birthday I had my second abortion, nearly two years after my first. The time between was an incubation period as I suffered terribly for the loss. Although there is no one that is any more or less traumatic in essence, the second pregnancy was very involved and complicated, and delivered not a life but a full-blown depression that consumed every bit of my being. I can recall significant events, but to this day I have difficulty remembering the sequence of events, and most troubling, the details. A great deal of this can also be contributed to my ensuing alcoholism that grew out of the depression. Only fueled by my mother's denial of my depression was I able to grasp an understanding of the grappling throes of my overwhelming torment. "Such incomprehension has usually been due not to a failure of sympathy but to the basic inability of healthy people to imagine a form of torment [so alien] to everyday reality."

More than a few therapists and psychiatrists had sat across from me while I attempted to put forth my senselessness. I was far too much of a wreck consumed by a constant cocktail of antidepressants and/or alcohol to ever express anything useful. I thought it was useless to describe myself to a doctor because I was always afraid of giving a wrong or insufficient answer that they might doubt my depression. Although the drinking could be questioned as a cause or interference with my progress, I knew then as I know now that my drinking grew out of the depression. Unfortunately, my brief vacation from my best friend plunged me even deeper upon my return. Styron captures his relationship with alcohol before his depression as I felt it throughout my own, as "a friend whose ministrations I sought daily . . . as a means to calm the anxiety and incipient dread that I had hidden away for so long somewhere in the dungeons of my spirit." Months of reality and sadness built a mountain of my grief and guilt. The only answer for me was time, as time distances us from that which makes us sad.

In retrospect, it was not my failed first attempt at a well-respected university or my eating disorders of many years that thrust me in a proverbial downward spiral that brought me to stay in a psychiatric hospital as well as complete an alcohol rehabilitation program. The melancholy I felt as I sat in my bedroom sophomore year of high school staring out the window hopelessly could be a sign that this depression could have been potentially a long time coming and instigated by the abortions and self-imposed guilt and secrecy. As Styron notes, "loss in all of its manifestations is the touchstone of depression—in the progress of the disease and, most likely, in its origin." I never belonged to a group nor could I identify myself as a unique individual. I was literally lost as a human being for many years. Styron sums the makings of depression quite well. "The danger is especially apparent if the young person is affected by what has been termed 'incomplete mourning'—has, in effect, been unable to achieve the catharsis of grief, and so carries within himself through later years an insufferable burden of which rage and guilt, and not only dammed-up sorrow, are a part, and become the potential seeds of self-destruction."

Much of William Styron's recollections ruminate upon suicide. This is a painfully disturbing and personal event for anyone to consider, and much more deadly under the torment of depression. It is a very real and wrenching process that cannot under any circumstances be justified. He presents the concept of suicide as a "fundamental question of philosophy" that is ulti-

mately an inappropriate means of relief for even the depths of depression. Fortunately I had the support from family and friends that he accounts as being necessary to nearly eliminating suicide as the last option, however I did scoff at the absurdity that life was worth living. William Styron's Darkness Visible *provides a discerning account that rendered the reader satisfied that if words should be used to capture such treachery, that they were well chosen from an insider's perspective. As a reader who experienced the same feelings of hopelessness and worthlessness that he expressed, his words regarding the outside world from the position of a depressed person were quite honest.*

Blythe begins her diary with a vivid dramatic irony: the green pants that she wore "faithfully" during the eighteen months of her depression suddenly rip as she begins writing the present entry, suggesting perhaps that writing has now allowed her finally to close this chapter of her life. Struck by the symbolism, she quotes the same sentence from *Darkness Visible* that her classmate Casey quotes. The knowledge that depression is incomprehensible to others is reassuring to both students, but it doesn't stop them from attempting to describe the indescribable. Agreeing with Styron that loss is one of the central symptoms, and perhaps causes, of depression, Blythe speaks authoritatively on the subject. She could not explain to her doctors what she was experiencing, perhaps because she feared they would not believe her; but she never doubts that the reader of her diary will understand the darkness of this period. She ends with a qualified affirmation of language to express reality: "if words should be used to capture such treachery, . . . they were well chosen from an insider's perspective."

Adrian: "I Could Not Get Myself Out of That Dark Place"

I did not feel anything for this book. I knew what it was going to be about. I knew that I would have to do everything I could to be emotionally detached. I unfortunately, like many other people, have suffered from a severe depression. This word, "depression," I would not have been able to say out loud about a year ago. Even now, it is difficult to write about.

My depression was slightly different from Styron's. Last summer I hit what felt to be the bottom. I knew around March or April that I was not feeling myself, but I refused to believe I was seriously depressed. I could only think and feel sadness and emptiness. I wanted to sleep all the time, even though I would wake numerous times throughout the night. I did not seem to care much about anything; such as school, family, work. Nothing seemed to be enjoyable and the only time I wanted to see my friends was if we were going out to a bar. At that time, I was also drinking alone at home most nights. I was miserable, and I had no idea why. I became even more miserable because I could not get myself out of that dark place.

The next phase of my depression I still feel very uncomfortable speaking out. I went through a period of burning and cutting myself. I was terrified by this and had no idea why I felt such a strong desire to do those things. I realize now that, among a few other reasons, I subconsciously knew where I was headed and wanted someone to help me. I also came to the same point of an emotional breakdown as Styron, the night of the dinner party, when he felt an "inner convulsion" of "despair beyond despair." All I can say about my experience was I also was with friends when I felt the same convulsion and left my friends, got in my car and drove away with a sense of determination. While Styron at this point threw out his notebook as an act of his decision to die, I went home and attempted to cut my wrist. Even now, while I write this, I cannot believe that that person was actually me. Very few people knew about my experience; only my parents and two of my closest friends.

When Styron was hospitalized, he thought of it as his salvation, and there the "tempest" in his head was quieted. When I hit that lowest point, and was forced to live at home with my father for a while, I too felt relief. It seemed as though I could finally relax because someone found out my secret, and they would take care of me, and help find the treatment I needed. In therapy, after this horrible experience, I was able to see how far back into my childhood this problem went. I always assumed that I was just going through a normal childhood, that periods of extreme unhappiness and hopelessness were all part of growing up.

In conclusion, I think it's great that Styron wrote this book. People need to see how disabling this illness is. Before writing this diary, I was unsure if I wanted to write about my experience; I thought about just writing a summary of the book. Even though this is something extremely personal to me, and I do feel a pinch of shame because of this illness still being taboo, being able to write about this does feel a bit cathartic, and I can understand completely why Styron wanted to write Darkness Visible.

Adrian begins her diary by stating that she did not "feel anything" for *Darkness Visible*, but as we continue reading, we realize that she needs to brace herself emotionally for Styron's story; she feels too much rather than too little. It seems remarkable that she is now able to write a diary entry about a word that she could not even express aloud a year ago. As she describes her suicide attempt during this period, she can hardly recognize the person she was. By the end of the diary, her lack of feeling for *Darkness Visible* has changed to unqualified enthusiasm—"I think it's great that

Styron wrote this book." One suspects that Adrian would not have been as moved by *Darkness Visible* if she had merely written a summary of it for her diary, as she thought of doing before deciding to write about how the book affected her life.

Griffen: "Depression Is Always There, Probably in Almost Everyone, and for Some More Than Others"

Before beginning this book, I had great fear of it. This book focuses on melancholia, an illness I myself have just overcome. No doubt my disease came in a milder form than Styron's, but at times it seemed almost as horrid. I feared reading this book because I believed it might cause me to slip back into this drowning pool of despair. In fact, the effect of reading this book was just the opposite.

This book entails Styron's illness from the inside out. It starts out by allowing the reader to delve into the depths of his depression, and then proceeds back to the beginning and portrays the unraveling of this mind state. He had heard accounts of the disease from several of his closest friends, and although he was sympathetic he could not relate to their state of mind. One of his closest friends is conquered by the illness, and ends his own life. Styron is not angry with him as many friends and relatives of suicide victims tend to be. At the same time he cannot understand why Romain Gary did this until he himself begins to become depressed. Styron's own malaise began at age sixty when his body finally started to reject alcohol intake. The drink had been a crutch for him for many years, it kept his demon's at bay. It also inspired his writing greatly (or so he says), and even more so his creative flow. I believe that this is false, and that creative minds are only distracted by drugs and alcohol. I once believed drugs enhanced my own creativity, but now I realize the truth.

I myself have experienced the state of depression. I cannot be sure if it was "clinical," because I never saw a doctor or a psychologist about it. Instead I sought help from my girlfriend, my music, sometimes even my parents, but probably most of all from marijuana. I told myself I enjoyed getting high because it relaxed me, which it most certainly did. My girlfriend and I (now x-girlfriend) use to get high every day during our last two years of high school. The first of these two years was like a fantastic euphoria. Our relationship was blooming; we enjoyed each others company so much that we didn't even feel the need to go out places like most couples do. We would just lie in bed together, smoking, making love, it seemed like heaven. We almost always hung out alone, and we became distant from most of our friends. I noticed this as it was occurring, but it had little affect on me because I was "in love."

Eventually she became bored with this routine and quit smoking. I how-

ever saw no reason to do such, and continued on this path. This slowly began to cause conflicts in our relationship. She would say hurtful things like, "Do you have to get high to enjoy being with me?" Of course I would always answer "no," but as time went by and our fights became more and more frequent the answer became yes. Our relationship grew further apart through senior year, until the time came to go to college. She was devastated, claiming she could not survive without me. I believed her because I had come to realize how dependent on me she had become. I tried to convince her that she would meet lots of nice people at school and make new friends, perhaps even meet a nice guy. At this point she was in tears, I could not end it even though I knew that's what would have been best for both of us. We were going to schools over 8 hours apart, and in my opinion we barely had anything worth holding on to. But, my guilt for taking two years of her life overtook me. I told her we would try and stay together.

Our relationship then consisted of emails and instant messages, calling each other only occasionally. We saw each other over breaks, but this was not cutting it. I told myself that if I met someone here in Albany that I would break this relationship off, but that never happened. In recollection, I realized this was because I still felt somewhat attached, almost morally obligated, and so I never really tried to meet anyone. Instead I buried myself in my schoolwork, and spent my free time as I pleased, which entailed a lot of smoking and laziness. This behavior, along with my increasing feelings of loneliness led to my depression's arrival. I felt useless, worthless, helpless. The friendships I made were superficial; they were almost solely based on smoking pot. I felt like I could confide in no one, and experienced not one bit of actual joy or happiness all year. Eventually summer came and we were back together everyday, but this did not seem to help matters at all. The fights continued to get worse, but somehow at the end we were still together, holding on to fond memories of the past.

We went back to school and barely contacted each other at all. On Christmas break I finally ended it, and it was not any easier than my first attempt to do so over a year earlier. Initially my condition worsened to the point where I had no desire to live. I could find nothing that brought me any happiness or pleasure at all. Even mary jane had no appeal to me. Getting high seemed only to make me feel confused and even more depressed at the same time. At many points I asked myself, is life worth living? Is it ever going to get better. Will I ever know happiness again? The thought of suicide crossed my mind several times during this time.

One night last semester I was invited by a friend to a yoga class. I had done yoga once before and enjoyed it so I figured I would try it again. At this point

I was willing to try anything to diverge my thinking from oblivion. I also had not been getting any physical exercise, as most pot-head's don't, so I thought it would be good for that as well. After the class my mind was crystal clear, and my body felt amazingly renewed. I realized that I had been attempting to mask my problems with weed, and that this substance was no longer enabling me to do this. I decided to take a serious cut back with smoking, and continued going to yoga class twice a week, every week. Within a couple of weeks I felt so much healthier, both physically and mentally. Through yoga I learned about meditation, and began practicing both every morning when I woke up. It became a great way to start the day. I came to terms with my addiction, and my depression. I saw these things for what they truly were, distractions. They were distracting me from living life, from enjoying life.

I realized that lack of exercising my mind and body, and lack of social interaction allowed my depression to commence and eventually thrive. After overcoming it, I spoke with my parents about it who revealed that I had been depressed as a child several times, and had overcome that through physical activity, creative artwork, and peer relations. This allowed me to see that depression is always there, probably in almost everyone, and for some more than others. I had survived probably a mild case, but the illness had not left, only subsided. I realize now what I have to do to keep it from ruining my life. The most important thing I try and tell myself every day is a saying I learned through yoga which is, "Baba nam ke va lam." This translates into, "love is all there is." Love for others, and most importantly, love for one's self. To remember how special you are, how to love who you are, helps you remember how worthy life is of living.

I believe in one way or another this is how almost all people (including Styron) conquer this vicious disorder. Some people may need professional help in doing this, such as cognitive behavioral therapy of pharmacology, or both combined. I was lucky enough to find a way to give myself cognitive therapy, and continue to do so every day. I believe that if I had not began to cure myself when I did, I may not have been able to do it alone. Perhaps I would not even be alive to write this paper. In addition to this self-therapy, this entire course has also been of great help in overcoming my depression. Partly because I was able to see that others (the writer's we read) were far more depressed than myself, but even more so because of these mandatory diary entries. They have enabled me to get out a lot of thoughts and emotions that I would be incapable to discuss even with a close friend. In writing about my feelings, I was able to analyze them, and see their true origins. This has helped me greatly in overcoming them. I have decided to start a journal of my own so that I continue to heal myself through the act of writing.

I have also began to re-commence my artwork, which I find an extremely rewarding activity, even while completely sober. This was my proof that drugs are not needed to be creative. They only relax you enough to become creative. Therefore, creative minds must only learn to relax naturally, and then their creative flow will be unobstructed, undistracted, and infinite.

Griffen begins his diary by conceding that he feared reading *Darkness Visible*, but the book had the opposite effect, helping him to delve into the depths of his past depression. Disagreeing with Styron's assertion that alcohol or drugs can enhance creativity, Griffen explains how marijuana contributed to his own depression. Like Styron, he believes that depression has always been part of his life and may return in the future, but he now seems better prepared to deal with that possibility.

The students' depression narratives reveal that what happened to them was frightening, confusing, isolating, and stigmatizing. In the beginning they could neither understand nor resist what was happening to them. They were *overcome* by depression, suggesting a loss of control and agency. Some can find causes for their depression while others cannot. Though many of them describe illnesses that occurred only a year or two ago, they imply that they felt like they were a different person, one to whom neither their closest relatives or friends could relate. Some, like Angie, describe loving relationships with their parents, while others, like Casey, describe distant relationships with one or both parents. All found it nearly impossible to explain to others what was happening. Since those who suffer from mood disorders may not have the overt symptoms associated with physical illnesses or injuries, such as a high fever, swollen glands, or a broken bone, it is much more difficult to explain these disorders to other people. The "invisibility" of these mood disorders heightens self-blame.

Three of the four women describe psychological illnesses that have a direct impact on their bodies. Angie speaks about losing sixty pounds in two months and being forced to eat while in the hospital. Blythe refers to an eating disorder, while Adrian recalls a period of burning and cutting herself. Another student, Christine, also describes cutting herself as a response to depression (see below). By contrast, none of the male students, including those who describe having been suicidal, mentions anything that might indicate an attack on the male body. Although the number of student diarists is too small to generalize, it is nevertheless striking that unlike men, women who write about depression often reveal violence against their bodies—either through dieting, sometimes to the point of starvation, or self-mutilation in the form of burning and cutting. Amber raised a similar observation in the preceding chapter, when she describes what it feels like for a woman to be ashamed of her body. As Susan Bordo argues in *Unbearable Weight: Feminism, Western Culture and the Body*, culture teaches women "to memorize on our bodies the feel and conviction of lack, of insufficiency, of never being good enough" (166).

The students' healing occurred in many different ways. Angie's healing was made possible by hospitalization and medication, which she continues to take. For Casey, healing came in the form of brief psychotherapy, diary writing, art, music, and friends. Blythe cited the support of her family and friends, while Adrian's recovery was aided by living with her father. Yoga, the decision to stop smoking marijuana, and cognitive therapy were helpful for Griffen. The coherency of their diaries suggests that they are on the way to having more control over their lives. They are able to write about the past as if it is a concluded chapter in their lives, and though only Griffen uses the word, they now see themselves as survivors.

Bearing Witness to Present Depression

Reading *Darkness Visible* proved most difficult to those students who feared that they were themselves becoming depressed. Although these students were in pain *before* taking the course, reading *Darkness Visible* and *Risky Writing* compelled them to confront frightening or disturbing aspects of their lives that they had heretofore denied. One of these students, Chloe, wrote about how reading *Darkness Visible* suddenly helped her to understand the meaning of her mother's dark "moods"—and her own as well:

Chloe: "Reading Styron's Words from His Experience Hit Me Like Lightning"

When I was small, I blamed myself for my mother's "moods." When I went away to school, I worried everyday that she would not be there when I came on my weekly weekend visits. When she cried every morning, I blamed myself and decided to transfer closer to her. I never blamed my mother, she is just who she is and I had to help when she couldn't face the world. This is just how it was, and none of us questioned it. By reading William Styron's account of his descent into the illness of depression, I was jolted into recognition of my mother's lifeline. The word depression was never spoken around my mother and it was only used in passing, not as a real disease with a real affliction and especially not to describe my mother's actions. Depression was a disease for the mentally ill and to be mentally ill was to be crazy! My mother is the most loving, giving and wonderful woman that I know. She just has "moods" sometimes. Reading Styron's words from his experience hit me like lightning. Depression hurts, depression is uncontrollable, depression is inescapable, and depression can kill. Depression doesn't mean someone is crazy; it slowly and methodically removes them from the world around them. My mother has a mood disorder that may very well be killing her slowly and I passed it off as "moods." I can't help but blame myself.

Styron writes that when he learned of his friend's fall into depression that he was "relatively indifferent." He writes that this "is important because such indifference demonstrates powerfully the outsider's inability to grasp the essence of the illness. [The] depression [was an] abstract ailment . . . to me, in spite of my sympathy, and I hadn't an inkling of its true contours or the nature of the pain so many victims experience as the mind continues in its insidious meltdown." It is almost impossible to understand or describe what it is like to be stricken so harshly and so inexplicably with a disease that has no real cure. It is harder to explain how you feel when you don't really understand yourself. My brother and I came to call my mother's episodes as "moods." When my mother would suddenly be so horribly sad and hated everything around her, my brother would ask me what was wrong and a simple "she's in a mood" would suffice. No further explanation was ever searched for, we would just be better children and tried to do everything perfect so she wouldn't be sad or angry anymore. After all, it was most likely that we did something to cause it, right? We never thought anything could be wrong with our mother, that's just the way it was.

I remember one time that I came home from staying at a friend's house and my brother was in our kitchen making a sandwich. My mother came out of her bedroom and started crying. She said the house was a mess, always a mess and that she would never be able to keep up with the mess. She then went back to her room and cried alone for hours. I asked my brother what was going on and he said, "She's in a mood." I just nodded my head and started cleaning the house. Nothing more was said, it never was. To this day, my brother will call me up and simply say "she's in a mood" and I'll go home to help. It is never questioned, that's just the way it is. Now I realize that my mother cannot control these attacks on her inner world and that she is suffering. I realize that it is not my or my brother's fault. I realize that this is out of our control and that my mother can find some help. I cannot figure out why we didn't see this earlier, why we didn't question, why we didn't get my mother real help and save her from the darkness that is suffocating her? I should have known, I should have seen and understood. I can't help blame myself.

The thing about reading this book, Darkness Visible, is that now I understand what my mother is going through just a little bit better. The thing *about reading this book is that now I can begin to see the darkness that clouds her beautiful eyes. The thing about reading this book is that I can see tendencies in myself. The thing about reading this book is that I got a peek at recognition and understanding, but for the first time a fear and a perception that this might come out to knock on my door tagged along. I was home, helping my mother when I read this book. It seems almost poetic, or a bit like fate. I could actually read the book, look up at my mother and see it in action. The thing about reading this book and actually watching it happen is that I began to watch myself. I do much of what my mother does. My mother has obsessive-compulsive tendencies and so do I. There are many days that I am inexplicably unable to get up and face the day and the world. There are many days that I want to cry and can never explain to others why. Just a couple of weeks ago, I was on break from work and just the thought of going back to work made me cry uncontrollably and I can't even tell you why. I love my job and my co-workers, but just the thought of going there, being there, not being able to just go and hide in my room made me feel stuck. I know you are now thinking that you don't understand. I know this because I always felt that way when my mother tried to tell me why she was crying. I could never really understand and I don't even really understand it in myself.*

From reading this book I have realized a great many things and one major thing I realized is that I really don't know or understand much. All I know is that William Styron had to come to the brink of "answering the fundamental question of philosophy" in order to get better. All I know is that I don't want my mother to get to that point. All I know is that I don't know. I don't know if she has felt that way, or if she does feel that way, or if she ever will. I don't know if I will ever feel that way and that scares the hell out of me. The thing about reading this book is that I got a glimpse of what it is to be at the bottom of a spiral down, I got a little bit of hope from Styron's survival, and I got an extreme realization that it is a very real possibility that my mother or even I might not. Most importantly what I got is a light at the end of that very dark and lonely tunnel. I cannot tell you how afraid I am of the darkness in between but at least I have that light to hold onto.

The power of Chloe's diary lies in its loving description of a mother who inextricably drifts into and out of "moods," which, before *Darkness Visible*, seemed to have no psychological explanation. The word "depression" does not make these moods less fearful, but it does help Chloe to accept her mother's condition. She remarks that Styron's words hit her "like lightning," and her own words strike the reader with nearly equal force. The incantatory clause "the thing about reading this book" highlights the urgency of her prose. One senses that Styron's story has changed her life, and that to do justice to his and her mother's dark moods, she must create a rhetorical self that will enable her to bear witness to depression. Her language is so emotionally charged that it threatens to become too emotional, hence, melodramatic; but what prevents this from occurring is that she doesn't claim to have discovered too much from Styron's memoir. It is negative knowledge, Socratic knowledge, to which she refers; now she realizes, perhaps for the first time, how little she has known about the meaning of the dark moods within her mother and herself. Nor does she claim too much hope at the end of the diary; she closes not with an image of lightning but with a ray of light, just enough to help her imagine undertaking a journey through a dark, lonely tunnel.

Some students intimated that they were struggling with a personal problem, though they didn't use the word "depression." Jerry notes in his diary on *Risky Writing* that the most disturbing chapter was the one devoted to binge drinking, with which he uncomfortably identifies.

Jerry: "I Had to Put the Book Down Because I Was on the Verge of Tears"

The one chapter entitled, "Writing Under the Influence," I found especially touching. I don't mean to begin a story about what I felt during the essays written, and what I am currently going through as of right now, but the entire topic of binge drinking really means something to me. There was a time in my life when I used to think that the more you could drink, the tougher you were. This probably took place right before my entry into college. This doesn't mean that I drank too much because I actually found that too much alcohol just made you feel really shitty during and after drinking. The turning point in my ability to put down a good amount to alcohol was when I took a semester to live in Spain. In Spain, people drink as a way of life. As the day begins, so does the drinking. This is not every Spaniard, but from what I have seen, a great amount. In that beautiful country was where I learned to binge drink. I hate to say it, but I was good at it. There is no need to express how much alcohol I put down in a night, but all I will say is that I would get home at 7:30 in the morning stumbling and hungry. This went on for 4 months straight, every night of the week. I never thought in my wildest dreams that I could drink so much and for so long without it effecting me. When I got back to New York, however, it did.

Besides going through culture shock, I was still greatly in the mood to party as I got so very used to it after doing it for 4 months straight. To jump passed some time right about now, here I sit 4 months later having trouble stopping drinking. The essays I read in Risky Writing *touched me because people actually questioned whether or not they had an alcohol problem. I felt just kind of relieved in a way that people questioned exactly what I questioned for quite awhile. In one of the essays, the writer comments that there is nothing else to do at night in a social setting. Another comments that he decided to cut down his drinking, but soon there after went back to the binge lifestyle. I found all of this really good to hear because it almost seemed to me that people never had any problems handling their alcohol intake, nor did it effect them in any way mentally. I actually vowed to myself to stay away from drinking for 3 weeks to see how my mental status will or will not improve. So far, I actually feel a lot healthier and my thoughts are beginning to clear themselves up. I was in such a hole with myself that I could not function to any degree unless completely inebriated. I'm really glad I found this out now instead of 10 years down the line. Having read this book, especially that chapter, it made me feel better about my decision for taking a break from my drinking, and also made me feel like a person who is not alone.*

I finished this book in two days. There I was sitting in my nice corner seat of the library surrounded by windows so I don't feel entrapped, reading this book with all of my attention. There was actually more than 5 instances where I had to put the book down because I was on the verge of tears. I don't normally get very choked up when reading a book which is not to say that it has happened, but I must say, with reading this one book, I have never been brought to the verge of tears so many times; it was like I was being emotionally poked by every journal I read. I am in no way mocking this book because it actually made me feel so much more human, so much more empathic towards other people that I feel like I am not alone in the world. So often and so easily can one feel alone in this world, but in truth, none of us are. All our problems and feelings run through others at every moment. It is simply difficult to remember that sometimes.

Identification can be either comforting or disturbing—or both, as it is to Jerry. His identification with students writing about alcohol problems makes him feel less alone and, presumably, less stigmatized, but it also brings him to the "verge of tears." Identification may also bring to the surface previously unacknowledged fears and conflicts. The simile he uses to describe the act of reading—like "being emotionally poked by every journal I read"—evokes the "hazards of reading." Such reading, he concludes, makes him feel more human, more empathic, and more connected to people.

Evaluating the Diaries

How did the students feel about the diaries they heard me read aloud? They had two opportunities to respond to this question: either in their diary on *Risky Writing*, in which they discussed the extent to which reading the signed essays of my past students resembled hearing the anonymous diaries of their classmates, or on the following final exam question:

> In *Darkness Visible* William Styron writes about his depression, in the process educating his readers about the seriousness of this disease. He concludes with the following observation: "But one need not sound the false or inspirational note to stress the truth that depression is not the soul's annihilation; men and women who have recovered from the disease—and they are countless—bear witness to what is probably its only saving grace: it is conquerable."
>
> Discuss what you have learned about depression from reading *Darkness Visible and* from hearing me read several *Darkness Visible* diaries aloud. To what extent have *you* borne witness to depression by being a member of Literature and the Healing Arts? Have reading and writing about depression been depressing or uplifting to you? Explain.

To begin with, many felt like they were in the position of the Wedding Guest in Coleridge's *The Rime of the Ancient Mariner,* who is transfixed by the Mariner's tale of the killing of the albatross. Struggling to free himself from the dark story that he "cannot choose but hear," the Wedding Guest finds his life changed:

> *went like one that hath been stunned,*
> *And is of sense forlorn:*
> *A sadder and a wiser man*
> *He rose the morrow morn.* (105)

Both *Darkness Visible* and the diaries were a revelation to those who knew little about depression before taking the course. One student, who had never experienced a mood disorder, observed, "I'm not being forced to listen to these stories, and yet I can't really leave without being changed. Each story is almost like a deep dark secret that they don't really want to tell me and at the same time, they want to share it with me. Each story is so powerful and all I can really say is, 'I'm lucky—No, not lucky—but it's been the grace of God that has protected me all this time.'" Some students realized that contrary to what they previously thought, they had *never* been seriously depressed:

I have always been one of those people who when upset or sad exclaims, "I'm so depressed!" I never really thought about what that means when it is actually true. From the book and my classmates I gained a better understanding as to what depression really is. My understanding of it now is that it occurs when someone experiences feelings such as sadness, gloominess or melancholy for an extended period of time which can inhibit the person's ability to function effectively. Up until this class I would have sworn that I was depressed. Those feelings would invade my life and last for what felt like eternity. In reality it was probably a day or two at the most. My classmates and Styron showed me that depression is very real and more intense than I could have imagined.

By being a member of "Literature and the Healing Arts," I bore witness to depression to a new extent that I had ever experienced before. For the first time I saw how many people really do suffer from depression. It affects more lives then I realized or could even imagine. No one that I know of in my life has experienced depression. This fact makes it hard for me to truly understand what someone with depression is going through. Being a part of this class has made me aware of how difficult it is to overcome depression. It has shown me the huge struggle that a depressed person goes through to cope with depression. It has also shown me that the people in that person's life can play a huge role in that recovery. People like me can either hinder or help someone's recovery. Bearing witness to depression in class was an educational experience for me.

Another student felt that although she never had suffered from depression, the course helped her overcome another "disease":

By being a member of "Literature and the Healing Arts," I feel that I have borne significant witness to the disease that is depression. Through reading Styron's memoir about his ordeal and triumph over the disease, I too feel that I have overcome the disease as well; but I have overcome a disease of a different kind — the disease of generalization. For me, being an eyewitness to this disease has opened up and cleared up many of the misconceptions that I had about this disease that has taken many lives of great writers. . . . Hearing the stories of fellow classmates who had gone through or had experienced depression via a loved one and how they helped to get their loved one through it whilst trying to cope with it themselves is an experience that many do not get to be a part of. Just like Styron's memoir gave an intimate portrait of his experience, thus too the reader response journals that were written by my fellow classmates gave me a view into their life, which up until that point had not been known to me.

Students wrote empathically about their classmates' diaries, and although they did not know the diarists' identities and could not always remember many of the details of individual diaries, they bore witness to what they had heard. Here is how Jerry referred to Angie's diary, which I had read aloud nearly three months earlier:

I can remember one certain diary read aloud in class earlier on in the semester about one girl who was placed in the psychiatric ward of a hospital for an attempted suicide. She got so deep into it that her parents had no choice but to place her in the care of doctors so as to try and pull her out of her own ending. The thing that really touched me in her writing was that no matter how depressed she knew she was, she still felt that she did not belong inside a psychiatric ward in a hospital filled with those who look like they should be in one. She expressed how alone she felt when her parents left her there, but in the end, thanked them for helping her conquer such a terrible period of her life. What I found absolutely amazing about this person was that such an extreme case of depression which almost lead her to suicide was sitting in class with me speaking about it through her diary. A survivor exists amongst our class, and she has the strength to speak about it honestly and truthfully. This strength amazed me in so many ways.

Often students reported that hearing a classmate's diary on depression reminded them of another person's situation or behavior. For instance, the knowledge that one person gained from hearing Casey's diary, which she assumed was written by a male, helped her to understand a friend's depression:

One of the diary entries that I heard made me wonder if my friend was going through the same thing. One entry talked about how the person would not be able to get out of his bed in the morning. He would look up at the ceiling or continue to sleep. He would get up only for meals. He always enjoyed the night better than the day because he could go out to drinking parties during the night. However, he hated coming to his room after a party because he hated the loneliness that he felt. He would be panic-stricken if none of his friends came over to go to dinner because he felt as though he did something wrong.

While I was listening to this particular diary entry, my eyes watered because I was reminded of my friend. I had recently found out that he was suffering from depression. He had a habit of constantly telling me that he liked the nights better because he felt that the darkness could hide his disease. He would stay in his room or go to an isolated area during the day when he had no classes because he felt that whenever people looked at him, they knew that he had depression. He felt that during the night, he could blend in with the rest of the world because no one would be able to tell that he was suffering from depression due to the darkness. He would ask me, "What's the meaning of life? Here's the point when you're born and here's the point when you die. But what's in between? Nothing." Whenever I heard him talk like this, I would ask him to stop talking because it scared me. I didn't know how to deal with these random thoughts. I just wanted him to snap out of it. Now I realize that he can't. It's all part of his depression.

I feel as though I bore witness to depression by being a member of "Literature and the Healing Arts" each time I heard a diary entry or read Styron's book. Whenever a new diary entry was read, I felt as though the diary entry had a strong force pulling me into the life of the diarist. I felt that the diary had life and that it had something important to tell. The diary was somehow beckoning me to come to follow him into the life of a diarist suffering from depression and I willingly followed. He wouldn't let go until I listened to the whole story. He wouldn't let me leave until I was awakened.

Another student wrote about how hearing his classmates' diaries helped him understand his roommate, who was struggling with depression:

I did not realize how many of my classmates had been through depression. I see how other people's experiences have influenced them and shaped them as they grew older in life. Some people's parents are manic-depressives and take medicine for this. Once I had heard about my peers' experiences, I was shocked to go home and find out that my roommate was just recently on anti-depressive medication and had stopped taking it. His mood was noticeable and I saw some of his symptoms. One of the main ones was that he was happy only when he drank. I felt it was my obligation to suggest he go back on the medication and take it easy on the drinking. He went back on the medication, but the drinking remains. At least during the daytime he does not worry me about his thoughts and actions.

Many students found themselves pulled in to their classmates' lives, sometimes involuntarily, and when they emerged, they found themselves changed, like the Wedding Guest. Without exception, those who remarked on this change felt that it was for the better. Here is how one person commented on Blythe's, Adrian's, and Griffen's diaries on *Darkness Visible*:

It is hard to understand depression, and many people don't even want to understand it. I suffered from minor depression, and reading Styron's story was very therapeutic for me. He overcame his depression and lived to tell about it. This book and the diaries read in class have all had a major impact on the way I look at depression.

The first diary read in class was about a woman [Blythe] who suffered from depression after her second abortion. Growing up, I was taught by the Catholic Church that abortion was wrong and sinful. We even watched a video on abortion to instill how horrible it was. As I have grown, I changed my views on abortion and consider myself pro-choice. I do however find it wrong when women use abortion as a form of regular birth control. I always thought that was selfish of them, but I never realized the torment that some go through. Prior to this diary, I would get disgusted whenever I heard the term second abortion. After hearing about her problems with alcohol and drugs, and how she suffered from an eating disorder, I realized she did what she had to do even though she did not want to. She had to deal with her own self-imposed guilt and who am I to judge her for that.

In high school, I knew a girl who used to cut her arms and legs. When the second diary [Adrian] was read I immediately thought of her. I wasn't that close with her but for some reason she told me what she was doing to herself. I made sure that she was seeing a professional about her problem and I asked her if her parents knew. She informed me that they both knew and took her to a psychologist, so after that I promised not to say anything. I never told anyone what she told me, but it troubled me because I couldn't understand why she would do that to herself. After reading Darkness Visible *and diary two, I came to understand a little more about her illness.*

The person who wrote diary three [Griffen] also suffered from depression. At first, he was afraid that reading Styron's memoir would bring him back down into a depressive state. But in the end his reaction was the same as mine, in that it was sort of a healing and therapeutic story to read. I could relate to him when he talked about him and his girlfriend and how they smoked weed together, and had so much fun together. It took me a long time to get out of my three-year relationship because every fight we had would end due to us smoking our troubles away. I never realized how badly I depended on weed. I needed it to function, and I needed it to be happy. I stopped smoking all together due to this diary. I came to the conclusion that it was just distracting me from living my life. Thanks to that diary I now lead a drug free life.

Angie: "A Commonality . . . with Each of the Depressed"

The diaries were especially valuable for those who had suffered from depression and who were able to learn something about themselves as a result of hearing their classmates' experiences. "During English 226," Angie wrote, "I began to realize a commonality that existed with each of the depressed. Prior to each episode of depression, each person seemed to develop their own methods of coping. Frequently these methods were quite unhealthy and self-destructive. For instance, Styron relied heavily upon alcohol. Several diarists also relied on drugs, including alcohol and marijuana. One diarist felt comforted by the self-harm acts of cutting and burning. It was usually when these methods cease to work that the depression became a serious and debilitating problem. I looked back on my experience with depression with this new realization. I found that I used controlled eating and exercise as a means of distracting myself from depression." Angie identified with those diarists who had difficulty discussing depression with their doctors. "I found it extremely hard to express to others what I was going through. I found my illness impossible to describe and my mind continually drew blank when I was asked simple questions. Thus, I greatly admired Styron's powerful words and my classmates emotional diaries."

Casey: "A Huge Weight Has Been Lifted"

Casey wrote on her final exam that she was anxious about the course syllabus at the beginning of the semester. "As I was buying my books all I could think was 'these look so depressing'; it worried me because I had spent a major part of last year in a depression. Now, however, I feel a huge weight has been lifted from my chest. In fact, another student shared that they felt the same way in one of the diaries read aloud. This course has showed me that many people have had similar experiences, and they too have overcome melancholia. It was a difficult subject to read about and discuss at first, but our open discussions in class have been like group therapy for me, and probably many others." Reading and writing about depression was unexpectedly uplifting for Casey. "A few days ago I completely surprised myself when I told someone I had recently met about my depression. Up until then, I had made up excuses about why I had to transfer schools. Even though it kind of scared me (and probably sounded weird to my friend), I felt like a burden had been lifted; I was finally being honest with myself and with others. While the hardship of depression is extremely difficult to bear and is unfortunately fatal for some, our discussions and readings have shown the class that the disorder can be overcome."

Blythe: "An Opportunity to Express Myself Honestly and Coherently"

Blythe was attracted to Literature and the Healing Arts because of the opportunity to write about her past. "Recovering from my traumatic depression I knew that being able to write out everything would be a means of recovery for me in many ways." She wanted to write a diary on *Darkness*

Visible that "truly merited being read aloud." Her diary was the first of the five that I read aloud that night, and she believed that she succeeded in conveying her grief during that dark period of her life. Blythe was impressed with the variety of points of view expressed by her classmates. "As a sufferer of depression, I tend to view the illness as one-sided rather than through the eyes of family members or friends. Many of the students suffered the same symptoms and I felt slightly more connected, although I still have the tendency to believe that my depression was in some way more severe, that it would be difficult to encounter a person whose suffering was near to mine." Blythe felt, as Casey did, that reading and writing about depression were uplifting. "I have climbed from the depths of depression to appreciate an opportunity to explore my pain in a productive manner today. Sharing my experiences has provided me with an opportunity to express myself honestly and coherently. Understanding the complexities of suffering through a piece of literature makes an experience seem real and valid, yet when it is expressed personally within a classroom of tangible people that I interact with, I am exposed on an entirely new level. I am a survivor and I want you to know because I am proud to be here today."

Adrian: "I Was Glad That I Made Myself Write on It"

Adrian believed that the diaries helped her see the "variety of emotions experienced by those who have suffered from depression themselves, or have had someone close to them suffer from this illness." Hearing the diaries was a unique learning experience. "In reality, the only depressions I have learned from were those seen in works like *The Bell Jar, The Awakening, The Yellow Wallpaper*, to name a few, and my own experience. In most novels which depict depression, I usually experience them on a superficial level, not letting myself become affected. However, the diaries did teach me the pervasiveness and uniqueness of depression." Adrian was unsure whether the class readings and diaries were uplifting or depressing. "The reading of and listening to diaries about depression occasionally uplifted me to hear about recoveries. On the other hand, these readings also affected me negatively by reminding and occasionally reliving my own depression. Furthermore, hearing these stories would depress me to see how huge and widespread this illness is. It saddens me to know the seriousness and the amount of people who suffer from depression, while people who have not directly or indirectly experienced it do not understand or care that depression is in fact a debilitating illness." Adrian felt ambivalent about her diary on depression. "The writing about that time not only brought back memories, but also the emotions of that point in my life. I was also unhappy to see how difficult it was, and still is, for me to write and discuss my own and others depression. On the other hand, I was glad that I made myself write on it, even if not very much in depth. I also believed my writing on my own experience made me feel good that I have been able to live through it, and remain to 'bear witness' to the effect of depression."

Griffen: "The Opening of Your Soul and the Unleashing of Your Demons"

Griffen believed that hearing about his classmates' lives enhanced his capacity for empathy. "I now try and listen empathically to every personal story I encounter, whether reading a novel, or being there for a friend." He was startled when he heard me read aloud his diary on *Darkness Visible*:

> *All semester I had hoped you would read one of my journals so that I could have the experience of having my personal life cracked open for a classroom full of students to see. I thought that it would not make me feel anxious or scared, but strong. It did in fact make me feel strong, but that was not until after it was done. As you began reading it was as if I could not control myself, my heart began to race; as the diary became more and more personal, the anxiety grew, and I literally began to sweat. I am not sure why even now, no one knew it was my diary, and even if they had I was quite confident that no one in the class would try and judge me. It must have been the feeling of extreme openness; the opening of your soul and the unleashing of your demons publicly is a feeling like no other I have experienced. For this reason I am glad you chose the most personal of my diaries to read aloud.*

Griffen's responses should give us pause, for his metaphor of the diaries as a public unleashing of demons suggests the unpredictable power of self-disclosing writing for good or ill. If a person who writes about past depression finds it difficult to remain in control when hearing his diaries read aloud, how do those who write about a present crisis react to hearing their diaries read aloud? Do they, too, experience their words as a public unleashing of demons? The two students who feared that they were at risk, Chloe and Jerry, both responded to this question:

Chloe: "I Learned That I Am Not Alone"

Chloe concluded from reading *Darkness Visible* and hearing her classmates' diaries that her mother probably suffers from depression and that she herself shows signs of this disease. This knowledge scared but did not dishearten her. "I learned that depression often shows in mild episodes in youth only to strike harder later in life. I learned that many people die from depression. I learned that many people survive. Although much of what I learned frightened me inexplicably, the last thing I learned from the book is what will save me. This I can count on." She believed that Literature and the Healing Arts was mainly about bearing witness and surviving the stories of survivors. "From listening to other students' diaries I learned something just as precious as the hope I got from the book, I learned that I am not alone. It's not shameful, it's not strange, and I am normal. My feelings aren't freakish and I don't have to shut myself up to the rest of the world. I don't have to hide when I am feeling 'not right.'"

Jerry: "We Are All People Alike and We All Feel Pain"

Jerry also believed that the strength he heard in his classmates' diaries would help him to come to terms with one of his own problems, binge drinking. He had spoken about this issue in his diary on *Risky Writing,* but he acknowledged on his final exam that the problem is more serious than he had implied earlier. "A lesson that I learned from 'Literature and the Healing Arts' concerning depression was that no matter what we as human beings are afflicted with, we are not alone. During this semester, I was in such a deep hole with myself over alcohol abuse that it eventually led me to a contemplation of suicide. I never told anyone about it because at that exact moment of serious contemplation, I automatically abandoned the thought, and decided to get help any way I could. My mother proved to be my savior in this situation, but what was most important in my realizing my depression was that of my classmates and their self-disclosures." Jerry felt comforted by the recognition that his classmates were struggling with similar problems. "It is so very hard to remember because all your talking sounds like complaining to any other person, but those who live under depressions hand can understand and will offer help to you. Going to class taught me this. I am nothing special to feel such terrible feelings and I alone am not the only one who has or is feeling those feelings. Listening to discussions and diaries about depression let me remember something long forgotten by me: that we are all people alike and we all feel pain. Others have been in my shoes before if not larger shoes. We need to be there to listen to each other so that we don't end ourselves."

Risky Reading

For Chloe, Jerry, and the overwhelming majority of their classmates, Literature and the Healing Arts lived up to its title, but for about ten students—including those who were glad they took the course—the class readings were more emotionally exhausting than they anticipated. They reported in their diaries that they experienced nightmares, insomnia, nausea, or dread—symptoms that ranged from moderately to severely upsetting before disappearing in a week or two. A statement by Kafka, which I used as the epigraph to *Surviving Literary Suicide*, comes to mind here:

> I think we ought to read only the kind of books that wound and stab us. If the book we're reading doesn't wake us up with a blow on the head, what are we reading it for? So that it will make us happy, as you write? Good Lord, we would be happy precisely if we had no books, and the kind of books that make us happy are the kind we could write ourselves if we had to. But we need the books that affect us like a disaster, that grieve us deeply, like the death of someone we love more than ourselves, like being banished into forests from everyone, like a suicide. A book must be the axe for the frozen sea inside us. (16)

Patrice: "The Most Traumatic Experience of My Life as a Reader"

The book that was most upsetting to my students was not *Darkness Visible* but *Survival in Auschwitz*. Despite the fact that Primo Levi is liberated from the concentration camp, the story literally sickened several readers. "Talk about literature having the ability to traumatize," Patrice states at the beginning of her diary:

There were times when I felt sick to my stomach. There were times when I became overwhelmed and just wanted to stop reading. But I was compelled to continue by more than a mere course requirement. I have had what I now consider to be an academic understanding of the Holocaust. I have seen the images in documentaries, I have heard the numbers; but from all of this, one cannot even begin to fathom how the individuals experienced such unimaginable horrors. Levi's autobiography is an example of the enlightenment that comes with literature that I never got out of a classroom. It was this sense of enlightenment, the feeling that I was developing a more personal understanding of what World War II meant for the people who lived it, that kept me reading despite my visceral reactions.

Now, books have made me laugh aloud as well as cry, but I cannot remember ever reading a book that gave me a nightmare. Last Wednesday I finished the final chapter, "The Story of Ten Days," and went to bed. That night I was haunted by those very same images I have seen at least a couple of dozen times in documentaries. However, not one of those documentaries ever gave me a nightmare, Primo Levi's book did. Human figures so emaciated I could see their bones through their gray skin. I felt scared, as if these lifeless bodies were ghosts, although none seemed to be aware of my existence. They all bore heavy loads of various types (one was pushing a huge boulder, another was carrying an old car on his back), and their heads were listlessly pointed towards the ground. It seemed like a sort of purgatory, with the putrid smell of human suffering that no stomach can handle. I honestly woke up scared! I think the last time I had a bona fide nightmare before this was about 14 years ago, when Freddy Kruger intruded into my unconscious.

I think that final chapter was the most traumatic experience of my life as a reader. It seemed like a scene of Armageddon. I can understand why so many of the Hafling (perhaps all) had as their worst of fears, "the ever-repeated scene of the unlistened-to story." Both, the prisoners of the death camps and the nazi officers, were aware of the fact that what was taking place was so unimaginable it was also unlikely to be believable. I never doubted the fact of the Holocaust, but now I have found an entirely new, more profound and dynamic perspective of the event.

I think Levi's nightmare has come true in that current generations learn a very white washed version of World War II in their high school history classes, and the Holocaust almost seems like a post-script. Textbooks are written very matter-of-factly and I have begun to doubt if anyone can sufficiently learn about such an event when no attempt is made to evoke any emotion in the reader.

On the other hand, I think Levi's dream has also come true. The events of September 11th, in addition to this autobiography, have me think about the reality of evil and realize why it is so important to maintain peace. I now have a scar that will forever remind me of that reality. Although I may forget what I learned in high school textbooks, I will never forget the gruesome images that were created in my mind by Primo Levi's words.

Patrice's response to *Survival in Auschwitz* recalls my discussion in *Risky Writing* of Chrissy's response to *The Diary of Anne Frank* and *The White Hotel*: both students found themselves literally sickened as a result of reading about the Holocaust. The violence of these stories was so intense that the two readers could not safely detach themselves from it. They found themselves pulled into the nightmare in a way that goes beyond the Wedding Guest's reaction to the Mariner's tale. Although many literature teachers, especially those who teach on a college level, might regard Patrice's response as unusual or excessive, I believe that their own students would describe similar responses. I am not suggesting that books like *Survival in Auschwitz*, *The Diary of Anne Frank*, or *The White Hotel* should not be taught—their timeliness is greater than ever—but I am suggesting that teachers should be sensitive to the students who find these works wrenching. *Survival in Auschwitz* had a Kafkaesque impact on Patrice, affecting her like a disaster, and reading it a few months after the September eleventh attack only heightened its horrific power.

Mac: "When I Try to Imagine It, I Get Sick"

Survival in Auschwitz allowed Patrice to imagine what it must have been like to be a prisoner during the Holocaust, but the story had a different effect on Mac, whose identification with Primo Levi reawakened memories of a different kind of incarceration:

"I feel myself threatened, besieged, at every moment I am ready to draw myself into a spasm of defense." Primo Levi uses these feelings to describe his deepest fears concerning the state of vulnerability that he finds himself in during his stay at the concentration camps in Auschwitz. In that one sentence, Levi echoes my deepest fear in life, being put into jail. Everything that Primo Levi says about the conduct of himself and the other prisoners makes me uneasy because I am so afraid of being just a number. As Primo Levi was tattooed with a number on his arm, I am afraid of ever being restricted to those numbers on my chest. I was once arrested and kept in jail for the short period of two weeks and I had never been so afraid before in my life. I felt like I was not a person, only another criminal in the eyes of the law. I know everyone says they did not do it, but I in all actuality did not. It was proven later, after those hellish two weeks that seemed like two years that I really had no idea what was in the trunk of my friend's car and that I was not lying to protect my friends and myself.

"A long training is needed to survive here in the struggle of each one against all, a training which young people rarely have." In a place like the concentration camp, survival is nothing short of impossible; no one was expected to live. It felt as though the torture was never-ending, the time spent would seem like an eternity. That is exactly how I felt during my stay in County. I would always sit and wonder when this would all be over. I felt like I was in there forever; there existed no concept of time. I was only 18 and like Primo Levi said, in that struggle of each one against all, the young rarely have the training to survive in that place. I did not feel I had to; I did not deserve to be in there. My friend's are the one's who decided to stash that crap in their trunks, not me. My dad is a cop for crying out loud, I know better than that. I thought I was going to get eaten alive in there. Worst than that though was the fact that no one believed I had nothing to do with it. My parents thought I was involved and my so-called friends took a while to admit that I had no idea that there were drugs in the car. I hated not being believed, it made me fear that I would be in there for along time. I could not bare that reality; I have nightmares to this day about being held prisoner.

Reading all about Primo Levi's experience serves as a reminder to me as to why I get so scared when I see a police officer. Being held captive against my will was definitely the most traumatic thing to happen to me. I never looked at things the same way; not my friends who would put me in such a position, my relatives and other friends who felt I was every bit as guilty as the law believed me to be, nor myself who has never been so scared before and will never let myself forget. To hear Primo Levi's accounts makes me sit and think about those dreams I always have; the one's when I wake up in that cell, wearing the bright orange of County, in a pool of my own sweat, trying to keep myself awake, and most of all afraid of every single shadow that passed. I never want to be just a number again. One loses all sense of self-respect and one loses his identity. Primo Levi was one among the masses persecuted against by the German's. No one believed he would survive the experiences at Auschwitz but he somehow gathered the strength to pull through. I have so much respect for this man. He has endured more than I can ever imagine and when I try to imagine it, I get sick, I get nervous, I start to sweat and I just can't talk about it anymore.

I will return to Mac's statement that he could not "bare that reality," but for now I want to point out that neither authors nor teachers can control a reader's response to a text. Mac may be responding to *Survival in Auschwitz* in a way that neither Levi nor I could predict, but this is what happens all the time: "real readers," as opposed to "ideal readers," bring to literature their own life experiences and "identity themes," to use Norman Holland's term. Levi's deepest fears triggered Mac's deepest fears—or to describe this in a way that attributes primary agency to the reader, Mac interpreted *Survival in Auschwitz* in a way that conformed to his own life experiences, in this case, a two-week incarceration that remains the most terrifying event of his life.

Christine: "I Am Unable to Get the Horrible Images and Thoughts Out of My Mind"

An even more extreme response to *Survival in Auschwitz* may be seen in Christine's diary, which was written over the course of several days:

I think this is the most disturbing, bleakest, novel that I have ever read in my entire life. I have had nightmares now for three nights. I can't stop thinking about it and I can't fall asleep. Last night I was up until five something in the morning, afraid to fall asleep because I know that then I will be there, in Auschwitz. I am unable to get the horrible images and thoughts out of my mind; I cannot stop thinking about it. I awoke from the nightmares and went into the kitchen late last night. I saw a sharp knife and I thought, maybe if I cut myself a little, it would make the pain stop. I made a small nick on my arm, just a few drops of blood, and I thought that maybe I felt a tiny bit better. Yes, I thought, it feels better. I looked in horror at what I had done and dropped the knife to the floor. I cried so hard after that, for over an hour, until my eyes were swollen and red, and my head ached. I thought, I deserved to be there, not Primo Levi, not all of those innocent people. Why would God allow something like that to happen? Doesn't He care? I used to think He allowed bad things to happen to test our limits, to show us what good is by showing us absolute evil first. Now I don't know; I am too stupid to understand. The world seems blackened with evil. Pain and sorrow are surrounding me, trying to get inside of me, to gobble me up and eat me alive. I need to find a way to make this stop, I needed it to stop; it's making me feel as if all the horror of the world is rushing into me. It is all so sorrowful and meaningless, there is nothing I can do to help any of it; I can't stop crying. (The following day)

I want to write about the story, but I have to let some time pass, I cannot discuss the novel objectively. Every time I think of it, my eyes blur up, so I will come back in a few days or so. Maybe if the sun would shine a little that would help. I don't know. I will be back.
(Two days later)

I slept for twelve hours last night and I still feel tired. I am going to force myself to write about this, and then I'll try to never, ever, ever think of it again. I doubt that I will succeed.

The novel begins with a grim sense that something very bad will happen. The narrator is young and naive and doesn't realize how bad it will be in the camp though he does seem to realize that the situation he is in is not good. From the beginning, things are bad for the prisoners. They hit them and pile them like animals into a train car to transport them to the camp. When they arrive after a nightmarish journey, they are subjected to horrific humiliation, their hair is shaved off and they are stripped of all their possessions and clothing. They are subjected to a bizarre disinfection ritual, which it seems is really done to break their spirits. Primo Levi gets through it somehow and his real enemy as the novel progresses is his stomach and the acquisition of extra soup and bread. He never loses his spirit. The Germans work him like a beast, and when he compares them to Satan with their knowledge of how to pick the evilest of men for leaders, it sent chills through me. I think this passage is a good example of why no one doubts the existence of evil, but we all ponder long and hard about whether there is good. When Primo's foot got hurt I became very worried about him; what would happen to him in the Ka-be? I knew just enough about nazi doctors to be truly afraid for him. I didn't know if he would make it out of such a hospital in one piece, or if they might do some horrible experiments on him, or what. It turned out to somehow be okay, and he got enough of a rest to continue to try and survive. I held my breath for him when the last selection began, they made him run out naked, and it was so crazy that I wondered how men could do such things. He made it. Somehow they passed him by, for what turned out to be the last time. When it was over, it wasn't really, because many men still died in the abandoned camp. Primo Levi tried to help as much as he could, I was so happy when they found the trench of potatoes. I thought that was a wonderful moment and that now he would really make it home again. I read later online that Primo Levi died from his own hand, that is, he committed suicide. I find this difficult to accept; I don't want it to be true. It is a terrible loss to the world. Maybe he could never get the ghosts of what had happened to him out of his mind. I don't think that is something anyone could ever get over.

I am so glad that there are no more nazi's in this world, though they make the tailban sound like that and there was Pol Pot and . . . I won't think about it, if I do I will go crazy. I have to detach myself from it or I will get pulled into it. It is so painful, so bad, that it might suck me down; I will die too. I am a coward. I am closing this book for as long as I can.

Christine's diary shows how wrenching reading can be for certain people, especially when they identify with a traumatic situation. With what is she specifically identifying? We cannot be sure from the diary alone. Her decision to cut herself does not imitate any of the scenes in Primo Levi's memoir, which she incorrectly calls a novel. Why does she feel that she "deserved to be there, not Primo Levi, not all of the innocent people"? The story of the Holocaust leads to a crisis of faith for her: inhumanity compels her to question the existence of God. Perhaps Levi's inability to find religious consolation further challenges her own beliefs. She ends the first entry with a feeling of grief and futility, unable to stop crying, but she seems more composed in the brief second entry written a day later. She returns to the diary two days later, more in control now, able to process the details of Levi's story. She recognizes that she must detach herself from the story lest she be "pulled into it" and die.

Does Christine's identification with Primo Levi lead to traumatization or catharsis? Again, it is impossible to judge from this diary alone, though her statement at the end that she must close the book for as long as possible suggests the absence of therapeutic relief. She identifies not with Primo Levi's survival but with his suffering, and unconsciously she suffers along *with* him, or perhaps *instead of* him. Her discovery that he committed suicide years after being released from Auschwitz is even more unnerving to her.

Christine's diary was unnerving to me as well, and I called her up and asked to speak with her in my office. She assured me during her conference that she was feeling better. The only personal question I asked her was whether she had ever cut herself before, and she replied that she had, several years earlier. A week later she asked me for the name of a therapist in the area. In her diary on *Darkness Visible*, she revealed a number of traumatic events in her adolescence, including "tormenting" a friend who later shot himself in the head when he was drunk. His suicide initiated her own suicidal behavior. "I began to think that dying was my secret life. I would climb high up, to the tops of tall buildings, and frighten myself senseless. Walk midway on bridges, in freezing weather, crying and trying to convince myself to jump, to not be such a pussy, to do it already. I would cut myself with razors, long thin ones, for relief to pay for my sins." Perhaps this last statement explains her wish to exchange places with Primo Levi. She admired Styron's courage to endure, and she ends the diary by suggesting that Literature and the Healing Arts has renewed her determination to seek professional help:

I think it was great that Styron went for help. I think that is a big step towards regaining one's emotional health. I myself have not been able to do it really. I have been to family doctors, but always for one or two visits only, just to get pills really. I just want to dull the pain, nothing more. I don't believe that they can really help. It would just humiliate me more to spill my guts to some guy who could care less really, probably he would just wish I would shut up already because he has better things to do with his time then to listen to some stupid hag whine about her life.

I made an appointment last week at the counseling center after a particularly nasty episode struck (thank you again for the referral) but I was too ashamed to really go to it. I like to imagine that I can solve this problem myself. Actually I am deeply ashamed of all this. I do not know why. If it was someone else I would not be able to understand why. I am so disturbed right now. Seeing all of this in writing is very disturbing somehow. I mean, I am not really crazy. I get all my responsibilities accomplished. I work hard. I try. I fight the sadness every step of the way; I refuse to give in to it. That is why I am in your class. I am trying to heal myself. I hope it works.

Christine gave me permission to read her diaries aloud but I didn't, fearing that they might have been too distressing to her classmates. I was also worried that hearing me read her diaries aloud would intensify her pain. Of the fifty-three students enrolled in Literature and the Healing Arts, Christine's reaction was the most extreme; her response confirms that a reading or writing assignment may "stir up" conflicts that may prove overwhelming. Opponents of courses like Literature and the Healing Arts will argue that Christine's story dramatizes the inherent dangers of the self-disclosing classroom. Surely the *potential* for danger exists, and at times I wondered whether the course was appropriate for her, at least during this time in her life. Yet to judge from what she wrote on the final exam, the course was valuable precisely because it taught her that she is not alone in feeling pain:

I have learned that when self-disclosure is allowed in a classroom, we suddenly begin to see the hidden faces of human suffering. Unfortunately, depression is all around us. It is a prevalent disorder in this country and in many parts of the world. Thankfully, however, it is conquerable for most of its sufferers.

When listening to Professor Berman read the depression diaries aloud, I often felt bombarded with pain. Several times my eyes welled up, and it felt as though there was suddenly so much suffering in the world. I wondered if their anguish was eased by their writing of it. I hope so.

I felt as though I was bearing witness to the melancholia of history when I read Primo Levi's Survival in Auschwitz. *This is the riskiest writing and reading that I have ever done in my life. And then, later again, I and my class bore witness to the sadness that had overcome many of the diarist's entries. I found out that, at different times in their lives, many other girls had also cut themselves. Why? Where does all of this come from? I don't know even though I have experienced it myself.*

When I was involved in the readings and then writing about it afterwards, it all felt very depressing to me, like the weight of the world was pressing down on me. But, afterwards, when I had gained some distance from it, I began to feel more hopeful. The feelings were less powerful.

Styron says that "depression is not the souls annihilation." During an attack of it, however, when the bell jar is descending; it feels like it is. And then one feels very alone. I know that the most dramatic lesson I learned this term is that there are many others out there who are in pain also. I think this was the biggest catalyst for change I have ever experienced. I no longer felt alone, that I was the only one, that no one could ever understand the pain or the madness of it; how could they? You have to feel it, I thought, to know it. Not true.

I think that you are right when you said that suicide isn't about courage or cowardice. It is about being in an irrational state of mind, and that is so hard to remember when you are in the middle of that kind of thinking, but I have done it. I have told myself this advice and it has worked and I am alive. Thank you. Thank you for helping me stay alive. I have slipped a few times, and forgot it for a minute. But then, you gently reminded me, somehow, that

I am not alone. That this is not rational, that it will pass, that someone out there is just as cold and lonely inside as I am. Oh, I wish I could say here that I am fine, that it is gone forever and that now I will be this really emotionally healthy person; but I know that isn't true, and that I am only on the road to recovery, I am not there yet. At least I am on the road though, and there is hope, and I am not just living forever in heaviness.

This would be an apt statement on which to end the chapter, for it reflects the nearly unanimous consensus of Christine and her classmates about the value of bearing witness to depression. But I would be remiss if I did not mention the following evaluation of one student who objected vehemently to classroom self-disclosure.

Rich: "Your Book Reads as If It Were a Supermarket Tabloid"

I have just finished reading your book, Risky Writing, *and all I can say is the worst thing about the book was that I liked it—for all the wrong reasons a reader technically should like this book. You told us in class your various reasons for writing this book, and I suppose (your reasons being your own) that you were honest. I cannot say, however, that I see the benefits of publishing such a book. This is not a personal attack on your writing style or anything of that sort, but your book reads as if it were a supermarket tabloid. The only interesting things contained in it are in the various traumatic experiences related by your students. I am not sure who this was written for, although I can only assume it was meant for your students to read (no offense, but I don't see many people wandering into Barnes and Noble and exclaiming, "OOOH,* Risky Writing!*), yet all of the text that is NOT written by your students is very contrived and hard to follow. In other words, it seems to fall into the trap of what your friend Michael Kaufman called PhD's only speaking to other PhD's. I also doubt the fact that it should be included in a course entitled "Literature and the Healing Arts," as I don't really see it as a piece of literature, but rather as a collection of essays and your analysis of them, but I digress. As I said before, I like this book for all the wrong reasons. The only thing that kept me interested was that I wanted to find out just how fucked up other peoples lives were from drinking, so on and so forth.*

It may not have been your intention, but this book is simply pandering to the reader. Maybe other college professors can sit around their fire sipping scotch and praise your work for its in depth analyses of the college mind, but to anybody other than the serious (and seriously overblown) academic, it just doesn't cut it. There is nothing to keep the reader interested save for the stories of peril and horror that your students were forced to offer you in fear

*of receiving a bad grade. Yes, I say forced. You see, no matter what you tell
your students about their degree of disclosure, or what relationship you feel
you may have with them, the simple fact remains that you are their teacher,
and they your students. No matter how many times you tell them that it does
not matter if they are personal with their writings, or that they do not have to
read it in class, they WILL feel pressured to do so, be it out of fear or as an
attempt to gain your favor. This is something that has bothered me about the
"Diary" entries all throughout the semester. As soon as I started with your
book, I knew what my final "diary" would be about, and that would be my
critique of the entire diary process, but, and here's the kicker: I can't do that.
Each "diary" is supposed to be a somewhat personal relation of the text to
our lives, yet how can 50 some-odd students ALL have a personal event
relating to the texts that you assign? By making these assignments, you are
forcing the hand of the writer. I know I myself have grasped at strands on
some of diary entries, as I had no personal reaction to some of these texts,
and I'm sure some other students feel the same way. One quick example
could be our last "diary" entry about depression. What are the chances of all
of your students in Eng 226 being depressed? Probably not as good as the
number of personal essays you received describing personal experiences with
depression. You said in our last class that most students feel that the rest of
the class is not being honest in their writings. This is not an effect of narcissism, but rather a tacit admittance of the wide spread lying that you encourage through these assignments. Nobody will come out and say it, but I somehow doubt that you receive 50 honest papers each time we have to hand
them in. Again, I have to stress that this is not an attack on your teaching
style, as I find your class to be somewhat interesting, and you seem to be a
very nice man (I also would not have to write this if you weren't my professor,
as the last thing I want is retribution for my writing). I guess all I can conclude with is that I agree with that nasty book review you handed out to us
in class. "Ravaging young minds," I believe that is what the author of that
nasty book review said you were doing. While I don't think it is that extreme,
I do agree with the fact that it is wrong to encourage such disclosures. You
say it yourself on page 9 in your introduction: shame is the key emotion in
risky writing. Do you really want to shame your students?*

Throughout the course I asked students to be honest about their feelings, and Rich did just that. Reading his diary, I couldn't help feeling amused
because not even in my most grandiose moments do I imagine professors,
at my university or elsewhere, sitting around sipping scotch while they
praise one of my books. The reality of academic publishing is that most

books, including my own, receive little scholarly or public attention. Generally one toils for years writing a scholarly book that, if modestly successful, may sell a thousand copies; rarely are the royalties sufficient to cover photocopying expenses. I've never thought of myself as the author of a "supermarket tabloid," and I'm not sure how a writer can be guilty of "pandering" to readers while at the same time writing a "contrived and hard to follow" book. Rich's inability to see the "benefits of publishing such a book" is, alas, shared by other, more influential arbiters of literary judgment. When, for example, I walked into my local Barnes and Noble to see whether they would order one copy of *Risky Writing*, I was told curtly that it was not the kind of book they would stock—not even for their "local authors" section. I had better luck with the local Borders bookstore but only because one of their employees was a former student.

I wrote on Rich's diary that while I was disappointed he felt so negatively about *Risky Writing* and his classmates' diaries, it was courageous of him to express this point of view: He knew that I would be displeased and was thus engaging in his own brand of risky writing. His diary is proof that students will express their point of view even when they fear that a teacher may seek "retribution." He was doing precisely what I wanted my students to do, conveying his feelings about the self-disclosing essays in *Risky Writing* and the reader-response diaries on *Darkness Visible*. His response is not what I had hoped for, yet I agree with him that "feelings are feelings." His critique, however, is based on a number of factual errors that may lead to misleading conclusions.

I explain in the final chapter the reference to the reviewer who believes that I am guilty of "ravishing young minds," but for now I want to respond specifically to Rich's factual errors. For example, he attributes to Michael Kaufman a statement I made when introducing his lecture: "At a time when literary studies has become increasingly narrow, over-specialized, and jargon-ridden, and where Ph.D.'s can speak only to other Ph.D.'s, Michael Kaufman has demonstrated how stories and plays can speak to anyone who is willing to listen." This is the same goal that I pursue in my own teaching and writing. Rich also misquotes a statement I made in class about the truthfulness of the diaries, from which he concludes that there is "wide spread lying." What I had said appears in the final chapter of *Risky Writing*, when I evaluated the results of the anonymous questionnaires students had completed at the end of each of the five sections of expository writing on which the book is based:

> Some of the most important questions I asked involved the honesty of students' writings. "How often were you honest in your writing? That is, how

often did you tell the truth as you saw it?" Eighty-one percent indicated "all of the time," 18 percent "most of the time," and 1 percent "some of the time." Interestingly, when asked "How often do you think your classmates were honest in their writing?" the figures were much lower: 40 percent indicated "all of the time," 56 percent "most of the time," and 5 percent "some of the time." I reported the same phenomenon in *Diaries to an English Professor*, where close to 100 percent of the polled students reported that they were honest in their *own* diaries, whereas only between 60 to 70 percent of the polled students believed that their classmates were honest in *their* diaries. (233–34)

My research thus suggests that four-fifths of the students believe that they themselves write truthfully *all* of the time in their diaries and personal essays. Slightly more than half of the students believe that their classmates write truthfully *most* of the time. The claim that there is "wide spread lying" has no basis in fact.

Rich states that the students in my expository writing course were "forced" to write about "stories of peril and horror" to avoid receiving a bad grade, but as I discuss at the beginning of *Risky Writing*, all the expository writing students were graded pass/fail. They knew that they would pass the course if they turned in all their written work and attended class. Although some students may work harder when they know their writing is being letter graded, I believe that a pass/fail grading system is preferable in a personal writing course, since it minimizes the element of coercion. Rich may have felt pressured into self-disclosure, but none of his classmates expressed this fear. It's true that reader-response diaries are personal, but that does not mean students are forced to disclose anything they regard as *too* personal. For instance, students could simply state in their diaries why they liked or disliked a story, or why they found it interesting or boring. To invite students to write about their "familiarity with depression," as I had done in the *Darkness Visible* diaries, is not to pressure them to disclose that they have personally been depressed. Moreover, contrary to what Rich states at the end of his diary, not everyone wrote about being depressed. Most of the male students did not write about being depressed.

To judge from the reader-response diaries and the anonymous course evaluations, Rich was the only student who felt coerced into self-disclosure, but I agree with him that it would have been better not to grade the reader-response diaries. Two students made the same suggestion in their anonymous course evaluations. The best way for teachers to minimize students' fear of coercion is by not grading personal essays and reader-response diaries; these writings can be a requirement, like class attendance, but not contribute to their final grade. As an aside, neither Rich nor any of his classmates objected to the grade he or she received on the diaries. The only aspect of the course to which several students objected was the section of the midterm exam in which they were required to identify quotations from the readings: they felt the quotes were "too hard" and "unfair."

Bearing witness to depression involves, for many people, "baring" one's most private feelings and thoughts, and not all students feel comfortable with such bearing/baring. Recall Mac's statement that he could not "bare" the reality of incarceration: he almost surely meant that he could not "bear" (tolerate) that oppressive environment, but in another sense it was hard for him to "bare" (reveal) this experience to his classmates—and it was equally hard for some students, like Rich, to hear such a disclosure. A pedagogy based on self-disclosure must be able to respond sensitively to those students who do not want to participate in such bearing/baring. There are a number of ways in which a teacher can try to accommodate a student's desire not to hear self-disclosing diaries. I tell my students that they are free to leave the room if they find a diary entry too painful to hear; those who choose not to hear any of the diaries are permitted to stand outside the classroom door and enter after I finish reading the diaries. Admittedly, students may feel self-conscious about doing this, but they know that they can always speak to me in my office if they have a problem with the course.

I don't wish to deny Rich's statement that there was a subtle "pressure" in the classroom, but I think this pressure had less to do with self-disclosure than with the need to remain empathic. "Pressure" may not be the most accurate word here, for there was an explicit agreement, from the beginning to the end of the semester, not to invalidate anyone's point of view. Those who stayed in the course beyond the first week agreed to this condition—and no one dropped the course. Students followed my lead in maintaining an empathic, nonjudgmental attitude during class discussions. I recall only two moments when the empathic atmosphere was threatened. The first instance occurred during a discussion of *Survival in Auschwitz* when a student questioned why the concentration camp victims did not try to rebel against their oppressors. "The Jews are a passive people," he stated, provoking the ire of many of his classmates. I pointed out the irony of the statement in light of current world events—the Israeli army was occupying Palestine, and none of Israel's many opponents was calling the Jews "passive." The following week I read to the class Primo Levi's convincing answer to this question, in which he said that escape from the concentration camps was virtually impossible. One student told me later that she wished we had had a more "open" discussion of this issue, but I was reluctant to do so, largely because it was unrelated to the focus of the course. The second incident occurred when a student said in class that she had been shunned by her friends for being depressed; she felt that some of her classmates, whom she had overheard talking about her before class, were unsympathetic to her. I sensed that she was now making her classmates feel uncomfortable and reminded everyone that we had an agreement not to criticize any members of the class.

Rich quotes me correctly when he observes that "shame is the key emotion in risky writing." Self-disclosures are dangerous, as films like *The Breakfast Club* dramatize, precisely because they expose the self-discloser's vulnerability. But why does he assert that students felt shamed in the class? No other student made this accusation at any point in the semester. Christine acknowledges feeling too ashamed to visit the counseling center, but nowhere does she suggest that I had shamed her. Quite the opposite: the empathic classroom atmosphere helped students to write about depression and thus to overcome the shame and stigma that inevitably accompany this disease.

I would have read Rich's diary aloud had he made it clear that he was expressing his own feelings rather than speaking for all of his classmates. Reading the diary aloud in its present form would have had, I believe, a chilling impact on the class. Students who had written about depression would have felt attacked and ridiculed, and they might have regretted their self-disclosures and lost trust in their classmates or teacher.

Eddie: "The Page Is the Analyst"

How, finally, did the students in Literature and the Healing Arts evaluate their role of "bearing witness to depression"? I believe that a majority of the students would agree with the following observation made by Eddie. "[*Darkness Visible*] certainly touched the authors of the diaries read aloud in class, and certainly others. The room was as somber as it ever had been before. The atmosphere was tense; there was a thickness to the air. It is not my intention to dramatize that particular night, but it cannot be disputed that there was less paper shuffling and bag zipping that particular night. My classmates were all frowning, every one of them. There was no sunlight in the room that night, and it seemed to affect the whole class. But there was some encouragement; it seemed that those diarists ended on a note that was almost optimism, much like Styron." Eddie acknowledges that hearing about so many people in his age group who suffer from depression made him cringe. "Somehow, before the class, this particular disease was not that close to home. And after the class, after hearing my classmates' voices, it occurs that it is exactly that close to home. Glancing at my diary for *Darkness Visible*, and the notes from the diarists, it becomes clear that Styron's memoir has been depressing to me, but it has provided me with knowledge. It has provided me with a book of guidelines, a rulebook of depression. It has cleared up the word 'depression'—it has defined the disease." Eddie then closes with an intriguing observation: "The page is the analyst. The job of the analyst is to find meaning in personal issues, to aid in the rise up out of trauma, and to listen. The page always listens, and people usually heal through the process of venting."

Reader-response diaries allowed Eddie and his classmates to write about a subject they had never written about before, and in doing so, they created their own survival narratives. Styron had "helped unlock a closet from which many souls were eager to come out and proclaim that they, too, had experienced the feelings I had described" (34). So did my students, through their diaries, help unlock a closet for their classmates. The empathic classroom prevented this unlocked closet from becoming a Pandora's box, unleashing all human ills into the world. We were able to glimpse depression from the perspective of hope—not the breezily optimistic assurances that Styron rightly rejects, but the recognition that depression is conquerable.

The Value of Depression

"Depression," remarks the early twentieth-century pediatrician and psychoanalyst D. W. Winnicott, "has value." He explains the paradox by saying that depression leads to suffering but *has within itself the germ of recovery.* This is the one bright spot in psychopathology, and it links depression with the sense of guilt (a capacity for which is a sign of healthy development) and with the mourning process. Mourning too tends eventually to finish its job" (*Home Is Where We Start From* 72; emphasis in original). One can best help a depressed person, Winnicott argues, "by adopting the principle of tolerating the depression until it spontaneously lifts, and by paying tribute to the fact that it is only the spontaneous recovery that feels truly satisfactory to the individual" (77). "To our surprise," Winnicott adds, "a person may come out of a depression stronger, wiser and more stable than before he or she went into it" (77). For this to happen, however, there must be a "facilitating environment"—one that has a "human quality, not a mechanical perfection" (144).

Empathic Understanding and Personal Knowledge

Our classroom became a facilitating environment that allowed students to write reader-response diaries in which they empathized with fictional and real characters who were suffering from depression. In the process, the students expanded their empathic understanding and personal growth. This empathic understanding was at times difficult and painful, even traumatic, but it transformed the course from an "academic" experience into personal knowledge. It is for this reason that I find Robert Samuels's criticisms of empathic pedagogy puzzling. Referring to the process of identification as a form of denial, he asserts that the "glorification of the personal emotional response to the pain of others can be derived from a faulty understanding of psychotherapy. Moreover, this mode of empathy has become a major form of popular entertainment" (142n 5). I agree with Samuels that "empathy with fictional characters may . . . have the negative effect of blocking all levels of critical thinking and analysis" and that "people's capacity to relate empathically to certain feelings does not guarantee that they have learned anything about the causes and actualities of the event in question" (138, 136). There is no guarantee of anything in life, except death, and empathy has its limits, as I suggest in chapter 3. Nevertheless, empathy remains the best way to learn about other people; and a pedagogy that encourages this form of learning leads to breakthroughs of understanding that might not otherwise occur. Moreover, most of my students expressed "empathic unsettlement," Dominick LaCapra's term for being "responsive to the traumatic experiences of others, notably of victims, [but without] the appropriation of their experiences" (*Writing History, Writing Trauma* 41).

Significantly, students who empathize with authors' or classmates' accounts of depression do not claim to have *complete* knowledge. Casey's observation is representative here. "Although William Styron was in a deeper, more life-threatening depression, we have shared the same feelings of extreme sadness, anxiety, and 'unfocused dread' that characterize this disorder." She then discusses the *differences* between Styron's depression and her own. The same process may be seen in Chloe's response to *Darkness Visible*. "By reading William Styron's account of his descent into the illness of depression, I was jolted into recognition of my mother's lifeline." She doesn't claim that now she has *complete* understanding of her mother; rather, she says that "now I understand what my mother is going through just a little bit better." The student who wrote that he or she was formerly "disgusted" by the term "second abortion" is now able to realize the "torment" of a classmate (Blythe) who went through this experience. The student doesn't claim a *complete* realization, but enough to feel a connection. "She had to deal with her own self-imposed guilt and who am I to judge her for that?"

It generally takes me about twenty-five minutes to read aloud five diaries; the thirty diaries I read during the semester constituted less than 15 percent of the total class time. From my perspective and, I believe, that of a majority of the students, this was the most enlightening part of the course. This was the time when the students spoke through me, disclosing their personal reactions to the class readings and discussions and revealing aspects of their lives that, in many cases, they had never shared with anyone else. Since nearly all the students were writing for the class, their reader-response diaries may be characterized as "speakerly texts," Henry Louis Gates's term for texts "whose rhetorical strategy is designed to represent an oral tradition" (181). The diaries created a dialogical relationship among the members of the class, with students commenting, through me, on their classmates' earlier writings. Without the reader-response component, the course would have been less meaningful. Given the silence and stigma surrounding depression, few students would have felt comfortable enough to talk about their own experiences, nor would they have developed the strong connection with each other and their teacher. They would have learned about Styron's experience with depression, along with those of the student writers in *Risky Writing*, but they would not have heard about the experiences of their classmates. Nor would they have had the opportunity to write about their own *lived* experiences.

I could have encouraged students to write diaries only on "positive" emotions. There is some evidence that such writing can be therapeutically helpful (see King), but most clinical and research psychologists who have investigated the "writing cure" would agree with Stephen Lepore and his associates that "exploring a broad range of thoughts and feelings, including negative ones, is on average, more beneficial than focusing on a restricted range of positive thoughts and feelings" (104). I agree with James Pennebaker's observation that "[p]eople must be given the freedom to invoke their feelings when writing about an emotional topic. . . . Emotions are part of virtually all important psychological experiences. Not allowing individuals to acknowledge them by definition restricts their exploring the impact and understanding of their topic" (Epilogue 283). Lest I misrepresent his position, Pennebaker argues in *Opening Up* that in his writing experiments, "people are unlikely to divulge their darkest secrets when writing in a classroom surrounded by their peers" (174). My own research suggests, however, that students are likely to divulge their darkest secrets when writing in an empathic classroom.

Trauma and Perception

Reader-response diaries stimulate students to reflect on the course after it ends. Sometimes they share their writings with relatives and friends, whose memory of an experience may differ from their own. An example of this occurred when I received an email from Gabriella five months after the semester ended. She told me that she had recently sent her diaries to her mother, who read them and pointed out that Gabriella's twin sister had been hospitalized for three weeks, not three months, as Gabriella had stated in her diary. "I didn't believe her at first," Gabriella wrote to me, "since I suppose my perception of the situation was so different. Interestingly enough, when I asked my best friend, who had been through the whole thing with us, how long she thought my sister was institutionalized, she said 'at least four months, right?' I guess we were all so upset and distraught by what was happening that it seemed so much longer in our memories." In a later email, Gabriella elaborated on the ways in which emotional trauma affects the perception of events:

I have to admit, I had a very painful argument with my mother about the whole thing, since her perception of things is very different than mine. Interestingly, my mother found out from my diaries a few things that had happened that she never knew about at the time, like my sister stealing alcohol from a friend's liquor cabinet. She became angry that I hadn't told her when it happened, but I reminded her to refer to my diary and to think back to my attitude about what was going on, that I was pretty much insensitive to my sister's plight and that I assumed she was doing it all as a rebellion to get attention. It sounds awful now, but that's how I felt.

My mother and I also discussed the way she had felt, and she denies having felt "guilty" although I remember that she was. She also insisted that my sister didn't look like a "zombie" while in the hospital, as I had originally written, although when I asked my friend who had also visited her at the time how my sister looked to her, her exact response was "emotionless, pale, eyes glazed over . . . like a zombie." Pretty interesting, the ways in which people perceive things. In writing this to you, I find myself wondering if the reason why my mother denies these painful memories is because she DOES feel guilty and would rather not think of my sister being in such an altered state. I don't mean to make it seem as if my mother doesn't take the situation seriously, because she obviously supported the therapist's decision to institutionalize my sister, but she did seem uncomfortable with my vivid memories of the ordeal. Nonetheless, writing this diary and having it incorporated into your book has been a reflective and often times painful experience for my family. However, I also feel that it has been more therapeutic than the years of professional help we as a family have all gone through on my sister's behalf.

In regards to my sister's feelings, she declined setting either of our memoies straight, and told my mother that whatever my perception is of the incident is what should go into your book. Of course, I want to fix any incorrect facts, such as the length of time she was hospitalized. However, as my sister requested, I will refrain from making any alterations regarding my personal memories. I want this diary to be as factual as possible, but also as true to my heart as possible. Thank you again for allowing me to be a part of this book.

It has affected me more than I could have ever expected last semester, which I suppose attests to the theme you are writing on.

"Most Truths Are Inherently Unretainable"

I began this chapter by quoting Styron's observation that depression is so "mysteriously painful and elusive" that it is "close to being beyond description," but just as *Darkness Visible* succeeds in conveying many aspects of this disorder, so do student narratives heighten our understanding. Rita Charon's observation about the therapeutic value of narration applies equally well to psychotherapy, medicine, and education, all of which rely on language and interpretation: "As in psychoanalysis, in all of medical practice the narrating of the patient's story is a therapeutically central act, because to find the words to contain the disorder and its attendant worries gives shape to and control over the chaos of illness" (1898).

There is no guarantee, however, that the illness that disappears today may not reappear tomorrow, with a vengeance; life is filled with uncertainties, and recovery is often ongoing and sometimes short-lived. This is especially true of depression, a cyclical disease that mysteriously appears and mysteriously disappears, with or without treatment. Lucy Grealy ends *Autobiography of a Face* with a disturbing observation: "I used to think truth was eternal, that once I *knew*, once I *saw*, it would be with me forever, a constant by which everything else could be measured. I know now that this isn't so, that most truths are inherently unretainable, that we have to work hard all our lives to remember the most basic things" (222). Grealy died in December 2002, at the age of thirty-nine, an apparent suicide; friends reported that she had been despondent over the failure of her reconstructive surgery. Hope may also be unretainable, especially during the onset of depression. Suicides of writers who have borne witness to depression are especially sad, highlighting the fragility of recovery. I can't predict how my students would have responded to Grealy's suicide, but I am certain that they would have been distressed, and that they would have welcomed the opportunity to write about their feelings in a reader-response diary.

The Best Treatment for Depression Is "Belief"

"It is my absolute belief," Andrew Solomon declares, "that in the field of depression, there is no such thing as a placebo." Unlike cancer, in which an exotic treatment that feels like it is working may not be successful in slowing the growth of the disease, "[i]f you have depression and try an exotic treatment and think you are better, then you are better. Depression is a disease of thought processes and emotions, and if something changes your thought processes and emotions in the correct direction, that quali-fies as a recovery." In Solomon's view, the best treatment for depression is "belief, which is in itself far more essential than what you believe in" (137).

There are many ways to achieve belief or hope, including reading and writing. An observation by Flannery O'Connor is relevant here. "People are always complaining that the modern novelist has no hope and that the picture he paints of the world is unbearable. The only answer to this is that people without hope do not write novels. Writing a novel is a terrible ex-perience, during which the hair often falls out and the teeth decay. I'm always highly irritated by people who imply that writing fiction is an es-cape from reality. It is a plunge into reality and it's very shocking to the system. If the novelist is not sustained by a hope of money, then he must be sustained by a hope of salvation, or he simply won't survive the ordeal." O'Connor concludes that "[p]eople without hope not only don't write novels, but what is more to the point, they don't read them" (78–79).

Bearing witness to depression is a way to maintain belief and hope, for as long as one writes about one's own illness, or a loved one's illness, then one refuses to succumb to despair. However painful a story may be to read or write, however shocking it may be to the reader's or writer's system, bearing witness is a way to describe and order the chaos of illness. Additionally, bear-ing witness allows the creation of what Cheryl Mattingly calls a "therapeutic plot" that may foster hope by pointing the writer in a new life direction when the "old directions are no longer intelligible" (108). Without excep-tion, the students who wrote about depression in Literature and the Healing Arts concluded that they felt psychologically strengthened at the end. Writ-ing about mood disorders heightened their empathic intelligence—which is all the more striking since depression usually inhibits empathy for others and oneself. They glimpsed the nature of depression and, in many cases, reached out to those from whom they were estranged. The students felt closer to relatives and friends who suffered from depression in the past, and closer to those who were presently depressed. They also felt more prepared to acknowledge their own vulnerability to depression and to seek treatment. They sought forgiveness from those with whom they could not empathize in the past, and self-forgiveness for blaming themselves for dark thoughts. Increased understanding helped them to destigmatize a disease that affects more people than they could imagine. They felt a connection with nearly every diary that was read aloud, and thus a connection with their classmates. In bearing witness to depression, students became storytellers, no less than the published authors on the reading list, and their narratives confirmed the power of literature as a healing art.

CHAPTER 6

Risky Teaching

ON BEING CALLED A PERVERT, A PREDATOR, AND A
NATURAL THERAPIST

Throughout this book I have argued that an empathic approach to teaching enables students to understand themselves and their classmates in ways that are impossible in more traditional argumentative classrooms. My students have been overwhelmingly positive about the pedagogy of self-disclosure, but some educators have called into question the motivation behind this approach and the value of opening up in the classroom. I don't challenge anyone's right to criticize my approach to teaching—indeed, I welcome public scrutiny—but much of this criticism has been of a knee-jerk kind, suggesting that the idea of what I am doing is so offensive that people have already made up their minds, without the need to read my writings, interview my students, or test my method in their own classrooms. I want to speculate on why empathic teaching seems so threatening and then suggest how this resistance can be overcome.

"You're Pervi"

In 2001 I attended a conference on psychoanalysis and culture at Rutgers University. After participating in a panel discussion on psychoanalytic pedagogy, I looked at the program guide for a description of the next set of talks and decided to attend a session on peer teaching groups. There were only about ten people in the room, and no designated speakers; instead, the facilitator was eliciting responses from each person in the group. He had heard my previous talk and asked me to comment briefly about psychoanalytic diary writing. I spoke about how reader-response diaries allow students to make connections between the stories and poems discussed in class and their own lives. With the students' permission, I read a few diaries aloud, always anonymously, before returning them. There is no discussion of the diaries; each student reaches his or her own conclusions about the entries read aloud. The diaries give a voice to students who would otherwise remain silent. They write about issues that are generally considered to be too personal for the classroom, such as divorced families, eating disorders, sexual abuse, drug-and-alcohol addiction, racial prejudice, depression, and suicide. The diaries are often better written than formal essays, perhaps because students explore topics that are vitally important to them.

As an example, I cited Vladimir Nabokov's *Lolita*, which has long been one of my favorite novels. Until I began reading my students' diaries, I never realized how painful, even traumatic Nabokov's story might be to sexually abused readers. These readers bristle at the suggestion—to cite the words from *Vanity Fair* appearing on the paperback edition's front cover—that *Lolita* is the "only convincing love story of our century." Sexually abused female readers tend to see *Lolita* not as a story about dark, obsessional, brooding love, as I view it, but as about pedophilia and rape, and they have difficulty appreciating the novel's exquisite language, ingenious plotting, and cunning puns. Only when I read these reader-response diaries could I begin to imagine how Nabokov's first-person narrator, Humbert Humbert, might awaken horrifying memories of humiliation in readers who were victimized in childhood or adolescence by sexual predators. Indeed, *Lolita* is so disturbing to some readers that they experience symptoms of post–traumatic stress disorder. I still teach *Lolita*, but I'm careful now to inform students that some of them might become at risk while reading it, and I point out that neither Humbert nor Nabokov was able to anticipate in 1955, when the novel was published, the short- and long-term consequences of child sexual abuse, a phenomenon that did not begin to receive public attention until the middle 1980s. Many of the diaries that students write on *Lolita* are about sexuality, but they are never explicitly sexual or arousing; rather, they are cautionary tales about the prevalence of child sexual abuse and the potential for retraumatization among certain readers.

Nearly everyone spoke during the panel on peer teaching groups, and the session ended harmoniously, without anyone raising serious objections to any of the suggestions offered. The conference concluded with a keynote address and a long, leisurely dinner attended by all the conferees. The dining room seemed to be flowing with wine, chatter, and good cheer, and I recall thinking how much I had enjoyed the day's events. As the dinner drew to a close and everyone began leaving, an English woman who had attended the peer teaching group panel approached and asked me if anyone had offered a reaction to my talk. No one had, I told her, though two people expressed interest in using reader-response diaries in their own literature courses. "No one told you you're voyeuristic?" she asked. Startled by the bluntness of the question, I began to tell her that I view myself as an empathic rather than a voyeuristic reader, but before I could finish my sentence, she cut me off with the comment, "You're pervi." The dining room was noisy, and I was feeling tipsy from two glasses of wine. When I asked her to repeat what she said, she replied, in a louder voice, "You're pervi, *pervi*." "I'm sorry," I said, my confusion deepening, "but I don't know what that word means." "Perverted," she remonstrated, "You're *perverted*." The grimness of her expression left no doubt about her seriousness.

How does one defend oneself against the accusation of being voyeuristic and perverted? My first impulse was to repeat Richard Nixon's infamous line, "I'm not a crook," but I doubt she would have appreciated the allusion. When I asked her why she didn't raise this issue at the panel discussion, she replied, "I was stunned into silence." Her reply left *me* speechless, for now I had become both a pervert and a silencer. She was not impressed when I told her that I was sorry that she felt that way, nor was she convinced when I told her that my students did not agree with her accusations. "How do you know that?" she demanded. I suggested that she read *Diaries to an English Professor*, where I discuss this question in detail, but she snapped, "I don't need to read your book; I know all I want to about you."

Had she read that book, she would have heard me raise a similar question: "In overhearing intimate aspects of students' lives, we may sometimes feel that we are voyeurs, gazing at private material that we have no right to witness. Students occasionally express uneasiness upon hearing their classmates' intimate revelations, and readers may feel similarly uncomfortable about portions of this book. Do self-disclosing diaries render us into Peeping Toms?" (29) My answer, then and now, is "no":

Nearly all students who comment upon their classmates' diaries do so sensitively and compassionately. An empathic reader is not a voyeuristic reader. Rarely will a student make a caustic or callous comment about another student's revelations. I have no reason to believe that students who do not comment on their classmates' diaries remain unmoved by them. Students do not exploit their classmates' vulnerability or derive pleasure from others' misfortune. The anonymity of the diaries prevents students from unmasking classmates' identities. Some students may surreptitiously gaze around the room during the reading of the diaries in an effort to locate a diarist's identity, but this is seldom a problem. Students are not rubbernecks, and diaries do not cater to prurient interests. (29)

I also explore this question in *Risky Writing*, where students generally sign their own names to personal essays, which they then share with classmates. At the end of each of the five sections of English 300 (Expository

Writing) on which *Risky Writing* is based, I asked students to fill out an anonymous questionnaire. To the question—"Did you feel like a voyeur or a 'rubberneck' when reading your classmates' essays (a 'rubberneck' is a person who takes pleasure in gazing at others' suffering)?"—7 percent indicated "yes," 81 percent indicated "no," and the remaining 12 percent were "not sure" (235). They did not believe that their classmates felt like voyeurs when reading their own essays; nor do I believe that I am voyeuristic when reading my students' diaries and personal essays. Why, then, do others find it impossible to believe that one can respond compassionately to a diary or personal essay? And how can one reject the charge of being a pervert or a voyeur without sounding defensive or self-justifying? When I put this question to my interlocutor—"Is there anything I can say or do to change your mind?"—the reply was a curt "no," at which point our discussion ended.

The next day, I spoke with a psychoanalyst who was at the panel discussion, and he told me that while he himself did not believe that I was voyeuristic in my use of reader-response diaries, he was not surprised that others might reach the opposite conclusion. The challenge, he said, was for me now to deal with the negative countertransference that her comments elicited in me. "And that," he remarked smilingly, "occurs all the time in therapy." I don't know anything about the English woman except the title of the talk she had given in an earlier panel discussion—"The Road to Hell Is Paved with Good Intentions."

She is not alone in ascribing voyeuristic motivation to my pedagogical approach, for when I told a friend at the conference about my encounter with her, he revealed that others who have heard me speak at past conferences feel the same way. He was reluctant to share this information with me, knowing it would be hurtful to hear, but I am grateful for his honesty. My approach to teaching elicits strong feelings, both positive and negative, as the next example confirms.

"Ravishing Young Minds"

An excerpt from *Risky Writing* appeared in the February 15, 2002, issue of the *Chronicle of Higher Education*. The excerpt, entitled "Syllabuses of Risk," focuses on three of my undergraduate students who had become at risk as a result of reading novels in English 447, The Historical/Hysterical Imagination, which explores the cultural and psychological implications of mental illness. Chrissy was the first student to tell me that she had experienced nightmares and insomnia while reading D. M. Thomas's *The White*

Hotel. She was horrified by the novel's graphic description of rape and murder at the infamous Babi Yar in Kiev. Chrissy told me that *The White Hotel* was not the first novel to have this effect on her, and she agreed to write an essay about this experience. The first book that evoked this response was *The Diary of Anne Frank*, which she read when she was ten. "As I read the book I noticed that I was more afraid of the dark than usual. I had trouble sleeping, and often had nightmares about being hunted and captured by the Nazis." She never finished the story. Chrissy's response to *The White Hotel* prompted me to inform my students, the next time I taught the course, that some of the books on the syllabus might place them at risk, and I urged them to speak to me if that occurred. Within a few weeks, two of the twelve students came to my office separately and revealed that they were feeling anxious and depressed while reading Kate Chopin's *The Awakening* and Sylvia Plath's *The Bell Jar,* both of which contained suicidal protagonists with whom they strongly identified. I concluded the *Chronicle* article by saying that we should not stop teaching emotionally charged stories, but that we need to understand their impact on our students. "Teachers can make themselves available to students who become anxious or depressed from a reading or writing assignment. They can try to be sensitive to the many students who, sitting alertly or perhaps not-so-alertly in their classrooms, struggle with personal problems that seem overwhelming" (B9).

I received two emails immediately following the *Chronicle*'s electronic publication of "Syllabuses of Risk." The emails could not have been more different. The first was from a female graduate student at a Midwestern university:

Hello Prof. Berman,

I just want to thank you for your article, and I hope that the awareness you expressed in the article about "risky" books becomes widespread. Of course, what comes next is that I too underwent the same experience with an assigned text, except that I'm a doctoral student, and should be able to deal with such things. The way the professor handled the situation in my case was so insensitive that I dropped the course as the only way to cope with the situation.

I read your article because I was at a loss of what to do with "risky" books; we can't stop assigning these books. So? I do think that addressing the possibility that emotional conflict may arise when reading particular texts is a good idea. Also the option of writing a reader-response essay seems as though that would work. Writing about the experience validates the experience for both the student and the professor, and also would present the student with the understanding that the crisis brought on by the book can be controlled, and therefore will not consume the student's life.

If you get this subject into book form, I'd look forward to reading it. Thanks again.

In a subsequent email, she elaborated on the reason that she had become at risk while reading an assigned text. "I have gone through a lot of therapy in order to heal, and in doing so I have realized that one of the reasons sexual abuse and sexual misconduct on all levels exists, continues, is not stopped until too late, comes from our societal desire not to speak of these things." She felt that because of our wish to "live in a perfect world," we try to maintain the belief that students are "innocents" and therefore unable to write about troubling events. She concluded by saying that each semester she seems to have at least one student whose depression interferes with his or her education. "I propose alternate ways for these students to complete the course requirements. I listen not as a therapist but as a person who understands that these things happen, and so far they [the students] actually do complete the course. For one student, mine was the only course she completed. I think the issues that you raise can keep students in school or can be the cause of why they drop out."

The second email was from Pierre Woog, professor emeritus of Human Service Studies at Adelphi University in New York. It contained a single sentence — "I want to call your attention to the letter I sent to the editor referring to your recent article in the *Chronicle of Higher Education*." Along with the email came an attachment. I don't generally open attachments from unknown people, but since he was an academic I assumed that I would not be "infected" by his words:

I don't think Jeffrey Berman, "Syllabuses of Risk" (February 15, 2002), gets the point. He wants to "inoculate" his students so that "just as physicians and pharmacists routinely inform their patients of possible adverse reactions to a drug, so might teachers alert their students to the untoward consequences of a novel or a writing assignment," as from his course, English 447, "The Historical/Hysterical Imagination." Well, has it occurred to him that he is no M.D. and the problem may be his course, not the students?

I have been a professor for 35 years, and I am the father of two daughters now attending college. I am appalled with what Mr. Berman has to say. While I have defended academic freedom and railed against censorship all these years, I can still discern silly-bad courses that should not exist. I remember several years ago reading *The White Hotel* and being distraught for months. I cannot imagine what a barrage of such literature under the yoke of "Pleasing the professor" might have done to me. And I am not a "young, vulnerable woman." I am a robust, albeit aging, white male. The course is patently offensive and dangerous to anyone with awareness and sensitivity. To merely ascribe the obvious threat to young women is condescending and misogynistic. The course is just a plain bad idea.

Furthermore, and most important, I believe Mr. Berman can be accused of ravishing young minds, to me the worst sin a professor can commit. *You* take these young energetic minds and from *your* position of power *you* bring them to the precipice and after a few sessions in *your* office *you* put them back together again; *you* rescue them. This is not teaching. It is predation. Mr. Berman can gussy it up all he wants by referring to himself and those in the healing arts, of which he is not a member. He would do better to heed the healing arts' primary dictum: Do no harm.

Although this attachment did not infect my hard drive, I could feel its toxins poisoning my heart. The letter was published in the March 22, 2002, issue of the *Chronicle*, though with three sentences deleted, including the charge that I am condescending and misogynistic. I always strive to obey the Hippocratic injunction to do no harm, and if Professor Woog had read "Syllabuses of Risk" carefully, he would have discovered that all three students concluded that they had learned a great deal from the course despite the emotional difficulties they experienced from the reading. It is easy for him to conclude that a controversial novel like *The White Hotel* should be banned from college courses, but does he feel the same way about *The Awakening* and *The Bell Jar*, two enormously popular and canonical novels? Would he also ban *The Diary of Anne Frank*, which is read by millions of high school students? If he did allow students to read Anne Frank's story, would he advise them not to talk or write about their reactions to it? How far would his censorship extend? What advice would he have given to the doctoral student who found herself becoming at risk; would he have said that she, too, was taking a "silly-bad" course? Would he permit courses on the Holocaust and books like Primo Levi's memoir *Survival in Auschwitz*? Would he reject the teaching of all "trauma texts," which Laurie Vickroy describes as a "kind of testimonial literary history, a means of recovering cultural memories and traditions of groups often neglected or suppressed by mainstream culture" (172)? As I discuss in chapter 5, several students in Literature and the Healing Arts wrote in their reader-response diaries that Levi's account of his concentration camp ordeal was horrifying to read, producing nightmares, insomnia, anxiety and dread, stomach pains, headaches, and prolonged crying. Christine wrote about cutting herself after finishing the book, an act that she had not committed for many years. Mac reported that the memoir revived painful memories of incarceration. Most students found *Survival in Auschwitz* a revelation, but they did not anticipate its wrenching emotional impact.

Professor Woog's email accuses me of being "condescending and misogynistic," presumably because I reported in the *Chronicle* article that the three students who became at risk were all women. He apparently ignored the question I raise immediately thereafter: "Does that mean that female students—who typically experience higher incidences of depression than their male counterparts—are at greater risk when reading psychologically dark stories, particularly when these stories are about vulnerable female characters?" Why is this question condescending and misogynistic? Perhaps Professor Woog reaches this conclusion because I am a male professor to whom female (as well as male) students entrust personal writings, but why should this automatically provoke suspicion and censure? And why should he imply that my metaphor of "inoculating" students to the potential dangers of a reading or writing assignment is transgressive because I am not a physician? Would he similarly condemn Seamus Heaney for suggesting that poems can "act like their society's immunity systems, going to attack whatever unhealthy or debilitating forces are at work in the body politic" (114)? Or condemn *New York Times* book critic Anatole Broyard, who observed, shortly before dying of prostate cancer in 1990, that sick people write stories in order to "detoxify" their illness? "The patient has to start by treating his illness not as a disaster, an occasion for depression or panic, but as a narrative, a story. Stories are antibodies against illness and pain" (20–21).

What is most troubling about Professor Woog's letter is the belief that I am a ravisher of young minds, particularly of young female minds, a predator. Here is where his characterization coincides with the English woman's judgment. Both accuse me of exploiting my students and taking advantage of my power in the classroom. If the English woman alleged that I was a wolf disguised as Little Red Riding Hood—or, in the context of *Lolita*, a duplicitous Humbert Humbert lusting after Dolly Haze—the American professor likened me to a sham psychologist, a Fraudian practicing without a license. He would probably agree with Humbert's mocking observation that the difference between "the rapist" and "therapist" is but a matter of spacing.

"Reading-Induced Behavior"

Reader-response criticism is a relatively new pedagogical approach, only about thirty years old, and so it is not surprising that little research has been done on the therapeutic and countertherapeutic implications of reading. As I suggest at the end of *Surviving Literary Suicide*, "literature has a transformative power, for good and for ill, and nowhere is this better seen than in suicidal literature, which records"—in George Eliot's words—"the roar that lies on the other side of silence" (262). Since the publication of "Syllabuses of Risk," I have received a number of emails from graduate students, professors, and administrators documenting the phenomenon of "risky reading," including the following from an assistant dean at a large California university:

> Dear Professor Berman,
>
> I read the article in the Chronicle about your observations of behavior changes induced by reading. I have long shared your concerns. In fact, they have recently affected me personally. My sixteen-year-old daughter read The Bell Jar, having chosen it from a reading list supplied by her high school English literature teacher. Immediately upon completing the book, she fell into a deep clinical depression from which she is only now emerging, thanks to antidepressants. Up until reading that book, she was a happy-go-lucky kid and had never shown any signs of depressive behavior. There are those who would dismiss the reading of this book as but a trigger for an underlying condition that would have emerged without reading the book. I think otherwise.
>
> I had read that book back in college and found it to be the sappy and boring chronicle of an uncharismatic protagonist. But my daughter—as have no doubt thousand upon thousands of young women—internalized it to a degree that placed her in suicidal jeopardy. Like cigarettes, this book—and many others—should come with a warning label that informs the female reader of its hazard to health. English literature teaching, like the science academics, is a legacy of male dominated pedagogy, one that does not recognize the mysterious mental life of females in groups. Though anecdotally well known—infectious vomiting and menstrual synchronization are two examples—and etymologically described in the word "hysteria," the psychic connection and persuasion between females is very little understood. If that connection involves depression, the results can be devastating, especially if—as Chinese folk-wisdom maintains—melancholy is catching.
>
> Sadly, in this rather primitive stage of our understanding of psychic phenomena and action-at-a-distance, recognizing this phenomenon is probably still considered a fringe belief. Worse yet, it is no doubt considered by many to be politically incorrect. But I believe you have touched upon yet another important facet of this phenomenon—reading-induced behavior. How many more females will needlessly suffer—and die—because of our ignorance? I hope your work will hasten the day when this natural reality is fully recognized.

The notion that "melancholy is catching"—the "Werther" effect—has been extensively documented by David Phillips and other researchers. I don't know how serious the writer of this email is in raising the issue of whether certain literary works should carry a warning label, but I raise the same question in *Surviving Literary Suicide*, concluding that such labels would be "self-defeating, only heightening readers' fascination with death" (177). But I believe that teachers need to be sensitive to this issue and take special precautions, such as the adoption of what I call a "therapeutics of reading":

> Based upon the principles of suicide prevention—knowledge of danger signals, the need to take suicide seriously, and the willingness to empathize and listen—a therapeutics of reading will help us respond to real and fictional suicidal characters. A reader's empathy for a suicidal character does not require acceptance of the fantasies associated with suicide: the belief that suicide leads to omnipotent control, rebirth, immortality, magical reunion with the dead, or reparation. Nor does empathy require acceptance of the dichotomous thinking and constricted logic associated with a suicidal crisis. Awareness of the countertransference feelings associated with suicide—including malice, aversion, and fear—enables a reader to avoid condemning or heroicizing self-death. Finally, the reader must guard against the temptation to blame a suicide on another character or agent, even when the text invites such a response. (*Surviving Literary Suicide* 197)

"A Natural Therapist"

A literature teacher need not be "a natural therapist" to respond sensitively and appropriately to these issues. I mention this because of an email posted on PSYART, the literature-and-psychoanalysis electronic listserv moderated by Norman Holland at the University of Florida, to whom I had forwarded "Syllabuses of Risk." The email was sent by Daniel Rancour-Laferriere, a professor of Russian at the University of California at Davis and a well-known psychoanalytic literary critic:

Dear Colleagues,

With great interest I read Jeff Berman's "Syllabuses of Risk," recently posted on this list. It continues a bold experiment at the intersection of psychoanalysis and pedagogy which Jeff has been conducting for many years now. The final sentence of the paper is too modest: "We need to realize that we can be caring without becoming caretakers." I think Jeff has, willy-nilly, become a caretaker, a therapist for his students. He essentially utilizes a "writing cure" for students who are "at risk." The cure may not be complete, and the students may go on to seek other kinds of therapy. But the first step—and the literary jumping off point—is therapeutic as well.

At the same time Jeff has parlayed for himself an immense research profit from his high-maintenance students. This is quite okay, however, as far as I am concerned. After all, psychoanalysts charge high fees, and sometimes even make progress in their research based on the sufferings of their patients. I think of Thomas Ogden's book The Primitive Edge of Experience (1989), which achieves enormous insights on the basis of interaction with some pretty bizarre sufferers.

Daniel's email generated a spirited discussion on PSYART, and another member of the listserv, Mary Ellen Elkins, wrote that he "misapprehended" my approach to teaching. She believed that I "profited" from my classroom experience in a way that exemplifies Thoreau's ideals of profitable business and philanthropy—that is, by engaging in an activity motivated by love of one's work. Daniel responded with another posting:

> Jeff is a friend, and I hold his writing in high esteem. (In fact I published one of his articles in *Self-Analysis in Literary Study* brought out by NYU Press some years ago.) I don't think I "misapprehend" Jeff's writing. I admire it, and I admire him. It feels "therapeutic" just being around him. I'm sure his students feel this way. He is a natural therapist—something I am not, and something most literature teachers are not. If he has profited from this, the rest of us have profited as well. If he has done the kind of research he has done without ever having been the target of a law suit, without ever having been called on the carpet by his dean—then he is to be congratulated. His is a great talent. In my opinion his research is as "risky" as the "risky reading" his students read. I am glad he has overcome the risks involved and has been able to publish his important findings.

I was pleased by the generous comments of a scholar whose work I have long admired and whose friendship I esteem. I do not want to appear ungrateful, but I believe that this positive characterization is as misleading as Professor Woog's negative one. I don't see myself as a "natural therapist" but rather as a person who tries hard to create an empathic classroom where students can write freely and safely about vexing issues. If one can learn to be argumentative or oppositional, one can also learn to be empathic or at least *more* empathic than one has been in the past. By calling me a "natural therapist," Daniel implies that other literature teachers will not be able to do what I do in the classroom. The reason I believe that teachers can be caring without becoming caretakers is because opponents of personal writing maintain that teachers will *inevitably* transgress boundaries and become therapists to their students—something that I strive to avoid. I do not dispense psychological advice to my students, nor do they want me to do so. Our class discussions in writing courses are limited to *writing*, such as pointing out strong sentences, revising weak sentences, and citing concrete details. My students are not "high-maintenance": they are as respectful of my privacy as I am of theirs, and they do not become dependent on me, nor I on them. There are many commonalities between the talking cure and the writing cure, and I believe that teachers can tap into the therapeutic benefits of talking, writing, and reading without playing the role of therapist, minister, or physician.

Paradoxically, only by not playing the role of therapist—that is, by not psychoanalyzing or diagnosing our students—can we unleash the healing power of reading and writing. Although healing is not my main goal in my literature and writing classes, it is an invaluable by-product. Like many teachers, I aim for an education in life, one that involves both intellectual and emotional growth. Such an education permits students to write about experiences that are rarely discussed in the classroom. These painful and shameful experiences are inherently risky, but these risks can be minimized through empathic teaching.

Can other literature teachers do what I do in the classroom? Why not? If psychoanalytically oriented teachers can educate themselves on a wide range of intellectually challenging subjects and master several languages, as Daniel has, why can't they learn the basic befriending skills necessary for empathic teaching, namely, listening attentively, suspending judgment, and being compassionate? People acquire these skills through experience, rather than at birth, and like other skills, they can be sharpened with practice. If scholars can learn the arcane theories of Lacan or Derrida, why can they not develop their empathic understanding, particularly if they are interested in ethnographic research? In the last few years many books and articles have been written about the *other*, but why don't we encourage the silent others in our classroom to write and speak about their experiences? We would surely learn a great deal about them if they did.

Walking out of the Classroom

Daniel and I have different approaches to risky reading that are worth noting. He states in his first PSYART posting that when he teaches a course in Russian folklore, he includes tales or *skazki* compiled in the middle of the nineteenth century by Alexander Afanasiev, the "Russian equivalent of the Brothers Grimm." Until recently, one of the six volumes was unavailable because of Russian censorship. Daniel feels compelled to teach a few of these previously censored obscene stories because he would be repeating the practices of the Russian censors if he excluded them. He alerts his students to this risky reading and tells them that they have the freedom to leave the classroom if they find the stories offensive; he also assures them that they will not be tested on these obscene stories so that there is no pressure to "know" them. While he was teaching these stories, a week prior to his PSYART posting, three of the seventeen students walked out of the classroom, as was their right. Daniel then had a lively discussion of the meaning of the stories with the remaining students. He concluded his posting by lamenting that "It is sad that the students who left remain ignorant of—or at least unconscious of—certain things."

It is no less sad, however, that Daniel and the remaining students did not know why three of their classmates walked out of the room. If they were my students, I would invite them to explain why they left the classroom, and I would also encourage those who remained for the discussion to write about their responses. With the diarists' permission, I would read several of the entries aloud so that students would be exposed to as many different points of view as possible. I would neither discuss nor interpret these diaries: rather, students would be free to reach their own interpretations and conclusions. It is possible that some students might decline to share their responses with their teacher and classmates, but it's far more likely that they would welcome the opportunity to express their point of view. Their responses would be an invaluable source of new information for the teacher, whose own attitude toward the stories might change as a result of this new information. Their responses would be of special interest to those who, like Daniel, investigate how literary self-analysis enables readers to gain a deeper understanding of themselves and literature.

Would teachers feel like voyeurs or predators when reading these reader-response diaries? I doubt it. If the diaries Daniel were to receive resembled those that I have received in the last quarter of a century, they would not contain sexually titillating content. Voyeurs gaze at forbidden material; empathic teachers, by contrast, read the writings their students *want* them to read. Why should we be so mistrustful of the desire to look closely at what our students want us to see? Since our training as literature teachers enables us to read closely, why cannot we read reader-response diaries and personal essays with the same engagement that we read scholarly texts?

Surveillance Anxiety

A generation of scholars has been influenced by Michel Foucault's theory of the panopticon, the image of the omniscient gaze that overlooks Enlightenment penal reform. In 1791 the British reformer Jeremy Bentham published his book *Panopticon* in which he advocated a circular prison where prisoners would be continuously seen and thus controlled by inspectors. Foucault read the book, which had never received much attention, and seized upon panopticism as an ominous metaphor of institutions' "all-seeing" power to discipline and punish. "We know the principle" on which Bentham's *Panopticon* is based, Foucault writes:

> [A]t the periphery, an annular building; at the centre, a tower; this tower is pierced with wide windows that open onto the inner side of the ring; the peripheric building is divided into cells, each of which extends the whole width of the building; they have two windows, one on the inside, corresponding to the windows of the tower; the other, on the outside, allows the light to cross the cell from one end to the other. All that is needed, then, is to place a supervisor in a central power and to shut up in each cell a madman, a patient, a condemned man, a worker or a schoolboy. By the effect of backlighting, one can observe from the tower, standing out precisely against the light, the small captive shadows in the cells of the periphery. They are like so many cages, so many small theatres, in which each actor is alone, perfectly individualized and constantly visible. The panoptic mechanism arranges spacial unities that make it possible to see constantly and to recognize immediately. In short, it reverses the principle of the dungeon; or rather of its three functions—to enclose, to deprive of light and to hide—it preserves only the first and eliminates the other two. Full lighting and the eye of a supervisor capture better than darkness, which ultimately protected. Visibility is a trap. (200)

Foucault asserts that "our society is not one of spectacle, but of surveillance. . . . We are neither in the amphitheater, nor on the stage, but in the panoptic machine, invested by its effects of power, which we bring to ourselves since we are part of the mechanism" (217). As Thomas Levin notes, Foucault's theory of the panopticon "has since become synonymous with the vast repertoire of surveillant practices that have so profoundly marked the modern world. When we hesitate to race through a red light at an intersection where we see a black box, not knowing whether it contains a working camera but having to suppose that it might, we are acting today according to the very same panoptic logic" (12). The resulting surveillance anxiety, anticipated by George Orwell and Franz Kafka, and a major theme in Alfred Hitchcock's 1954 film *Rear Window*, Francis Ford Coppola's 1974 film *The Conversation*, and Peter Weir's 1998 film *The Truman Show*, leads to what Levin calls a "rhetorics of surveillance" revealing the increasing fear of being watched, controlled, and monitored by a totalitarian government.

Visibility may be a trap in Foucault's panoptic dystopia, where an elaborate technology of surveillance exists, but the kind of looking that occurs in an empathic classroom is radically different. Students have the power to

show—or not show—their writings to the teacher. Students decide for themselves both the degree of self-disclosure and whether to share their writings with classmates. They are sometimes apprehensive when they read
their writings to the class, or hear me read them anonymously, but this is
not surveillance anxiety so much as the fear arising when repressed emotions are expressed for the first time. Nor is the looking that occurs in the
empathic classroom similar to what Freud calls "scopophilia," the "pleasure in looking" that may lead to voyeurism and exhibitionism. "[A]nyone
who is an exhibitionist in his unconscious," Freud writes in *Three Essays
on the Theory of Sexuality*, "is at the same time a *voyeur*; in anyone who
suffers from the consequences of repressed sadistic impulses there is sure
to be another determinant of his symptoms which has its source in mas-
ochistic inclinations" (167). Unlike Freud, I do not believe that all knowledge derives from sublimated sexuality, nor do I believe that the desire to
see what others wish to show, in this case, diaries and essays, should be
pathologized into voyeuristic or exhibitionistic urges.

Sympathy and Sadomasochistic Desire

Nor do I believe that the sympathy that arises in the empathic classroom
can be reduced to sadomasochistic desire, as contemporary theorists assert. Building upon Foucault's writings on perversion, Laura Hinton claims
in *The Perverse Gaze of Sympathy* that sympathy is a cultural formulation
of male desire, the embodiment of a controlling gaze. "[S]adomasochistic
desire underlies the experience of sympathy, through the perverse narrative spectator who creates and reflects sentimental image-making" (3). She
insists that sympathy, "even more than the figure of the panopticon, *con-
ceals* the desire for and use of power through identification. Through sympathy, the aggressivity of sentiment is safely, perversely, released" (16). It is
unsettling to see how Hinton strips the words "sympathy" and "compassion" of any positive qualities. (Nowhere does she mention empathy.) Thus
she endorses the eighteenth-century philosopher David Hume's description of compassion "as a spectator's inertia, when, 'safely at land,' he contemplates the idea of 'those who are at sea in a storm,'" and she distinguishes sympathy from compassion by the "greater 'nearness' of the
spectacle, as the ship actually appears 'to be driven . . . near me,' and the
spectator 'can perceive distinctly the horror'" (234).

Hinton does not mention Nietzsche, but she would have gained a powerful ally had she done so. As Joel Black observes, "[t]he philosophical
project undertaken by Nietzsche entailed nothing less than the dissolu-

tion of the established metaphysical categories operative in both ethics (good versus evil) and in epistemology (truth versus lie), and the exposure of such 'absolute' values as merely provisional, functionally related determinations that are actually motivated by the ceaseless interplay of various competing manifestations of the will to power" (78). This will to power may be seen in *Human, All Too Human,* where Nietzsche offers one of the most withering critiques of sympathy. "The reason why someone powerful is grateful is this. His benefactor has, by his act of benevolence, violated the sphere of that powerful person and forced his way into it: now, in retaliation, he violates the benefactor's sphere by the act of gratitude. It is a milder form of revenge" (51). Echoing Jonathan Swift, he proclaims that "people are grateful to the same extent that they nurture revenge" (51). In Nietzsche's view, sympathy leads inevitably to hypochondria and illness. "There are people who become hypochondriac out of sympathy and concern for another person; the resulting form of sympathy is nothing other than a sickness" (53). Nietzsche agrees with La Rochefoucauld that "one should *exhibit* pity, but guard against *having* it: for the unfortunate are simply so *stupid* that the display of pity does them the greatest good in the world" (54; emphasis in original). Sympathetic people are, in Nietzsche's opinion, merely trying to gain advantage over others. "Natures that are sympathetic and always helpful in misfortune are rarely as likely to share in joy: when others are fortunate, they have nothing to do, are superfluous, feel as if they no longer possess their superior position, and hence easily manifest discontent" (201). Nor is he keen to bestow love on others. "There is not enough love and goodness in the world to allow us to give any of it away to imaginary beings" (98).

Joseph Conrad was no less mistrustful of compassion than was Nietzsche, and he dramatizes in his 1896 novel *The Nigger of the "Narcissus"* the near-catastrophic consequences that occur on board the ship *Narcissus* when the crew, manipulated by a vicious man named Donkin, befriends the dying West Indian Negro, James Wait. Among Conrad's extensive cast of villains, none is more malevolent than Donkin, whom the narrator—a collective "we" who is essentially the novelist himself—identifies as the "pet of philanthropists and self-seeking landlubbers. The sympathetic and deserving creature that knows all about his rights, but knows nothing of courage, of endurance, and of the unexpressed faith, of the unspoken loyalty that knits together a ship's company" (301). Conrad implies that the crew's compassion for James Wait is nothing more than callous self-interest: they are so fearful of his impending death, which threatens to paralyze their will, that they will do anything to keep him alive. It is not simply that their compassion is misplaced—both Donkin and Wait are masters at exploiting weakness—but that compassion is seen as a disruptive force. In one of the most cynical statements appearing anywhere in Conrad's fiction, the narrator states that the "latent egoism of tenderness to suffering appeared in the developing anxiety not to see him die" (421). It is never clear why Conrad equates compassion with selfishness, an attribute of the self, rather than with selflessness, recognition of the other. Such compassion in Conrad's world generally leads to heightened vulnerability, self-deception, and paralyzed overidentification. Through their devotion to Wait, "we were becoming highly humanised, tender, complex, excessively decadent: we understood the subtlety of his fear, sympathised with all his repulsions, shrinkings, evasions, delusions—as though we had been overcivilised, and rotten, and without any knowledge of the meaning of life" (421–22). In Conrad's world, those who give way to their compassionate instincts—in Levinas's words, taking responsibility for the other—find themselves in a "weird servitude" (332). The crew is released from this disabling condition only when Wait dies and his body disappears into the sea.

These reductive or cynical analyses of sympathy do not resonate with me; I don't feel "inertia" or "servitude" when my students write about tempestuous experiences but rather concern for their well-being. My students appreciate my concern, as I appreciate theirs. Contrary to Nietzsche's assertion, I feel gratitude to the many people who have helped me over the years—parents, teachers, friends, and colleagues. This gratitude contains none of the unconscious desire for revenge of which Nietzsche speaks. I feel a special gratitude to the hundreds of students who have entrusted their personal writings to me. Nor is my desire to befriend others an effort to gain power over them. Nietzsche may have "sought to strip the dialectics of pity—in which the sufferer inflicts pain on others by arousing pity—of its sentimental coating, thereby revealing the power struggle beneath the surface," as his latest biographer, Rüdiger Safranski, observes (187). Nevertheless, Nietzsche omits the altruistic motives, which are no less powerful or real than darker motives.

What word would I use, then, to describe how the members of an empathic classroom look at each other's writings? Curious. The word conveys, without the pejorative implications of either Freudian or Foucauldian theorizings, the desire to understand more about classmates' lives. We are all curious about each other's lives and stories, and this curiosity is as fundamental as the desire for human connection.

If, as I suspect, some of the people who walked out of Daniel Rancour-Laferriere's class had been sexually abused, they would probably write about their feelings of shame over this experience and the ways in which it has affected their lives. They might also express their anger or indignation toward the professor for including disturbing material on the reading list. By writing about this traumatic experience, the students would gain a degree of mastery over it. By hearing their professor read these diaries aloud, in an empathic and nonjudgmental voice, the students would educate their classmates about a terrifying reality that is seldom discussed openly inside or outside the classroom. Finally, by reading these diaries aloud, without invalidating the feelings contained therein, the professor would help to defuse their verbal violence. Similarly, if the English woman were a student in my class and turned in a diary in which she accused me of being voyeuristic and perverted, I would read the diary aloud if she gave me permission to do so. By doing so, I would allow her to voice her criticisms: she would no longer be stunned into silence. She might not change her opinion of me, but at least she would express herself and reflect on her words. Her diary would give me a better understanding of why she felt that my approach to teaching was so harmful—perhaps each of us would then be able to narrow the mistrust between us. And perhaps Professor Woog would be in a better position to evaluate my teaching if he sat in on my classes and interviewed my students.

"Why I Write"

What is the motivation behind my teaching and writing? I believe that motivation almost always involves a combination of self-centered and unselfish impulses. The best discussion that I have read appears in George Orwell's brief essay "Why I Write," in which he argues that, apart from the need to earn a living, there are "four great motives for writing": (1) "Sheer egoism," which he characterizes as the "desire to seem clever, to be talked about, to be remembered after death, to get your own back on grownups who snubbed you in childhood, etc."; (2) "Esthetic enthusiasm," that is, "perception of beauty in the external world, or, on the other hand, in words and their right arrangement"; (3) "Historical impulse," the "desire to see things as they are, to find out true facts and store them up for the use of posterity"; and (4) "Political purpose," which he defines as the "desire to push the world in a certain direction, to alter other people's idea of the kind of society that they should strive after" (315–16). After acknowledging these four impulses, however, Orwell adds that "at the very bottom" of writers' motives lies mystery: "Writing a book is a horrible, exhausting struggle, like a long bout of some painful illness. One would never undertake such a thing if one were not driven on by some demon whom one can neither resist nor understand. For all one knows that demon is simply the same instinct that makes a baby squall for attention" (320).

Orwell recognizes the complexity of motivation, the coexistence of egotistical, aesthetic, historical, and political impulses. He might have mentioned a fifth motivation, "psychological," in which we write about troubling experiences in order to achieve self-mastery and self-healing. As Arthur Frank observes in *The Wounded Storyteller*, "As wounded, people may be cared for, but as storytellers, they care for others. The ill, and all those who suffer, can also be healers. Their injuries become the source of the potency of their stories. Through their stories, the ill create empathic bonds between themselves and their listeners. These bonds expand as the stories are retold. Those who listened then tell others, and the circle of shared experience widens. Because stories can heal, the wounded healer and wounded storyteller are not separate, but are different aspects of the same figure" (xii). Judith Harris's book *Signifying Pain* demonstrates eloquently how writers as diverse as John Keats, Charlotte Perkins Gilman, Derek Walcott, Jane Kenyon, and Robert Lowell have used their writings to work through personal traumas. Other books, including *Writing and Healing*, edited by Charles Anderson and Marian MacCurdy, affirm the therapeutic power of verbal expression. In *True Notebooks* Mark Salzman shows how youthful offenders in a Los Angeles detention facility write movingly and honestly about their lives. In the words of a member of the Inside Out Writers program, "[our teachers] give us something we never had: a voice that we could use so we would be heard by people that make the decisions that affect us. With our newfound voice, we can give our opinions on the way others are guiding us. With that voice we can explain to the people who have never been in our situation who we really are, and why we do the crimes we do" (169).

In the last decade my writing has focused on teaching, and the motivation behind both includes precisely what Orwell and Frank discuss. There is the "sheer egoism" of writing and teaching, in which I see my name in print. I don't wish to deny the existence of these egotistical impulses. "Let us conduct a little thought experiment," Avishai Margalit proposes in *The Ethics of Memory*:

> If I ask you which you prefer: that a momentous work of yours will survive after your death, but only anonymously, or that your name will survive but none of your works will (as happened to the legendary Dedalus), how would you answer? Miguel de Unamuno, the Spanish philosopher, knew his preference, and believed that he knew yours. He believed that you, as he, would opt for the survival of your name rather than survival of your work. I don't

share his preference, and I don't know your preference. Yet the mere fact that I do not know your preference is enough to underline Unamuno's point: how strong the desire is for even such an insubstantial immortality as that of a name. (25)

I would opt for survival of my work but only after conceding the powerful temptation to choose survival of my name. I would like to believe that pride in my work is stronger than pride in my name, but perhaps the truth is that my guilt would be the deciding factor. In any case, I agree with Orwell that one motive behind writing is the desire for fame and recognition, however minuscule and fleeting they may be—far less than the fifteen minutes claimed by Andy Warhol. The same motive helps to explain why my students are so excited about seeing their writings in my books. The egotistical motivation behind writing becomes less troubling when we realize that it reflects the desire for validation and affirmation, the recognition that our lives have significance not only to ourselves but also to others. "It is certain," wrote Novalis, in a passage that was so important to Joseph Conrad that he used it as the epigraph to *Lord Jim*, "my conviction gains infinitely the moment another soul will believe in it."

My "esthetic enthusiasm" derives from the pleasure of polishing my language. I don't like to write—it feels as if I'm writhing rather than writing when the words do not flow—but I love to rewrite, crafting words into essays and books that others may read. Immersing oneself in writing is one of the most intense experiences imaginable, resulting in what the psychologist Mihaly Csikszentmihalyi calls "flow," in which we may lose all sense of time. These flow experiences, Csikszentmihalyi explains, often involve "painful, risky, difficult activities" that stretch a person's capacity and involve elements of novelty and discovery (110). I also feel a "historical impulse" to understand my students' lives, to teach them how to read and write so that they can tell their own stories. This historical impulse enables us to bear witness to suffering, memorializing those who are no longer here and preserving a record for posterity. My "political purpose" is to push the world in a more empathic direction, a difficult goal to achieve in an age that privileges argumentative and oppositional speech over attentive listening. And my psychological intention is to show that literature can indeed be a healing force for writers and readers alike.

As interesting as it is to write about fictional characters, it is more interesting to write about real characters. As I note in chapter 3, my students' world is startlingly different from the world in which I grew up, and the men and women who sit in our classrooms have lives that are far more complex than I could ever imagine. I take pleasure in writing about my students, and, to judge from what they say years after they have studied with me, they take pleasure in seeing their own writings in my books. This may well be a narcissistic pleasure for them and for me, but it is, I believe, healthy narcissism, one that fully acknowledges the existence of others. Their writings often reflect anguish, but they don't regret writing on painful subjects, and nearly all experience therapeutic relief. They give me permission to use their writing and know in advance exactly how I contextualize it; they are neither coerced nor exploited. I never tell students more about themselves than they already know. They are the ones who interpret their own lives, and if they write about past breakdowns, they also write about recoveries. I do not rescue them; they rescue themselves.

I don't claim that empathic teaching will revolutionize education, but I believe that it has the potential to make a difference in students' lives, as it has with many of my own students. I have not discovered anything new; Heinz Kohut and Carl Rogers were tireless advocates of the use of empathy in psychotherapy, and they both recognized its application to education. Other teachers and researchers have investigated the dynamics of self-disclosure in a variety of settings. My contribution is to show how empathy and self-disclosure can be combined safely and productively in the classroom. I have been using this approach now, in one form or another, for more than a quarter of a century, and the question for future research is not whether empathic teaching works but how others will adapt it for their own classrooms.

A colleague from another university visited my writing class a couple of years ago and later told me that he was struck by how ordinary the class appeared. He meant this as a compliment. He said that he was relieved that I was not a charismatic teacher and that there were no emotional fireworks in the class. There was no high drama, nothing resembling fictional or filmic representations of high school or college teaching. It was an ordinary class in every way, except for the fact that the essays were unusually self-disclosing and the students were unusually constructive in their comments on each other's writings. The implication, with which I agree heartily, is that other teachers could adopt this approach in their own classrooms.

Is this approach to education risky? Yes, but the risks are manageable. "The one overriding lesson from the mountains of literature generated by the science of risk analysis," writes John Ross in *The Polar Bear Strategy,* "is that a risk cannot be assessed and managed along only one dimension, like a mountain peak waiting to be conquered. In fact, risk management, both individually and collectively, involves a world of trade-offs and demands a certain finesse" (148). Indeed, it may be far riskier *not* to allow students to write about their fears and conflicts. Donald Murray's observation is relevant here: "Donald Barthelme told us to 'write about what you're most afraid of.' When I do, I survive the terrors that silence me. While writing, the dark clouds rise, the monster shadows retreat. Graham Greene explains, 'Writing is a form of therapy; sometimes I wonder how all those who do not write, compose or paint can manage to escape the madness, the melancholia, the panic fear which is inherent in the human situation.' Writing is my therapy" (56).

Would literature teachers need to be "natural therapists" in order to apply my approach to their own classrooms? I don't think so. I can imagine that teachers will feel anxious at first when receiving personal writings on emotionally charged topics such as divorce, depression, and suicide, but they will become more experienced over time. They will learn, along with their students, that traumatic knowledge creates the opportunity for posttraumatic growth. They will learn that their students want them only to listen to their stories rather than to intervene in their lives. They will learn that students who are encouraged to pursue an education for life will achieve new breakthroughs of understanding for themselves and their classmates; to paraphrase the ending of *King Lear*, students will speak what they feel, not what they ought to say. They will learn that teaching is one of the most exhilarating activities imaginable, leading to heightened empathy, openness, trust, and understanding for teachers and students alike. They will learn that their departmental chairpersons and deans will not reprimand them for being empathic teachers. They will learn that they will not need to fear lawsuits if they observe the protocols I discuss in *Risky Writing*. And they will learn, after receiving their students' grateful letters long after the semester has ended, as we see in Ben Gordon's poignant letter that I quote in the introduction to this book, that they have truly made a difference in their students' lives, which is the greatest profit that teaching can offer.

APPENDIX

English 226: Literature and the Healing Art

Spring 2002
T, Th 5:45–7:05   HU 137   Course No. 1787
Jeffrey Berman

Many writers would agree with D. H. Lawrence's observation that "one sheds one's sicknesses in books—repeats and presents again one's emotions, to be master of them." In this course we will explore the therapeutic implications of reading and writing, including the relationship between creativity and illness. We will read poems, novels, memoirs, and autobiographical essays that explore illness, injury, and death. Lest this seem unduly gloomy or depressing, our focus will be on the ways in which literature enables the writer and reader to confront and master painful events. We will emphasize trauma theory, bearing witness, and empathic reading. There will be five guest lecturers who will be giving public lectures that you will be expected to attend. The lectures, which will be open to the general public, will take place on Tuesdays or Thursdays from 7–9 P.M. (Most of the lectures will be in the Chapel House.) There will be no regular class that day, but you will be expected to attend the lecture that evening, and attendance will be taken.

Required Books

Leo Tolstoy	*The Death of Ivan Ilych*
Lucy Grealy	*Autobiography of a Face*
Albert Camus	*The Plague*
Primo Levi	*Survival in Auschwitz*
William Styron	*Darkness Visible*
Jeffrey Berman	*Risky Writing*

Requirements

There will be a midterm and a final examination, each constituting one-third of your final grade. The other third of your grade will be determined by six reader-response diaries, one for each of the required books on the reading list. Each diary should be between 2–3 pages long, typed and double-spaced. I have indicated on the schedule when the diaries are due; late diaries will be penalized. The diary should give evidence that you have read and engaged with the book. You can be as personal as you wish in each diary: you determine the degree of self-disclosure. At least half of the diary should focus on the book, including the beginning, middle, and ending. I will not grade each diary, but I will comment on each one before returning them to you the next class. On the last day of the semester, May 7, I will ask you to resubmit all six diaries to me in a folder (remember that I will have already read and commented on them); I will then grade the diaries and turn them back to you on the day of the final exam, May 14. You will not be graded on the degree of self-disclosure but rather on your ability to discuss insightfully the book you have read.

What am I looking for in the diaries? I'm mainly interested in your ability to illuminate the story under discussion and to show how the story affects you—both intellectually and emotionally. These are diaries, not formal essays, and therefore I will not have the time to discuss the strengths and weaknesses of your writing (the class is too large for me to do that). Nevertheless, I do value good writing, and a well-written diary is bound to receive a higher grade than a poorly written one. I would like to read about five diaries aloud before I hand them back to you the next class. If you do *not* want me to read your diary aloud, please indicate so; otherwise, I will assume that you are giving me permission to read your diary aloud. I will always read the diaries anonymously—no one will know the diarist's identity. Nor will there be a discussion of the diaries afterward. Your grade will not be influenced by the number of your diaries I've read aloud.

Schedule of Guest Lectures

Feb 7   Iliana Semmler: "Fashioning Nature: Literature's Judgment on Aesthetic Surgery"
Feb 19 Lucy Grealy: A Reading
Mar 19 Sophie Freud: "The Reading Cure"
Apr 4   Michael Kaufman: "McMedicine: Tolstoy's Anatomy of Human Frailty"
Apr 16 Rita Charon: "Narrative Medicine"

Class Schedule

Jan 24   Introduction
Jan 29   Coleridge: *The Rime of the Ancient Mariner*
Jan 31   Hawthorne: "The Birthmark"
Feb 5   Richard Selzer: "Minor Surgery"
Feb 7   No class; guest lecturer: Iliana Semmler
Feb 12   Grealy: *Autobiography of a Face*
Feb 14   Grealy: *Autobiography of a Face*
Feb 19   No class; guest lecturer: Lucy Grealy; first diary is due

Feb 21 Camus: *The Plague*
Mar 5   Camus: *The Plague*
Mar 7   Camus: *The Plague*; second diary is due
Mar 12 Levi: *Survival in Auschwitz*
Mar 14 Levi: *Survival in Auschwitz*
Mar 19 No class; guest lecturer: Sophie Freud
Mar 21 Levi: *Survival in Auschwitz*; third diary is due
Mar 26 Midterm exam
Apr 2   Tolstoy: *The Death of Ivan Ilych*
Apr 4   No class; guest lecturer: Michael Kaufman
Apr 9   Tolstoy: *The Death of Ivan Ilych*; fourth diary is due
Apr 11 Charon: essays (to be given out in class)
Apr 16 No class; guest lecturer: Rita Charon
Apr 18 Styron: *Darkness Visible*
Apr 23 Styron: *Darkness Visible*; fifth diary is due
Apr 25 Berman: *Risky Writing*
Apr 30 Berman: *Risky Writing*
May 2   Berman: *Risky Writing*; sixth diary due
May 7   Conclusion; all six diaries are due (Please place them in a folder.)
May 14 5:45–7:45 Final exam

English 226: Literature and the Healing Arts

Final Exam: May 14, 2002
The final exam will be a take-home exam; it can be turned in no later than May 14, 7:45 P.M., at my office (HU 348). You can turn in the exam earlier if you wish; either slip it under my office door or place it in my mailbox in HU 380. If you do not personally give me the exam, be sure to make a photocopy in case the original gets lost. If you want to find out your final grade early, either include a self-addressed, stamped postcard with the exam or send me an email. I should have the final grades determined by May 17.

The final exam should be typed, double-spaced; my expectations are that the exam will be between 9–12 pages. I will be grading you on both content and form, so make sure the exam is as well written as possible. I want you to write on all three questions. This is not a collaborative exam, so please do not discuss your answers with anyone else.

1. Summarize in a paragraph or two Rita Charon's argument in her essay "Narrative Medicine: A Model for Empathy, Reflection, Profession, and Trust" and then apply that argument to Tolstoy's *The Death of Ivan Ilych*. Contrast the ways in which Ivan Ilych's doctors treated him with how you imagine Dr. Charon would treat him. If you wish, you can write up "Dr. Charon's" notes about her patient. What are the major issues that would arise when an em-

pathic physician treats a dying person? What would empathic physicians learn about themselves when treating a patient like Ivan Ilych? Be sure not to reduce the complexity of a physician's efforts to treat a dying person.

2. In *Darkness Visible* William Styron writes about his depression, in the process educating his readers about the seriousness of this disease. He concludes with the following observation: "But one need not sound the false or inspirational note to stress the truth that depression is not the soul's annihilation; men and women who have recovered from the disease—and they are countless—bear witness to what is probably its only saving grace: it is conquerable."

   Discuss what you have learned about depression from reading *Darkness Visible and* from hearing me read several *Darkness Visible* diaries aloud. To what extent have *you* borne witness to depression by being a member of Literature and the Healing Arts? Have reading and writing about depression been depressing or uplifting to you? Explain.

3. Write a review of *Risky Writing*. Make sure you discuss both the strengths and the weaknesses of the book. (You will not do well on this answer if you discuss one without the other.) Include in your discussion at least one student writer from the beginning, middle, and ending of the book. Also include in your review your responses to my paper that I read aloud, "Risky Teaching: On Being Called a Pervert, a Predator, and a Natural Therapist." Finally, did your experience writing and hearing read aloud reader-response diaries in English 226 resemble the experiences of the students in *Risky Writing*?

Aberbach, David. *Surviving Trauma*. New Haven: Yale University Press, 1989.

Adams, Henry. *The Education of Henry Adams*. Boston: Houghton Mifflin, 1961.

Agosta, Louis. "Empathy and Intersubjectivity." In *Empathy 1*, edited by Joseph Lichtenberg et al., 43–62.

Albert, Arielle Berman. "Parental and Peer Support as Predictors of Depression and Self-Esteem among Late Adolescents: An Attachment Theory Perspective." Ph.D. diss., Loyola University Chicago, 2003.

Albert, David Brian. "Prevalence and Patterns of Post–Traumatic Stress Disorder among Persons with Severe Mental Illness." Ph.D. diss., Northwestern University, 2002.

Alcorn, Marshall. *Changing the Subject in English Class*. Carbondale: Southern Illinois University Press, 2002.

————. "Ideological Death and Grief in the Classroom: Mourning as a Prerequisite to Learning." *JPCS: Journal for the Psychoanalysis of Culture and Society* 6 (2001): 172–80.

Althusser, Louis. "Ideology and Ideological State Apparatuses." In *Lenin and Philosophy and Other Essays by Louis Althusser*. Translated by Ben Brewster. New York: Monthly Review Press, 1971.

Amato, Paul, and Alan Booth. *A Generation at Risk: Growing Up in an Era of Family Upheaval*. Cambridge: Harvard University Press, 1997.

American Psychiatric Association (APA). *Diagnostic and Statistical Manual of Mental Disorders*. 3rd edition. Revised. Washington, D.C., American Psychiatric Association: 1987.

————. *Diagnostic and Statistical Manual of Mental Disorders*. 4th edition. Washington, D.C., American Psychiatric Association: 1994.

Anderson, Charles, and Marian MacCurdy, editors. *Writing and Healing: Toward an Informed Practice*. Urbana, Ill.: NCTE, 2000.

Antze, Paul, and Michael Lambek, editors. *Tense Past: Cultural Essays in Trauma and Memory*. New York: Routledge, 1996.

Arendt, Hannah. *The Human Condition*. Chicago: University of Chicago Press, 1958; 2nd edition, 1998.

Austen, Jane. *Pride and Prejudice*. Norton Critical Edition, edited by Donald Gray. New York: Norton, 1966.

Austin, J. L. *How to Do Things with Words*. Cambridge: Harvard University Press, 1962.

Barth, John. *The End of the Road*. London: Secker and Warburg, 1962.

Bartlett, Thomas. "Guidelines for Discussion, or Thought Control?" *Chronicle of Higher Education*, September 27, 2002.

———. "Why Johnny Can't Write, Even Though He Went to Princeton." *Chronicle of Higher Education*, January 3, 2003.

Batson, C. Daniel. *The Altruism Question: Toward a Social-Psychological Answer*. Hillsdale, N.J.: Lawrence Erlbaum Associates, 1991.

Belenky, Mary Field, Blythe McVicker Clinchy, Nancy Rule Goldberger, and Jill Mattuck Tarule. *Women's Ways of Knowing: The Development of Self, Voice, and Mind*. New York: Basic Books, 1986.

Bellow, Saul. *Seize the Day*. In *The Portable Saul Bellow*. New York: Viking, 1974.

Berman, Jeffrey. *Diaries to an English Professor*. Amherst: University of Massachusetts Press, 1994.

———. *Narcissism and the Novel*. New York: New York University Press, 1990.

———. *Risky Writing: Self-Disclosure and Self-Transformation in the Classroom*. Amherst: University of Massachusetts Press, 2001.

———. *Surviving Literary Suicide*. Amherst: University of Massachusetts Press, 1999.

———. "Syllabuses of Risk." *Chronicle of Higher Education*, February 15, 2002, B7–9.

Bernard-Donals, Michael, and Richard Glejzer. *Between Witness and Testimony: The Holocaust and the Limits of Representation*. Albany: State University of New York Press, 2001.

Bernstein, G. A., C. M. Borchardt, and A. R. Perwien. "Anxiety Disorders in Children and Adolescents: A Review of the Past Ten Years." *Journal of the American Academy of Child and Adolescent Psychiatry* 35 (1996): 1110–19.

Black, Joel. *The Aesthetics of Murder*. Baltimore: Johns Hopkins University Press, 1991.

Blake, William. *Complete Writings*. Edited by Geoffrey Keynes. London: Oxford University Press, 1967.

Blanchot, Maurice. *The Writing of the Disaster*. Translated by Ann Smock. Lincoln: University of Nebraska Press, 1995.

Blum, Virginia. *Flesh Wounds: The Culture of Cosmetic Surgery*. Berkeley: University of California Press, 2003.

Bok, Sissela. *Secrets: On the Ethics of Concealment and Revelation*. New York: Vintage, 1983.

Boker, Pamela. *The Grief Taboo in American Literature: Loss and Prolonged Adolescence in Twain, Melville, and Hemingway*. New York: New York University Press, 1996.

Bordo, Susan. *Unbearable Weight: Feminism, Western Culture, and the Body*. Berkeley: University of California Press, 1993.

Bouson, J. Brooks. *The Empathic Reader*. Amherst: University of Massachusetts Press, 1989.

Bowlby, John. *Attachment and Loss*. 3 volumes. New York: Basic Books, 1969–80.

_____. *The Making and Breaking of Affectional Bonds*. London: Tavistock, 1979.

Bracher, Mark. "Identity and Desire in the Classroom." In *Pedagogical Desire: Authority, Seduction, Transference, and the Question of Ethics*, edited by Jan Jagodzinski, 93–121. Westport, Conn.: Bergin and Garvey, 2002.

Breuer, Josef, and Sigmund Freud. *Studies on Hysteria. The Standard Edition of the Complete Psychological Works of Sigmund Freud*. Translated by James Strachey. Volume 2. London: Hogarth Press, 1975.

Briere, John. *Child Abuse Trauma*. Newbury Park, Calif.: Sage Publications, 1992.

Britzman, Deborah. *After-Education: Anna Freud, Melanie Klein, and Psychoanalytic Histories of Learning*. Albany: State University of New York Press, 2003.

Broun, Heywood. *Collected Edition of Heywood Broun*. Freeport, N.Y.: Books for Libraries Press, 1969.

Broyard, Anatole. *Intoxicated by My Illness and Other Writings on Life and Death*. Edited by Alexandra Broyard. New York: Clarkson Potter, 1992.

Bruner, Jerome. "Life as Narrative." *Social Research* 54 (1987): 11–32.

Caesar, Terry. *Traveling through the Boondocks: In and Out of Academic Hierarchy*. Albany: State University of New York Press, 2000.

Calhoun, Lawrence, and Richard Tedeschi. "Posttraumatic Growth: Future Directions." In *Posttraumatic Growth: Positive Changes in the Aftermath of Crisis*, edited by Richard Tedeschi et al., 215–38.

Caruth, Cathy. "Traumatic Departures: Survival and History in Freud." In *Trauma and Self*, edited by Charles Strozier and Michael Flynn, 29–44.

Ceci, Stephen, Michael Toglia, and David Ross, editors. *Children's Eyewitness Memory*. New York: Springer-Verlag, 1987.

Charon, Rita. "Narrative Medicine: A Model for Empathy, Reflection, Profession, and Trust." *JAMA* 286 (October 17, 2001): 1897–1902.

Cherlin, Andrew. *Marriage, Divorce, Remarriage*. Revised edition. Cambridge: Harvard University Press, 1992.

Chodorow, Nancy. *The Reproduction of Mothering*. Berkeley: University of California Press, 1978.

Clark, Candace. *Misery and Company: Sympathy in Everyday Life*. Chicago: University of Chicago Press, 1997.

Code, Lorraine. "'I Know Just How You Feel': Empathy and the Problem of Epistemic Authority." In *The Empathic Practitioner: Empathy, Gender, and Medicine*, edited by Ellen Singer More and Maureen A. Milligan, 77–97. New Brunswick, N.J.: Rutgers University Press, 1994.

Cohen, Richard. *Ethics, Exegesis, and Philosophy: Interpretation after Levinas.* Cambridge: Cambridge University Press, 2001.

Coleman, J. C., and L. B. Hendry. *The Nature of Adolescence.* 3rd edition. New York: Routledge, 1996.

Coleridge, Samuel Taylor. *The Portable Coleridge.* Edited by I. A. Richards. New York: Viking Press, 1965.

Conrad, Joseph. *The Nigger of the "Narcissus".* In *The Portable Conrad,* edited by Morton Dauwen Zabel. Revised by Frederick Karl. New York: Penguin, 1976.

Cottle, Thomas. *A Sense of Self: The Work of Affirmation.* Amherst: University of Massachusetts Press, 2003.

Cotton, Kathleen. "Developing Empathy in Children and Youth." School Improvement Research Series (SIRS). July 13, 2001. http://www.nwrel.org/scpd/sirs/7/cu1.3html.

Covey, Stephen. "The Mind-Set and Skill Set of a Leader." In *Leading beyond the Walls,* edited by Frances Hesselbein, Marshall Goldsmith, and Iain Somerville, 149–58. San Francisco: Jossey-Bass, 1999.

Cross, Amanda [Carolyn Heilbrun]. *Death in a Tenured Position.* New York: Ballantine, 1982.

Csikszentmihalyi, Mihaly. *Creativity.* New York: HarperCollins, 1996.

Darlow, Michael, and Gillian Hodson. *Terence Rattigan: The Man and His Work.* London: Quartet Books, 1979.

Davies, Jody Messler, and Mary Gail Frawley. *Treating the Adult Survivor of Childhood Sexual Abuse: A Psychoanalytic Perspective.* New York: Basic Books, 1994.

Davis, Lennard. *The Sonnets.* Albany: State University of New York Press, 2001.

Des Pres, Terrence. *The Survivor: An Anatomy of Life in the Death Camps.* New York: Oxford University Press, 1976.

Dobson, Joanne. *Cold and Pure and Very Dead.* New York: Doubleday, 2000.

Eble, Kenneth. *The Craft of Teaching.* 2nd edition. San Francisco: Jossey-Bass, 1988.

Elder, Joseph. "Expanding Our Options: The Challenge of Forgiveness." In *Exploring Forgiveness,* edited by Robert Enright and Joanna North, 150–64.

Enright, Robert, Suzanne Freedman, and Julio Rique. "The Psychology of Interpersonal Forgiveness." In *Exploring Forgiveness,* edited by Robert Enright and Joanna North, 46–62.

Enright, Robert, and Joanna North, editors. *Exploring Forgiveness.* Madison: University of Wisconsin Press, 1998.

Erikson, Erik. *Childhood and Society.* New York: Norton, 1963.

Farrell, Kirby. *Post-Traumatic Culture: Injury and Interpretation in the Nineties.* Baltimore: Johns Hopkins University Press, 1998.

Felman, Shoshana, and Dori Laub. *Testimony: Crises of Witnessing in Literature, Psychoanalysis, and History.* New York: Routledge, 1992.

Fenichel, Otto. *The Psychoanalytic Theory of Neurosis*. New York: Norton, 1945; reprint 1972.

Fiedler, Leslie. "Bernard Malamud and the Marginal Jew." In *The Fiction of Bernard Malamud*, edited by Richard Astro and Jackson Benson, 97–116. Corvalis: Oregon State University Press, 1977

Fitzgerald, F. Scott. *The Crack-Up*. New York: New Directions, 1945.

———. *Tender Is the Night*. New York: Scribner's, 1962.

Fitzgibbons, Richard. "Anger and the Healing Power of Forgiveness: A Psychiatrist's View." In *Exploring Forgiveness*, edited by Robert Enright and Joanna North, 63–74.

Fonagy, Peter. *Attachment Theory and Psychoanalysis*. New York: Other Press, 2001.

Foucault, Michel. *Discipline and Punish: The Birth of the Prison*. Translated by Alan Sheridan. New York: Vintage, 1995.

Fowles, John. *The Magus*. Revised edition. New York: Laurel, 1978.

Frank, Arthur. *The Wounded Storyteller*. Chicago: University of Chicago Press, 1997.

Freire, Paulo. *Pedagogy of the Oppressed*. Translated by Myra Bergman Ramos. Revised edition. New York: Continuum, 1993.

Freud, Sigmund. "Analysis Terminable and Interminable." *The Standard Edition of the Complete Psychological Writings of Sigmund Freud*. Translated by James Strachey. Volume 23. London: Hogarth Press, 1964.

———. *An Autobiographical Study. The Standard Edition of the Complete Psychological Works of Sigmund Freud*. Translated by James Strachey. Volume 20. London: Hogarth Press, 1959.

———. *Beyond the Pleasure Principle. The Standard Edition of the Complete Psychological Works of Sigmund Freud*. Translated by James Strachey. Volume 18. London: Hogarth Press, 1974.

———. *The Ego and the Id. The Standard Edition of the Complete Psychological Works of Sigmund Freud*. Translated by James Strachey. Volume 19. London: Hogarth Press, 1961.

———. *Fragment of an Analysis of a Case of Hysteria. The Standard Edition of the Complete Psychological Works of Sigmund Freud*. Translated by James Strachey. Volume 7. London: Hogarth Press, 1975.

———. "General Subject Index." *The Standard Edition of the Complete Psychological Works of Sigmund Freud*. Translated by James Strachey. Volume 24. London: Hogarth Press, 1974.

———. "Mourning and Melancholia." *The Standard Edition of the Complete Psychological Works of Sigmund Freud*. Translated by James Strachey. Volume 14. London: Hogarth Press, 1975.

———. *The Origins of Psychoanalysis: Letters to Wilhelm Fliess*. Translated by Eric Mosbacher and James Strachey. New York: Basic Books, 1977.

———. "Recommendations to Physicians Practising Psycho-Analysis." *The Standard Edition of the Complete Psychological Works of Sigmund Freud*. Translated by James Strachey. Volume 12. London: Hogarth Press, 1975.

————. *Three Essays on the Theory of Sexuality. The Standard Edition of the Complete Psychological Works of Sigmund Freud.* Translated by James Strachey. Volume 7. London: Hogarth Press, 1975.

Freyd, Jennifer. *Betrayal Trauma: The Logic of Forgetting Childhood Abuse.* Cambridge: Harvard University Press, 1996.

Fulk, Mark. *Understanding May Sarton.* Columbia: University of South Carolina Press, 2002.

Furst, Lilian. *Idioms of Distress: Psychosomatic Disorders in Medical and Imaginative Literature.* Albany: State University of New York Press, 2003.

Furst, Sidney. "Psychic Trauma: A Survey." In *Psychic Trauma*, edited by Sidney Furst, 3–50. New York: Basic Books, 1967.

Gabbard, Glen, editor. *Countertransference Issues in Psychiatric Treatment.* Washington, D.C.: American Psychiatric Press, 1999.

Gabbard, Glen, and Eva Lester. *Boundaries and Boundary Violations in Psychoanalysis.* New York: Basic Books, 1995.

Gallagher, Robert. "Treating Troubled College Students." *Chronicle of Higher Education*: Colloquy Live Transcript, February 12, 2002.

Gallop, Jane. *Feminist Accused of Sexual Harassment.* Durham, N.C.: Duke University Press, 1997.

Gates, Henry Louis, Jr. *The Signifying Monkey: A Theory of African-American Literary Criticism.* New York: Oxford University Press, 1988.

Gilbert, Sandra, and Susan Gubar. *Masterpiece Theatre: An Academic Melodrama.* New Brunswick, N.J.: Rutgers University Press, 1995.

Gilligan, Carol. *In a Different Voice.* Cambridge: Harvard University Press, 1982.

Gilman, Sander. *Creating Beauty to Cure the Soul: Race and Psychology in the Shaping of Aesthetic Surgery.* Durham: Duke University Press, 1998.

Goldstein, Arnold, and Gerald Michaels. *Empathy: Development, Training, and Consequences.* Hillsdale, N.J.: Lawrence Erlbaum Associates, 1985.

Goleman, Daniel. *Emotional Intelligence.* New York: Bantam Books, 1995.

Gordon, Benjamin. *Sea Monkeys and Other Disappointments.* New York: Raise Giant Frogs Publishing, 2002.

Grealy, Lucy. *Autobiography of a Face.* New York: HarperPerennial, 1995.

Haber, Joram Graf. *Forgiveness.* Savage, Md.: Rowman and Littlefield, 1991.

Hacking, Ian. "Memory Sciences, Memory Politics." In *Tense Past: Cultural Essays in Trauma and Memory*, edited by Paul Antze and Michael Lambek, 67–88.

————. *Rewriting the Soul: Multiple Personality and the Sciences of Memory.* Princeton: Princeton University Press, 1995.

————. *The Social Construction of What?* Cambridge: Harvard University Press, 1999.

Hampton, Jean. "The Retributive Idea." In *Forgiveness and Mercy*, by Jeffrie Murphy and Jean Hampton, 111–61.

Handelman, Susan. "'Knowledge Has a Face': The Jewish, the Personal, and the Pedagogical." In *Personal Effects: The Social Character of Scholarly Writing*, edited by Deborah Holdstein and David Bleich, 121–44.

Harris, Judith. *Signifying Pain: Constructing and Healing the Self through Writing*. Albany: State University of New York Press, 2003.

Heaney, Seamus. *The Redress of Poetry*. New York: Farrar, Straus and Giroux, 1995.

Hemingway, Ernest. *The Sun Also Rises*. New York: Scribner's, 1926.

Henderson, Michael. *Forgiveness: Breaking the Chain of Hatred*. Wilsonville, Oreg.: BookPartners, 1999.

Henke, Suzette A. *Shattered Subjects: Trauma and Testimony in Women's Life-Writing*. New York: St. Martin's Press, 1998.

Herman, Judith Lewis. "Crime and Memory." In *Trauma and Self*, edited by Charles Strozier and Michael Flynn, 3–17.

———. *Father-Daughter Incest*. Cambridge: Harvard University Press, 1981.

Herzog, James. *Father Hunger: Explorations with Adults and Children*. Hillsdale, N.J.: Analytic Press, 2001.

Hilton, James. *Good-bye, Mr. Chips*. New York: Little, Brown, 1962.

Hinton, Laura. *The Perverse Gaze of Sympathy*. Albany: State University of New York Press, 1999.

Hoefner, Joel. "Democracy, Pedagogy, and the Personal Essay." In *Cross-Talk in Comp Theory: A Reader*, edited by Victor Villanueva Jr., 511–23.

Holdstein, Deborah, and David Bleich, editors. *Personal Effects: The Social Character of Scholarly Writing*. Logan: Utah State University Press, 2001.

Holland, Norman. *Death in a Delphi Seminar: A Postmodern Mystery*. Albany: State University of New York Press, 1995.

———. *The I*. New Haven: Yale University Press, 1985.

Holland, Norman, and Murray Schwartz. "The Delphi Seminar." *College English* 36 (1975): 789–800.

Howes, Carollee, and Sharon Ritchie. "Changes in Child-Teacher Relationships in a Therapeutic Preschool Program." *Early Education and Development* 4 (1998): 411–22.

Huddleston, Rodney, and Geoffrey Pullum. "Of Grammatophobia." *Chronicle of Higher Education*, January 3, 2003.

Hunter, Evan. *The Blackboard Jungle*. New York: Simon and Schuster, 1954; reprint 1999.

Hynes, James. *The Lecturer's Tale*. New York: Picador, 2001.

Ickes, William, and Jeffrey Simpson. "Managing Empathic Accuracy in Close Relationships." In *Accuracy*, edited by William Ickes, 218–50. New York: Guilford Press, 1997.

Ingersoll, Earl, editor. *Conversations with May Sarton*. Jackson: University Press of Mississippi, 1991.

James, William. *Talks to Teachers on Psychology*. Cambridge: Harvard University Press, 1983.

Jamison, Kay Redfield. *Night Falls Fast: Understanding Suicide*. New York: Knopf, 1999.

———. *An Unquiet Mind*. New York: Knopf, 1995.

Janoff-Bulman, Ronnie. *Shattered Assumptions: Towards a New Psychology of Trauma.* New York: Free Press, 1992.

Jarrell, Randall. *Pictures from an Institution.* New York: Knopf, 1954.

Jones, D. J. H. *Murder at the MLA.* Athens: University of Georgia Press, 1993.

Jordan, Judith V., Alexandra G. Kaplan, Jean Baker Miller, Irene P. Stiver, and Janet L. Surrey. *Women's Growth in Connection: Writings from the Stone Center.* New York: Guilford Press, 1991.

Jourard, Sidney. *The Transparent Self.* New York: Van Nostrand Reinhold, 1971.

Kafka, Franz. *Letters to Friends, Family, and Editors.* Translated by Richard Winston and Clara Winston. New York: Schocken, 1977.

Karp, David. *Speaking of Sadness.* New York: Oxford University Press, 1996.

Kaufman, Bel. *Up the Down Staircase.* Englewood, N.J.: Prentice-Hall, 1964.

Kesey, Ken. *One Flew over the Cuckoo's Nest.* Edited by John Pratt. New York: Viking Critical Edition, 1973.

Kierkegaard, Soren. *The Sickness unto Death.* Translated by Alistair Hannay. 1849. London: Penguin, 1989.

Kilborne, Benjamin. *Disappearing Persons: Shame and Appearance.* Albany: State University of New York Press, 2002.

Kindlon, Dan, and Michael Thompson. *Raising Cain: Protecting the Emotional Life of Boys.* New York: Ballantine Books, 1999.

King, Laura. "Gain without Pain? Expressive Writing and Self-Regulation." In *The Writing Cure: How Expressive Writing Promotes Health and Well-Being,* edited by Stephen Lepore and Joshua Smyth, 119–34.

Kirmayer, Laurence. "Landscapes of Memory: Trauma, Narrative, and Dissociation." In *Tense Past: Cultural Essays in Trauma and Memory,* edited by Paul Antze and Michael Lambek, 173–98.

Klugman, David. "Empathy's Romantic Dialectic: Self Psychology, Intersubjectivity, and Imagination." *Psychoanalytic Psychology* 18 (2001): 684–704.

Koestler, Arthur. *The Act of Creation.* New York: Macmillan, 1964.

Kohut, Heinz. *How Does Analysis Cure?* edited by Arnold Goldberg. University of Chicago Press, 1984.

_____. "Introspection, Empathy, and Psychoanalysis." *Journal of the American Psychoanalytic Association* 7 (1959): 459–83.

_____. "Introspection, Empathy, and the Semicircle of Mental Health." In *Empathy 1,* edited by Joseph Lichtenberg et al., 81–100.

_____. *The Search for the Self.* Edited by Paul Ornstein. 2 volumes. New York: International Universities Press, 1978.

_____. *Self Psychology and the Humanities: Reflections on a New Psychoanalytic Approach.* Edited by Charles Strozier. New York: Norton, 1985.

Kottler, Jeffrey A. *The Language of Tears.* San Francisco: Jossey-Bass, 1996.

Kristeva, Julia. *Black Sun.* Translated by Leon Roudiez. New York: Columbia University Press, 1989.

LaCapra, Dominick. *Representing the Holocaust*. Ithaca: Cornell University Press, 1994.

———. *Writing History, Writing Trauma*. Baltimore: Johns Hopkins University Press, 2001.

Lawrence, D. H. *Studies in Classic American Fiction*. New York: Viking, 1969.

Lepore, Stephen, Melanie Greenberg, Michelle Bruno, and Joshua Smyth. "Expressive Writing and Health: Self-Regulation of Emotion-Related Experience, Physiology, and Behavior." In *The Writing Cure: How Expressive Writing Promotes Health and Emotional Well-Being*, edited by Stephen Lepore and Joshua Smyth, 99–117.

Lepore, Stephen, and Joshua Smyth, editors. *The Writing Cure: How Expressive Writing Promotes Health and Emotional Well-Being*. Washington, D.C.: American Psychological Association, 2002.

Levi, Primo. *Survival in Auschwitz*. Translated by Stuart Woolf. New York: Touchstone, 1996.

Levin, Thomas. "Curatorial Statement." In *CTRL [Space]: Rhetorics of Surveillance from Bentham to Big Brother*, edited by Thomas Levin, Ursula Frohne, and Peter Weibel. Cambridge: MIT Press, 2002.

Levinas, Emmanuel. *Discovering Existence with Husserl*. Translated and edited by Richard Cohen and Michael Smith. Evanston: Northwestern University Press, 1998.

———. *Is It Righteous to Be?* Edited by Jill Robbins. Stanford: Stanford University Press, 2001.

———. *The Levinas Reader*. Edited by Sean Hand. Translated by Sean Hand and Michael Temple. Oxford: Blackwell, 1989.

Leys, Ruth. *Trauma: A Genealogy*. Chicago: University of Chicago Press, 2000.

Lichtenberg, Joseph. Introduction to *Reflections on Self Psychology*. Edited by Joseph Lichtenberg and Samuel Kaplan. Hillsdale, N.J.: Analytic Press, 1983.

Lichtenberg, Joseph, Melvin Bornstein, and Donald Silver, editors. *Empathy 1*. Hillsdale, N.J.: Analytic Press, 1984.

Lichtenstein, Hans. *The Dilemma of Human Identity*. New York: Jason Aronson, 1983.

Light, Richard. *Making the Most of College*. Cambridge: Harvard University Press, 2001.

Lodge, David. *Changing Places*. New York: Penguin, 1992.

———. *Small World*. New York: Penguin, 1995.

———. *Thinks*. New York: Viking, 2001.

Lopate, Phillip. "Couch Potato: My Life in Therapy." In *Tales from the Couch: Writers on Therapy*, edited by Jason Shinder, 75–87. New York: William Morrow, 2000.

Lurie, Alison. *The War between the Tates*. New York: Random House, 1974.

Lutz, Tom. *Crying: The Natural and Cultural History of Tears*. New York: Norton, 1999.

Malamud, Bernard. *A New Life*. New York: Farrar, Straus and Cudahy, 1961.

Malcolm, Wanda, and Leslie Greenberg. "Forgiveness as a Process of Change in Individual Psychotherapy." In *Forgiveness: Theory, Research, and Practice*, edited by Michael McCullough et al., 179–202.

Margalit, Avishai. *The Ethics of Memory*. Cambridge: Harvard University Press, 2002.

Margulies, Alfred. *The Empathic Imagination*. New York: Norton, 1989.

Masson, Jeffrey Moussaieff. *The Assault on Truth: Freud's Suppression of the Seduction Theory*. New York: Farrar, Straus and Giroux, 1984.

Mattingly, Cheryl. *Healing Dramas and Clinical Plots*. Cambridge: Cambridge University Press, 1998.

McCourt, Frank. *'Tis*. New York: Simon and Schuster, 1999.

McCullough, Michael, Kenneth Pargament, and Carl Thoresen, editors. *Forgiveness: Theory, Research, and Practice*. New York: Guilford Press, 2000.

McFarlane, Alexander, and Giovanni de Girolamo. "The Nature of Traumatic Stressors and the Epidemiology of Posttraumatic Reactions." In *Traumatic Stress*, edited by Bessel van der Kolk et al., 129–54.

Mead, George. *Mind, Self, and Society*. Edited by Charles Morris. Chicago: University of Chicago Press, 1934.

Meissner, W. W. "The Problem of Self-Disclosure in Psychoanalysis." *Journal of the American Psychoanalytic Association* 50 (2002): 827–67.

Miller, Jean Baker, and Irene Pierce Stiver. *The Healing Connection: How Women Form Relationships in Therapy and Life*. Boston: Beacon Press, 1997.

Mitchell, Stephen. *Influence and Autonomy in Psychoanalysis*. Hillsdale, N.J.: Analytic Press, 1997.

———. *Relationality: From Attachment to Intersubjectivity*. Hillsdale, N.J.: Analytic Press, 2000.

Morris, David. *Illness and Culture in the Postmodern Age*. Berkeley: University of California Press, 1998.

Murphy, Jeffrie. "Forgiveness and Resentment." In *Forgiveness and Mercy*, by Jeffrie Murphy and Jean Hampton, 14–34.

Murphy, Jeffrie, and Jean Hampton. *Forgiveness and Mercy*. Cambridge: Cambridge University Press, 1988.

Murray, Donald. *Crafting a Life*. Portsmouth, N.H.: Boynton/Cook, 1996.

Natterson, Joseph, and Raymond Friedman. *A Primer of Clinical Intersubjectivity*. Northvale, N.J.: Jason Aronson, 1995.

Neill, A. S. *Summerhill: A Radical Approach to Child Rearing*. New York: Hart, 1960.

Newberg, Andrew, Eugene d'Aquili, Angie Newberg, and Verushka deMarici, "The Neuropsychological Correlates of Forgiveness." In *Forgiveness: Theory, Research, and Practice*, edited by Michael McCullough et al., 91–110.

Nietzsche, Friedrich. *The Genealogy of Morals*. In *The Philosophy of Nietzsche*. Translated by Horace Samuel. New York: Modern Library, 1954.

_____. *Human, All Too Human. The Complete Works of Friedrich Nietzsche.* Edited by Ernst Behler. Translated by Gary Handwerk. Volume 3. Stanford: Stanford University Press, 1995.

Noddings, Nel. *Caring.* Berkeley: University of California Press, 1984.

North, Joanna. "The 'Ideal' of Forgiveness: A Philosopher's Exploration." In *Exploring Forgiveness*, edited by Robert Enright and Joanna North, 15–34.

Nussbaum, Martha. "Compassion and Terror." *Daedalus* (winter 2003): 10–26.

_____. *Upheavals of Thought: The Intelligence of Emotions.* Cambridge: Cambridge University Press, 2001.

O'Connor, Flannery. *Mystery and Manners.* Edited by Sally Fitzgerald and Robert Fitzgerald. New York: Farrar, Straus and Giroux, 1969.

Offer, Daniel, Eric Ostrov, and Kenneth Howard. *The Adolescent: A Psychological Self-Portrait.* New York: Basic Books, 1981

Offer, Daniel, Eric Ostrov, Kenneth Howard, and Robert Atkinson. *The Teenage World: Adolescents' Self-Image in Ten Countries.* New York: Plenum, 1988.

Ogden, Thomas. *Conversations at the Frontier of Dreaming.* Northvale, N.J.: Jason Aronson, 2001.

Orwell, George. "Why I Write." In *A Collection of Essays.* Garden City, N.Y.: Doubleday, 1954.

Palmer, Parker. *The Courage to Teach.* San Francisco: Jossey-Bass, 1998.

Park, Crystal. "Implications of Posttraumatic Growth for Individuals." In *Posttraumatic Growth: Positive Changes in the Aftermath of Crisis*, edited by Richard Tedeschi et al., 153–78.

Parson, Michael. *The Dove that Returns, the Dove that Vanishes: Paradox and Creativity in Psychoanalysis.* London: Routledge, 2000.

Pennebaker, James. Epilogue to *The Writing Cure: How Expressive Writing Promotes Health and Emotional Well-Being.* Edited by Stephen Lepore and Joshua Smyth, 281–91.

_____. *Opening Up: The Healing Power of Expressing Emotion.* New York: Guilford Press, 1997.

Pennebaker, James, and M. Francis. *Linguistic Inquiry and Word Count: LIWC.* Mahwah, N.J.: Erlbaum, 1999.

Pennebaker, James, T. Mayne, and M. Francis. "Linguistic Predictors of Adaptive Bereavement." *Journal of Personality and Social Psychology* 72 (1997): 863–71.

Peters, Margot. *May Sarton: A Biography.* New York: Knopf, 1997.

Petrey, Sandy. *Speech Acts and Literary Theory.* New York: Routledge, 1990.

Petronio, Sandra. *Boundaries of Privacy: Dialectics of Disclosure.* Albany: State University of New York Press, 2002.

Philips, David. "The Influence of Suggestion on Suicide: Substantive and Theoretical Implications of the Werther Effect." *American Sociological Review* 39 (1974): 340–13. Reprinted in *Essential Papers on Suicide*, edited by John Maltsberger and Mark Goldblatt, 290–313. New York: New York University Press, 1996.

Polanyi, Michael. *Personal Knowledge*. Chicago: University of Chicago Press, 1958.

Popenoe, David. *Life without Father*. New York: Free Press, 1996.

Rancour-Laferriere, Daniel, editor. *Self-Analysis in Literary Study: Exploring Hidden Agendas*. New York: New York University Press, 1994.

Rattigan, Terence. *The Browning Version*. In *The Collected Plays of Terence Rattigan*. Volume 2. London: Hamish Hamilton, 1953.

Rogers, Carl. *Freedom to Learn*. Columbus: Charles E. Merrill Publishing, 1969.

——. *A Way of Being*. Boston: Houghton Mifflin, 1980.

Ross, John. *The Polar Bear Strategy: Reflections on Risk in Modern Life*. Reading, Mass.: Perseus Books, 1999.

Roth, Philip. *The Professor of Desire*. New York: Farrar, Straus and Giroux, 1977.

Rothberg, Michael. *Traumatic Realism: The Demands of Holocaust Representation*. Minneapolis: University of Minnesota Press, 2000.

Russell, Diana. *The Secret Trauma*. New York: Basic Books, 1986.

Russo, Richard. *Straight Man*. New York: Vintage, 1997.

Safranski, Rüdiger. *Nietzsche: A Philosophical Biography*. Translated by Shelley Frisch. New York: Norton, 2002.

Salinger, J. D. *The Catcher in the Rye*. Boston: Little, Brown, 1951. New York: Bantam, reprint 1964.

Salter, Anna. *Transforming Trauma*. Thousand Oaks, Calif.: Sage Publications, 1995.

Salzman, Mark. *True Notebooks*. New York: Knopf, 2003.

Samuels, Robert. "Teaching about the Holocaust and the Subject of Objectivity: Psychoanalysis, Trauma, and Counter-Transference in an Advanced Writing Course." *JPCS: Journal for the Psychoanalysis of Culture and Society* 8 (2003): 133–43.

Sarton, May. *The Small Room*. New York: Norton, 1961; reprint 1976.

——. *May Sarton: Selected Letters, 1916–1954*. Edited and introduced by Susan Sherman. New York: Norton, 1997.

——. *May Sarton: Selected Letters, 1955–1995*. Edited and introduced by Susan Sherman. New York: Norton, 2002.

Schlender, Elizabeth Anne. "Images of Self as Teacher in Seven Selected Novels." Master's thesis, University of Alberta, 1995.

Shaw, Daniel. "On the Therapeutic Action of Analytic Love." *Contemporary Psychoanalysis* 39 (2003): 251–78.

Skorczewski, Dawn. *Teaching One Moment at a Time*. Amherst: University of Massachusetts Press, forthcoming.

Slatoff, Walter. *The Look of Distance*. Ithaca: Cornell University Press, 1985.

Smiley, Jane. *Moo*. New York: Fawcett Columbine, 1995.

Solomon, Andrew. *The Noonday Demon: An Atlas of Depression*. New York: Simon and Schuster, 2002.

Spellmeyer, Kurt. *Arts of Living: Reinventing the Humanities for the Twenty-First Century*. Albany: State University of New York Press, 2003.

Spiro, Howard. "Empathy: An Introduction." In *Empathy and the Practice of Medicine*, edited by Howard Spiro, Mary Curnen, Enid Peschel, and Deborah St. James, 1–6. New Haven: Yale University Press, 1993.

Steiner, George. *After Babel*. Oxford: Oxford University Press, 1975; 3rd edition, 1998.

Stengel, Richard. *You're Too Kind: A Brief History of Flattery*. New York: Simon and Schuster, 2000.

Stiver, Irene P. "The Meanings of 'Dependency' in Female-Male Relationships." In *Women's Growth in Connection: Writings from the Stone Center*, by Judith Jordan et al., 143–61.

Stowe, Harriet Beecher. *Little Foxes*. Boston: James Osgood, 1873.

Strozier, Charles. *Heinz Kohut: The Making of a Psychoanalyst*. New York: Farrar, Straus and Giroux, 2001.

Strozier, Charles, and Michael Flynn, editors. *Trauma and Self*. Lanham, Md.: Rowman and Littlefield, 1996.

Strupp, Hans, and Suzanne Hadley, "Specific vs. Nonspecific Factors in Psychotherapy: A Controlled Study of Outcome." *Archives of General Psychiatry* 36 (1979): 1125–36.

Styron, Rose. "Strands." In *Unholy Ghost: Writers on Depression*, edited by Nell Casey, 126–37. New York: Perennial, 2002.

Styron, William. *Darkness Visible*. New York: Random House, 1990.

Sullivan, Harry Stack. *The Psychiatric Interview*. New York: Norton, 1954.

Sykes, Charles. *ProfScam: Professors and the Demise of Higher Education*. Washington, D.C.: Regnery Gateway, 1988.

Tal, Kalí. *Worlds of Hurt: Reading the Literatures of Trauma*. Cambridge: Cambridge University Press, 1996.

Tannen, Deborah. *The Argument Culture*. New York: Random House, 1998.

Tanner, Laura. *Intimate Violence: Reading Rape and Torture in Twentieth-Century Fiction*. Bloomington: Indiana University Press, 1994.

Tedeschi, Richard, Crystal Park, and Lawrence Calhoun, editors. *Posttraumatic Growth: Positive Changes in the Aftermath of Crisis*. Mahway, N.J.: Lawrence Erlbaum, 1998.

Tennen, Howard, and Glenn Affleck. "Personality and Transformation in the Face of Adversity." In *Posttraumatic Growth: Positive Changes in the Aftermath of Crisis*, edited by Richard Tedeschi et al., 65–98.

Terr, Lenore. *Unchained Memories: True Stories of Traumatic Memories, Lost and Found*. New York: Basic Books, 1994.

Thoresen, Carl, Alex Harris, and Frederic Luskin. "Forgiveness and Health." In *Forgiveness: Theory, Research, and Practice*, edited by Michael McCullough et al., 254–80.

Tolstoy, Leo. *Anna Karenina*. Translated by Constance Garnett. Edited by Leonard Kent and Nina Berberova. New York: Modern Library, 1965.

Tutu, Desmond. *No Future without Tears*. New York: Doubleday, 1999.

van der Kolk, Bessel. "The Black Hole of Trauma." In *Traumatic Stress*, edited by Bessel van der Kolk et al., 3–23.

_____. *Psychological Trauma.* Washington, D.C.: American Psychiatric Press, 1987.

van der Kolk, Bessel, Alexander McFarlane, and Lars Weisaeth, editors. *Traumatic Stress.* New York: Guilford Press, 1996.

van Manen, Max. *Researching Lived Experience: Human Science for an Action Sensitive Pedagogy.* Albany: State University of New York Press, 1990.

Vickroy, Laurie. *Trauma and Survival in Contemporary Fiction.* Charlottesville: University of Virginia Press, 2002.

Vida, Judith. "The Role of Love in the Therapeutic Action of Psychoanalysis." *American Imago* 59 (2002): 435–45.

Villanueva, Victor, Jr., editor. *Cross-Talk in Comp Theory: A Reader.* Urbana, Ill.: NCTE, 1997.

Wahl, Otto. *Telling Is Risky Business.* New Brunswick, N.J.: Rutgers University Press, 1999.

Wallerstein, Judith S., and Joan Berlin Kelly. *Surviving the Breakup: How Children and Parents Cope with Divorce.* New York: Basic Books, 1980.

Wallerstein, Judith S., Julia Lewis, and Sandra Blakeslee. *The Unexpected Legacy of Divorce.* New York: Hyperion Books, 2000.

Warren, Robert Penn. *All the King's Men.* New York: Bantam, 1973.

Weinfield, Nancy S., L. Alan Sroufe, Byron Egeland, and Elizabeth A. Carlson. "The Nature of Individual Differences in Infant-Caregiver Attachment." In *Handbook of Attachment: Theory, Research, and Clinical Applications,* edited by Jude Cassidy and Phillip Shaver, 68–88. New York: Guilford Press, 1999.

Winnicott, D. W. *Home Is Where We Start From.* Edited by Clare Winnicott, Ray Shepherd, and Madeleine Davis. New York: Norton, 1986.

_____. *The Maturational Processes and the Facilitating Environment.* New York: International Universities Press, 1965.

_____. "Transitional Objects and Transitional Phenomena." *International Journal of Psycho-Analysis* 34 (1953).

Wispé, Lauren. *The Psychology of Sympathy.* New York: Plenum Press, 1991.

Wolitzer, Meg. *The Wife.* New York: Scribner, 2003.

Womack, Kenneth. *Postwar Academic Fiction.* Houndsmills, England: Palgrave, 2002.

Wordsworth, William. "My Heart Leaps Up." *William Wordsworth: Selected Poems and Prefaces.* Edited by Jack Stillinger. Boston: Houghton Mifflin, 1965.

Wurmser, Leon. "Shame: The Veiled Companion of Narcissism." In *The Many Faces of Shame,* edited by Donald Nathanson, 6–92. New York: Guilford Press, 1987.

Woog, Pierre. Letter to the Editor. *Chronicle of Higher Education,* March 22, 2002.

Young, Allan. "Bodily Memory and Traumatic Memory." In *Tense Past: Cultural Essays in Trauma and Memory,* edited by Paul Antze and Michael Lambek, 89–102.

_____. *The Harmony of Illusions: Inventing Post–Traumatic Stress Disorder.* Princeton: Princeton University Press, 1995.

Young, Jeffrey. "Prozac Campus." *Chronicle of Higher Education,* February 14, 2002.

Zornberg, Avivah Gottlieb. *The Particulars of Rapture: Reflections on Exodus.* New York: Doubleday, 2001.

STUDENT WRITERS

INDEX

399

JEFFREY BERMAN is professor of English at the State University of New York at Albany, where he has received the Chancellor's Award for Excellence in Teaching. He is the author of *Joseph Conrad: Writing as Rescue*; *The Talking Cure: Literary Representations of Psychoanalysis*; *Narcissism and the Novel*; *Diaries to an English Professor: Pain and Growth in the Classroom*; *Surviving Literary Suicide*; and *Risky Writing*.